Men in Crisis

Men in Crisis
Human Breakdowns in Prison

Hans Toch
State University of New York at Albany

with contributions by
John J. Gibbs, Robert Johnson, and James G. Fox

Aldine Publishing Company/Chicago

034358

ABOUT THE AUTHOR

Hans Toch received his undergraduate training in psychology at Brooklyn College and received a Ph.D. in social psychology from Princeton University. He has contributed numerous articles to the literature and his published works include: *The Social Psychology of Social Movements* (1965, Bobbs-Merrill) and *Violent Men* (1969, Aldine). Dr. Toch is currently Professor of Psychology in the School of Criminal Justice, State University of New York at Albany.

First published 1975 by
Aldine Publishing Company
529 South Wabash Avenue
Chicago, Illinois 60605

ISBN 0-202-25126-8 clothbound edition

Library of Congress Catalog Number 74-18214
Printed in the United States of America

Contents

Acknowledgments

The study of which this book is based was supported by an NIMH research grant (5 RO1 MH 20696–02 "Self-Destruction Among Prison Inmates") from the Center for Studies of Crime and Delinquency, and the Center for Studies of Suicide Prevention. The work was made possible through the cooperation of Russ Oswald, the New York State Commissioner of Correctional Services, George McGrath, the Commissioner of Corrections of New York City, Deputy Commissioners Robert Fosen and George Camp, and the wardens and superintendents of major correctional facilities. Barbara Meilinger shouldered our administrative burdens and coordinated the data transcription.

The most direct debt I owe is to over six hundred inmates, who spent countless hours sharing their thoughts, feelings, and concerns with us. Primarily for their sake, I hope that this book will add to knowledge and contribute to reform.

Men in Crisis

1

The Scope of Our Concern

Mental health, however one defines it, varies not only across groups and persons but for each person over time. The most regressed psychotics have days in which their lethargy or helplessness is more—or less—evident than it is the remainder of the time. And the most outgoing and cheerful of us face moments of despondency, self-doubt, worry, or apathy. Freud, whose patients were anxious or obsessed, wrote about the "psychopathology of everyday life" to show that nuances of neurosis appear in the mental life of "normal" persons. And Freud also discussed the universal phenomenon of grief (such as is occasioned by the death of loved ones) as a short-term version of chronic depression.[1]

Students of crises tell us that situations encountered in most people's lives (like moving to a different environment) often produce serious coping problems.[2] And drastic experiences, such as natural disasters, may offer difficulties to which few persons can adjust with calculated equanimity.[3] Extremely inhospitable settings, such as concentration camps, can evoke pathological reactions in a great many of their victims.[4]

A wide range of social circumstances or institutions can be called "generally stressful," in that they circumscribe, frighten, disappoint, bore, or challenge people exposed to them.[5] Investors caught in a stock market crash, soldiers patrolling enemy-held jungles, passengers "bumped" from flights, discharged employees, students who fail courses, and preoperative

1

patients share common fates—noxious, disheartening, and disturbing discoveries or impingements. Reactions to such situations will differ from
person to person. While most displaced airline passengers, for instance,
meekly adjourn to their lodgings, others explode at the reservations clerk;
while most patients stoically await the knife, others fret or complain. The
responses of some individuals in the face of stress are even more extreme
and may be seriously disabling. Soldiers who panic may become perma-
nently afraid of minor challenges. Students who fail a course may drop
out of school altogether. Investors may take their lives over financial re-
verses. Hospital patients may lose the will to live. Such reactions are
"breakdowns," in the sense that they make it impossible for the person to
continue functioning as he would ordinarily.

Though society has an obligation to reduce the stressful features of the
institutions it controls and to ameliorate the stressful properties of scheduled events, it may be utopian to rely on institutional restraints for
prompt, wholesale solutions to the problem of personal breakdowns. For
one, establishing and maintaining any institution requires human
strength and endurance. Society need not be a jungle to test our mental
health. And there are some persons so maimed in early childhood that
even the mildest upset in later life may prove disabling for them.

Stressful conditions are also not direct products of structural variables
which are easily diagnosed and remedied. For instance, viewed from the
patient's perspective, the most technologically advanced hospital may be
an inhumane environment. Moreover, expectations can outstrip or be
irrelevant to the ameliorative properties of settings. Scandinavian coun-
tries, whose institutions are protective and supportive, have unconscio-
nably high suicide rates.[6] The central concerns of Danes or Swedes, such as
human contact or success, create problems in situations which are comparatively innocuous for persons with different orientations. Conversely,
such groups of people as the Eskimo and slum dwellers survive in settings
which men raised elsewhere would find impossibly difficult.[7]

On the other hand, it seems obvious—on both ethical and pragmatic
grounds—that social institutions must never be run or sustained in igno-
rance or defiance of human costs. Attention must be given to the problems
created by environments, and this demands study of the reactions to concrete settings of the persons who function within them.

Information about environmental impact is required not only for reform but for the continued operation of necessarily stress-producing milieus. In our day we have outlived the view that those who fall by the
wayside are undeserving of assistance. For one, our concept of man has
become more tolerant and flexible. Today we know not only that "war is
hell," but that it is more hellish for some men than for others. While a
modern army does not see itself in terms of "Catch 22," it also recognizes

that it is not populated by Audie Murphys or John Waynes.[8] And it seeks to regenerate its shell-shocked members not only in order to maintain its strength, but also because it considers war neuroses and psychoses to be consequences of combat conditions. In addition, it may try to modulate the wartime experience and to minimize the consequences of stress through such devices as "rest and recreation."

Though information about human breakdowns under stress has been obtained, the available data have somewhat limited import. At times the information is circumscribed by the specificity of the environment studied. We may know about the impact of extreme cold and isolation, or about the liabilities of trench warfare, but we find the information hard to apply to other circumstances.[9] The existing literature also overrepresents clinical or physiological research. It may tell us about idiosyncratic individuals, or about physical reactions of the human organism, but it conveys little feeling for the concerns and perspectives of persons who suffer. Where the portraiture is more sensitive, as in studies of disasters, the analysis traces ideal-type reactions.[10] While of value, these have limited practical implications. If we are to respond effectively to people in crisis, we cannot do so in general terms. We must view personal breakdowns differentially—as unique manifestations.

The concern which shaped and inspired the work reported in this book is with mapping a wide spectrum of despair—with cataloging the feelings and thoughts of a variety of men who break down in a variety of ways under shared stress. We have sought to define the problem in vivo so as to make it possible to think of a realistically relevant range of crisis interventions and institutional reforms.

For the sake of neatness we have confined our research to one manifestation of breakdown and one type of stressful environment. Our mapping is thus not really exhaustive. But the range built into our survey is sufficiently generous to insure that our observations apply elsewhere. The stressful setting we have surveyed—that of confinement—is a complex of situations which have properties in common with other stressful settings. And the type of breakdown we have studied—self-destruction—reflects an impressive universe of motives and concerns.

Ultimately, it is the method of our inquiry which enhances the generalizability of our observations. We have taken pains to explore the evolution and climax of crises strictly from the perspective of the individual in crisis. This approach takes us closer to the process of breakdown under stress than would standard inventories focused on tangible reactions to parameters of stressful settings. We have tried to reconstruct the ineffable shapes taken by human extremity as fully and faithfully as possible, so as to explore feelings and assumptions that define experienced crisis states. Though this approach involves subtle classifications, and dispenses with information about the concrete behavior of men under stress, it provides a more full-blooded view of breakdowns as psychological phenomena than do standard inventories.

We have tried not to subdivide our universe in ways that would distract us from the goal of letting the process of crisis take its natural shape. We have explored the reactions of major groups of subjects with substantially divergent experiences and concerns, but we have not tampered with the integrity of our portraits by allocating crises to nature, nurture, or milieu. We have faithfully spelled out the reactions to situational pressures and the dominant concerns of comparatively "normal" individuals and of persons who would be clinically diagnosed as seriously disturbed. Though ultimately we do categorize our data, we do so in terms of the concerns of our subjects rather than of considerations extrinsic to the process of breakdown.

In focusing our research on the jail and the prison, we do not imply (as some critics do) that these milieus are malevolently designed to make men suffer. We are aware of the timely trend to divert people from prisons and to mitigate the experience of incarceration. We also know that most correctional administrators decry the role of "punisher" allocated to them by segments of the public. We know that in the criminal justice system prison is viewed as a necessary evil, to which one reluctantly consigns people because one feels that one must.[11] By the same token, we know that the prison is a consciously harsh human environment. We are also aware that, given the mission of the prison, it is slated to remain harsh indefinitely. For if prisons should ever move in the direction of benignity, segments of the public would resist the "coddling" of muggers and "country club housing" for adjudged rapists.

Historically, the use of penitentiaries as an intervention tool was premised on the assumption that environments that segregate people can also change them. Long before recidivism figures cast doubt on prisons as rehabilitators, less inaccurate but more dramatic statistics raised questions about jail cells as settings for survival. Uncompromising solitude proved an invincible challenge to inmates. Some died, and a large number emerged incurably disturbed.[12]

In contemporary institutions, the lot of inmates has improved. Meals are balanced and adequate; there is cleanliness and sanitation, medical and dental care, exercise, entertainment, and opportunity for talk. There are also the obvious "pains of imprisonment": enforced intimacy and segregation, uniformity and routine, unreality and insularity, separation from love and status. There are norms and conventions to cope with these pains: the guard-inmate chasm, the exploitation of peers, insularity, dissembling and posturing. There is the required stance of inviolability and autonomy in the face of captivity.

Paradoxically, some men flourish in this context. Weaklings become substantial and influential; shiftless men strive and produce; pathetic souls sprout unsuspected resources.

It stands to reason that others will do less well. The artificiality of the milieu must overtax some and overwhelm others. Adversities must grate on susceptibilities: pain or strain must smother. These, however, are inferences, since indices of prison breakdowns are hard to obtain. To be sure, inmates become ill and die in prison, but illness and death occur in all settings. Health care is usually better in prison than in the neighborhoods where the inmates originate. There is violence in prison, but prisons harbor men who have been violent elsewhere. Prisoners become mentally ill. But many of those transferred from prison to psychiatric settings have had past histories of civil commitments and diagnosed disturbances.

By the same token, we can rest no case against the Alice in Wonderland flavor of the inmate world. Admittedly, prison events seem strange, puzzling, and "abnormal." Displayed elsewhere, much prison conduct would suggest twisted personalities or strained psyches. But inmate acts fit the prison situations. They may be no more than extreme, evanescent adjustments to extreme, temporary trials.

To locate prison breakdowns, we need behavior that is rare in the world, deviant in prison, and potentially damaging.

It is easy to find objectively undesirable conduct among inmates—but it is hard to find dysfunctional acts. Too many seemingly undesirable prison acts are rewarded by staff or reinforced by peers. They are purposive, and they are related to norms.

Self-injury or mutilation is a possible exception. It involves pain, self-affronts, danger. It raises questions about one's stamina and stability. It annoys staff and puzzles peers. It invites sanctions and segregation.

In the outside world, self-destructive acts are comparatively rare; in prisons, they occur frequently. Unfortunately there are few hard facts. Public attention focuses on occasional suicides and sporadic waves of protest-mutilations. But routine inmate self-injuries remain unrecorded, are buried in infirmary records and disciplinary logs, and are dismissed as inconsequential oddities of prison life. Staff make light of inmate "attention getting"; they note that in most cases physical harm is confined to scratches or cuts and that for the most part damage is limited to surface scars.

Every stressful setting has norms which dictate unrealistic adjustments. The soldier must be brave, and the hospital patient must be "patient." These norms help get the job done, but they dictate pretense and blind us to cues of stress. A patient may pretend to ignore his fear, may display a veneer of stoicism, may even accept staff pretense that they take his behavior at face value. The anxious patient—the lady whose buzzer disturbs the peace of the nursing staff—is classified as an amusing nuisance or as an insufferable hypochondriac.

Similarly, beachheads are presumably taken by individuals who value their lives lightly or are blind to the odds. Manifestations of fear are classed as surface idiosyncrasies disguising the dedication pointing (with informed consent) to a hero's grave. Pluralistic pretense—silence or clichés —creates a climate that discourages panic in landing craft or parachute jumps or jungle patrols. And any man who defies the taboo against fear and breaks down is seen as being different from his peers, as having a character defect, or as manifesting pathology.

Concepts which discount the seriousness of prison breakdowns are a product of prison myths. These myths—shared by staff and inmates—proscribe feelings of despair, weakness, and vulnerability. They dictate "manliness," rationality, invulnerability, and a pragmatic orientation. They presume coolness, toughness, and a capacity to negotiate obstacles.[13] Even the weak are provided for: these are the ill-prepared, ill-equipped manipulators who use others as crutches to achieve rational, selfish ends.[14]

The Manly Man, like the Dedicated Soldier, the Stoic Patient, Rational Man, or Economic Man, is a conceptual tool, shaped for convenience rather than validity. The Manly Man, devoid of depression, free of anger, and immune from despair, is a product of closed opportunity settings which create impotence. It is an image (and self-image) which permits men to face emasculation devoid of self-doubt, entitled to respect, dependable, and predictable. It saves face, insures stability, confers status.

Leaving such ends aside, the myth of the Manly Man has built-in risks. If every man is presumed Manly, what about un-Manliness? What about experienced impotence? And what about lapses among subscribers to the norm?

Deviations and exceptions call for pretense and collusion. Pretense requires credence—A's need, matching B's, shapes a bargain: if A grants B's steel-and-concrete image, he can expect reciprocity. His claim to calm in the face of adversity is safe. An equivalent pact binds keeper or staff. If A (inmate) is vulnerable, and B (staff) is helpless to deal with vulnerability, B may support A's facade. B may do more than lend credibility to A: he may suggest that indices of vulnerability are in bad taste.

More generally, a system for the discounting or suppressing of stigmata of unmanliness can be created. Flippant formulas and surface descriptions cover personal or interpersonal difficulties. Critical events are deindividualized and merge into less sensitive or innocuous categories. Themes such as manipulativeness, politics, ethnicity, or psychosis become "respectable" explanations, and are invoked to characterize inmate conduct.

Worse, breakdowns may be discounted out of existence and expunged from the record. They may become part of the unwritten knowledge of prison sophisticates. Inmate homosexuals, for instance, are known to custodians and peers, but they are nowhere compiled in rosters. Nor are lists kept of inmate isolates, peer-rejects, victim-prones, staff-dependents, or other men with problems.

Self-injury is similarly subterranean. If files are kept, they list only damage serious enough for medical risk, incidents relevant to disciplining, and patterns considered psychotic. Unremarkable inmates are disinfected, bandaged, and discreetly sent back to their cells.

What is more serious is that inmates who break down (in defiance of norms) are expected to make light of their problems, to deny their manifest despair. If they fail to do so, they risk being seen—and seeing themselves—as weak, unmanly, impotent, sick.

To illustrate this phenomenon and its consequences, we will review major excerpts from one of our more laborious interviews. The subject, whom we call Sam, harbors accumulating rage which bursts forth when he feels under pressure. Yet—in line with the Myth of Manliness—Sam must view himself as pragmatic, unfeeling, and controlled. This prevents insight, spawns incongruence, and compounds his problem.

In our interview, Sam tries (at least, at first) to project and document his "respectable" self-image. He makes light of his difficulties and presents himself as manly, manipulative, cool. He tries to make the facts about himself conform to the norm. In time the true situation emerges—not only as a problem for Sam but as a crisis of concern to his keepers.

Sam is an inmate of Clinton Prison, in New York. He is a white man in his twenties, large, muscular, and of rigid, military bearing. His offense is homicide. He speaks distantly, formally, as if reciting. During the long session with us, he sits upright without moving or shifting.

We begin our interview (as we usually do) with an exploratory, open-ended question:

INTERVIEWER: Why don't you just begin with what happened?

SAM: The situation that I was involved in, in Comstock Correction Facility, arose through matters of financial debt that I owed. During the time of the debt I had a fight with another inmate and I was unable to get that money. So I was locked up in this fifteen-day keep-lock, and this party came to me and stated that if I didn't get his money for him he would cut me with a razor blade. Now I'm white and he's black, and I'm from the South anyway, which caused my actions at this time. So the doctors came to me, and I told them I wasn't going to be responsible for my actions if they kept me in this cell. So they asked me what was making me depressed, and I told them it was a home situation and home difficulties and things like that to do with my family. But it was really on account of this action with this other inmate, and him cutting me with a razor blade. And before he was going to cut me, I was going to get him first. And so, rather than getting another fifteen years on top of this ten, I portrayed to the doctor that I was depressed and asked him to transfer me to a mental institution to see if I couldn't straighten out my thinking abilities and get myself straightened out on a line that would alleviate my depressing mania. But I could not see myself in a situation where I was worrying about some guy causing me to get fifteen years because he was worried about a carton of cigarettes. So I just pulled a night like I was sick and I got out. So the board gave me another sentence.

INTERVIEWER: During that act did you in any way harm yourself?

SAM: No. I threatened to cut my wrists. I had a razor blade, and I made scratch marks, and I showed them to the doctor, and he asked me why I didn't go through with it. And I told him I didn't see no sense in carrying it to such extreme measures, by actually harming myself. I could just get transferred by doing this. And he asked me if I wanted to get transferred. And I said yes, because I didn't like the atmosphere I was residing in now. But I didn't say nothing about the conflict with the other inmate. So I was shipped from Comstock to Dannemora State Hospital.

INTERVIEWER: Do you think in that situation that he believed that you just wanted to get transferred, or do you think he believed that you were really depressed at the time?

SAM: I believe he really thought I was depressed because I portrayed myself in such a way that he had to believe me.

INTERVIEWER: You mean your actions indicated that?

SAM: Yeah.

INTERVIEWER: You said you gave yourself some light scratches, but you couldn't see going through with it.

SAM: Right. I saw no reasoning in taking my life when there was actually nothing wrong. I was just trying to avoid a fight that would give me another fifteen-year sentence. So this was a confirmation of my depressive state of mind at the time that I was talking with my psychiatrist. . . .

INTERVIEWER: When you want to do this for proof, is that something that's rather difficult to do, or is it easy?

SAM: Well, a person has to work himself up to an emotional state where he can actually carry through with the act of destruction on his body.

INTERVIEWER: Can you give me some idea of what that is like? Or what you do?

SAM: You sit there, and you have to put yourself in a mental position where you have to think of the supposedly wrongs that have been done to you and the wrongs you have done to other people, to yourself and to your family and to your loved ones. And you've got to keep running this through your mind until you get in a paranoid state of mind that "I'm no good to myself and to anybody." Somewhere along that line your mind blanks out, and you have no recollection of what it does to you then. And from that state on, you can carry out almost any act that you want, whether it is self-destruction or destruction of another individual. You have no control over your emotions whatsoever. You just function like a machine.

INTERVIEWER: How much of this were you aware of at the time? Was this something that you planned out, or did it begin in any sort of particular way?

SAM: I planned it right from the beginning, when I found out my sentence and right on up through the whole thing.

INTERVIEWER: Oh, you purposely tried to get these things in your mind?

SAM: Right. It was premeditated, and I was able to carry it through.

INTERVIEWER: This may sound silly, because you say you have complete control, but when that gets going do you believe those things? Do they become real to you? Is that part of the idea?

SAM: If a person can put himself in a state of mind where paranoia gets to him, to a certain extent, yes he can.

INTERVIEWER: Did that happen to you?

SAM: I came close to it.

INTERVIEWER: Was that part of the idea, that you have to sort of start believing it so that it helps you work it out?

SAM: Yes it is.

INTERVIEWER: You were saying that this is also something that you can do if you want to harm someone else?

SAM: Right.

INTERVIEWER: Is it the same type of process, more or less? What do you think about?

SAM: No, you don't think about the depressive atmosphere when you're been perpetrated towards you. How you're being motivated by some inner push to do this thing. It's like some force working on you where you get paranoid and your idea of this person is constantly messing up your life, pushing you, seeing how much you can take until you get to the point where everything and anything that he does is interfering with your life. To where your way of life is so that you can't react anyway and you have to resort to violence.

INTERVIEWER: Is that like you're depending on what your goal is, you bring in all kinds of things into your mind that would support your developing, like a tense feeling to act on?

SAM: Yes. Because each individual has a certain goal in his mind that he is trying to achieve. And if he's paranoid from the beginning, and something gets in his way or obstructs his pathway leading to this goal, he reacts with violence. Such as I did. And I wasn't going to let anything interfere with my reaching my goal. I was bound to get my way, regardless of who I hurt or what I did to obtain it. I was persistent to get there.

INTERVIEWER: Now that process that you told me about, when you're going through this—and you said you almost got to the paranoid bag part of it, you almost started to believe it—now when you get to the contemplating of this thing. You think of unjustified wrongs to the point that you can harm yourself—can you describe some of those feelings or thoughts?

SAM: You mean the feelings you experience when you put yourself in this trance?

INTERVIEWER: Yeah, when you're getting near there. As it goes through you.

SAM: Working toward feelings toward the other individual or yourself?

INTERVIEWER: Toward yourself.

SAM: You've got to keep running things through your mind, saying to yourself, "Why, what good am I to myself or anybody else? I'm never going to do anything worthwhile. I've left no mark on this earth. I'm twenty-one years old. I've achieved nothing, left no mark. What is my existence here?" And you keep running this through your mind until you reach a point that you've convinced yourself that you're a worthless human being, toward the human race or anything else. And you realize that you've been no good, and you're not going to be any good, so what's the reason for your existence? From that point on there's really nothing to do but to take your life.

INTERVIEWER: This question may be very difficult, but when you were going through this experience, was there some way that you could control so that you don't cut yourself too much? Is there some way that you can stop that from going all the way?

SAM: Your mind has an automatic, built-in protective system toward bodily harm. . . .

INTERVIEWER: After you've gone through this, is it a painful experience? Does it make you feel good? Is it an exhilarating experience? Or does it make you feel pretty unpleasant?

SAM: It depends on the person's nature. Myself, it might mean a blank state of mind where I didn't care. If somebody was to point me in a direction with a gun and say, "Shoot," I would have shot. That's the state of mind that I can put myself into. If I wanted to be self-destructive to myself, I could have carried the trance farther and been self-destructive.

INTERVIEWER: Are there any times where this state of mind you mentioned has led you to punching something kind of violently? Like these same kind of feelings, but anything will do, like a wall or something? You just want to release some tension?

SAM: Yes, quite often I get that.

INTERVIEWER: Has anything ever happened as a result of that?

SAM: Well, for instance, two years ago I got a letter from my wife stating that she wanted a divorce. Now naturally I was disturbed about it, and when I received the divorce papers I was upset. And I punched on my locker in my cell. The only thing I'd done was scrape my knuckles and let out some of the frustration I'd built up. But it don't take much to set some people off. I've learned to control my temper quite a bit, but I still can be set off at times. At the drop of a hat I can react violently toward somebody else or toward myself.

INTERVIEWER: These times that you do something, like you have enough violence to bruise your hand or scrape your knuckles, those situations, you're saying that the things that trigger them could go either way, or is there something unique in the event that makes it violent, either on yourself or on somebody else?

SAM: It's the frame of mind you're in at the time of the happening. Like, if someone would have crossed me then or said something out of the way, more than likely I would have hit him instead of the locker. Like, when I got this ten years, it started December 2, 1962, and it started off that morning when I went to see a friend about buying a car. And then I was walking home, and I went over to another friend's house, and I went out drinking with him at night. And we met some of his other friends, and I asked this one guy that I'd seen before if he would take us to another city where they were having a dance. And he made an off-the-wall statement. And I took it wrong, 'cause I was in a mess that night. And I took him outside, and I hurt him. And I put him in the hospital for some time, plus I took his money. Because of the statement and my wrong frame of mind that it happened.

INTERVIEWER: Then you had a mental set. You were describing that you had a lot of self-doubt the time that you scratched yourself and cut up a little bit. In other words, it could be the same amount of tension that was building up inside because of events, like a letter from home, or the divorce, different things you hear, but then it depends on whether or not they make you doubt yourself. You're describing that you didn't see any purpose. You didn't leave a mark. When are the times that you turn this tension inward?

SAM: Some people tend to conserve it inside theirselves, where they don't want people to know what's going on in their minds and thoughts. They don't want people to know what's going on in their minds, and they don't want people to know what's happening to them, the bad things from the outside or the inside. They don't want them to know, so it comes to a point where it is so built up inside of them that they explode one way or the other, either toward themselves or toward somebody else. It's a variety of things that can cause a person to get in this frame of mind. Like you said, it can be an emotional outlet for problems in the streets, from inside the institution, or it can be his own self-thinking toward himself where he's placed himself in a position where he thinks he's no good and never will be any good. Or he never was going to amount to very much. A person will put himself in a state of mind where he will just want to commit an act of violence where he can obliterate everything from his mind at one shot without having to go through the process of rationalizing everything out toward himself and towards others. All he wants to do is just react in a violent way. . . .

When I received a letter from my wife stating that she wanted a divorce, the service room that sorts the letters stopped it, and that afternoon they called me down, and they interviewed me about it in the service room. And they showed me the letter. And I read it. And she stated that she wanted a divorce, and she didn't give a specific reason why. Now the service unit retained that letter until that night. And I had all that afternoon to think about it. And even still knowing that I was going to get the letter that night, I was in the shape of a shook-up frame of mind. And that night, when I got the letter again, that's when it penetrated me what my wife had stated. And once it penetrated, I reacted violently by assaulting my arm. I had to release the frustration and agony I had built up unconsciously during that afternoon. So upon reading the letter, I just exploded in a burst of violence. . . .

Because when I read the letter the first time in the service unit office, my mind just blanked out. I was too shocked to react in any way or manner. I couldn't think. It was automatic. I just went from the office back to my job. And I reacted like I was out. Nothing could penetrate. I was like a walking statue, you might say. With no thought of living or anything else. And then when I got the letter that night, reality just closed in on me, and I had to react one way or the other. If I hadn't reacted I would probably still be walking around in that state of mind. And when it did finally penetrate, I would have probably reacted toward an individual for making some kind of statement. But as it was, it penetrated while I was alone in the cell that night, and nothing could get hurt except possibly my hands, from assaulting my locker or the wall. And I took out my frustations on that. . . .

INTERVIEWER: During this whole period when this happened, what time in there can you say that you felt more relieved?

SAM: After the doctor stated that he was going to commit me to a mental institution. I felt relief that I would not have to put up with any more of this miscellaneous baloney that I was going through in this institution. And I wouldn't have to be harassed by inmates threatening me with knives, razors, and whatnots. I wouldn't have to be under the pressure of hurting another individual because of this threat. . . .

INTERVIEWER: Since we've been rapping about this, is there anything else that you've thought about that? Other people that we talked to have said that they thought of things while we were talking to them. Was there anything in this interview that you thought about new since we've been talking about it?

SAM: Another thing I have thought about my past actions, referring to the sense that in 1964 I brought this story down to the doctor, I always regretted that time because I've had self-doubts about myself and this individual, and whether I could have avoided the conflict of violence with this individual and made peace with him and worked it out without means of violence. And also I'm sorry I did carry it through because it's on my record, a blot on my record that I was in a mental institution. And this is a serious setback for a person that tries to obtain good employment. And if the people have a reference checkup on you they might say, "What's this, not only is he a felon, but he's also a manic-depressive who was in an insane asylum. What am I going to have him working for me for? What is he, a nut?" I've been lucky so far that it has never come up. I have committed perjury a number of times when I have taken out applications for a driver's license and things like that.

Where people have asked me if I was ever in a mental institution, I've told them no. Because it would be a block, and it would stop me from procuring the objects that I needed at that time.

Our first paradox emerges early in the interview. Sam presents himself as intent on avoiding trouble from a fellow inmate. Yet he confesses no fear, and sees himself as a potential aggressor ("I was going to get to him first"). He hints at being disturbed ("the doctors came to me . . . asked me what was making me depressed") but claims to have dissembled ("I portrayed to the doctor that I was depressed"). He also claims he invented a new set of problems to secure transfer.

Sam confesses and yet denies self-injury ("I made scratch marks"); he recalls threats of self-destruction and disclaimers ("I threatened to cut my wrists. . . . I told him I didn't see no sense in carrying it to such extreme measures"). He slides over his various problems and talks of situational complaints ("I didn't like the atmosphere"). Finally, he tells us that his symptoms were such as to compel transfer.

Sam next qualifies his claim to dissembling by explaining that "a person has to work himself up to an emotional state where he can actually carry through with the act of destruction on his body." He discusses the content of obsessive pain and self-degradation ("you . . . think of the supposedly wrongs that . . . you have done . . . until you get in a paranoid state of mind that 'I'm no good to myself and to anybody' "). He even realistically describes his breakdown and complete loss of self-control ("your mind blanks out. . . . You have no control over your emotions whatsoever").

Yet the helplessness of despair becomes transmuted into a claim of potency. Sam sticks to the assertion that "I planned it right from the beginning. . . . It was premeditated, and I was able to carry it through."

The picture Sam presents of his violence to others runs parallel to his account of self-destructive violence. Again he describes pain and obsessive thought. He feels cornered to the point of helplessness ("you get to the point where everything and anything that he does is interfering with your life"). He sees his opponent as an ever-present obstacle, with no possible circumvention.

Sam talks in detail of feelings of worthlessness that engulf him. He speaks of not deserving life. Yet—at least, at the start—he claims to control these feelings: "You've got to keep running things through your mind," he tells us, "saying to yourself, 'Why, what good am I to myself or anybody else?' . . . And you realize that you've been no good, and you're not going to be any good, so what's the reason for your existence?"

Ultimately, Sam's self-description breaks down as he recounts two other episodes, one precipitating a self-destructive act and the other an assault. In the first, Sam's wife notified him that she wanted a divorce, and Sam admits to having reacted with extreme pain. In the second (somewhat parallel to Sam's commitment offense), he recalls injuring a man in response to an insulting comment.

Sam next describes, in deceptively general terms, the buildup of tension that results from pent-up grievance. He explains how a pretense of imperturbability leads to an outburst of destructiveness. "They don't want them to know," he says, "so it comes to a point where it is so built up inside of them that they explode one way or the other, either toward themselves or toward somebody else." He then illustrates the sequence by describing the agonizing aftermath of his wife's message.

Finally, Sam refers to prison in ways suggestive of fears and doubts about his safety. He talks of being "harassed by inmates threatening me with knives, razors, and whatnots." Nevertheless, he renews his claim to a tailor-made bid for psychiatric transfer.

Sam's case illustrates not only the difficulty of maintaining a consistent stance of autonomy, but also shows how this stance can contribute to violent outbursts. Sam has doubts about his adequacy which are easily mobilized. When this occurs, he pretends calm and pursues business as usual. Meanwhile, the resentment, frustration, and self-hate which Sam feels but cannot admit build up to the point where they dominate his thinking. Since expressed feeling is excluded, the process cumulates in a self-destructive or punitive explosion.

Sam illustrates for us the most serious consequence of the Manliness Myth. If feelings are deemed illegitimate, they cannot be acknowledged or voiced. With insight and verification ruled out, an obsessive, self-destructive cycle sets in. Ultimately, feelings express themselves, but they cannot be faced for what they are. This produces cognitive and emotional spirals in the form of compulsive acts. The illusion of omnipotence and autonomy then promotes their opposites: it spawns helplessness, defeat, and loss of control.

Sam's case is admittedly extreme. He went to unusual lengths in distorting information about himself so as to accommodate his self-image, and persevered to an extraordinary extent in his elaborations of his myth. More typically, the manly self-portraits traced for us by inmates crumbled rapidly as our interviews progressed. As the men told us about the antecedents of their breakdowns, the magnitude of their despair was easily reawakened in them. And as they resuscitated their feelings, they relinquished (with gratitude) their postures of pragmatic planfulness and inviolability.

Our interview procedure enhanced our chances of surfacing crisis connotations, because (1) we dealt with the subjects' view of their acts, and (2) we dissected their self-perceptions in follow-through questioning. The interview with Sam illustrates the process. We see how Sam's first, casual self-characterization ("I portrayed to the doctor that I was depressed") was picked up by the interviewer and explored. If Sam was willing to admit to feelings, he was provided with opportunities to do so. In response to a neutral query ("is that something that's rather difficult to do, or is it easy?"), Sam expands on his self-engineered-tantrum formula. "You sit there," he tells us, "and you have to put yourself in a mental position. . . . And from that state on . . . you have no control." Sam's detailed statement permits us to explore the emotional release component he admits to. We do this in a fashion that minimally penalizes frankness. We self-deprecatingly ask, "This may sound silly, because you say you have complete control, but . . . ," and are rewarded with the first deviation from Sam's party line.

Sam's interview illustrates the sequential exploration of crisis stages (including assumptions and feelings) which forms our interview structure.[15] Sam is asked about triggering or catalytic experiences, about the direction of his thinking, about his cumulating feelings, about the climax of his difficulties, and about his postcrisis reactions. His interview is atypical only because Sam—unlike most of our subjects—prefers to talk about himself in safe, generalizing terms. Most of our subjects relate one or more incidents of personal breakdown and—in response to our step-by-step probes—fill in details and expand on their narratives. The bulk of each interview consists of chronological reconstructions of specific incidents, including the subject's feelings and perceptions at each stage of crisis. Questions dealing with commonalities in incidents or general observations the interviewee might have about his own difficulties (or the problems of other inmates) are posed at the end. These questions involve our subjects as observers and (in a restricted sense) as coresearchers.[16]

All our interviews were tape-recorded. Despite this fact—and despite the consent forms and "blind" interview requests sometimes required by law or by the institution—our turndown rate was low. Of the men we approached who were capable of being interviewed, only 5.5% (19 men) refused to talk with us. (We lost 29 additional interviews—5 because of language difficulties, and 24 because psychotic subjects proved incoherent or unresponsive.) In our interviews with female inmates, we had no turndowns, but lost one of our 53 interviews, due to a broken cassette.

More important than our low turndown rate is the level of rapport we achieved with our subjects—which often bordered on the therapeutic. We obtained information withheld from staff during their investigation of incidents. And at times our interviewees told us that they were sharing concerns that they had never communicated to anyone. If these observations are valid, there are probably several reasons for the willingness (and frequently, the eagerness) of our respondents to deal openly with us.

For one, we may have succeeded in creating a client-centered climate. We communicated our interest in the inmate's perspective not only through our open-ended questions but also through the care we took to explore any theme initiated by a respondent, no matter how tentatively he introduced it. This enabled our subjects to expand on sensitive areas which they usually deemed it unsafe or less than respectable to broach. Though we cannot claim that all our subjects were fully open with us, we discovered that at least some of them felt able to explore areas which they had previously regarded as private, unshareable, or damaging. In the words of our subjects:

GM 9:   This is the first time in a long time that I feel that I can trust somebody. Even a psychiatrist couldn't get it out of me.

D 38:   It was just good to get out and talk to somebody, because I haven't talked with anybody. I didn't talk to anybody about it from the beginning.

CX 49:   Right now, this is a very good feeling to me, because I'm looking back on it. . . . I'm virtually having it out in my mind, and it's a good feeling.

M 52:   It's beautiful. Like, I'm here right now running down everything to you that you wanted me to run down, and I'm being specific. I never took no time to run it down to anyone else. So I've had it in me before this. Now I'm letting it all out, and it makes me feel good.

Our relative success in obtaining data was not exclusively a function of our interview style. Often, the information we obtained had been unavailable to others because they had never posed the relevant questions. In other instances, the fact that we approached our subjects as historians of crisis rather than as crisis prevention agents proved crucial. Whereas at the climax of crisis a person may be willing—even anxious—to share his experience, he may be uncommunicative and self-contained at earlier stages:

C 49:   Even if anyone walked by my gate, "Get the fuck away from the gate! Get the fuck out of my gate!" I was really upset. Even one of my closest friends here couldn't talk to me because I wouldn't let him, and I didn't want to talk to anyone. I wanted to think this out for myself. This is the feeling that I had.

GM 1:   I quit talking to people. I moved to myself, and I didn't like anyone asking me anything what my problem is. I just like to be by myself.

D 19:   I don't think there would be a right person to talk to, the way I felt. See, like now I could talk about it, but before I wouldn't have been able to.

We were also aided by our freedom from institutional ties. Prison inmates feel vulnerable because they assume that self-disclosures are self-incriminating or, more important, provide ammunition to exploiters. They are concerned about the possibility that confidences will find their way into dossiers or become public knowledge. Even prisoners who know that they could benefit from advice or emotional support may feel compelled to try to "work through" their problems on their own. Yet they may share their concerns eagerly if they are assured of safety. The first "outsider" to approach such a man may find him ready and willing to provide data:

MHDM 40:   Like, you came and talked to me, and I talked to you, right? As a man to another man. You have no ties with this joint. And I'm talking to you like another guy. But if you were to sit there and say you work for the institution, "What's bothering you?" Well, "Nothing's bothering me."

I: Just as an aside, like, why wouldn't you talk to the psychiatrist, but you'll talk to me?

MHDM 41:   Well, what you're asking me can't do me no harm and it can't do me no good. So I'll give you the information. Like you said, maybe that will help someone else. . . . The psychiatrist didn't ask me these questions anyway. He just wanted to know why I did it, that's all. And I just told him that I was tired of everything.

I: You told him that, and he just left it at that?

MHDM 41:   He had to leave it like that because I didn't feel like talking.

Our own disaffiliation with the correctional system was communicated not merely through verbal assurances (though we took pains to describe our role) but by the nature and scope of our questions. The message was carried by our de-emphasis of matters related to culpability and judgment and the stress we placed on the interviewee's feelings. Thus the interview sold itself in part because its lines of questioning contrasted with those conventionally pursued by custodial and treatment staff.

We achieved dramatic successes among some types of subjects who had reason to be unapproachable. The reserve we encountered among black inmates, for example, dissolved after we had conducted several interviews. Our initial successes included a number of militants. One of our early subjects—highly respected among his peers—not only helped us recruit others but also assisted in interviews and analysis. Puerto Rican inmates served as group interviewers and translators. Following the same interview pattern with psychotic inmates as with other subjects produced rich retrospective data. These men vividly described their dissociated states and reviewed their delusions from an almost clinical perspective:

46: As I say, it's like a combination of voices, you know? It's very difficult for me to explain.

I: You mean, it is like a chorus of the same voice?

46: Right, solid, right.

I: Like sometimes on records they'll have one guy singing, but they record his voice over and over again so it sounds like about fifty of them singing the same thing?

46: Right, that's how it is, right.

I: Does it come on in a regular voice or is it sort of a singsong-type voice?

46: Very like a monologue, one thing, only very high-pitched but spaced. In other words, where you'd think a high-pitched voice would be rapid, it's not like that. It's like—

I: Smooth?

46: Yeah. But high, very high, but spaced. The words are spaced.

I: Does it ever go higher or lower, or does it keep that same tone?

46: It keeps the same tone.

I: So all right, you're saying that it gets down on you, it says derogatory things about you. Now can you get into the things that it says about you a little more deeply than you already did? I know it may be painful for you, but—

46: No, I'll try.

I: What type of indication did you have that they were going to rape you? Did anybody say anything to you, or did you see other guys being raped before?

24: No.

I: It just came to you out of the blue that they might rape you?

24: Well, the way they were talking. And since it was kind of a family affair. When they want to bug you out they bug you out.

I: Usually, why do they want to bug you out?

24: Well, to make you suffer. When they know you're paranoid they do it.

I: Were you paranoid?

24: Yes.

I: And they knew this?

24:   Yes.

1:   And you think that both guards and inmates were picking on you?

24:   Well, they didn't actually pick on me, but they always seemed like
they was going to. So rather than have them beat me up or rape me like
I thought they was going to do, I just wanted to commit suicide.

Our interviews were conducted in all major facilities of the New York
State Department of Correctional Services and the New York City Department of Corrections. We also talked to inmates in a medium-sized county
jail. The state institutions we covered included the maximum security
prisons, an institution for youthful offenders, the women's prison, and two
facilities housing inmates with psychiatric problems or special treatment
requirements. In New York City, we interviewed detainees at the Man-
hattan House of Detention, the Adolescent Remand Shelter, the Rikers
Island Hospital, and the Correctional Institution for Women.

Our survey enjoyed the support of key officials in two of the nation's
major correctional systems. This support, and the expenditure of time
and manpower it implied, testifies to the hospitality of at least some allegedly closed systems to unsolicited incursions by uninvited guests. The
reason for cooperation was probably the desire of officials for relevant,
trustworthy feedback. Despite the portrait traced by critics (some of whom
may never have met a correctional manager), in our experience the custodians of inmates do not seem oblivious to the suffering of their charges.
They appear concerned about their impact and about possibilities (within
the limits of the available options) for ameliorating the experience of incarceration. We were probably also aided—given the goals of our research
—because we shared a specific concern about a practical problem that worries prison administrators. And the warmth with which we were received
may have been due in part to the fact that our credentials and our past
involvements implied that we would approach our task with an effort at
objectivity.

Whatever the reasons, our interviewers had access to nearly all the inmates in our sample.[17] Institutional staff contacted the interviewees, escorted them to the interview site, and provided facilities for unimpeded
contact. Though in crowded settings we occasionally resorted to the use of
semiprivate rooms, most of our interviews occurred in quiet, undisturbed
surroundings. We also had access to recorded data of relevance to our
study, including inmate folders and central ledgers.

We aimed at an exhaustive inventory of inmates incarcerated between
January 1971 and August 1973 who had committed acts of self-injury or
had attempted suicide. While most of the inmates in our pool had experienced breakdowns during that period, some showed incidents only
prior to 1971 or had injured themselves at some unspecified time. And

though our pool included all inmates for whom incidents were recorded, it did not exhaust the universe of inmates who injured themselves. Records were sparse in central offices despite the fact that New York City has a roster of dramatic incidents and that at our request New York State instituted critical incident reporting covering the period of our study.[18] Institutions seemed to vary in the completeness of their data about inmate behavior. In one facility we amassed our sample by combining the use of disciplinary logs, the warden's file, deputy warden's cards, and infirmary logs. And at most interview sites our subjects were able to locate other subjects for us, though the referred inmates had no incidents on record (other than in their folders). Our control sample, which is reasonably representative, suggests that the sample population underestimates the incident rate by at least 7%—this being the proportion of controls who had injured themselves.

We attempted to reach as many of the inmates in the sample population as we could, and interviewed those inmates wherever in the system we could locate them. We reached 45% of the projected sample—381 out of 847 interview candidates. The principal loss occurred in the city system, which has a sharp population turnover. Whereas we reached two thirds of our prison population we reached only 25% of the New York detention pool.[19]

We interviewed a systematic random sample of 175 control subjects. The purpose of these interviews was to verify the applicability (or nonapplicability) of our findings to inmates who had not injured themselves. We also aimed at a comparison of randomly selected inmates on demographic and other variables with our self-injury group. From the folders of all our subjects, we collated and coded all available background information, including criminal histories and institutional careers.

Another source of data for the study was provided by four inmates who committed suicide in prison during the final stage of our survey. In each case, we deployed a team to the setting of the tragedy within days after it took place. We interviewed key staff members and inmates who had known the victim, and questioned them about their observations, impressions, and inferences. The data were collated into individual clinical case studies (psychological autopsies).[20] These case studies are recorded in Part III of this volume.

Our interviews were transcribed from tape and subjected to content analysis. In line with standard criteria for the construction of typologies, we aimed at a classification which would give us complete coverage of our population, as well as describe each individual without violating the shape of his dominant concerns. We insisted on clear-cut, nonoverlapping categories, internally meaningful and consistent, and parsimonious. We also aimed at a code formulated with sufficient precision and concreteness to permit reliable classifications by trained raters.[21]

At first our analytic procedure evolved inductively. We grouped our interviews (15% of our sample)—subcategorizing them according to dominant "themes." By a "theme" we meant the difficulties described by the subject, his main concerns, the focus of his despair. Each interview was assigned such a theme.

We tested out the coding scheme on a new subsample. And we discovered that while the themes "fitted," the fit was sometimes uncomfortable. One theme might characterize the dominant concerns of some but violate the integrity of others. Even a single incident could be overdetermined. A variety of concerns contributing to breakdowns could (and did) emerge conjointly. Men felt literally "crowded" or "cornered"—smothered by overlapping problems.

Interviews began with statements such as:

M 7:   And when I was in the cell, my mind was running, I was having so many delusions. Like seeing things come out of the toilet—things like that. And I was worried about my family, that they wasn't coming down to visit me. And when I went to court I thought I was going to walk right out. And they told me they were going to send me up to the supreme. I came back. I was real depressed.

MHDM 27:   I'm here on an armed robbery charge. I'm married, and when I first came in, my wife was very understanding. She got a lawyer for me. She wrote to me every day. And after I had been here two months I discovered that my wife was seeing someone else. And subsequently she left me for somebody else. Now, just about at the same time I realized that my situation in here, and how I got myself in here, I could have avoided anytime in the three weeks prior to my arrest. And it all came down on me at once.

MHDM 39:   I got a visit from my uncle, and he told me that my mother was still sick. She was dying from cancer. She had a cancer operation. And that just kept playing on my mind. It just kept building up. And then my court cases were coming down on me. And you've got nothing to do up there. And it builds up, and I was thinking about it. . . . I'd be thinking about something, and then my case would come in front of me, and then my mother would come in front of me.

We addressed the shape of this reality by increasing the flexibility of our procedure. For a given interview, we would assign a single theme if possible, but allow for two or more themes where multiple concerns led to breakdowns. Such composites (which cover half our sample) denote overdetermined crises, or point to patterns in which some incidents are differently motivated than the rest. Where two or more themes are used

to classify an interview, one has been selected as the *primary* theme—
meaning that it stands out as the dominant motive or concern. This procedure proved reliable. Independent codings yielded 85% to 90% agree-
ment for primary themes, and 75% to 80% for secondary themes.[22]

The change to a nonmonothematic emphasis is more than a procedural
shift. It alters the typology from a *classification of persons* to a *classification of personal difficulties*. It presumes a richer, more eclectic mix of
psychological events. It stipulates, for instance, that a person may be
enmeshed in crises that reflect pressures from both the outside world and
the prison, or that combine "normal" difficulties with neurotic or psychotic overtones. And it presumes that men who have serious emotional
problems can simultaneously experience coping difficulties that are equivalent to the crises of far less disturbed persons.

A second discovery is related to the structure of our typology. We
found that when we arranged our inductively derived themes in logical
order, they clustered into categories which revealed a conceptual model.
This should not have come as a surprise. Given a complex stimulus array,
it is nonsense to assume that classification occurs with carefree promiscuity. Unconscious assumptions govern the selection of material that is
deemed worthy of classification. And even if this were not the case, we
might have expected that the person's perspective (whether "healthy" or
"disturbed") would reflect psychological mechanisms, which were apt to
be revealed as themes were grouped. Our typology is therefore probably a
mix of theoretical bias and observed process.

The "model" that emerges from our classification is schematized in
Table 1.1. The columns represent types of crises which we regard as qualitatively different. The first category ("coping") connotes "concrete" or
"situational" problems—those having to do with difficulties in adjusting to
contextual pressures or demands. The second category ("self-perception")
refers to crises in which doubts about personal or social adequacy seem
to be the principal issue. The last category ("impulse management") comprises difficulties arising out of struggles with feelings or impulses.
Whereas all crises are responses to environmental stress, the responses (if
our scheme is valid) may be to different connotations of the environment.
In the first type of crisis, the connotation is, "I am unable to handle
noxious impingements"; in the second type, stress gives rise to the inference, "I must be inadequate or unworthy"; in the third, the milieu helps
trigger the ultimate question, "Am I real, and in control of my conduct?"

What we suggest is that situational coping, self-doubts, and rampant
impulses are arenas in which adjustment is played out—arenas in which
mental health can be cross-sectionally gauged. We feel that stress—depending on the dispositions of the persons who encounter it—can translate into
issues of surviving, facing oneself and others, and maintaining control.

The side headings in Table 1.1 summarize dominant concerns which

TABLE 1.1   *Typology of Personal Breakdowns*
(Gross Theme Clusters)

Relevant Psychological Dimension	*Type of Difficulty*		
	Coping (self and environment)	*Self-perception (self and others)*	*Impulse management (self and others)*
Impotence	Helplessness and resentment	Hopelessness and self-doubt	Catharsis and self-hate
Fear	Isolation panic	Fear of prison pressures	Projected or subjective danger
Need for support	Staff	Significant others	Mental health

pervade all three types of crisis. These are universal motives—or, at least, they seem to be involved in varying degrees in different kinds of crises. For example, "fear" can mean panic in overwhelming settings, the defenseless stance of self-defined victims, or terror in the face of irresistible forces that seem to be taking possession of one's mind. In this most general form, the dilemmas of our subjects seem to be issues of mastery over fate, the capacity to stand up under pressure, and dependence. These issues—as we see it—represent existential questions running through crises of every kind in every setting. In the account that follows, we shall explore how these questions concretely manifest themselves for men in confinement.

In the next three chapters, we describe our typology in detail and also try to illustrate the way in which our themes take shape in the accounts of our subjects. We begin with a listing of categories and definitions. That listing is our "code"—the instrument we used to classify the crises of inmates. We then describe the substance of our findings for each theme. Next we trace the shape each theme takes and describe its typical variations. Chapter 2 covers the coping difficulties subsumed under the first category (Column 1) of Table 1.1; Chapter 3 deals with self-assessment problems (Column 2); and Chapter 4 discusses difficulties in the management of impulses (Column 3).

Part II of the book (Chapters 5–8) deals with the relationship of crisis themes to personal background factors and milieu variables. Here we explore the differential impact of jail and prison, of cultural experience, of sexual socialization on the shapes of personal crises. In Part III we turn to irreversible breakdowns—suicides. In our account of these tragedies, we emphasize the cumulative development of crisis themes over time.

In the last chapters, we review our control interviews, and we take up the implications of our findings for crisis intervention efforts. We also explore some issues related to the prevention, management, and amelioration of breakdowns.

NOTES

1. Freud, S. "Mourning and Melancholia," in *Collected Papers*, Vol. 4, (London: Hogarth Press, 1925) pp. 152–173; *The Psychopathology of Everyday Life* (New York: New American Library, Mentor Book, 1951).

2. As early as 1909 W. I. Thomas defined a crisis as "simply, a disturbance of habit" (*Source Book for Social Origins* [Boston: Gorham Press, 1909], p. 18); with F. Znaniecki, Thomas studied the dislocating role of migration in their classic *The Polish Peasant in Europe and America* (Boston: Badger, 1927). Statistical relationships between migration and serious emotional disorder were documented in the thirties by B. Malzberg (see, for example, "Rates of Mental Disease among certain Population Groups in New York State," *Journal of the American Statistical Association*, 1936, *31*, 367–72; see also B. Malzberg and E. Lee, *Migration and Mental Disease* [New York: Social Science Research Council, 1956]). A. Toffler, in *Future Shock* (New York: Random House, 1970), cites evidence to show that "alterations in life style" can produce illness. Research studies on the psychological damage stemming from dislocation range from those showing differential incidence of mental disease with reduced stability of neighborhood (in tradition of the Chicago School) to observational or clinical surveys. Among the latter is a report on persons forcibly relocated in Boston, in which mild disturbances lasting over a period of months were noted in three fourths of the group (M. Fried, "Grieving Over a Lost Home," in *The Urban Condition*, ed. L. J. Duhl [New York: Basic Books, 1963], pp. 151–171). The crisis intervention literature contains discussions of low-level crises (crises of everyday life). In a book edited by H. J. Parad, for instance, there are chapters on relocation and on entry into kindergarten (*Crisis Intervention: Selected Readings* [New York: Family Service Association of America, 1965]).

3. Probably the best-known studies of the impact of disaster are those of A. F. C. Wallace and Martha Wolfenstein. It was Wallace who coined the term "disaster syndrome" to describe the withdrawal and anxiety typically observed among disaster victims (A. F. C. Wallace, *Tornado in Worcester* [Washington, D.C.: National Research Council–National Academy of Sciences, 1956]). Psychiatric studies of disaster victims include not only Wolfenstein's work (*Disaster: A Psychological Essay* [Glencoe, Ill.: Free Press, 1957]) but also a frequently quoted paper by J. S. Tyhurst ("Individual Reactions to Community Disaster," *American Journal of Pyschiatry*, 1951, *107*, 764–69). In a recent summary of available research, F. Hocking notes that "if the stress is sufficiently severe, virtually all individuals will develop what would be, in an everyday setting, neurotic symptoms" ("Extreme Environmental Stress and Its Significance to Psychopathology," *American Journal of Psychotherapy*, 1970, *4*, 4–26, p. 5). The literature on breakdowns of soldiers in war began with studies of "nostalgia" during the Civil War; 5,213 cases of breakdown were observed during the first year of the war, and the rate rose as the war went on. Civil War soldiers were also discharged with diagnoses of "paralysis" and "insanity" (W. A. Hammond, *A Treatise on Insanity in Its Medical Realtions* [London: H. K. Lewis, 1883]; A. Deutsch, "Military Psychiatry: The Civil War," in *One Hundred Years of American Psychiatry*, ed. American Psychiatric Association [New York: Columbia University Press, 1944], pp. 376 ff). In World War II, 500,000 men were released for psychiatric reasons; the casualty rate reached 101 per 100,000 for the American invasion forces in Europe (W. J. Tiffany and W. S. Allerton, "Army Psychiatry in the Mid-'60s," *American Journal of Psychiatry*, 1970, *123*, 810–21). Studies of stress in wartime include the classic work by R. R. Grinker and J. P. Spiegel, *Men Under Stress* (New York: McGraw-Hill, 1963). Another classic in this area is the research by I. L. Janis on the impact of bombing on civilian populations (*Air War and Emotional Stress* [New York: McGraw-Hill, 1951]). Janis found that although bombing did not produce gross psychopathology, it resulted in psychosomatic symptoms ranging from peptic ulcers, dermatitis, and coronaries to bed-wetting. Freud concerned himself with the problem of "war neurosis" in the first World War. In a letter to Ernest Jones he wrote, "Anxiety is a protection against shock. Now, the condition of the Traumatic Neurosis seems to be that the soul had no time to recur to this protection and is taken by the trauma unprepared. Its defense against stimulation is overrun, and the principal and primary function of keep-

ing off excessive quantities of stimuli, frustrated. . . . The difference between peace and war is that in the former the ego is strong but surprised, with the latter it is prepared but weakened" (E. Jones, *The Life and Work of Sigmund Freud* [New York: Basic Books, 1955], *2; 253–54*). William James also concerned himself with the disequilibration produced by disasters; in *Memories and Studies* (New York: Longmans, Green, 1911) he discussed the plight of earthquake victims.

4. The psychological breakdown of concentration camp inmates is described in B. Bettelheim, "Individuals and Mass Behavior in Extreme Situations," *Journal of Abnormal and Social Psychology*, 1943, *38*, 417–52; in E. A. Cohen, Human Behavior in the Concentration Camp (New York: Norton, 1953, chap. 3; and in V. E. Frankl, *From Death Camp to Existentialism: A Psychiatrist's Path to a New Therapy* (Boston: Beacon Press, 1959). There have also been studies of the long-term impact of the concentration camp experience. L. Ettinger, for instance, reports that "the most predominant sequel to the concentration camp captivity seems to be the deep changes in personality, a mental disability which affects every side of the personality's psychic life. . . . in short, the inability to live in a normal way [is] among the most characteristic symptoms of the condition" (*Concentration Camp Survivors in Norway and Israel* [London: Allen and Unwin, 1964]).

5. The definition of stress as a taxing or threatening situation may be reduced to the concept of "imbalance" employed by Lazarus. Lazarus also emphasizes that events threatening to all people exposed to them can mean different things to different people and result in qualitatively different coping problems. See R. Lazarus, *Psychological Stress and the Coping Process* (New York: McGraw-Hill, 1966).

6. H. Hendin, *Suicide and Scandinavia* (Garden City, N.Y.: Doubleday Anchor, 1965).

7. The Eskimo tribes provide a telling case, because they live with a chronic disaster situation, in which sudden "icequakes" can destroy their fishing parties. One observer has noted that the physical environment of some Eskimo groups has not been experienced by Western man since prehistoric times (J. Bilby, *Among Unknown Eskimos* [Philadelphia: Lippincott, 1923], p. 58). The issue of "socialization for survival" in the slums has been discussed in H. Toch, "The Delinquent as a Poor Loser," *Seminars in Psychiatry*, 1971, *3*, 386–99.

8. The most detailed available explorations of morale and the adjustment problems in a wartime army are S. A. Stouffer et al.'s studies of the American soldier in World War II (*The American Soldier: Adjustment during Army Life* and *The American Soldier: Combat and Its Aftermath* [Princeton, N.J.: Princeton University Press, 1949]).

9. J. P. Zubek notes that "in surveying the literature on sensory restriction, one is struck not only by the variety of procedures and techniques that have been employed to reduce the variety and level of environmental stimulation . . . but even more so by the innumerable terms used to describe this experimental condition" ("Behavioral and Physiological Effects of Prolonged Sensory and Perceptual Deprivation: A Review," in *Man in Isolation and Confinement*, ed. J. Rasmussen [Chicago: Aldine, 1973], pp. 9–83). A bewildering inventory of situations explored in "stress" studies is catalogued by J. E. McGrath, in *Social and Psychological Factors in Stress* [New York: Holt, Rinehart & Winston, 1970]. The limited generalizability of the research is apparent from the impact measures deployed by the investigators, which (according to Zubek) include flicker frequency, psychogalvanic skin responses, electroencephalograms, thematic apperception test, and Rorschach inkblots.

10. In her classis study of *Disaster* Wolfenstein discusses such reactions as an upsurge of positive feelings, a sense of unreality, psychological paralysis to major calamities, tormenting memories, endemic fear, and a calculus of losses.

11. See, for example, the Corrections Task Force Report of the National Advisory Commission of Criminal Justice Standards and Goals (Washington, D.C.: U.S. Government Printing Office, 1973).

12. D. Lewis, *The Development of American Prisons and Prison Customs, 1776–1845*, reprint (Montclair, N.J.: Patterson Smith, 1967), p. 82. As recently as 1972, a lower court decision in New York State (Sostre) limited the use of solitary confinement on the grounds that "human isolation might endanger the prisoner's sanity" ("The Constitutional Status of Solitary Confinement," *Cornell Law Review*, 1972, *57*, p. 483).

13. G. Sykes, *The Society of Captives* (New York: Atheneum, 1966); D. Clemmer, *The Prison Community* (Boston: Christopher, 1940).

14. An exception is the discussion by E. Johnson of the inmates labeled "rats" by other inmates. Johnson notes that many inmates find themselves stigmatized in this way because of limited coping skills rather than because of any actual "informing" they may do. ("Sociology of Confinement Assimilation and the Prison 'Rat,'" *Journal of Criminol Law, Crimonology, and Police Science*, 1961, *51*, 228–33).

15. The interview procedure is similar to that used in studies of violence-experienced offenders (H. Toch, *Violent Men: An Inquiry into the Psychology of Violence* [Chicago: Aldine, 1969]). It centers on incidents which are obtained through open-ended questions. These incidents are explored from their initiation to their culmination, by means of questioning about sequences of events, premises, and feelings.

16. H. Toch, "The Convict as Researcher," *Trans-Action*, 1967, *4*, 72–75. In their sensitive and humane book-length essay on survival in a maximum security prison wing S. Cohen and L. Taylor note that "the subjects of our research had the habit of becoming researchers in their own right" (*Psychological Survival: The Experience of Long Term Imprisonment* [New York: Random House, Vintage Book, 1974], p. 33). Not only did the idea for Cohen and Taylor's research originate in discussions with inmates, but two-way communication was preserved throughout the study by providing the subjects with relevant reading material and letting them put their thoughts in writing for shared review.

17. Attempts were made to reach the entire self-injury population. However, institutional routines and regulations, transfers, and court appearances limited our sample size. This was especially the case in the jails, where men would enter and leave the system before we could approach them, and where court appearances are more frequent than is the case in prisons.

18. This reporting system helped us to locate some subjects, but otherwise proved of limited value. Given a tradition of autonomy among correctional institutions, centralized communication systems cannot be established by fiat. Consequently, the return rates for our report form ranged from adequate to zero, and the respondents' interpretations of incident categories varied.

19. The first jail interview was not obtained until 11 February, 1972; thus, most of the 1971 self-injury population in addition to suicides during the interview interval were excluded from the available interviewee population. Refusals, denials, insurmountable language problems, prisoners too psychotic to interview, interviews not completed because of recording problems accounted for another fourteen exclusions. The remainder of the attrition in the New York City sample can be accounted for by court appearances, in-system transfers, transfers to state institutions, and releases. In many instances the exact reason for a man's absence from the institution could not be ascertained.

20. The "psychological autopsy" procedure originates with E. Shneidman and his associates at the Los Angeles Suicide Prevention Center.

21. The importance of such classification criteria in offender typologies is discussed by M. Q. Warren in *Classification of Offenders as an Aid to Efficient Management and Effective Treatment*, working paper, The President's Commission on Law Enforcement and Administration of Justice, mimeographed (Washington, D.C.: 1967).

22. Reliability was determined for all male interviews. Each transcribed text was coded by the interviewer and an independent coder. The few remaining discrepancies were resolved in conference.

I

Varieties of Human Breakdown

2

Solving Insoluble
Problems

It is easy to be uninformative about breakdowns. In explanations of prison crises one often hears such statements as, "He couldn't handle it," or "He couldn't take confinement," or (shift of emphasis) "Prison was too much for him."

Such formulas tell us nothing because they are too vague. What couldn't the person handle? In what way was he unable to cope with confinement? What aspect of the prison situation proved "too much"?

This chapter tries to deal with such questions. We list—and explore—ways in which men succumb to situational pressures. We examine specifically how they succumb. Human failure is not a syllogism, a logical consequence of excessive pressure or insufficient stamina. It is a multifactorial, cumulative sequence, which comprises a person's changing circumstances, perceptions, expectations, and requirements for survival. A man will uniquely explore, fail, and feel stymied; a situation otherwise bearable may become a subjective problem, a stalemate—a crisis.

The crises we review here are junctures of life in a very trying setting which are found overwhelming by some persons. These junctures encompass problems of managing, enduring, manipulating, relating, husbanding, assimilating, living with, and surviving. Our focus in examining these breakdowns is neither on weaknesses or defects of the individual nor on drawbacks or difficulties of the environment. It is, rather, on the "trans-action" between individual and environment—the relationship between personal areas of susceptibility and the difficulties presented by concrete situations. Specific tests are posed by the environment which specific persons fail. Other persons may surmount the same difficulties. And the same persons might have found the same junctures manageable at other stages of their personal and social development or in other settings.

Coping problems relate to the type of environment in which a person finds himself. Some coping themes are more or less common to a wide range of stressful settings; others acquire new connotations in different contexts. The emphasis in this chapter will be on the pressures of a prison environment and on the coping problems generated by that milieu.

However, in the two chapters that follow (Chapters 3 and 4) we will explore personal crises that transcend here-and-now adjustment problems. If the portraits we paint in those chapters are valid, they should apply in all kinds of institutions and in the community at large.

I.   Themes Related to Coping (Problems in the Adjustment of Man to Prison)

(A, B: Overstimulation and Resentment)

A. Sanctuary Search: An effort by the inmate to escape from redundant preoccupations—particularly with regard to problems in the outside world or in his own situation—to which he finds no solution or closure. The object of his effort is to break the unproductive cycle and secure peace of mind.

B. Self-Victimization: A statement by the inmate of his inability to endure the self-defined status of victim of continued arbitrariness, inequity, or abuse by the criminal justice system or its personnel. The prisoner gives notice of his helplessness (demanding a truce) or advertises his accumulated resentment, where he feels retaliation is unsafe.

(C: Understimulation and Fear)

C. Isolation Panic: A demand for the inmate's release from isolated confinement which he finds fear-inspiring, intolerable, and obsessive. The prisoner dwells on the duration and/or circumstances of his situation, on his discomfort, and on his inability to engage in prison activities and social life.

(D, E: Quest for Assistance in Selective Coping)

D. Self-Classification: An inmate's effort to communicate to staff the seriousness of his need for a specific milieu among those available in prison. Here the inmate differentiates between social or physical environments within which he can function and settings he finds it impossible to adjust to. He underlines the seriousness and importance of the distinction.

E. Aid Seeking: An inmate's demand for staff services which, as the inmate sees it, cannot be ignored by staff. Such a demand occurs when a physical problem becomes the focus of the inmate's discontent, and he becomes obsessed with the need for attention to his complaint and upset about staff failure to comply with or respond to direct requests.

II. How Do Coping Themes Manifest Themselves?

A. SANCTUARY SEARCH

We presuppose that all people at given junctures in their lives are faced with events which they find disappointing, disheartening, or difficult to accept. For all of us, life is a continuing process of assimilating or de-emphasizing disappointments, of working out alternative behavioral strategies, of changing frames of reference, of reducing negative feelings, or of obtaining social support.

Imprisonment can present extraordinary obstacles to all of these modes of adjustment. Alternative goals can become harder to achieve because the inmate is physically immobilized; assimilating a problem can become more difficult in the absence of full information and in the context of more immediate demands on resources; inattention to and suppression or de-emphasis of difficulties can be precluded by a barren environment which forces a person to live with and face his problems during long hours of solitude and inactivity.

This impact of prison can represent a dramatic departure for persons used to fast-paced lives, anesthetized existences, or extroverted careers. Unable for once to escape painful stimuli, such men may react to untoward events in their lives by dwelling on them, becoming obsessed with them, and involuntarily and inescapably replaying them. They end up with psychological "overload," feeling confused, overwhelmed, helpless. They try to terminate their internal ordeal, to diffuse it, dispel it, "release" it.

As one inmate describes the sequence:

CL 2:   See, in the street, you'd say so-and-so is the point, and you'd try and straighten it out. But being that you can't straighten it out, all you can do is brood about it. Now if the brooding goes on to any extent, something's got to give.

The intimate relationship between person and environment is fairly clear here. The environmental setting does not offer the coping tools with which certain individuals customarily grapple with negative experiences. In such conditions a man faced with a state of mind he has previously been able to bypass may conclude that to shut off the painful and confusing feelings and thoughts that engulf him, he must attack their remaining source—his own mind.

A typical situation is that of an inmate who has been disappointed by news from home, has created difficulties in the prison (which he blames on unresolved tension arising from his unhappiness), and is placed in segregation. During the first days of his confinement, he tries to escape from "bad feelings" by engaging in physical activity, but finds the activity insufficient to accomplish that end:

cx 28:   At the time I tried to get this thing off my mind. Washing my socks, doing things to get this off my mind. But I found out that it didn't work. It didn't work right. After I did this here, I laid down on the mattress on the floor again, and I'd get all these bad feelings again. I'd start thinking real bad and this and that. So I really got a bugged feeling in here. I started stomping around the room. This is on the third day. Trying to get these things off my mind. And this didn't seem to work. On the third day I got to stomping around my room, and I built into this thing. I smashed the window up there, and I said to myself, "I'm going to kill myself." . . . And meanwhile all these things were still hitting me in the head.

The inmate describes a cumulating sequence of painful and inescapable thoughts. He tells us he was confused, he "couldn't think straight." This complaint is amplified with a description of failure to "make sense" out of his situation. There is a suggestion that the unfamiliarity of problem-solving makes the man tackle too much too soon. This taxes his capacity to sort through parameters and arrive at closure and resolution:

cx 28:   You say things to yourself that do make sense, but they can't fit in then. They just don't fit in at this time. They get all confused. You're thinking about so many things at once. You're trying to think about this, and you're trying to think about that, but they just don't fit in there.

Obviously, the free world poses its complex, multidimensional problems. But the free world offers an illusion of options even for those who do not really cope, who suffer from temperamental impediments, or whose access to opportunities is limited. The prison is experienced as qualitatively different—as presenting *insoluble* problems rather than difficulties which can be attacked, dealt with, or avoided:

cx 12:   I don't know, I couldn't cope with not solving a problem because I never had a problem I couldn't solve. Not necessarily solve, but to cope with. Like, the time, I could cope with that. But I never had a problem where, like, what could you do? It's like if you put a newborn child in the middle of the street, and a truck comes down, he ain't going to know that that truck's going to kill him if it hits him, he's going to sit there looking at the truck, right? It's just like with me, I didn't know what to do with it, like, what can you do? You rake your mind for a solution, but there's just no answer. You don't know the answer. There's got to be an answer to everything, but there just wasn't no answer to this.

B. SELF-VICTIMIZATION

One self-saving formula which often emerges is that the world (particularly the immediate world) is grossly unfair, and dooms one's struggles from the start. This formula deals with impotence by defining the cards as stacked. It permits disengagement or self-exoneration. But it forces a man to live in a world he has defined as overpowering, and as malevolently arbitrary. Ultimately, the perspective can prove uninviting:

5:　I was sitting contemplating on where do we go from here. And knowing the court system, it'll be extremely improbable that I could get a favorable decision on my appeal. And I just came to the conclusion, or rather reaffirmed and decided to act upon a decision that I'd made long before that, that to carry it past this point would really be an act of absurdity in terms of attempting to deal with them on their terms.

1:　I see. Pointless?

5:　Yeah. Well, you know, it would just be, you already know the ending. It's like watching a movie three or four times over. The climax or the conclusion is known.

Prison punishes, under the presumption that the punishment fits the crime. Inmates who are punished may share that presumption. But many inmates find grounds for questioning the equity of their treatment. Some even react out of a preexisting tendency to see themselves as perennial victims. They react not so much to individual acts of injustice as to existential inequities. For them, incidental coping problems become foreordained strokes of fate. They view their lives as chronicles of victimization and even see themselves as the victims of incidents which they themselves provoke:

16:　Well, I got pushed around a lot, you know? Not by inmates, by officers. I got a few write-ups. I went to court for them, to get out of them. I got one write-up for sassing an officer back. I told him to get off my back, and he locked me up. They get on your back a lot, because they think you're kids here.

Such an inmate may claim that he is continuously put upon by peers and/or authorities. He may present a number of cases in point, which may prove to be routine encounters cumulatively skewed or reinterpreted:

16:   He made me scrape benches, when I'd been in the shop since September, and every day he made me scrape benches. Scrape the shellac off. It got so I didn't like it. I told him I didn't like it and I wanted to do something else. He said, "No, no, you better scrape benches." I got mad because of that. I didn't get mad—tight inside. I went back to work, and then he said I wasn't doing a good job on the benches. I looked it over, I did the same kind of job every day. And then he comes up on one certain day—this is Tuesday—and he said, "You didn't do too good a job on the table." It was tables and benches, and that day I did a table. I told him I did the same kind of job every day. And then he said, "Well, that don't look like the way you done it when you first come in the place." He just about come out and said I was lazy. From five-thirty to one o'clock I'm in the kitchen, and then he tries to drive me in the afternoon.

An inmate of this kind reacts with the resentment appropriate to his perspective, and the reactions he generates feed his original premise. Ultimately, he may explode with rage. Thus one inmate began his interview by defining a near-homicide as a reaction to victimization. He said:

4:   So that inmate had no right to be on that block in that gallery, and he kept wanting to fight. So you can just take so much. You know, the one straw that broke the camel's back. So I could take just so much, and I stabbed him in the neck. And I said, "Damn." Because I was just playing. I didn't mean to take it that far, but it was already done.

Every subsequent situation was seen by this man as a new imposition on his sensibilities:

4:   So they said, "We're going to put you in the shop. You can stay there for three months. And then, if you're good, we'll give you your old job back." I said, "Bullshit, I'm not going." They put me in the shop anyway. They took me out of E block and into F block, in the garment shop. After one day I told the officer that I didn't enjoy that kind of work and that I had never done it before. And I said I didn't want to do that shit. It was for girls. So the next afternoon I was out of the shop. . . . So I didn't know where I was going till I got there, and I found out I was going to keep-lock. I said, "Shit, I'm not going in there." I slammed the door. Now they put me in there, and they didn't even tell

me why I was there. I was there all by myself, with no explanations. I
didn't even have a mattress or some cigarettes. It was neglect.

When a man fails to see his own contribution to situations that backfire
on him, he predefines countermeasures as gratuitous harassments. As he
states his objections, he creates new problems and provokes new "harassments." Ultimately, he may feel pushed beyond the level of tolerance.

However, Self-Victimization need not be a function of distorted perspective. The prison and the criminal justice system have built-in features
that feed the view that life is unfair to the inmate. Disparate dispositions
—different punishments for the same crimes—and gaps between theory
and practice are endemic; rationales for decisions are often cryptic; hopes
and expectations are violated; and channels of appeal are lacking.

Few convicts see themselves as untouched by injustice. The average inmate may see his arrest as unfair, his sentence as disproportionate, his
classification as arbitrary, or his integrity as violated by staff. But this
view does not usually disable, obsess, or fill with hate. For most men, the
fact of inequity remains within the realm of unwelcome but assimilable
adversity.

It is not the most maltreated inmate who breaks down. It is, rather, the
inmate whose norms about the way one must be treated are most violated,
the inmate who holds uncompromising expectations of his environment.
A case in point is an interviewee who had strong convictions about his
integrity as a rational man. He felt that interventions directed at him
were appropriate only insofar as adequate justifications or reasons were
offered. In his view these requirements were not met during plea negotiation, or when prison regulations about haircuts were applied to him:

MSHC 5:   The district attorney said that if I would cooperate with this I
    would be released. You know, needless to say, I refused to cooperate
    with them, because I didn't like the way they were going about it. Try-
    ing to put me under pressure, either I cooperate with them or I would
    be penalized. Any information I could have given them would have
    been vague information anyway. . . .

    And in Clinton I was told I would have to shave off my beard and get
    a regulation haircut. And when I asked for the rationale behind this, I
    was given the stock answer, "Security demands it." Upon further in-
    quiry into it, what it is they figure if you wear a beard you're hard to
    identify, if you have long hair you can conceal weapons in your hair.
    Both reasons have been demonstrated to be absurd when you look at
    the situation in Massachusetts, the prison up there. They're allowed
    beards and long hair, and they're not endangering the security of the
    prison.

The inmate expressed his general premise with statements such as:

MSHC 5:   Yeah, well, I don't see why, I'm already incarcerated, why should I be forced to debase myself in order to fit into the system? . . .

Well, just being in a prison itself, it's really absurd. The rules, they don't make any sense. Some of them do, but most of them don't. You know, with my orientation I would always be in segregation. . . .

It's when you're totally stripped of any option, then you have a decision to make, whether you become a tool, whether you will conform and suppress your own ideals, principles, orientation, and conform at least overtly with theirs. . . . Knowing it's only a matter of time before that overt conformity will definitely influence your principles.

For this inmate, the end of the road came with the realization of the obdurate inflexibility of the prison environment. His struggles to impose terms on correctional staff not only failed, but produced increased regimentation. Ultimately, the hopelessness of the battle became inescapably obvious. The man set fire to his cell, having decided that "it was no longer worth the effort to live under these conditions."

Self-Victimization—like Sanctuary Search—is a problem relating to environmental flexibility and coping flexibility. In both responses, the inmate's minimal requirements for events with which he can deal are unmet. In Sanctuary Search, the difficulty is cognitive—the requirement is problems the inmate can solve. In Self-Victimization, the inmate has requisites relating to interpersonal dealings which he is incapable of relinquishing. In both circumstances, breakdown occurs because the environment fails to provide the options a man feels he requires.

C. ISOLATION PANIC

Almost every penal institution has settings in which, for varying periods of time, men are confined alone, with limited stimulation. Some inmates seek such settings as a refuge from specific dangers, such as fights; most inmates can survive these occasions, though with some discomfort, by employing such modes of adaptation as sleep, distraction, or exercise. There are certain inmates, however, whose tolerance for isolation is low. These men feel caged rather than confined, abandoned rather than alone, suffocated rather than isolated. They react to solitary confinement with surges of panic, despair, or rage. They lose control, break down, regress.

The most immediate impact of isolation is sensory deprivation and physical circumscription. There is boredom, a feeling of immobilization, a sense of resourcelessness. Quite often, there is also a buildup of physiological and psychic tension:

10:   You're locked up in a strip cell, and you have nothing to read for about thirty days. All you have is a Bible. I read the Bible. . . . There's no way to go, you know. You want to get out and move, and there's nowhere to go. Back and forth from wall to wall is only eight feet long, and there's nowhere to walk. And then I started getting falling sensations in my chest. Anxiety built up so much it was a physical thing. My heart beat fast, my heart pounded, I had a flying sensation in my chest.

c 7:   And you get in a quiet position all day long where you don't make a sound and nobody else is making no sounds. It gets to you. So I wanted to make some type of noise. I didn't care what it was that I made, what it might cost me.

Isolation also signifies social deprivation, which for many inmates is an unfamiliar, panic-producing experience. For the isolated inmate, prison activities, a guard, or a cellmate can acquire unexpectedly positive attributes:

cL 3:   If I had had somebody sitting on the side of the cell to talk to me about anything, it doesn't matter. If I had had somebody in the cell with me, I wouldn't have gotten depressed. I was isolated from people, except I could hear the guy next door. But that didn't take the place of this guy being there where I could see him.

c 7:   Well, you know, what can really get you is this, that you can hear the cats outside playing basketball and all. And you being young and active, you want to be out there too. You can hear them playing basketball, talking to each other. You say to yourself, "Damn, man, I got myself locked up."

Isolation highlights not only the advantages and liberties of movement in the population but also the larger losses sustained through imprisonment. Isolation can dramatize the pains of imprisonment per se and also make those pains more acute. Thus Sanctuary Search reaches its most pathetic levels in segregation cells:

d 57:   I feel that the cell is the only thing that's pressuring me, and I want to get out. And then I started thinking about my sentence. Why did I take these four years? And I try to put it all together, and it don't make no sense. . . . I think about the outside at the same time. Sometimes I feel so miserable I have to do something. I jerk off or anything just to forget about it. Many things that I'll be thinking about when I'm in the cell.

Isolation removes even the coping instruments ordinarily available in prisons, and is thus the most trying test of an inmate's coping competence. It is ironic, therefore, that isolation tends to be used disproportionately with inmates who are comparatively weak and resourceless.

Isolation may backfire most with men who have developed an acute sense of victimization or injustice. This attitude sets off clashes with staff that are often punished by isolation, a measure which serves to accentuate the state of mind that provoked it. However, isolation evokes panic more readily if it is not accepted as just or fair. The cycle that culminates in panic may be initiated by the inmate's concern about the arbitrariness of his assignment or by worries about its indefiniteness. Finite sentences imposed for acknowledged acts seem less prone to inspire panic. More often than not, the process starts with feelings of injury and indignation, which are dwelt on to the point of obsession:

cx 17:   This shit that "we'll hold you for investigation." What kind of investigation? What's up? What's going on? Investigation, you want to know, what need have they to hold you for investigation? . . . You just say, "Why me?" That's just what you say, "Why me? Why did this have to happen to me?"

d 34:   I thought I was right in what I had done. And then I felt, you know, I shouldn't be punished. I shouldn't get this treatment, you know? And then I felt the world was against me, people was against me. You know, you feels all kinds of things. You know, I had gotten the feeling that the walls was closing in, you know?

In time, a sense of uncertainty or unpredictability is added to the issue of perceived arbitrariness, making the setting even more intolerable. Status and physical setting become a combined stimulus to fear:

c 43:   I'm thinking, "Well, damn, when is this shit going to be over with? They could hold me in this joint here for how long? I just barely made it to hold out for these couple of days. They going to hold me up here longer?"

cx 17:   I would have felt better if I had just went in there and they had said, "Five days keep-lock." I would have went back, and I wouldn't have even thought about it. I would have been looking to come down on Wednesday. But then, when they put this investigation, you don't know what they're digging into, you don't know what's going on.

Interpersonal connotations may add complexity to such a sequence. There may be protest against the sentencing body, implied appeals, or the desire for a hearing. Finally, the symbolic connotation of being caged combines with substandard living conditions to create the impression that one is viewed as subhuman:

CL 10: So when they don't know how to handle it they take people and throw them in a cell and just forget about it. And they expect them to act like human beings. But when you're in an animal stage and animal conditions you got to try to help yourself in some way or somehow.

D 34: I felt that I'm a man, and I'm not going to be treated like an animal. If I'm going to be treated like an animal, I'd rather die. Something like that. I'm going to die as a man, you know? I'm not going to die like some motherfucking animal, some creature or something.

Irrespective of dominant concerns, the reaction to isolation is a panic state. It is a back-to-the-wall, dead-end desperation, an intolerable emptiness, helplessness, tension. It is a physical reaction, a demand for release or escape at all costs:

9:   It feels like you're all alone in the world. No one cares, no one listens, no one answers. Nothing, you're just by yourself.

CX 20:   I'll be sitting there, and just about the second or third night I get nervous. I start pacing back and forth, and my heart will start beating, boom-ba-boom. I break out like into a light sweat, perspiration. And I'm saying, "I've got to get out of here, out of this room," and the tension builds.

D 34:   I had started walking around the cell, you know? And then I had started going to wall to wall banging myself, you know, my body into the walls. And, like, then all of a sudden I started crying and shit, you know? And then I started jumping up and down and, you know, I guess I just got—I don't know why. I was mad, you know? But I wanted out, you know?

Personal breakdowns in isolation do not square with manly self-images and reputations. Not surprisingly, when they are reviewed in population, such episodes have a way of becoming casual gestures or ploys, lightly and airily dismissed:

CX 17:   Well, it's like I say, I have no situation where I would harm myself. That's ridiculous, for me to harm myself. But like I don't consider this harming myself, putting little scratches on my arm, you know? So they tell me that I harmed myself.

ɪ: What do you think it is?

cx 17:   Well, at the time I just wanted a little bit of attention. I had
gotten into a little bit of trouble, and I went up to this place they call
A-3. It's like solitary there. I didn't like being up there, I wanted to get
from out of there. So I was willing to do anything I can to get from out
of there. I was thinking, "What could I do, what could I say that maybe
they'd let me back downstairs?" So I came up with this idea, and I said,
"They don't let people downstairs for cutting themselves. But maybe
if I tried, they might let me out."

The "I-sat-down-and-scratched-my-arm-a-bit" pose does not, as a rule,
survive a scrutiny of the events preceding the incident. Self-injury entails
the defiance of taboos and fears, usually with considerable incentive:

cx 17:   I was kind of scared of doing it, because I knew I was going to
really hurt myself if I was going to really do what they'd been doing.
I mean, the real way they do it, some of them, they just cut their whole
fucking arm. That's why I didn't really figure that I would do the whole
thing. I just put a couple of scratches on my arm. While I was doing
this I was kind of scared. I had to close my eyes to do that. I couldn't
look at that shit and do it. . . . Like I say, I was scared, I had to work
up to it. When I had it on my arm, I was just saying, "What should I
do, man, should I really fuck my arm up or what?" I had to build
enough heart to even put those few scratches on my arm.

But even if a man realizes the extent to which his reaction involves
panic and despair, he must suppress this fact in his dealings with fellow
inmates. Fear connotes weakness, and weakness unmanliness. Indices of
fear must be disguised or explained away. The truth—if revealed at all—
must be cautiously and circumspectly broached:

cx 43:   You come out with any old bullshit: "Yeah, man, well you know
how it is, everybody was fucking with me, and I had to do something."
You're bullshitting now, you dig? "I tried to do this, but it didn't work,
so I had to do this. I fucked around and did this and did that, and it
didn't work." You're bullshitting. He's not looking at it as serious as he
was before, you know? So then after you stuff it off, he don't look at you
as serious—well, he don't look at you like, "Damn, man, you ain't shit
in my eyes, you couldn't even do that shit up there." He don't look at
you like that after you got through stuffing it off. . . . Then you come
back, and then you run it down to him as it is, you dig? But only you
don't bullshit this time. You come back and you say, "No, man, but
this is on the up. I had to do it because I was feeling this way here and

feeling that way there. You know, it was just one of those things." Shit like that. Then he accepts it more.

Since prison involves degrees of incarceration, Isolation Panic is not confined to formal solitary confinement. It is, however, most sharply prevalent in segregation. And irrespective of its physical setting, Isolation Panic marks a dichotomy in the minds of men—a distinction between imprisonment, which is tolerable, and isolation, which is not.

D. SELF-CLASSIFICATION

Coping differentiation is sometimes made along lines other than population-isolation. Inmates may see within the prison or prison system some environments that contain the prerequisites of survival, and others that do not. Self-injury becomes a means of alerting staff to the fact that placement within the appropriate environment is literally a life-and-death matter. One interviewee posed the issue in these terms:

MHDM 10:   What they were trying to do is force me out of my environment into another environment. I can make it on another floor. I know I can make it, but why should I be in constant unpleasantness? For what? It's just unpleasant being in jail. Why should I make it more unpleasant? I'm asking to be with my own people. I ain't asking nothing. I'm not taking nothing out of their pockets. Nothing that will put them out of their way.

Usually Self-Classification is described as a two-stage process, the first a routine request for reassignment, the second a dramatic act to emphasize the seriousness of the request:

CX 2:   So about five days ago, I guess, I went to see this lieutenant— he called me up to see about going on the farm. And I went in there, and I knew it was hopeless as soon as I walked in, because as soon as I walked in, he writes down my name and then wrote down, "Farm," which means that no matter what I said to him I was still going on the farm, you know? So I rapped to him, and I told him that I needed all the music that I could get because I'm behind the kids now as it is. . . . So I said, "I'm in two-part harmony now—I'll be in three-part harmony." I said, "Three-part harmony will put me much closer to these people than if I was just in two-part harmony." And he said, "Well, you're going on the farm, you're going to be a farmer." . . . And so I just said, "OK, so long," and walked out. And so then I came down to work on the farm, and all this time all this is building up in me, you know? . . . And I felt just like I was being busted all over again.

The emphasis in Self-Classification may be positive or negative. For instance, some inmates regard a congenial peer group as a requisite of survival:

M 1:   If they put me in with Spanish guys, it would be all right. And the officer says, "No, we're going to put you in a cell." I said I would feel better if I could talk to this other Spanish guy. I can't talk English too much, you know? With a colored guy or a white guy, I can't rap too much English.

By the same token, uncongenial peers are seen as making life impossible, as creating an environment that contains too many handicaps:

M 1:   They put me up on the tenth floor. I've never been up to that floor. That's for flaky people. I do it in my cell. I don't want a lot of noise. A lot of flaky guys in there. I don't belong to that floor.

Prison coping problems are partly determined by extrainstitutional relationships, self-appraisals, temperament, dependency needs, and other qualities of self. These create special preferences and aversions. One man's meat can be another's poison: some men require contact, others solitude; some communication, others privacy. In all cases, however, these are not simply favored options. They are environmental qualities needed to maintain stability and pursue the routine of living.

The prevalent view in correctional circles is that self-injury is usually a manipulative tactic designed to attain relocation. In a sense, the self-classifier fits this model. In another sense, however, he does not, for his is not a cool, calculated, premeditated gesture, but rather a product of needs. Moreover, it is generally a precipitate, self-defeating, magical move. Different settings within the system are sufficiently alike to make it probable that any process interrupted by self-injury will be reinstituted in the presumably more desirable location. New cells more often than not breed old thoughts.

One itinerant inmate summarized the syndrome, somewhat confusedly, in the following words:

D 33:   I went to Maryland to get married. I came back, and my wife went on the methadone program, and six days later she passed away. About a month later time came to go for sentence, and I got sentenced for three years, and I went to Sing Sing. After about three months, from Sing Sing I went to Elmira. . . . Even at the time of sentence I specifically asked the judge to send me to state prison. I figured I'd get treated better at a state prison, not treated like an adolescent. . . . So besides my going to Elmira from Sing Sing, plus—it started catching up with me—I started thinking about, you know, I lost my wife, so one night I broke an ash-tray, and I cut my wrists. One of the purposes was I wanted to get out of Elmira, plus I was depressed.

Like most self-classifiers, this particular man was primarily concerned with the setting he wanted to escape. A solution could be any different location:

D 33:   Well, from the minute I got to Elmira I wanted out, and I thought the best thing to do is come through here and go to another prison. So I figured I had to do something outrageous. . . . I didn't really care where I went just as long as I was out of Elmira.

The self-defeating character of the pattern is highlighted by the fact that the inmate may repeatedly use self-injury to obtain transfers, only to find himself again and again in situations he sees as intolerable:

D 33:   They gave me a job in this one part of the prison where it is very strict, and I couldn't do a bit in this kind of atmosphere. It was a bad joint. So I saw a psychiatrist, and I told him I was hearing voices. So they sent me to the hospital, and from the hospital they sent me to this isolated cell block. They had mental observation on one side of the block and homosexuals on the other. I didn't know this; so as I left the hospital I went into this block and, like, I just couldn't believe what I saw—blankets on the floor and guys making out with fags like they were on the beach, and I said to myself, "No, I don't belong over here." Plus I had slight conflicts; first I was in a reformatory, then a penitentiary. So I made up my mind I'm getting out of here. I didn't even want to be identified with that block. So I'd seen somebody I knew, and I got a razor, and I went to my cell and cut my wrists.

A 1:   I got tired of going back to the hospital from Block 2 to one here to Bellevue to Block 2 over here. I got tired of that. And where am I right now? In Block 2. Where I don't want to be, but I am now. Whether I like it or not, I am in Block 2. . . . And why should I cut up? If I go to the hospital, where am I? Still in jail. If I go over here, where am I? Still in jail. It might be a sweeter bit, but I'll be doing it. But still, it's jail. These things in life come along, these things that you don't like, you're going to have to accept.

Inmates attribute Self-Classification bids to staff responsiveness to self-injury, and staff unresponsiveness to other modes of appeal. They claim that they are forced to engage in demonstrative acts which cannot be ignored when staff do not respond to requests made within the framework of the system, in accordance with formal rules:

cx 21:   You know, you've got to lay up in the cell, and you keep waiting until somebody tells you he'll see you. And they finally don't say, and it's the same as people lying to you. . . . The warden and everybody tells you that in the rule book it states that if you have any problems, see somebody about it, drop a bomb and do this and that, and that's exactly what I did. I followed the rules to the tooth. And they don't want to do nothing.

Self-injury is viewed as the only effective medium of appeal. Less drastic moves are ignored, and more drastic moves (such as extrapunitiveness or destructiveness) bring retribution. The virtue of self-injury is that it requires staff response of a positive nature. At minimum, someone must clean and close the wound, and someone must inquire into motives. This opens lines of communication which are believed to be closed ordinarily:

cx 21:   You can cut up, smash your cell up, something like that. That's the best way to do it. If you do something violent, they'll put you in the jacket, they'll put you between sheets, and you're in trouble.

cx 2:   I like to be noticed in here, you know, noticed as a person, and they want to be noticed as a person, so they break up their cell, and they say, "Wow, look, I'm alive, I'm a person. You see this? I cut myself, I'm bleeding, I have blood in me just like you." And this is their way of expressing themselves, of trying to prove to somebody, you know, "Why do you do this to me when I'm just like you? I'm just like your son," and things like this.

Since Self-Classification is an assertion of humanity and an appeal to humanity, it poses problems for the self-image of both the perpetrator and his target. The former must see himself as coldly exercising an option; the latter may take the message at face value, or pretend to. Thus, one of our inmates classified himself as a "cutup artist." He told us:

10:   This is going to shock you. This is what you call a bag. The bag is try to be committed to a state hospital. That's called bagging. It's a phony act. The quickest way to get results is to cut up.

As an afterthought, this inmate added:

10:   Now maybe there's something behind it, and I admit it. Most people would never harm themselves. Maybe there is something behind it. This is why I did it.

I: Well, why did you want to get here, if I may ask that?

10:   I got sick in prison. I got claustrophobia, and I couldn't stay in the cell.

In responding to this inmate, staff could and did ignore the point of his despair. But they responded by arranging for a psychiatric transfer. In this fashion, they could remain nominally unconcerned while providing relief. And the inmate could retain, superficially, his sense of autonomy.

E. AID SEEKING

The self-sufficiency issue may become moot with the inmate's continued awareness of despair. Or rather, his dilemma may become more complex. The inmate may feel an acute need for support, understanding, or help which peers and custodial personnel cannot satisfy because he doesn't trust them, views them as unsympathetic to his requests for aid, or sees them as incapable of assisting him. However, he may assess psychiatric and medical staff differently: he may attribute magical powers to them and exempt them from the social norm relating to Aid Seeking.

One interviewee arrived at this view of professional staff while he was experiencing withdrawal symptoms. Peers were no help in this crisis:

D 32:   We could rap, right, but that was no time for a rap. What would you say? "Help!" That's all you felt like saying. You knew there was no conversation. You wanted something for the pain.

The inmate considered all sorts of desperation moves designed to invoke contact with mental health staff:

D 32:   I was cursing the establishment, and every hack that came by I'd spit at him. You know, just to get a beating so they'd take me to a doctor or something. This was what was going through my mind—let me grab a hack, maybe they'd give me a beating, they'd take me down to the doctor or take me to the hospital. And professional people would see that this is what's happening to me.

Self-destruction was one lower-level option this man considered during a process characterized by considerable floundering:

D 32:   I wanted to do something, and I couldn't do something, and I was thinking of this and thinking of all this violence and everything, just to get myself together. There was a lot of hurt there.

I: You say you were thinking of suicide. Was that flashing in and out too?

D 32:   Yes. That would come, and I would say, "Later for that, man.

That ain't me, that's not my bag. Let me dig myself for as long as I can."

When self-injury did emerge as an option, the inmate had to edge up to it by degrees.

D 32:   And I called the hack. I told the hack, "Man, I'm going to die. I need something now. I'm seeing things, the walls are starting to crawl up on me. Like, this is a hell of a time for me." So I told him, and he told me, "Punk, lay down and shut up." One of these things, you know? So I took some water and threw it at him, hoping to get a beating. But, like, he knew what I was trying to do. So I couldn't get no help—they wouldn't let me out of the cell. So I got one of my friends to get me a razor blade, that's when I decided. I didn't decide really until I got the razor blade, until I seen it. I said if they ain't going to help me, I'm going to help myself, and this is the only thing available really.

At the point of self-injury, the agenda gets contaminated. What begins as an act of Aid Seeking acquires connotations of self-release, with lethal intent:

D 32:   I didn't really have my mind made up. I thought if I asked for the razor blade, like, one of the dudes might not give me the razor blade, call the man and tell him I'm asking for razor blades, and the man might come. But the razor came instead of the man, you know? So I got the razor blade and I cut on my bed. This was about eleven o'clock at night, and I cut my arms. I cut my arms pretty bad. I cut them, and then I cut them again. I cut on the inside, and then I cut my throat. I cut my throat three times, and then I laid down and went to sleep.

Coping problems sometimes focus on detailed, specific complaints (as happens in conversion hysteria). An advantage of focused complaints is that they facilitate Aid Seeking. Their disadvantage rests largely in their artificiality. Aid-givers can sense the exaggerated quality of symptoms, and respond accordingly, supplying aspirin or placebos.

In such situations suicide attempts may result because the inmate feels that his problem has not been addressed, and in a sense he is right, since the real problem here is not the symptom for which alleviation has been sought but the more diffuse anxiety symbolized by the complaint.

Aid Seeking may be discouraged by the fact that it often does not work. The institutional response may not take the form hoped for, and in fact cannot do so, because the inmate's objective is unrealistic or unrealizable.

Staff response may also, at times, intensify rather than ameliorate the coping crisis:

M 9: Well, they took me out of my cell and took me downstairs and put me in a cell they got down there and they call the bull pen. They handcuffed me with my arms in the air, and they let me stay there for a while. I stayed in there close to two days. . . . They don't give me nothing. All they did was wash my arm off and put on some Band-Aids on it and leave me in the cell.

M 11: The doctor felt that I needed some peace and quiet and some rest and relaxation. Agreed, it could have been used, and I accepted it. But I didn't know that I was to accept it in the form of solitary confinement, on bing status, where I was deprivileged from all my privileges.

The noncorrespondence between needs and responses does not indict the staff or the institutional setting. Messages communicated by self-injury are unclear even to the actors themselves. Conflicting norms produce fictional perceptions and self-perceptions. The chief fiction, as always, is the ascription of casual connotations to self-injury in order to rescue illusions of manly self-sufficiency and of imperturbability in the face of crises.

3

From Losing Battles
to
Losing the War

Thus far we have reviewed personal breakdowns produced by adaptational crises or coping failures. The person's concern was with the present or the immediate past, and the person's suffering was usually restricted to difficulties he faced at a given time and place.

Now we will review crises in which the victim's perspective extends into the past and future. Here his despair is not a product of the moment but a verdict rendered on his entire existence—on his potency and reputation and worth. It entails an inventory not only of his immediate circumstances but of his lifelong contributions and actions and prospects. It is a skewed inventory, yielding a record of failure and a vista of defeat. Such a crisis can be a disabling experience if it is unrelieved, redundant, self-confirming.

A cycle is built into self-doubt and self-defeat. When a man holds himself in low self-esteem, this fact colors his entire outlook on life. His past documents his failures and negates his hopes. He deals with others not as an equal but as an inferior. His peers are judges, sponsors, enemies, threats. Love is not for him but for the worthy; as substitutes, he buys loyalty, pity, or (at best) restraint.

By the same token, self-doubt is a *product*—a *social* outcome derived from encounters with other men. It is nurtured by guilt, shame, fear. It is magnified by the looking glass he finds in every face he sees—his jaundiced self-image finding its reflection in the neglect and gloating and contempt of others.

Self-doubt is also a motive. It paralyzes, intimidates, isolates. It dictates dependence. It prescribes unimpressive roles—foil for barbs, or passive, sullen yielder.

With help, the seeds of doubt become fruits of doubt. Other men play into the games of the weak, eagerly feeding off their low self-esteem. The timidity of the weak builds the egos of the brave, provides rungs for the ambitious, helpless victims for the cruel, pawns for exploiters.

In prison, the weak bear a special burden. The outs who are left out, the twice-rejected rejects are the means whereby other inmates can regain status in their own or their fellows' eyes. In effect, the stronger inmates elevate themselves on the backs of their weaker fellows, and the weak are further weakened in the process.

I. Themes Related to Negative Self-Assessment (Problems Based on the Relationship between Self and Others)

(A, B, C: Hopelessness and Self-Doubt)

A. Self-Deactivation: A lack of interest in day-to-day life, which is seen as an extrapolation or continuation of past failures. This stage follows an inventory which makes the person increasingly apathetic and discouraged —he sees no future role for himself, and loses interest and drive.

B. Self-Sentencing: An effort to cut losses and provide relief to others. This stage follows an inventory of past and current conduct vis-à-vis friends and relatives, which sparks shame, guilt, self-condemnation, and a dismal prognosis for the future. The person adjudges himself a complete liability to himself and others and sees no prospects for improvement.

C. Self-Retaliation: A person experiences self-hate or engages in self-punishment because he attributes his intolerable position to his own past acts, and feels justifiably angry and resentful at himself.

(D: Resourcelessness and Fear)

D. Fate Avoidance: A stance stemming from a person's inability to survive current or impending social situations which he fears because he sees himself as weak, ineffective, or unable to appropriately respond.

(E, F: Need for Significant Others)

E. Self-Linking: A person's protest against intolerable separation from significant others, against perceived abandonment by them, or against his inability to function as a constructive member of a group. The person rejects the possibility of an independent life, feels that his well-being is inconceivable without the continuation of certain vital relationships, and that no satisfactory existence is possible without them.

F. Self-Certification: A person's effort to convince the other party in a degenerating or terminating relationship of his seriousness about the relationship and his inability to survive its dissolution. The effort takes the form of a dramatic demonstration of resentment, self-pity, or personal sincerity.

II. How Do Negative Self-Assessment Themes Manifest Themselves?

A. SELF-DEACTIVATION

For some men, crises are declaration of bankruptcy. When such men break down, they feel that the lives they have led and can expect to lead were and will remain devoid of highlights or rewards. They tell us that, given their pasts, no satisfying future is possible for them, that the future will inexorably replicate a past that was not worth living. They see themselves as inescapably relegated to the junk heap.

Theirs is a linear extrapolation of failure. For them unemployment in the past signifies a jobless future, rejection betokens loneliness, jail or imprisonment promises a life behind bars. There is no recourse, and no escape from such trends:

cx 56:   I said "these people ain't going to never let me go home. . . . Like Al Capone, that guy was in prison, he died of syphilis." I thought, "Well, they're going to keep me in prison just like him, like I killed somebody out in the streets. I never killed nobody—they can't keep me in jail forever." I'm thinking this. It seems like they're doing it to me. They keep me in all these homes and jails and prisons, stuff like that. It seems like they're never going to let me out on the streets again.

cx 12:   I started on the line of thinking, "Jesus Christ, what am I doing here anyway? There's nothing in front of it. What am I going to do when I get out? I have no ambitions, I don't want to do anything." I said, "My past life has been shitty. I don't want to live through this again when I get out. And back to jail again, and get out, and back to jail." I said, "It's going to be a never-ending thing." I said, "What the hell, ain't nobody knows I'm here anyway, nobody really cares. If I died right now, who's going to know about it? No one. They don't give a shit here if I die right now. Just a bunch of fucking cattle in here."

This projection is often invoked by men whose lives are in reality bleak and devoid of opportunities. But it is not forced by the facts. It is not provoked by the discouraging experiences themselves. It signals a trauma-produced failure of defenses, and marks the death of a hope that would otherwise tend to defy the odds.

The experience of bankrupcy represents a "discovery" which is arranged and purposive. It is a response to a failure that hurts. It is (paradoxically) a face-saving formula which wards off a searching—and self-critical—inquiry:

CX 12: And once they turned me down, I went back to my cell. And I was thinking, you know, "I just came off the streets, I came back to jail again, what am I going to do when I get out of here?" I had no hope or nothing. I had nothing to look forward to.

MHDM 50: Well, I believe why it happened this time was because I was in jail, and this time the crime that I committed was a more serious crime than the ones that was in the past.

I: You mean, you could get more time for it?

MHDM 50: Right, right.

Superficially, what the person experiences seems to be the outcome of an "objective" summary of his career, the product of a long-term review of discouraging facts about himself, often starting with childhood. The review makes a cumulative case:

CX 56: See, I've been in a lot of foster homes, myself, and a lot of jails, and a lot of prisons, I've been through in one lifetime. I've only seen the streets three times in my life. The first time I got sent away I was just ten years old, I was just a young kid.

CX 12: I looked at not only the problems that I had, but I looked at everything, all of my past problems, and they all seemed to be right there, in the present. They all were there, all the problems that I'd done. When I was little, back when I was eight, nine years old, everything. And they all seemed to be there at the present. And I said, "Look at my life, it's always been the same. Always been in trouble." And I said, "What makes you think you can change now?"

But the inventory which leads to despair is not open-ended. It is systematic and selective, and seems bent on proving its painful point unambiguously:

MHDM 50: Your mind is like on a highway, and it's going at a very fast pace, just like a car. You know how a car pick up speed? Your mind is going along them terms, and as it's running along this highway, you go back and you pick up incidents. And one incident leads to another incident of your failure in your life. You say, "well, I've been drinking," and then I remember I did this and I did this, and they just keep adding on.

D 51:   The good things wouldn't register on me at all. I mean if you have
a relationship with a person, there's good things and bad things, and I
guess normally you think about all of them. But I couldn't think about
the good times. The good times they just didn't come. They didn't register. The thoughts were just all the bad things that happened.

As the "evidence" accumulates, it brings discouragement, depression,
a de-cathexis from life, a loss of interest in living. This mood may build
gradually, or it may eventuate in an apparent resolve to give up:

D 51:   I just kept pushing and pushing, and every day just seemed harder
and harder to get through. I stopped reading, and I stopped doing
things. I stopped washing up in the morning. I lost everything. What
ambition I had I lost. And over a gradual period of four or five months,
until I was worn down to a point where I didn't want to go on anymore.
. . . It would be like compared to falling asleep. Everything just got
duller and duller. Things got more difficult. Everyday things, especially
my relationship with people, they got more difficult to handle. And loss
of interest and everything. Even like, prior to that period when I
first got sent to prison, I'll go down and see if I can better myself. Take
courses at the State University. And I even stopped working the courses.
I just stopped everything. I just ground to a halt. Anything that had
any value just lost its value.

MHDM 50:   It's a real down feeling. You know, it's a feeling where you
don't care nothing about life no more. You know that you're sleeping
and eating every day, and breathing. But all of a sudden you want to
cut all that off, you don't want that. You don't even want that. You
don't want nothing.

As part of a state of mind, the man sees himself as no longer active and
influencing, as having no way of affecting his own life for the better. He
abdicates his autonomy:

CX 12:   And the other voice said, "Well, what am I going to do when I
get out of here?" And I just didn't have an answer. I don't know what
I'm going to do when I get out of here. I said, "Yeah, I'll come right
back to jail. End up shooting drugs again, and this and that."

D 51:   It's like being caught in something you have no control over.
That's the way I thought of it. I didn't have any control over the situation. There was nothing I could see that I could do to better myself. To
bring about any changes. It started getting worse, and there was nothing I could do about it. What could I do about it?

Existence becomes not only pointless, but flat. The experience of incarceration, extrapolated into the future, is a scenario ready-made for boredom. Such a "revolving door career" includes a vivid perspective of endlessly replicated routines, of redundant eventlessness and boredom:

D 47: It gets to you after a while. The same thing. Tomorrow morning you'll do just about the same thing that you did this morning. The constant thought that it's there. Each day is just about the same. Wash up, go to the bathroom, go to breakfast, go to the shop, just sit around. It's like a bore. Just really boring. . . . The thought of having to do each thing, not for a month or six months, but for years, year in and year out. Celebrate the holidays, so on and so forth. Each day just about the same.

CX 12: I just don't see how a person can stay in jail for the rest of his life. Just lives day by day, . . . Like a robot, get up when they tell you and lock in, that was it. I just couldn't bear the thought of that.

But life outside the walls may present qualities no different from prison. For many, life has been a continued fight against the realization of failure. One inmate, a sophisticated drug addict, described typical experiences variously linked to his addiction. He recalled adversities and asperities from which drugs had protected him; he saw his addiction as an index of indifference to living—a deliberate risk-taking and devaluation of loss-of-life:

MHDM 3: Take a shot of dope, and I can sit in the auditorium full of KKK and all of them calling me, and I would just sit there, and it would just bounce off me. So taking a shot of dope is an umbrella, a blanket over the individual. Right? It blocks out the sensitivity. That's why after a time he doesn't love his mother, he doesn't care about his family, no family, no friends. You dig that? Because what do you need with family and friends? You've created your own sanctuary. Through outward things, through chemical things, you've found a way to escape. Everybody's on an escape. One way or another. One guy spends his whole paycheck balling prostitutes; another guy doesn't do anything but fix cars; another doesn't do anything but buy clothes. All these things are addictions. . . . When I was in the army I used to fight. But still if I had the needle full of hell, and I got it in my hand, I could push it in my arm. . . . You know every time you do it, you take a shot that could be your last shot. You know that. That's a fact. That's not a myth. You know that is for real. . . . Maybe that's what you want anyway; maybe you won't admit it. But inside that is what you want, that's actually what you're looking for. Something to take you, 'cause you haven't got the guts, something to take you off the calendar.

Despite its extreme form, this insightful statement describes the usual context of Self-Deactivation—the reason why Self-Deactivation crises occur as they do when they do. It refers to the dominant concerns which enable most of us to avoid facing existential questions that could disturb our routines. It points out that we act as short-term problem solvers, and that we stipulate the rationality and meaningfulness of the activities we engage in.

The statement also refers to the risk we take when we anesthetize ourselves to the import of our self-destructive acts—to our assumption that our failures have no bearing on the pattern of our careers. The risk we take is that when our defenses collapse, events whose import we are ordinarily able to ignore emerge en masse to haunt us. They emerge in inventories designed to document failure. And rather than inspire constructive reevaluation, they spark despair, apathy, and a sense of defeat.

B. SELF-SENTENCING

Self-deactivation is face-saving, because it blames fate and externalizes responsibility. This perspective may be reassuring if it can be kept within bounds. But once unleashed, the formula is very hard to control. Its pessimism tends to breed despondency; its passivity spawns a sense of worthlessness. The formula lowers self-esteem, since it implies that a person is not as potent or effective as he might be:

D 28:   I kept on thinking that I was a complete failure. Like, all my friends made good. You know, they raised a family, they kept their jobs. And all my family was the same way. And I just kept on seeing myself as a nothing, just useless. . . . I kept on thinking and thinking about it. You know, how useless I am. That I'd never amount to anything.

Moreover, blaming fate does not obviate the continued risk that a man will ask himself whether he has been a completely innocent victim of unprovoked providence:

CX 12:   And I was thinking, all these people, they just stuff me off. But then I started thinking in terms of why they stuff me off. "Maybe it's me. Maybe I don't deserve it. Maybe I don't deserve to be put in a school, you know? Or maybe the guy thinks I'm a wise guy or something." And then I started thinking about myself, and I said, "I guess I don't deserve it. Look at me—here's all these things that I have, and all these traits are in myself." And the realization of it really had a big impact on me, really brought me down a lot. And I was looking back, just the bad things—you never think of the good things when you're in that state of mind. You think, "Look what happened here, look what happened there, look what I did there," you know? And all these things just mounting up, mounting up. And I said, "Jesus Christ, I'm really a rot-ten guy." I said, "Here I'm thinking about these guys shouldn't be here. I shouldn't be here myself, really."

Most personal careers (even those of saints) are studded with instances in which the needs of other persons are violated or disregarded. Asocial conduct rarely reflects blindness to the feelings and concerns of others—a sociopathic orientation or outlook. More often, persons who are otherwise prosocial suspend awareness of the deleterious impact and consequences of their acts. When success requires asocial or antisocial dealings, conscience and social feedback are bypassed.

Failure to face the facts about one's interpersonal dealings does not mean that such information is not acquired and stored. What it means is that the information is not retrieved, assessed, or incorporated into one's self-view. These defenses can prevail as long as the strategy works. But if a person has been rejected or unsuccessful, or if circumstances suspend his pursuit of antisocial concerns, he may seek out the suppressed import of his past acts:

16: Things happen too fast. Like, we could do something. It's not even on my mind what we're doing until after. When I start thinking about it, then, "Wow, how the hell did I get mixed up in this?" . . . I don't think at the time when I'm doing it. And after it's all done with—you know, me, I just let everything get to me. And I don't know which way to get out, which way to go.

L: You don't feel it, you know, when you're a drug addict. But when you're not a drug addict anymore, you start feeling these things, you start feeling a little bit of sympathy. . . . You start thinking of the way you used to get your money. The way innocent people used to get their feelings hurt for you, for your habit. For something that you didn't really need, but it was all your mind, thinking that you did need this, you know? And you start thinking of this type of stuff. You start thinking, "Wow, man, why did I do this? It wasn't necessary. I could have got it some other way." But the harm was done already.

When the occasion for crisis is failure, inventory serves the function of documenting or explaining failure. Thus, when suppressed data about one's destructive impact on others reach awareness, one does not view them objectively and dispassionately but tends to see them in a manner which transforms one's peccadilloes into horrendous crimes. The inconsequented weakling thus turns into a betrayer of trust, a villain, a monster.

16: She left, she started fucking around with all the guys in the neighborhood, right? She was nothing like this. She was a very nice girl out there. Now this is building in my mind. . . . Because if I didn't treat her

the way I did, this probably would never have happened. . . . I think it
was me, wanted too much out of her. You know, because I don't know,
like, when I come home I want things my way. This is how I been. I
just started being like this. I wanted everything done the way I wanted
it. Now when I really come down to it, this is wrong. When I find out
it's wrong, and I know I should be ashamed of myself for it, I don't
know how to go about it.

45:   Well, I have guilt feelings about my mother. She died when I was
in jail, and I had given her a rough time when I was using drugs. She
died at sixty-four, and I felt very guilty about it. The doctors even
brought it out and showed me that she had coronary thrombosis and
she had a pretty bad case of diabetes. They brought it out that she was
a pretty sick woman, and they said that I didn't bring these things on
her.

As memories evoke each other through the common thread of one's
villainy or inadequacy, the accumulation of incidents can cement the import of their self-degrading implication:

L: You start thinking of more and more people that you let down. . . .
when you start thinking about everybody, everybody, wow, man!

cx 12:   They all were there, all the problems that I'd done. When I was
little, back when I was eight, nine years old, everything. And they all
seemed to be there at the present. And I said, "Look at my life, it's always been the same. Always been in trouble."

Three negative implications are commonly drawn from a review of
destructive or nonconstructive encounters. The first is discouragement
with one's capacity to be an effective interpersonal agent. A man can see
himself as congenitally disloyal, untrustworthy, undependable, or noxious
to others:

cx 12:   I was thinking about everything. I started thinking about my
family. And I come to the conclusion I'd be better off, and they'd be
better off without me. Because I'd bring them nothing but trouble, and
to me I wasn't much of a son. I was always in trouble, they had to pay
for lawyers. I never really had done anything for myself. And I kind of
proved they would be better off without me.

The second negative implication is the assumption that one is unregen-
erable, that one's future must be shaped inescapably by the fruits of one's
worthless past:

29:   I thought about how if I went back on the streets I'd do the same thing again. I could tell people, tell you, that I'm going to stop, I'm not going to do this, I'm going to do that. But when you go out there, and you know you can get it—I didn't think much of me or my life, because I knew what I'd do.

D 28:   Even when I got out of here, I thought that I would go back to drugs. It would be a complete merry-go-round. Get completely messed up. It bothered me. It still bothers me now, you know? Knowing that if I got out—I only have six years, and I figure I'll be out in three. But I'm scared to go back out in the street and maybe use drugs again.

The third implication is that, given one's defective relationships with other persons (one's intrinsic unlovableness), there is no prospect of continued loyalty from significant others:

16:   I look at my mother. What could I possibly say to her? What can I possibly say to her that's going to make her feel good when she comes up here every week to see me?

L: All the time you're growing up, your mother tells you, "Be a good influence to your brothers so they'll do something good when they grow up." You don't think of these things until finally you're in a position that's so messed up. Then you start thinking, "Wow, man, I should have took my mother's, what she was telling me, I should have took everything that she told me under consideration." It's true. Like, your mother starts telling you your friends are nothing. It's true. I don't have no friends.

The conclusions drawn from such inferences are often defeatist and destructive. One becomes convinced that friends and strangers alike would benefit from one's demise—that given a future in which one functions as either a burden or a source of misery, as a person unaccepted and unacceptable, the world would be a better place if one could remove oneself from it:

D 28:   I just felt like I was better off dead, you know? I took everything into consideration, like my family and everything.

16:   I've put enough on them, and I wanted to end it before, just leave it at that, die and that's it.

Self-Sentencing comes close to a type of experience which, viewed abstractly, is regarded as "healthy." A man blind to himself—with no in-

sight into the contributions he makes to his fate—is apt not to change, no
matter how destructive his behavior may be. He sees himself as effective
(or as ineffective) because of external constraints, and is impervious to
resocialization efforts.

In voluntary treatment models, a patient seeks intervention because he
has questions as to his personal effectiveness. In involuntary settings, similar doubts are deemed desirable, and if they are absent they are delib-
erately fostered. The experience of the early prisons ("penitentiaries")
shows how this strategy can boomerang. These institutions were seen as
settings in which—with the help of social rejection and the impact of a
Bible—a man's thoughts could be turned to the import and ethics of his
career. Some men responded to this pressure with depressions and insanity.

The reasons for such reactions are not difficult to understand. "Insight"
may be a requisite, but it is not the whole, of personal reform. To gain
new options, a man must pause and rethink his past; but he must never
lose his supports or resolve. He must be able to embark on a fresh course,
assured of his potential, of rewards, of allies. A self-sentencing crisis contains no positive ingredients of this kind. The past—being the past—is a
given. A perspective centered on past failures is intrinsically discouraging
and devoid of implications for constructive actions. A view centered on
lost alliances, particularly at a time when help is most needed, is discouraging and painful. And a self-view imbued with disdain or doubt is paralyzing. At best, it is nonproductive; at worst, it leads to the loss of faith
and the death of hope.

C. SELF-RETALIATION

Along the same dimension as hopelessness and low self-esteem is the type
of inventory which results in self-hatred and self-condemnation. The difference is that in the latter a person tries to punish himself for his inef-
fectiveness rather than to escape it. The dominant tone is not despair and
remorse but bitterness and self-contempt. As one inmate puts it, "I didn't
cut up to kill myself. I cut up to kick myself in the ass." He elaborates by
saying:

1:   I wanted to hurt myself. I wanted to get myself in trouble. Get myself
     in trouble for fucking the whole year up, for not being able to get out
     there. For being so stupid.

Another inmate speaks of a preference for punishment administered by
others:

10:   I was hoping that they would take me to the wall. By "take me to the
      wall," I mean take me out and shoot me or hang me or burn me or

something. . . . I was hoping that they would burn me. When I finally knew that I wasn't going to die, even though I hadn't gone to trial or anything yet, this was pretty much predisposed, I think that's when I really decided if they aren't going to do it, then I have to do it myself.

A man often hopes that, in punishing himself, he will eliminate undesirable personality traits by eliminating the physical being which contains them. The strategy here is one of moral or psychological surgery. Self-punishment is an effort to produce a new—purer—self, to remove the basis for feelings of shame or guilt:

34: In one way I felt if I did hurt myself, I would feel better later on.

48: It might sound strange to you, but after I done it, the next day I felt different. For some reason . . . it made me feel better. It made me feel that I had cut something out of myself, I started making a new thing.

The need for self-punishment or self-removal is sparked by a special review of past acts. The incidents reviewed are generally suggestive of congenital weakness, or of an inability to control undesired conduct:

34: And I felt that I had done something wrong, setting that factory on fire. And working there, and knowing the people, and doing what I done . . . plus being I was drinking too much and family problems. . . . So I drink a little, but every time I drink just a little bit, I want more. I want to get higher. Get that higher feeling. Then after that I get in trouble. I explode, I get in trouble. And then I say, to myself, "What did I do wrong? I didn't do nothing wrong." I look around. I see the big mess. I did it, you know? And I didn't know I done it. . . . A trap I'll never be able to get out of. I feel sometimes that if I had a chance right this moment, I'm a drinker. It's out of my control, completely. Because I have tried before to restrain myself from doing these things. It's out of my control.

10: It was sex, young children. I was ashamed of it. I lived a double life. Everybody out there that knew me respected me. I had a good business, good family, good everything. But this was a skeleton in the closet. . . . I'd get spells where my wife would be laying in the bed next to me, and I'd get up out of bed and go looking for somebody to hurt—for three or four hours. I'd come back and get into bed, and she'd never know that I left. I guess some people would refer to it as being a werewolf.

Though impulse-ridden violent offenders can most easily document

their unworthiness, the sequence toward self-hatred may start with a
particular item of unwelcome news. An inmate may hear about an ugly
situation for which he holds himself partly responsible or learn about
undesirable events he feels he could have prevented. There may be self-
reproach for causing oneself to be imprisoned, and thus destroying his
own chances or harming those he left behind:

D 28:   One day I got a letter from home, and it said in the letter my
   brother was up for statutory rape and my sister was committed to Rochester State Hospital for observation. I started thinking about it, and
   I'm the oldest in the family of the children. And this kind of bugged
   me because I always looked out for them when I was out there. . . . I
   kept saying, "Well, if I was out there, if I hadn't got busted, I could
   have helped out. But I'm in here, and there ain't nothing I can do."

52:   I would say when I left Green Haven I had myself really bullshitted,
   I would say. Because I actually believed that this was it. And I've been
   locked up, if you've read my record, I've been locked up for about, I'd
   say, twelve years now. Different hospitals and here. So when I went out
   in 1970 I really thought, "If I could make it now, this is it." But when
   I got out there, and I was disappointed with a few things, I knew and I
   said, "Fuck it, I give up," and I went back. But even when I was going
   back I thought I could avoid jail. I thought I could avoid jail. But I
   didn't. When I got busted I thought, "I don't believe it." I really didn't
   believe it.

Instead of looking for explanations or remediable deficits, the person
arrives at a blanket judgment; he sets himself up as his own prosecutor,
judge, and (at times) executioner. He divorces himself from his own acts
by showing how much he despises them and hates himself for them. Each
"incriminating" incident sparks uncritical, purifying self-reproach, self-
contempt, self-hatred:

52:   After that I felt bad. 'Cause, like I said, I had myself bullshitted that
   I was a real strong person. I felt, "Damn, you ain't a man. You ain't
   been standing up to none of these obstacles." And I was more or less
   disgusted with myself. . . . I look down on myself.

Like Self-Deactivation and Self-Sentencing, Self-Retaliation is not a
problem-solving effort. The verdict is devoid of regenerative potential or
implications for action. Rather than come to grips with himself, a person
sets himself aside as a lost cause, and in his guise as self-observer he divorces himself categorically from the past he subjects to scrutiny. The
process is painful, but less painful than facing oneself as a continuing

enterprise and coming to grips with the complexity of one's motives and conduct. By showing good faith through self-hatred, a man can abrogate the responsibility and obligation for his regeneration and reform.

D. FATE AVOIDANCE

Reviewed with self-doubt, the past produces guilt and self-recrimination. Similarly viewed, the future inspires fear. Persons who see themselves as weak are apt to prize stability. They see new environments as tests they cannot pass, as obstacles they cannot surmount. Change is threatening because it leads to the unknown, unstructured, and unproved.

Given enough self-doubt, novelty brings a fear of failure that borders on panic. This explains repeated crises where the setting requires changes of environment. It also explains chronicity of crisis among individuals who are extremely lacking in self-confidence.

The following is an example of a fear-produced pattern of chronic self-destruction. The first incident, which occurred at the early age of nine, was a response to threatened transfer:

D 52:   That's when I drank the turpentine. I had been in a foster home before that, and I couldn't get along in a foster home. I was sent to another foster home. . . . And one day I was down in the basement, and I came across some turpentine. And I just drank glassfuls. And I started throwing up, and they rushed me to the hospital. . . . I think I was upset, but I didn't realize it at the time, that I was being moved around so much. I believe that was it. Because I was being moved around so much.

The most recent self-injury occurred in response to a similar announcement, involving an impending move from one prison to another:

D 52:   I had a friend that worked in the dep's office, and he told me, "You're going to Comstock Tuesday." So that was another real big disappointment. To some guys it wouldn't be a big disappointment, but to me it was a very big disappointment. . . . The first thing I tried to do, I tossed it around in my mind a little while. Then I tried to think of Comstock as acceptable, and I couldn't. No matter how I tried, I knew what Comstock was and I didn't want to go there.

Although a person may not be able to verbalize the link between self-doubt and fear, it is a discovery he must face sooner or later. The syllogism is built into the definition of maleness, from the perspective of the caveman to that of Hemingway. If a man is seen as afraid, other men are deemed to produce fear in him. If others can inspire fear, they are seen as stronger. To display fear is thus to admit weakness or submission, and to inspire fear is to proclaim power and dominance.

The extreme form of this syndrome is the interaction between bullies and targets of violence. This interaction may be idiosyncratic (as with the schoolyard terror) or institutionalized (as in German concentration camps). A milder form of the game is played among all-male groups (particularly young working-class groups), where indices of status are hard to come by and the group must feed on itself to supply self-esteem to some of its members. Pecking orders in such groups are often established by determining who can intimidate whom. The process may be functional for the inspirers of fear, but it is potentially traumatizing for their victims. This holds particularly true if premises regarding status are shared by those who are deprived of it.

Such juggling for dominance is more visible in the prison than in other social settings because the prison is blatantly status-depriving and thus creates a particularly acute need for indices of relative status. The juggling process can become almost ritualized, and the game can be played with uncanny skill. The process can also be more obviously productive of trauma, since the losers of the game tend to be men who have lost other, similar games.

Entry into prison, particularly among young, slight, or otherwise vulnerable men, often features a formal "testing" experience, in which efforts are made by some older prisoners to ascertain whether the newcomer is generally susceptible to intimidation or dominance. This "testing" can range from subtle interrogation to forceful attempts to secure physical compliance:

31: Everybody's out to test you out, you know? Sometimes they have to test you out for homosexuality, and sometimes they have to test you out to see if you've got money. See if they can get you to go down to the commissary for them. Or some guys like to walk around the penitentiary starting trouble. So when you first come in, for the first couple of weeks, you're under observation by all these different groups of guys. And, like, if you pass that observation period, you've just generally got it made. You might get into a fight or something, but it's not a constant thing, it's not like everybody picks on you. The first couple of weeks, that's the time when most everybody's got you under observation.

52: What I'm saying is that there are individuals that are just waiting to see how you react. . . . You may be a guy who had paranoia, or you may have certain ways. They may see another picture of you than what you are. It's all how you look to them. You may be an expert in karate or something, but they don't know this. They only see you. Once you show them the first time that you aren't a weak individual, then they leave you alone.

The process can cause considerable strain for the prospective victim, even if he fails to submit to his assailants. This is especially true because of cross-pressures and ad seriatim games—sequences which make survival a matter of walking a long tightrope. One inmate gives a vivid account of what this type of experience is like:

64:    And when you go in there you get all these eyes, man, all these mean stares. So lock into your cell, and your celly or someone else propositions you quick. "I can do this for you, I have commissary, and if you want something, I can get it for you." So you get in your cell, and your celly gives you this off-the-wall bullshit. They say they don't have any friends, and they jump on you right away. "I've been down for a long time, and my collar is tight." "What do you mean by your collar's tight, man?" "I ain't had no sex for something like eight or nine months out of this year, and there ain't no homos running around. Like, there's homos around, but they don't want to give up a lot of times if they're with somebody else." And he says, "I can guarantee, man, that it won't hurt or nothing 'cause we've got plenty of grease here and medication." So he says, "Will you go down?" . . . And they have Muslims and five per-centers and black guards and young guards, and when you're a new fish you're nothing. So you've got pressure coming from all sides. When you first come in the ward, anyway, their first intention when they look at you is that they're going to make this man my pussy, my girl and shit. And, "I'm going to stick this dick in him quick as hell when I get the opportunity in the shower." Now, through all this part here, you'll be waiting until you get to the shower. Here's a hundred motherfuckers at the shower, and they can see you're going to take a shower, and they're just waiting for you. So quite sensibly you're not going to take no shower then. I'm not no fool.

So then you go through a variety of different changes. And somebody says, "So-and-so is after you, and they're going to take you off." And he says, "You have to do something, so why don't you give it to me, and I'll see that nobody jumps on you." And, man, I'm not going to fall for this shit. I'm a man, and they aren't going to take nothing from me. Especially coming from the ghetto. So you come out of your cell the next night, and your celly is all frustrated and shit, and you're thinking he may cop. So you come out of your cell, and all these people are say-ing, "Hey, baby, how you doing? Did it hurt?" . . . They come around to a different degree of operation where they aggravate you. They say, "We're going to test this motherfucker. I know he ain't hip to the jail-house box, so we'll knock the motherfucker out quick. Just drag him out to the back of the tier and do it out there." So you come along back from the cell and shit, and you lock in and see these guys, big guys, running down. So, bang, you lock out, and here's everybody lined up in front of you. "How would you like to box, man?" "No, man, I don't know how to box." So he says, "Come on in the back, and I'll show you how to do it." And they're just waiting back there for you. They are conniving people. But my mentality is way further than that, to let them knock me out and fuck me. "No, man, You've got it all wrong."

Besides the magnitude of the onslaught, other aspects of the situation can make it difficult. A man may not know, for instance, what responses will discourage further "testing" and what responses will invite escalation. There is enough subtlety and ambiguity in the game to create confusion about the role one must play to buy freedom from fear:

cx 7:   I didn't know how many fights to get into, 'cause after you go to a place, you have to fight a couple of people. And I don't really like fight-ing. There's nothing to fight for. But when you go into a place you have to fight or do something to hurt somebody, to let somebody else know that if they come over to you and start something they're going to get something back.

52:   And one of the major mistakes that I made in doing my bit is that you've got individuals that come over to you and offer you things, like cigarettes, or to iron your clothes, things like that, and all the time they've got a mask on and they want to get to you. But they're doing it in a way that you won't see what they're doing. . . . These people even had me going that I had to project some type of image. Like a tough guy or something, so that they would respect me. But the guys would get together and have a conference about who was the chicken out there and try to grab him. So if this is your first bit, and you don't know what's going on, you can fall into this hole.

Frequently, responses designed to gain relief from pressure are per-ceived (from the power-centered perspective of one's assailants) as indica-tive of weakness, susceptibility, and compliance:

5:   Prior to my release time these guys had me buying them cigarettes in commissary and other items. And I was doing this to avoid getting beat up or in any kind of scuffle. So this went on for quite a few months. And each week it got larger and larger. And they were calling me names: "punk" and "easy to bulldoze." I knew that practically everyone was taking advantage of me. . . . And this particular day I was in my cell, and these three colored guys who I had been paying off from the commissary came in and started laughing, and they wanted to indulge in some sexual behavior. I was frightened and punched around a few times, and I was sexually assaulted. I was deathly afraid of going to the officer or any of the brass, that I would be held back from being cut loose.

From the reactions of peers a man learns about the substance of his image. He may discover his assigned role as victim, and the fact that the stigma may be built in and beyond his control:

5:   He seen me, and he smiled from ear to ear. He knew what kind of guy he had, and he knew a lot of his problems were solved.

52:   And the first vibration that I picked up was that everybody was looking at me. Right away they say, there's a young good-looking dude. Or sweet kid, or something. So I didn't pay no mind to it. I wasn't interested. So I thought, "Why can't I go to a place where the people are just like me?" These were men, and I was like a baby in the whole place. I looked like I was young. There were old men there and everything. So anyway, I let it bother me. It really got to me. . . . I've said to myself, "Is it my looks or the way I walk or the way I conduct myself or the way I react to things?" I've looked at myself in the mirror a lot, and I say, "Yeah, I am a reasonable-looking dude," and then I say, "This is in the family, and this is my mistake."

A man who is stigmatized as weak also discovers that his reputation may spread insidiously. This happens because men faced with powerlessness respond readily to rumors about the weaknesses of other men who can provide them with cannon fodder in their war against anonymity:

58:   It's one guy that starts it. And everybody listens to it. And they don't go to verify it first. They just go assuming that this guy isn't telling any lies. They stick with him. . . . A little bit at a time, and then it got worse and worse. And then some of them went home, and I relaxed again. But it goes from one guy to another, like a grapevine. Like, "Watch that guy. He's in here for this and that."

31:   Yeah, there were a lot of people riding me, because, like, guys were coming by, guys would say in a crowd, "I would get him myself, but I don't want to get the extra time for it." Because the word was already out that I was a rat; it was put out by the two guys that came up to prison with me.

The problem may also be aggravated by the set or expectation of the potential victim. Having been sensitized to the power game, an individual may approach his peers fully expecting to be ostracized, victimized, or attacked. When the pressure comes, he may thus be overintimidated by it.

cx 7:   When you're on the street you hear about so-and-so going to jail, and they ripped him off in there. And I'm thinking to myself, "These people are all up on me. If they want to rip me off, it's going to be rough on me. I'm going to have to see if I can get out of here."

1:   When I got here I asked for protective custody in the beginning. I'm only twenty-one and coming to a prison. All through my life I've heard rumors about prison, and this police officer who is a friend of our family, he told me 'cause I prosecuted sixteen guys out of the prison, three years ago, that if I ever went back to a prison somebody is bound to recognize my name, 'cause it was in all the papers there in Pennsylvania. And I got officers fired from the jail and started a big investigation. They had to change the prison wagons all around so the guards can see the inmates at all times. That if anybody recognized it, there would be trouble. This thought is always in my head.

A man's past experience may also provide him with a poor prognosis of his social effectiveness and of his chances for making friends and influencing people:

31:   I believe that might be a reason that people might want to stay away from me, because they probably figure that here's a guy that doesn't want to make any friends. Maybe they was thinking that I was the type of guy that would be violent towards people or something. Because I stayed too much to myself.

Self-doubt translates into fear when a man thinks that the odds against him are overwhelming. Once he classes himself as victim, the man, like the proverbial sacrificial lamb, must await his preordained fate. This set can entail considerable tension and bring acute emotional upset:

31:   The anticipation of waiting for something to happen to me was too much.

58:   I knew they couldn't get me, but that fear that they might. Not knowing that [the riot] was going to happen, that might happen too. This scared the hell out of me.

Since the dominant issue here is the person's self-image as prospective victim, the fear he experiences may be more diffuse than the danger he faces. It may make him feel generally helpless and devoid of recourse:

58:   It's not fair. They may get at you. They might hit you when you're
      going down the line or get at you when you're not looking. . . . I couldn't
      go through it again.

31:   I wouldn't have been scared if I had known it was just one group or
      two, or just one guy. Because I would have said, like, "The best he
      could do is beat me up or something." But I said, like, "I don't know
      where, I don't know who. Maybe I can get him first. But if I don't know
      where it's coming from I don't know who to attack. Or who I'm going
      to be attacked by."

A person may even become paralyzed and obsessed by fear. He may stop
following his daily routine and may find that his customary coping strategies are inoperative:

5:    I have no defense for it. I can't let my mind off of it. I try to paint,
      and it's there, and I get disgusted and throw the paintbrush down and
      put the earphones down and listen to the radio. It keeps me awake, and
      it's messing up my system, my nerves, and I bite my nails down till they
      bleed, and it's making me hate my wife. I told her I don't want her to
      come up no more. I won't write home.

58:   This harassment just stops my normal procedure, my everyday life.
      Everything just seems to stop immediately. . . . You get scared and you
      don't eat or sleep or use the toilet regular. Everything tightens up on
      you. That fear . . . you lose interest in doing anything.

Fear is also isolating in a physical sense. With danger in the air, social
interaction seems hazardous and freedom of action is restricted. This
means that one may give up a good part of one's life to purchase a sense of
safety.

1:    I'd never come out of my cell. I'd sit by myself and eat by myself. If
      somebody said something wise, I'd just keep my mouth shut. I just went
      into my own bag, stayed by myself.

5:    I lock in the cell, and I can't get out. If I go down the corridor or go
      to talk to someone, it's there.

The individual also finds that the comforts he has obtained (at a price)
are unstable and precarious. His refuge can become a trap; his self-insulation is unreassuring; his obvious caution makes him look vulnerable to

potential aggressors. Most important, a man can find himself with no further options for retreat:

31: I felt that there was no way out. I said, like, "Here I am trapped up
here. I can't go to the yard. I can't do nothing." . . . at this point I felt
disgusted, I felt completely disgusted with myself. Because, like I said,
all this running away that I caught myself doing, trying to avoid trouble. I said, "I'm still over here in the box. Now there's no place to go,"
I said. "I can't walk about in fear because I never done it before." I
never knew how it feels to be walking around constantly in fear. That
someone is going to attack me. So I said, "My God, if I've got to go
around walking the rest of my time like that, I'd rather be dead."

There is a dead-end flavor to this dilemma. The individual comes to feel
that no moves are available to him. Since he sees himself as cornered,
he can become disoriented, paralyzed, or helplessly self-destructive:

5: It just all hit me. It seemed like spots in front of my face. I was told
to move up in the line, and I was told to eat. I seen where I was, but I
didn't know where I was headed. I was in a fog. Things were reeling in
my head. I just wanted to scream. It was such a short period of time
before I got back to the cell, and I threw my head down, and I just
wanted to die.

31: The way I was thinking, I had a one-track mind, there was no way
out. . . . I couldn't think out different solutions. I couldn't think about
the things that there's more than one way to solve the thing, you know?
. . . I just knew that being dead would relieve me of this particular
situation.

The sequence holds, whether or not an individual has been threatened
or abused in the past. But previous victimization aggravates and accelerates the process. A man's memories of pain convert danger cues into flesh-
and-blood terrors. They diagnose and spell out threats, and reawaken the
shape of fears. They use small but familiar indicators to derive a detailed
prospectus of danger. They do so not only from familiarity with threats
but from knowledge of self—from knowledge of proven vulnerability:

64: It never left me, and then when I got rearrested accidentally, going
back into the place again and seeing the bull pen again brought back
the memory. And I said, "Oh, shit, here I go again." I went through the
formalities of going through the d.t.'s and the rest of the shit, and then
it was the same old shit again. It didn't change. The same thing
happened.

5:   The next morning we locked out to go to chow. And going to chow you see practically the whole population with everyone running around. And on the way I saw the guy I had a problem with in 1965. And all I saw was his glasses, and then, I don't know why, but I really got upset. . . . I didn't know what to do. I went back to my cell and all I thought about was cutting up or hanging up, because I knew what I was going to have to go through. . . . In the cell my mind was right back to Rikers Island with 300 men all screaming. I put my pillow over my head and cotton in my ears. And this went on until about one-thirty in the morning. I just said, "Wow, I've got to go through this now. It's not going to be like before where you get out in a few months. It's going to be a few years." . . . I started to shake. I felt like I was back in Rikers Island. I don't know how I got back to the cell.

A special problem that may arise for a person who has been victimized is that he may have to cope, or may believe that he has to cope, with the reputation of being weak. Since he has no way of knowing how widely his past is known, he may conclude that it is widely known. The problem is a continuing one. There are not only the concerns about reputation but also fears, worries, and self-doubts relating to the future. If a man has been compromised, he cannot avoid struggling with questions concerning his adequacy as a person and his impressiveness as a human being:

5:   Something I'm going to have to face for the rest of my life. "Forgive myself," that's what I keep telling myself. But I just keep looking at the way it happened and what has happened to me. I'm not quite a full man. Maybe I should become a homosexual. It's been in my head for seven years, and I don't know if I'll ever forget it.

64:   In reformatory, you have a person that's willing to knock himself out to prove to himself that he can stick you in the ass. Now if you let the man do this to you, you can't look at nobody in the face. So right there you're a self-failure if you let the guy knock you out. The man screwed me and got his thing off, and what are you supposed to do? You can't talk to your friends, they reject you. I can't tell my people about it because they get angry. The main thing is actually your people. If you confront your mom or your dad or your sister or brother, and say, "These people are trying to fuck me and turn me into a woman." . . . I have two more years to go. But the question is, After the incarceration, when I get out, what am I going to do? It fucked me up so much when I was out there last time, what is it going to do to me when I go out there this trip?

The relationship between victim-status and self-esteem is not one to which others tend to be sensitive and responsive. Peers are apt to view the victim exploitatively, or, more commonly, they may attribute his difficulties to a defect of character or a social deficiency. Knowing themselves to be nonvictims they can thus reassure themselves of their membership in a qualitatively different, stronger, superior group.

Institutional staff are apt to see victims in classification terms. Even if they respond to a man's fears, they are more concerned about the management implications of his problem than about its subjective and psychological consequences. This approach, which reflects not callousness, but staff roles, is described by one inmate as follows:

64:   Going into a form of paranoia, this is like being in between two bricks and being squashed. But not being squashed downward but your brain being squashed and people attacking. Now you try to explain this to the doctor, and he gives you medication. And if he sends you to the psychiatrist in the prison, the first place they send you is a mental institution. And then, if they tried to turn me into a homo, then the man puts down that I had tendencies of being a homosexual. Now if you don't work or go by their thing and eat when they want you to eat, then they say the man is sick. He don't want to go with the system. They send you someplace else. . . . So who am I going to look for help to? And then when I talk about killing myself, they put me down as suicidal tendencies and throw me in seclusion. . . . I cut up and went to the third floor in the hospital. And if you go to the third floor in the hospital, there's no one hounding me. I'm by myself, and I'm watching television. I'm going to the mess hall, and I can get something to eat at night, and I listen to the radio. The dude next to me is rapping to me like a natural person. There ain't no side action. And I enjoy this. And the psychiatrist comes around and shoots you right back down to population, and it starts all over again. So you cut up just to get back up on the third floor. And they get hip to that. And instead of getting hip to the people that are trying to take you off, they get hip that you're trying to get to the third floor all the time.

To raise his self-esteem and obtain hope and reassurance, the victim—or prospective victim—needs social support. Abandonment by significant others makes a person feel more vulnerable and increases the chances that he will see himself as worthless. It also makes him more fearful when threatened because he comes to feel that he has no one on whom he can count in crises:

64:   For a man to kill himself, it takes two things. His people cuts him loose, including his wife or girl friend or whoever is involved, and then a motherfucker tries to fuck him. My people cut me loose because I got locked up. Just because I committed one crime, I was a dope fiend. Can you help being on dope? I couldn't help it. It's that kind of thing. They had to degrade me for this and abandon me just for this one thing? Why must they leave me? Why must people constantly harass me about fucking me? So I would give up all hope totally. It's what the preachers are talking about, man, death is beautiful.

52:   So I wasn't getting no visits, and I didn't get no mail, and I had all types of people that really were finding excuses and ways of communicating with me. To these guys that were doing life and shit, I must have looked real attractive to them. . . . I have a whole list of things, what it is when you disrespect your family, and then you find yourself in the hole, and you get away from somebody that wants to help you but you just don't believe it, and then you run away from him and fall into a deeper hole. And then you turn around looking for him, but he's not there anymore.

41:   It was like I was drowning and nobody was there to save me or nothing. I couldn't swim. That's the way it was.

The combined perspective of a degrading immediacy and a rejecting world converts a crisis of fear into a more substantial, and more disabling, crisis of hopelessness.

Fear, in other words, is more—much more—than awareness of danger. It is that too, and in this sense it represents an indictment of settings in which the unscrupulous are left free to terrorize their fellows. But fear is also an index of self-worth, and it is used for this purpose by victims and predators—and spectators. And fear is paralyzing and incapacitating, and leads toward self-entrapment. Fear also makes men vulnerable: fearful men become more dependent than most on the support of their fellows. It is ironic, therefore, that men who are afraid are unlikely to evoke sympathy, understanding, fellow feeling, and support. For by virtue of the stigma such men carry, they promote distance, manipulation, and contempt. They do so because they remind other men of the thin and precarious line that stands between respect—and self-respect—and social opprobrium. For in the power-centered male society those who are down tend also to be out. They are rejected because, by virtue of their degradation, they make the rest of us manly.

E. SELF-LINKING

Experienced abandonments can give rise to survival-related inventories centered on the question of one's self-sufficiency and one's capacity to live

an independent life. Some persons feel their fate to be so intimately inter-
twined with the fate of others that they cannot conceive of continued
existence on their own:

2: See, if I were to have their support, I know I could make it. But seeing
   though as my father turned me down, and then my mother turns me
   down, that was the only support I had.

N: You're by yourself. You're just like a piece of paper, and somebody
   tears you up.

There is also the matter of coming to terms with loss of social support.
Men who are abandoned often feel themselves betrayed. A frequent reaction to abandonment is to perceive oneself as having been arbitrarily deprived of support to which one is entitled. There is a notion of an implicit
or explicit contract which the other party has summarily and unjustly
violated:

19: In '68 I went to Attica, and up until that time my wife and I were
    on pretty good relations. And she'd been writing me and sending me
    money. But then all of a sudden in July of '68 I received a letter from
    her stating that that was it. But the way she went about it, I didn't like
    it. In other words, she was hiding behind my crime. She says, "Well,"
    she says, "honey, we can't get together. I'm going to get a divorce be-
    cause of your crime." She was using this as a stepping-stone to, let's put
    it this way, to do as she wants.

15: Like, I'd been in this county jail for five days, and she don't know
    what I was in there for, she don't know nothing about the circum-
    stances. It's just that her parents, I guess, got to her head. "Cut this
    dude loose. He's nothing. Look at him, he's in jail already." So they
    called me up to the bars, they said, "We got something here for you."
    I said, "Wow, a letter from Chris. Maybe she wrote." . . . So I said,
    "What is it?" And they said, "You'll see when you open it up." Boom,
    a decree of absolute divorce. I said, "Wow, you got the wrong guy or
    something."

The problem may be compounded if an individual perceives his experience, as many do, as the latest link in a career of abandonment. A single
experience of rejection may be seen as an ultimate demonstration of untrustworthiness because it comes at a time when the man defines himself
as in special need of love and support:

15: Like, eleven years old they put me in a state hospital, and they wouldn't even come up and see me, and they was five miles away. And they left me up there for five years. Finally the authorities at the hospital got so pissed off about it that they said, "Well, if you don't take him out, we're going to cut him loose to another family." So I guess that scared them or something. So I came out, and he says, "You're going in the service." I said, "Oh, I am, huh?" He says, "Yeah, I'm going to take you down and sign the papers." . . . Everything just turns out bad, your marriage, your family life, your home life, but yet every time you try and do something the way society says is right, it just don't get done. You always end up incarcerated again. And then, when my marriage went, they put me in the county jail, and that was just the last straw. That's all I could take.

The crisis here is a partial reflection of the self-defined juncture at which a man admits unashamedly and openly his acute need for external support. The betrayal includes the failure by significant others to be aware of and responsive to special needs for love and contact. Institutionalization or combinations of physical distance and hardship are productive of situations in which information available to significant others is small but the presumption that such information exists is strong. In some of the most heartbreaking statements made by inmates, they detail an overwhelming need for love which is not forthcoming despite efforts to communicate the extremity of the need:

59: See, I write every week, once a week I write, and I don't get any back. See, I've written my mother a letter not too long ago telling her that, you know, I got braces on my teeth, right? And I told her that if she was willing to pay for my braces, my guidance counselor was going to arrange a furlough, a leave, so I can go home so I can get them fixed. I thought she'd write back real quick like for that one. I still haven't heard from her.

N: It's just like the fellows in the block, say, they get a letter from their moms and their women, they're in another world, you dig what I'm saying? Because what they're listening to, it's just like they hear whoever's voice that wrote this. They're hearing their voice in their own head. And, like with me, it's funny though. When I get mail from my woman, you dig it, or my mom, I read it, and then I go over it again. I read it again. It's just like you pick up something and read it, and it's from your mother, and you think, "Wow, my mom sent this." It's just like you're talking to her. Or the dudes in here, they'll get pictures. They'll look at the pictures and just stare, and it seems like the pictures are realistic moving. This has happened. I don't know, it's weird sometimes. . . . Well, after the first two months I haven't got any letters or anything like that. Because my mother, she told me when I come to jail she wasn't coming to see me. And, like, I took it for a joke. . . . Well, I'll tell you, man, to tell you the honest truth though, man, my visiting days are what? Wednesdays and Fridays? Like every time, say, Wednesday comes around, I'll be sitting down and they'll call the first person, and I can just swear to God my name is on that visiting list. Or Friday comes, boom, I didn't get no visit or nothing, right? Or before they call, I actually get on my knees and, "Mama this and mama that. Please come to see me." And I mean, like, for a lot of people it would seem funny to them, you understand? This really feeling something for somebody. I guess it's because I'm in here.

When an individual feels that he has been betrayed or rejected, he generally experiences self-pity and anger. Both reactions are apt to cause problems in interpersonal relationships and, if he has been institutionalized, difficulties in adjusting to his setting:

49:   I got pissed off right away. And I still got the same attitude. As you probably noticed my attitude when you walked in here. The sinister attitude I had since then. . . . This is the feeling that I had. . . . A feeling that she rejected me, by leaving me, and just an out-and-out feeling that everyone was against me. Because she had left, I actually believed that the institution was taking her away from me. This is what I believed. . . . Now if you can imagine the traits of being angry and concerned, in other words worried, but being angry at the same time, also a feeling of un-self-reliance and a feeling of pity for yourself, all rolled into one, you could pretty much get a good picture of what I was like at that time.

2:   Sure, I got a lot of feelings, right? That's one thing. And sometimes, like somebody hurt my feelings, I might lose my head. You see? Sometime I could do to somebody, and I don't even know I did it maybe, 'cause I got like crazy. And then when I was in there, what I would have done is violence.

Men of an intrapunitive bent are more apt to review their contributions to degenerating encounters and to see themselves as responsible for their abandonment. Here the crisis is one of self-hatred rather than of resentment. Such individuals feel that their credit has been used up and that they can count on no further support from others:

59:   See, I love my people, and I care about them, especially my little sisters. I did them wrong a lot, yeah, by getting in trouble. You know, whenever a cop car came by our house, "Steve's in trouble again." They were scared of me more or less. And, you know, cops would come in the house and get me. And then, after my mother kicked me out of the house because I gave her a hard time—she got mad at me and kicked me out—and I broke into this house. That's what I'm up here for. And the cops went to the house, about three, four, five dozen times, looking for me, you know? And my little sisters usually answer the door for them. And they got scared, you know? . . . the house that I broke into, I don't know why I did it, but they were good friends of mine. I guess it was because it was the only house I knew a lot about, and I knew what they had, stuff like that. . . . I felt stupid about it. I think back to what's going on where I live, a day or two after I got busted, people were laughing at them, "ha, ha, ha, you're good friends with _____, and he stabbed you in the back," you know? Laughing about that. And people will never trust me again, and I lost a lot of friends because of this. . . . It makes me feel like a traitor to a friend, and it shows that I can't have a friend or I'll round on him. . . . It was hard for me to make those few friends that I had. People didn't trust me, you know? A lot of parents didn't want me hanging around because, what the hell, "he was in jail, he's no good, keep away from him."

Self-Linking breakdowns are not simple fractures of interpersonal links. They are crises in which the total configuration of a person's relationships to others is invalidated. Though the stress in some instances is on the brittleness of the support system and in others on the man's own contribution to degenerating encounters, there is a common theme here of the individual suddenly adrift on the waves, deprived of his moorings. A reconsideration of basic assumptions relating to dependency and the stability of human relationships may be a component of the problem as it unfolds:

49: I seen it as a stress and strain to my mind. I didn't take it as just my relationships with Paula, but as my relationships with human beings on the outside of these walls and also within it.

2: Oh, I was feeling like the whole world tear apart me, like I was the only one in the world. . . . Sometimes even now, when I'm in here, I feel like that sometimes. Empty. You know, an empty life. Like I never done nothing for my people or somebody else, and I feel empty. . . . Like there was nothing left for me, nothing else to do.

Such generalized assumptions are apt to lead to the pseudosolution of declaring one's independence of others, one's immunity from involvements, or one's doubts about the significance of significant others. This formula, which minimizes the impact of abandonment and proclaims immunity from future hurts, sounds hollow even in the telling because it makes no provision for the individual's continuing needs for outside support:

59:   No, see, I feel when I don't get a letter, I say, "This is it, man, I'm writing a Dear John letter, telling her to get the hell out of my life." Even though she already is—I think she is, at least. And I write her a Dear John letter, what the hell, I'll go to a halfway house. I'll get out earlier that way at least. Then I'll go, "What the hell, I'm not going to write her either." Then I'll think about not writing her, and then I'll ask for a letterhead and write her.

19:   Yeah, it gave me quite a bit of strength because the way I feel is, What's a woman? There's a lot of women around, there's a lot of women that are looking for men. I mean, this isn't the only woman in the world. But then again, she's the only woman that bore me three children. And I do love the three children, and I still love her. But I mean, she wants to go her way, and I can't stop her. And this is the way that I've got in my mind now. It's all up to her. I can't do nothing about it.

N: Look at it this way. When you was small, or when you was in junior high school, right, you say, "Mama, I need this. Mama, give me money. Mama, I dig them shoes." You didn't ask daddy for this here, dig it, because daddy would say, "Ask mama." You always run to mama, You dig it? Or when you was a baby, mama was feeding you this, or mama was feeding you a lot of presents. You stuck onto mama all the time. You're asking mama to do this, and mama's cooking for you, mama's buying clothes for you, mama's doing this, mama's doing that. And a lot of niggers say now they reject their mother. But when they get in a place where they're enclosed, you dig it, and like places where they're hurting, then they think about it. Or when they get arrested. "Where's mama?" They may not tell you this, but deep down inside it's in their head.

Given a man's need to minimize his hurt, his unwillingness to admit his dependency, and the unmanly connotations of a need for love, he is apt to harbor the residues of trauma in isolation, with efforts at denial and self-deception. But Self-Linking crises do tend to leave painful gaps between real needs for support and environmental rejection and unresponsiveness.

F. SELF-CERTIFICATION

Since hurting oneself is painful and difficult, one can do so to convey depth of commitment. An act of self-injury can thus testify to the sincerity and intensity of one's affection for another. Such certification is never employed in a stable relationship. It denotes a credibility gap between lover and beloved so great that more conventional assurances are discounted. More precisely, it marks a breakdown in relationships which the offending party sees no other way to mend.

One inmate reported two incidents in which he employed self-injury to recapture forfeited affection. Once his target was a girl friend who had broken off with him, after he had become an obvious embarrassment and nuisance. In this case, he threatened self-injury and finally felt compelled to carry out the threat. The girl friend, who had appealed to the police for protection prior to the act, yielded in response to the gesture. She briefly reestablished the severed relationship in the hospital emergency ward:

cx 26: And it took quite a bit until I really rapped right down to her. I knew she was listening then, you know? Because you could see she wanted to hear. I just rapped it right down to her. I think it was the idea that she was listening and really trying to understand that brought me back down. . . . I was saying, "I haven't lost it, it's there, it just took this—what I done—to make her realize and myself realize it."

Having experienced some success in recapturing alienated affections, the man felt the incentive to employ self-injury again, in comparable circumstances. On the second occasion, he used it to enlist the aid of his family, who had turned their backs on him when he was incarcerated. The inmate knew that he had forfeited his trust with his family, and that routine efforts to reinvolve them would fail. He sensed that he must demonstrate that he was an object of legitimate pity and a man in irrefutable need:

cx 26: Well, you say to yourself, "I can write a letter," and then you say, "What will happen if I do write a letter? They'll read it, but it won't mean nothing to them." And you say to yourself, "Well, what if I tell somebody here, and they write a letter home?" Then I said, "No, you don't want them to think they're forced to write to you. If they wrote me because people had wrote and asked them to write to me, they'd say, 'Well, yeah, this kid—.'" I said, "That isn't the answer." I said, "What can I do to show them that I need them?" . . . I figured if I cut up they'll write a letter home saying that I cut up because I feel as though people don't want to help me and stuff like this. And then I felt they'd say, "Man, look what he done." And it would shock them. Like a person trying to take his life is not a normal thing, you know? It's not an everyday thing. . . . I just figured, "well, this is going to snap them out of it, they're going to want to help."

We interviewed another inmate with a closely analogous pattern, except that his first incident occurred in childhood and represented an effort to introduce affect into a degenerating family relationship:

D 35:   My father kept coming home and bugging my mother and throwing bottles and stuff like that at her and broke her arm and her leg. So I figured life really wasn't worth living for it. So I took the knife out of the dresser drawer, and I went out in the back woodshed, and I tried to cut my arm. But I just couldn't put myself in a position to really do it. So I figured I'd just make scratches. This is mostly what the doctors would say is people that would need attention. Because they haven't been shown attention in the family when they were small. And this is mostly what they were looking for. I thought if I tried to cut up or something like this, maybe someone in the family would start loving me and baby me or something like this. This is mostly the reason why I did it, really.

The incident did not result in the intended rapprochement. Instead, it produced a new, painful act of rejection:

D 35:   My sister come out, and she saw the blood on my arm, and she went back in and told my father. My father came back out and took me in the bedroom and stripped me and blistered me with a belt.

Despite this experience, the man employed self-injury on several other occasions. The most dramatic incident occurred in prison, vis-à-vis a homosexual partner. The two men had reached a stalemate, and self-injury was intended to underscore the urgency of the man's sexual requirements and demands:

D 35:   Well, we got these sexual relations going and stuff like this, and things didn't exactly work out my way. He got angry with me because he was trying to be a woman and I was already one. So I told him to cut it out or I'd knock his head off. . . . I told my husband that I would cut up if he didn't straighten up, and he said, "Go ahead, I don't think you've got the heart." So I figured, "We'll see." So that night I actually cut up . . . when I did wake up and found out I was still on the tier and there was no guards around, I went downstairs screaming like a maniac that I was going to kill this guy. So about seven or eight officers came over and handcuffed me and took me over to the hospital.

The attempt was a serious one. The inmate wrote a testamentary letter, disposed of property, and cut himself after setting fire to his cell:

D 35: I wrote a letter to my mother that night—just wrote a couple of words on a letter and told her I was sorry for what I was going to do. And I signed it and mailed it out. And then I started cleaning out my cell and everything, and giving it to this inmate. And I set my cell on fire, and then I cut myself. I kept pacing back and forth in the cell getting up enough courage to really do this.

The gesture, in this case, shows that such acts can incorporate complex and ambivalent feelings. There were self-destructive overtones to an interpersonal message, and the message combined demand and rejection. As this inmate communicated his needs to the other, he also revealed the assumption that there was no hope for renewed contact on his terms:

D 35: I could have actually told him that the relationship was over, but we had broken up Lord knows how many times, and we had always gone back to each other again. But people say that I was forcing this guy to go with me. That if he didn't do the things that I wanted to do that I would beat him up. This person was actually very scared of me. . . . I felt that I had the power in me to direct and run this person's life. He either had to do the things that I wanted done or it wouldn't have worked out.

Paradoxically, persons who exploit other persons are sometimes ultrasensitive to being manipulated themselves. For example, one inmate who had repeatedly exploited the women in his life describes himself as follows:

4: I've always been sort of lucky with women, you know, in understanding them. . . . I could pretty much tell when they were lying. I don't know if this is a blessing or not, because it got me hurt several times. But I could always tell. It's difficult for them to lie to me. So I find out things that I really don't want to find out.

This man indicates that his image of manliness calls for submissiveness in women, but that his own wife, whom he has beaten, is unacceptably self-assertive:

4: My mother was very domineering. And I used to look at her and look at my sisters—my sisters were coming up just like her. And even when I was a kid I used to think, "Boy, if she was my girl friend, I'd break her jaw or something." You know, because she was really domineering. And then it killed me that I ended up with my wife. My wife was just like her, you know, and she's the only woman that I've ever been involved with like that. But in that respect, I mean, extremely domineering. She was so aggressive in sex I had to tell her, you know? And, you know, hitting her was a very poor solution. And she made me aware of the fact that it was a very poor solution.

The man admits unfaithfulness before and after marriage, but regards his wife's resentment as unreasonable and uncalled for. In turn, he becomes consumed with jealousy on the flimsiest pretexts, works himself into a crisis, and stages suicide attempts to promote guilt in his wife:

4:   I found a picture of her that she had taken backstage at the _____, it's a theater in New York where they have groups and stuff. And this entertainer was sitting in a chair, and it was her and another girl too, and she was leaning on his leg. And I don't know, this got to me. And I started imagining all sorts of things. I also had a drinking problem at the time, and this certainly played a part in it. . . . I went and got some whiskey, and I drank it, and I did it. Then right after I did it, she came home. And I think I knew she was coming right home. I think I might have waited till she got there. So I know I didn't really want to die. . . . I was definitely feeling sorry for myself. And the only thing I can even remember while doing it, was thinking, "Yeah, well she'll be sorry now," something to that effect. Because I knew that she cared for me too, I was really sure of that. And hitting her, I don't really like to. Well, I have hit her, but it makes me feel worse.

An extreme reaction occurs in situations in which the man has blatantly overextended his credit. Having driven his wife to the breaking point, he faces her announced departure. After beating her, he injures himself to communicate the intensity of his need for her:

4:   And I told her, "Don't say anything to me." And she started talking, and I hit her. And I really hit her so it hurt bad. . . . And she started screaming, and she was always threatening for the cops. And I know that I felt bad about hurting her, and I don't know what it was. I just took a razor blade, and that was a real attempt to kill myself. Because I just mutilated myself.

Men who are vulnerable often assert an independence they do not feel, and defy those whose goodwill they need. The danger built into this gambit is that it may be taken literally. The bluff may be called, exposing the unimpressive hand. An example of this sequence is the following interaction between an inmate and his parole board:

8:   So I said, "He's a liar, and if you're going to believe it you might as well hit me with the rest of my time and rub the rest of it on your chest. Keep your parole, who needs it?" So they hit me with the whole thing, and my maximum expiration date fell on December 27, that's two days after Christmas. Now at that time I wasn't out for Christmas for, like six years. You know, I always happened to get locked up around Christmas. So I wanted to be out there. So I saw the institutional parole officer, and I asked him, "Can you do anything about this two days after Christmas? Can you give me a two-day—?" So he says, "Well, I don't know, I'll see if I can do anything." So he went to the meeting, and he spoke to the commissioner or somebody, and he called me back a few weeks later, and he said, "No, you told them to rub the parole on their chest, and that's what they're going to do." I said, "For two days, they're not going to give me two days?" And he said no. And I got really messed up in the head, you know, over this two days. And I cut up. But I don't think I wanted to die. I did it just to impress upon these people how much the two days meant to me.

The reaction of the man when he is passed over is to stage a dramatic gesture to counteract the impression left by his cool and defiant front. He seeks to convince officials of the intensity of his desire, which translates, as he sees it, into the meritoriousness of his request or appeal. This strategy of making a demand bid when in trouble is pursued by the same inmate in a letter to his wife:

8: My wife had this thing going with her cousin before she married me. Now they were kids, and it wasn't anything really deep. There was no sex involved or anything. But they used to do a lot of heavy petting and shit. Now I never knew this, and this cat was in Vietnam, and he was writing to her. So I said, "Well, who is this guy anyways?" And she said, "He's my cousin." I says, "who?" And she says, "Well, it's _____ son." And she's telling me he's been in Vietnam for a year or something like that, she just got a letter from him. So I says, "Yeah, well let me see the letter." So I'm looking at the letter, and there's like all sorts of little funny things implied. You know, "I always loved you." So I said, "Hey, write this guy and tell him you're married." So she says, "He knows I'm married." And I said, "Well, remind him that you're married, because I don't like what he's got here." You know? So now at the time I still didn't know that she had anything going with him when they were kids. So she wrote him, and she says, "I'm married, and I got two kids, and blah, blah, blah, and it's not right. I don't know if you're trying to start anything up, but I want you to know it's not right and it'll never happen." And he wrote to her and says to her, "I don't care about your being married, and I still love you." So this whacked me out. I said, "What does it mean, he still loves you? He's your cousin." She says, "He went with me when we were kids." I said, "kids. What did you do when you were kids?" She says, "Nothing. You know, just kid shit." So I told her that's got to stop. So he gets killed, you know? She starts crying when they found his body. He was missing for something like two months, and then they found his body all decayed and shit. They were able to tell by the dog tag. . . . So now she writes and tells me, "Gee, I just saw my cousin Dean, I haven't seen him in such a long time. He's nineteen years old. I can't believe how good he looks. He used to be fat when he was a little kid, and he got tall, and he lost all the fat, and he really looks good." So I wrote her back and told her, "What the fuck do you mean he really looks good? What are you trying to do, tease me? If you make it with one cousin, you'll make it with another one." So I got a whole lot of shit in that letter, because it really bugged me just reading it. Now she probably didn't mean anything by it, but the thought ran through my head, "What is she looking at this guy so hard for?" You know, like I'm an extremely jealous dude. I walk down the street with my wife, if you look twice I'll punch you in the face.

In this case, the bid is a threat, but the aim, once again, is to relay the intensity of feeling, to make it hard for the other party to ignore a request. And, again, impotence explains the explosiveness of the bluff:

8: Well, I realize there's nothing I can do while I'm here, so I tell her in the letter I'll kill the guy when I get out. "If I find out you and him got anything going on, I'll kill him." And I still don't know what her response is going to be. She knows if I get mad I'll take the guy off the count.

Another illustration of hollow self-sufficiency that boomerangs is provided by a Puerto Rican inmate who arranges for rejection by his mother, and then reacts with despair when his family takes him at his word:

A 1: She came to visit me. She told me, "How are you doing?" And I want to make her feel that I'm a man, that I don't need her. So I told her, "I'm all right, you don't even have to come to see me. I'm doing beautiful. I'm all right."

I: But you don't really mean it?

A 1: I don't really mean it. I love my mother a lot, but I want to prove to her that I'm a man. I said, "As a matter of fact, you come to see me every two weeks, make it a month. Come see me every month." And I would say, "Don't even come see me." So she was telling me, "We're planning to move to Puerto Rico. We're waiting for you to get out so we can go to Puerto Rico." And I said, "You might as well go to Puerto

Rico without me. I'm not going with you. I'm going to go out there and get me an apartment, and I don't even want to see you people anymore. So I don't know why you even bother to come see me."

I: Did you mean that?

A 1: I didn't mean that. No, I just say that. My mother loves me, but she don't want to tell me. She acts like she don't care really, but inside I know she cares about me. And I went up to my cell and I started crying, because my mother had told me, "I'm going to Puerto Rico," and she's going to leave me, desert me, you know? Just leave for Puerto Rico in two years. What if I don't get out in two years? I don't have nobody in New York City I could go to. I'd be all alone in the world.

The emerging theme is that of dependence with its double-edged connotations. Our man protests his self-sufficiency while feeling completely unself-sufficient:

A 1: She's just going to go to Puerto Rico and forget about me for the rest of her life. But I was saying to myself, "Man, I can do it. I don't need anybody. Fuck it, when I get out there, I'll get a job. I'm not even going to go to her house when I get out. When I get out I'm not even going to let my mother know."

At one extreme of the spectrum of degenerating interactions is the manipulator whose manipulations come home to roost. The turning point in such relationships is the juncture at which other persons—who are viewed (and treated) as objects—acquire unexpected life of their own. At the other extreme is the completely nonassertive individual—the self-defined object who invites manipulation by others. If cast in the wrong company, such a person may be subject to more victimization than he has bargained for, more than he can tolerate. Such a man's breaking point (or points) may be uncharacteristically extrapunitive, or suffused with self-hate.

A case is provided by an ex-parolee who found himself rejected by everyone he knew while on parole. The man reacted by arranging for his reconfinement, then discovered that prison brought new rejection experiences. The sequence is worth summarizing because it illustrates the link between incidents, including the contributions of the self-defined victim.

A continuing theme in this story is the man's self-image, a compound of selflessness, unassertiveness, and pessimism:

1: I'm not happy unless I'm doing for somebody else. I mean, the officers and the psychiatrists said, "Well, Art, you've got to do for yourself." I said, "Well, damn myself, I don't give a shit if I've got any clothes or not, as long as I can see D——————— or my mother or somebody else happy, this makes me feel good. . . . I've always condemned myself. I have a defeatist attitude. You can say now, "Art, I know you can reach over and pick up that carton of cigarettes." And I say, "I can't do that, I'm going to muff it." I think this goes back again to my childhood when my father would say, "He can't do that. He'll screw it around somehow."

The childhood situation to which the man refers was a triangle involving his mother, his father, and himself:

1:   Dad idolized Mom—he had her on a pedestal. Anything she wanted, she could do no wrong. And this is where I think the trouble with he and I came. Because when I was little I was in the hospital a lot. I had blood poisoning, pneumonia four times, I had tonsillitis. You name it, I had it. And all this time it took, Mom had to be with me instead of being with him. So he built up this resentment: "He's taking her away from me," and he's always had this in mind.

The father's resentment—according to the son—took the form of beatings, hostility, and open contempt. In a conversation with his father, he recreates an early episode as typical of the relationship:

1:   "And you were sitting on the edge of the couch. You were reading a *National Geographic* magazine, and the reason I remember the magazine is the outline of their design with the yellow cover," I said, "and I got up off the floor and I came down to the couch and sat on your lap. You laid the book down, reached over and picked me up and put me down on the floor and went back to reading the book. Mom looked up over the top of her chair, and she used to wear those old wire-rimmed glasses." He said, "Yeah, I remember the glasses she wore." I said, "And she said to you, 'Bud, why don't you play with your son?' And you said, "Playing with him is like playing with a rattlesnake.' " And I said, "You tell me, dad, what did I do at six years old to deserve that kind of treatment from you?"

There is no question in the man's mind as to the "kind of treatment" he "deserves." His memories of Attica thus include the assessment that he himself should have been among the victims:

1:   And I just couldn't figure why these guys had to die when probably a lot of them had wives and kids on the outside, and they had a reason to live. "And you haven't got a reason for even existing, yet you walk off the yard without even a scratch. Now why? Why do things work that way, that you should get off and the other guys should die?" . . . It was just something that stuck in my craw. I couldn't figure out after seeing all them other guys that got shot down and everything else. And their families were so broken up. My people didn't even write to me, for crying out loud—they could care less whether I got bumped off or not. I said, "Why is it that you walked off and they had to stay?" I think it more infuriated me than it puzzled me as to why. It pissed me off. "Well, ain't this a bitch? I walked off, and I didn't get shot, and these other guys all got the hell blown out of them." It just irritated me. As far as I could see, I didn't have anything to live for.

Assuming the role of sacrificial lamb represents a challenge to the world to disprove the hypothesis that one isn't wanted. It carries the cautious hope that one is or might be loved, appreciated, or accepted by somebody. Various experiments along this line are arranged, but they are almost designed to make affirmative findings improbable.

The gambit is dramatically illustrated in the relationship between this man and his wife. Here the test involves his marrying a woman with a reputation for promiscuity, and leaving her alone in the evenings, to prove his ability to retain wifely loyalty. The experiment fails when the man discovers that his wife is being flagrantly unfaithful:

1: So one night I went up to the fire department, and one of the guys made a remark to the effect that "we don't want jailbirds on this truck." So I got mad, and I put my stuff up, and I went home early. I went home about seven-thirty. And I came through the backyard, and I noticed this maroon Oldsmobile in the driveway, and it was only about seven-thirty. So I opened the door downstairs real quietly, and I went upstairs. The door was locked, and I kicked the door open. And there she was in the most awkward position. One guy watching, the other guy was doing his thing.

The experience gives this man a further chance to establish his own unworthiness and unlovability. Having been humiliated by his wife, he begs her to return to him, and is predictably and summarily rebuffed:

1: I had a change of heart. I called her back—I was a damn fool, I know that. Everybody else said, "You crazy asshole, call her back?" And she said she didn't want to come back. She said, "I get sick of people giving me looks and everything else because they know where you've been, they know what you are. It's just not going to work out."

Three other experiences help the man see himself as an object of contempt: (1) his employer displays distrust in him; (2) his volunteer fire

company makes it obvious that he is unwelcome; and (3) his landlady
throws him out of his apartment. These events all partly result from the
fact that the man has withheld information about his parole status, setting the stage for inauspicious discoveries of his criminal past:

1:   One day I was sitting outside with five other employees, and he approached me and said, "I'm missing five-hundred dollars out of an en-
velope that was on my desk." And he asked me if I had seen it, and I
said, "No sir, I haven't." He said, "You're the only one on parole out
here, and naturally you're going to be the one suspected of taking that
money." And I said, "Mr. K——————, I didn't take that money."
He took me to the back room where he shook me down. He came back
about an hour later and said, "Art, I'm really sorry. I found the money.
It was in my suit-coat pocket." And I said, "Well, Mr. K——————,
I'm sorry too, because I quit." I walked out. . . . The reason I stayed so
close to the area was because I was in the fire department. This is something I've always enjoyed, helping people. But when the word got out
in the fire department that I was on parole, I got the freeze from them.
I wasn't good enough to ride the trucks anymore; they just gave me
jobs like cleaning up. On top of my wife leaving and my job and now
the fire department, everything was piling up pretty fast. . . . And then
she said, "Arthur, I just don't feel comfortable having a person of your
caliber around here." She said, "I'll give you thirty days to find another
place to live in." And I said, "You can just give me the weekend. I'll
be out by then."

In self-defeating efforts to secure acceptance from others, our man now
proceeds to set fires that attract his volunteer fire department, and arranges his own reimprisonment:

1:   I had moved into another apartment. I was all alone. I didn't really
have any friends to speak of. I sat there talking to myself. I didn't have
anybody to go to. My dad and I didn't get along, and I couldn't go out
and see my mother on account of him being there. So I really blew the
works. I went out and started a couple of fires. And everybody said,
"Why did you start a fire, Art?" And I did it because I knew the guys
from the fire department would come out, and I would have somebody
to talk to. So I went and broke into a store. With no intentions of
stealing anything, but I just thought that this had gone far enough.
Instead of burning places down, nobody to talk to and no place to go
or no job, I thought I would go back to prison. They were the only
type of people that I knew how to associate with. At least back there
they wouldn't frown on me and call me a'crook or say I was an oddball.
I was in with guys that I knew. So I sat there on the counter, and the

detective came in. And he said in court later that he did feel a little ridiculous coming busting in the door and seeing one fellow sitting on the counter there, breaking down and crying and everything, saying "Take me away, I'm ready." He said, "I've never experienced this before in the twenty years that I've been on the force."

Inevitably, prison, with the help of self-defeating moves, becomes a rejecting environment. It adds to the stigmatizing record, produces snubs from impatient peers, and causes problems with family members who have become irritated:

1: I had been writing on and off to my mother, but Mom wasn't well at the time, and she was under a psychiatrist's care, and she had her own problems. I hadn't heard from her since after the riot. She said, "Your letters are too upsetting. Don't write anymore." And my sisters had never wrote, and my dad hated my guts, so I wasn't getting any mail. Everybody else was getting mail and I wasn't. . . . I'm just a prisoner. There's nothing exceptionally good about me, and there's nothing exceptionally bad about me. They can take me or leave me. It's not like a lot of the guys around here that the prisoners look up to. They're always saying, "Hi, how are you?" But with me it's one or two guys saying, "Hi, Art, how are you?" This weighs heavily on my mind a lot of the times.

New rejections bring depression and self-pity. Relief arrives in the form of a new experiment. This time our man decides to "prove" his unworthiness by trying to end his life:

1: I think what actually pushed me over the edge, January 26 or 27, after not hearing from my sisters or my mother or anybody for three or four months, all of a sudden I got birthday cards. "Wish you a happy birthday, we still love you." And that just pushed me over the edge. And I said, "How could they do it?" One of my friends here and one of the officers had noticed that I used to walk around with a "I could give a shit" attitude. And they told me later they noticed that all of a sudden I seemed happy in the last couple of days. They said the psychology and psychiatry books say that when a person does this, they'll go along most of the time feeling rejected, and then all of a sudden they perk up because they know they're going to try suicide. And they know that whenever they decide or whenever they set that final date to do it, their troubles will be all over. And they're happy. And this is the way I was. . . . When I look back on it now and try to visualize my state of mind at the time, I thought I would never have to worry about prisons anymore, and I wouldn't have to worry about getting shunned by girls and every-

thing. That's been one of my problems. I can get along with girls eighteen and nineteen years old, but when they get up to my own age—I'm
twenty-nine now—I can't compete with them. They look at me like I'm
a little kid.

In his self-destructive gestures, the man issues a multidimensional message to his tormentors. This message includes such themes as, "I'll arrange
for you not to hurt me anymore", "I understand that you wish me dead",
and "Even if I have to die, somebody is bound to accept me."

The crisis embodies the tragic components of a self-defeating cycle. A
child's birth spawns hate. In response, the child seeks acceptance at any
price, with the fear that the pursuit is hopeless because the end is not
deserved. As the last move, the grown child offers to destroy himself to
efface the hostility occasioned by his birth.

The relationship between rejection in childhood, the pattern of self-
doubt and testing, and the suicidal gesture to secure redemption also
emerges in the story of an inmate who is subject to homosexual pressures.
This man's account of his family problems reads as follows:

6:   It seems that my mother wanted a girl instead of a boy for her first
child, and she got me. Whether that's fortunate or unfortunate is a con-
troversy. And anyway she never really loved me, at least that's the way
it was put to me, and I was always doing these things because I wanted
to be loved. I wanted to be noticed. And all this time I keep getting in
trouble, keep getting in trouble, they were there all the time, to help
me. And I more or less took it for granted. And, like, I didn't really
think they loved me because of what was drilled into me. I thought
more that it was they were obligated because I was their son. And after
this last time, they just dropped me. And it hit me like wow, you know?
And then I started thinking about it. "They really didn't love me, but
now they didn't come this last time, and they aren't there to help me, I
guess they really didn't love me, they don't care about me. And I have
nobody to care about, and nobody to care about me, you know?"

The inmate views his prison homosexual involvements as efforts to purchase friendship, and feels that they misfire because of the exploitative
nature of his partners:

6:   See, I was under the illusion that there were people that were friends.
It seems that everybody that tries to be my friend, they all, because of
where we are, they all want to have sex. . . . I've noticed that it really
can't be a warm relationship, not with eleven hundred other inmates,
and they've all got one thing on their mind, and that's their own physical desires which they want to get taken care of. . . . And then people,

they seem to reject people that engage in this type of activity. And I've already been rejected enough, and I didn't need this to get rejected anymore.

The crisis for this inmate culminates in a suicidal gesture designed to express helpless resentment, to reproach and promote shame in those who have rejected him. He thinks of suicide as an effort both to hit back at his tormentors, and to purchase posthumous positive affect:

6: Well, I picked out one person particularly, one black person that had been pressuring me. I put down that I heard he was a punk and he was a creep. And if there was a life ever after, he's always a creep. . . . Then I started reminiscing, like I said, about girls again. I wrote down different girls that I had known, and their addresses if I could remember them. And I wrote some gibberish down there that I loved them all and they didn't return that love. I left a will, I think, something like that. To the effect that all my money and everything be divided among all my people by the laws in New York State.

I was hoping that it would stick in people's minds that supposedly had cared about me or were supposed to care about me. People I was supposedly close to. Maybe in a way I thought maybe I might be punishing them. I don't know. Maybe they'd think back and say, "He wasn't such a bad kid, we should have given him a chance" or "We should have done this." Some type of feeling, something. Because I wasn't getting anything at the present time.

Self-injury is used not only to underwrite declarations of love and need but also to underscore fear, panic, helplessness, and pain. The magnitude of defeat is dramatized by the person's willingness to sustain physical hurt rather than continued harassment. The message combines surrender with an appeal to pity, fellow feeling, and sportsmanship. The person acknowledges his vulnerability and invokes norms or conventions relating to pointless attack and injury.

Some inmates can offer "success stories" involving breakdowns used to neutralize threats. In each such case, a man puts himself off limits by demonstrating his vulnerability; in each case, he classifies himself as emotionally unstable:

6: I was in there for, like, eight months, settled, you know? I had a few guys that I did my time with. And I just wasn't going for this. And when they came and got me in the morning, I told them, "Look, I'm not going. I don't dig this being herded like cattle into another joint and then waiting to go into Sing Sing." I said, "I'm going to stay right here, or else I'm going to cut up." So the brass called my bluff, you know? So I says to them, "Look, I got a mental history, don't trifle with me" about whatever it was. So I guess he didn't pay it too much mind, because the van came. They called twenty guys out. I'm the last guy they called out, so they say, "Let's go." I said, "Wait a minute," and I cut up. So they stitched me up, sent me back upstairs. . . . This was to show them that I wasn't bullshitting, you know? And they didn't move me.

cx 7:   Well, they didn't give me much of a hard time because one guy there, Smitty, he was a spook, and he remembered me. "Wasn't you that guy that jumped off that tier?" I said, "Yeah." And he spread the word to all the spooks around that "this guy is crazy, you stay away from him." So everybody stayed away. Nobody bothered me.

Though humans, unlike lower forms of animal life, are comparatively willing to exploit the weak and vulnerable, their cruelty has limits. A convention honored by all but the most sadistic protects men who demonstrate that they have been pushed to the brink. If a breakdown signals extremity of despair, it can bring immunity.

The impact of such an act derives from its spontaneity. Others respond to the victim because his act demonstrates that he really does feel impotent—that he knows he has been defeated. A cornered man may thus be spared if he presents ironclad evidence of his complete helplessness.

4

Caging One's Tiger

Our third category comprises persons who carry with them a substratum of susceptibility to crisis which is made up of unwanted feelings and needs whose press and constraint is peremptory and disturbing. The equilibrium achieved by these men is one of inner battles lost and renewed. Their past is studded with shameful and unassimilable acts; their present is a nightmare of confusion; their future is threatening and uncertain.

Typically, these men have adjusted by shutting off some of their faculties—by forgetting and ignoring—by transmuting troublesome urges into threats from without. They have achieved a strained, unstable, paralyzing resolution of their difficulties, a resolution that is precarious under conditions free of temptations and challenges, volatile and explosive in situations that pose tests.

I. Themes Related to Impulse Management (Relationship of Self to Self)

(A, B: Capitulation to Internal Pressure—Catharsis and Self-Hate)

A. Self-Alienation: A reluctant or passive compliance with alien impulses and commands that direct the person to destroy himself.

B. Self-Release: A catharsis or strategic loss of control designed to discharge aggressive feelings and to end tension and discomfort related to such feelings. This occurs as a temporary loss of contact with reality after a cumulation of resentment, tension, and anger, and is followed by emotional drain and experienced relief.

(C, D: Projected or Subjective Danger)

C. Self-Escape: An effort to preserve sanity—or to escape—that is made when the person experiences strong, tension-provoking destructive impulses. The person may feel disturbed by imagined threats combined with experiences of his own destructive potential.

D. Self-Preservation: An attempt to escape cumulating harm, made when the person builds up the conviction that he is in substantial physical danger from pervasive, all-powerful enemies. The person may destroy himself because he fears imminent destruction by others.

(E: Need for Assistance with Internal Control)

E. Self-Intervention: A demand for professional help in the understanding and control of one's own impulses and moods. The person makes a last-ditch effort to secure such help through action because verbal requests for help are seen as nonproductive.

II. How Do Impulse Management Themes Manifest Themselves?

A. SELF-ALIENATION

The disturbed individual must live in two worlds. One is the workaday world of his daily routine; the other, his internal world of turmoil and conflict. The two worlds are incongruent:

D 46:   One time I sit down in the back, and I feel my face with the beard and my hair like Jesus Christ. I told myself that I was Jesus Christ. The next morning I woke up and I didn't know what to do. I know that I was supposed to wash my face and brush my teeth and start the new day. But I don't know what to do. I took my toothpaste and my toothbrush, and I'm putting a little toothpaste on my toothbrush, and I don't know what to do.

The abruptions between the two worlds of the self-alienated can be quite drastic. In one world, the person responds to events around him, gathers information, and takes action. He feels himself in charge of his acts, exercising volition. The other, "alien" world is one in which needs and impulses have a life of their own, in which a man is impelled rather than in control. He may respond as a helpless pawn to commands he feels originate outside himself; he may see himself as a passive recipient of sights and sounds imposed on him in improbable ways. From being a self-determined individual, he becomes a helpless spectator to undesired actions and strange sensations that involve him as a physical being:

D 27: Sometimes I'll be speaking, and I'll all of a sudden think about throwing myself in front of a truck or something and get hit. I'm pressed by this feeling. Like it's really no big thing. Like, "man, this is what's happening. Throw yourself in front of a truck." . . . It's out of my control. It just takes control. It's not like I have an opportunity.

4: Usually they tell me to do it, you know what I mean? I don't know how to say it. Not telling me really to do it, they're giving me ideas. Telling me, "I think it would be a good idea, I think you'd be doing the right thing if you did it." Or, "You're doing this time for nothing, you're never going to leave, you'll be here the rest of your life. You've been here thirty-two months already, you might be here another thirty-two months," or "you're never going to leave. Why don't you just end it all, get it over with?" . . . Right now I'm telling you I don't want to kill myself. And I could be talking to you, and like a minute later they could make me change my mind. You know, they have control of my mind. I don't know, they make me change my mind, and I could be sitting here talking to you, telling you I don't want to kill myself, this and that, and a minute later I could tell you I want to kill myself and try to kill myself. It's this kind of a thing, you know? I can never tell what's going to happen. . . . You know what would happen? Like a cop would be talking to me, telling me to get out of the shower maybe, right? And I would tell him, "OK," but he wouldn't hear that, you know what I mean? I don't know if it was the voices or what, but they would say something. I think they can turn their voices. I think they get different channels or something. Where they can say something so only I can hear it, or they can say something to make other people think that I'm saying it. So they would tell the cop, "Fuck you." And the cop would think it's me. They do it just to get me in trouble, things like that. You know, I don't really curse too much, myself. They would do things like that. See, I don't know, it has me all mixed up. I don't know if they control my mind to make me say that, to make me say it—I'm pretty sure this is what they do. I'm pretty sure they get different channels for their own voices and they can switch channels. And one way's so only I can hear them, so nobody else knows what they're telling me. And maybe they can never be caught, something like this. Maybe if they're caught, they'll have to leave me alone. I think their life depends on bothering me or something, you know? I think that's their only goal in life, to bother me. . . . It's not right. It's not supposed to be like this. They're supposed to let me think for myself.

The question of what is real and unreal has been described by sensitive observers as the key dilemma of schizophrenia, a dilemma which permeates the concerns of the patients themselves.

Some men describe the agony and confusion involved in not knowing whether trust can be placed in information transmitted through their senses or available to them in consciousness. Doubts about the validity of what is real can fill one with terror and make life precarious, even while one gives the appearance of lending credibility to voices or other delusions; even the "sickest" person must cope at some level with the encroachments of his surroundings:

4:   I don't know, it's funny and it's stupid at the same time. I get these dreams, right, that I'm the only person in the world. Like God made me to test me out, to see how man would do if he made a lot of other people. And I know you're real now, and I know he is and he is, but after these dreams, I get—and, like, all these other people around me, the whole world, nothing is really there. This table isn't really there, this isn't really here. I mean, they're not real. Like he's going to take them away, he's just testing me. And sometimes I think about, when I'm walking down the street, the sidewalk is just there to test me, or they put stores up to test me, see what kinds of stores I go into, see what kind of things I like, what kind of people I get along with. Things like this. Nothing or no one is really real. I mean, I could touch it. I don't know how to explain it. You know, the time, especially the time. Like, the clock on the wall, it says three o'clock. And it ain't really three o'clock. He wants to see how I would act, just see how I would act. To different things. Like there wasn't any such thing as three o'clock. You could say, "let's see, we have a clock, we have twelve numbers, each one is for an hour, sixty minutes for an hour, sixty seconds in a minute, like this, we'll see how you act." You go to bed at a certain time, eat at a certain time, go to work at a certain time, to test me to see if He should make other people, because the people aren't real anyway. The rest of the people around me, you know, they're not real. And maybe I'm just the only person, maybe the earth isn't even real. Maybe it's just something, maybe it's just something . . . I could touch and everything, but I know it ain't there, something like that. It's hard to explain. Can you understand?

D 35:   And I said to myself at the time, "I'll see how it would feel," and I tested it out, and it was like the whole thing was like the building was talking. Like there was no building and no walls, you know, just open space. It's like—I don't know if you'll understand what I mean—it's like you could have mixed the physical with the nonphysical, and the physical disappears. The nonphysical doctrinates the presence. And this is what I felt at the time. I said, "Well, I'm going to check it out." And after I did it, I said, "No, I don't want to do this." And the officer passed by me, and I said to him, "Officer, do me a favor and stay here, or maybe you can get me off this floor."

A problem of concern to the self-alienated—and a pressing problem for society—is that men often act while they feel dissociated and controlled. Impulses that originate "outside" them may dictate actions that are bizarre, vicious, cruel. Sometimes men destroy themselves in response to self-destructive urges and commands.

Self-alienated acts pose difficulties for the actors, not only because of their consequences, which are sometimes tragic, but because of the questions they pose about the actors' capacity to control their own conduct. Self-alienated acts also raise questions (particularly because of the amnesia that may follow them) about a person's responsibility for acts he disowns:

D 59:   A lot of people don't understand that when you do something, when you actually still remember that you did it and it's in your mind, maybe it takes a week or a day later, but you sit down and you can remember the whole thing. But then you say, "Why did I do that? I couldn't have done that." But then you say, "I did, but why?" At the time, though, like myself, there's many things that I've done in my life, but at that time I really didn't want to do it. And after I did it I saw that it was wrong. Not before. Before I did it I felt like it was the only thing to do. . . . it's like a lot of pain to go through. It's like quitting cigarettes. You don't want that cigarette, but you like it. And you know three hours later you're going to be all kinds of shook up so you might as well light it now. Do it now and get it over with. And this was the same way—do it now and get it over with and have that relief. But I don't think the doctors understand that.

The issue of where a man's own conduct begins and ends arises most directly in relation to thoughts and feelings he experiences both as his own and as externally imposed. Such messages may appear in consciousness as coming from "out there"—as having a life of their own—but bear an obvious relationship to thoughts and feelings a man may recognize as his. One may thus believe himself to be explored, exposed, and exploited by hostile forces and yet feel that one deserves this fate:

4:   They're funny voices, you know? Talking like this [weird noise]. They talk funny, they try to disguise their voice, you know? Maybe I know who it is, but they don't want me to know. . . . Sometimes I could say something to one, you know what I mean? I don't talk to them with my mouth. I talk to them with my head, and sometimes they answer me back. But I could say something to one, and later on a different one will come and say, "Why did you tell him this and this, you know you're lying?" So they don't talk about me while I'm there. They must go someplace and talk, have conferences or something about me. . . . See, they're trying to destroy my mind. They're trying to get me confused and mixed up, you know? You know, I could know something that happened, and I might tell one of them, or they might ask me a question and I answer them. And the other one would come back and say, "No, this and this and that happened. Don't you remember, don't you remember, don't you remember, don't you remember?" You know, trying to get me confused. I really know what happened. Trying to get me confused. And then the other one will come back, you know, they're playing with my mind. . . . The thing is, they're trying to do these different things, and then they give me the hint that it's not real, all of this is not real, so they want to see if they can drive me crazy. God or whoever it is, He wants to see how much pressure I can stand. And then they give me a hint that all this ain't real. You know, He told me that He's just testing me and everything. He wants to see how much I can stand, how much pressure I can take. They're testing me.

Since the content of self-alienated states bursts through brittle defenses and controls, a man finds himself impotent when he tries to fight off the incursions that flood his awareness. He may struggle to shut out the alien presence, but soon discovers that it can hold its own. A schizophrenic does not *invoke* his delusions—he experiences them as a painful fact of life:

4:   And they keep coming back. "Remember what I said, remember what I said, think about it." So they tell me these things. And I'm thinking and thinking and thinking, and they keep coming back, "remember what I said, remember what I said. It's the best thing to do. You'll be doing the right thing. It's your only way out. Thinks like this."

23:   I tried to put cotton in my ears, but it didn't help. . . . Sometimes I would tell them to shut up.

I: And what would they do?

23:   Get louder.

But the self-destructively alienated man must not only deal with evidence of his helplessness in the face of self-destructive urges. He must also face the self-contempt that prompts such urges. While he is told to do away with himself, he is furnished with unflattering but familiar reasons and motives:

M 46:   It's always derogatory stuff about myself that I hear.

I: What kind of stuff is it?

M 46:   Well, it's kind of funny for me to say, but I'll say it anyway. The voices would say things to me like, "You're no good, you're a faggot, you're a punk, you're this, you're that, look what you did to the family.

You got your mother doing this, you got your whole family in an uproar, worried about you here and there. You're no good."

23: They told me the same thing all over again. This time they started telling me that I was a bungler and a failure. And they started using profanity at me. They started using profane language on me. All sorts of things they said to me. I don't want to mention them, because you probably don't want to hear them.

I: No, you can mention them.

23: They decided to call me a cocksucker and a motherfucker and all that. I was stupid, and I couldn't even kill myself right. So I said, "If I can't do it right, then I'm going to show you that I can do it right." And then I went to do it again. . . . Telling me that my mother didn't love me no more and that I was going to stay in jail for the rest of my life. And I was a killer.

To the extent to which a man is not completely overwhelmed, he may concur with the negative assessment of his alter ego. The crisis may thus be partly one of explicit self-contempt and partly one of Self-Alienation:

M 46: I think back that it's right, there's no question about it, it's right.

I: Well, do they ever tell you how and why you're ruining other people's lives?

M 46: Yeah, by messing them up and always being in trouble. Always in difficulty. Or causing friction in the family. Through something that I have done.

4: Who knows, I may think about it for ten minutes or a half hour. And it depends on how good a thing. If they have a real good one, a real good reason, I might only think about it for five minutes. If it ain't good, I got to think about it. Sometimes they don't leave me alone till I do it. Sometimes they just get me frustrated, like I don't think it's a good enough reason, but they keep bugging me and telling me over and over again. And sometimes they try to make me believe it. And sometimes I don't believe that's a good enough reason, but I do it just to make them happy so they'll get the hell away from me. . . . You know, sometimes they don't have to convince me. Sometimes they tell me something, and I know it's true, and they don't have to convince me.

Conversely, conscious self-destructive intent, halfheartedly entertained, may be buttressed and reaffirmed by delusions, and thus lead to action.

The precise relationship of such acts to one's motives and volitions is confusing and ambiguous:

23:   They knew all my secret thoughts. Whenever something would pop into my mind, the voices would go along with it and say, "Yeah, that's right." When I wanted to kill myself, the voices said, "Right, that's what you got to do because it's the only way out. The only way you're going to find any peace."

4:   They used to tell me what to do, you know? They used to control my mind. You know, if I did anything, I didn't do it on my own. They used to tell me, "Get on the bus," I'd get on the bus. Then they'd tell me when to get off, and I'd get off. . . . See, I don't know if they knew where I was going or anything. I didn't tell them, but usually they got me where I wanted to go.

Theories of schizophrenia have stressed the contribution of rejecting mothers (and of relatives who send love-hate messages) in producing self-contempt and occasioning confusion as to reality. Self-alienated men can often recall incidents—particularly incidents involving mothers—in which the genesis of crises of confidence seems to emerge:

4:   Something happened around that time, you know? I got a letter from my mother. Well, I didn't get a letter from my mother. What I mean is, my grandmother and my mother, their handwriting is almost the same, you know what I mean? So my mother had came up to visit me, she told me she was going to get an operation, a hysterectomy operation. But she told me a few months. What happened was that she didn't want me to worry, she had to get it right away. She told me that she didn't want me to worry. And I got a letter, and my mother was sending me five dollars a week. And I got the five dollars, the receipt for the five dollars and the letter. I think my mother told my grandmother what to write to make it sound like her, but the handwriting was slightly different. So I took all my letters out from my grandmother and all my letters out from my mother. And I laid them out on the table. And I was asking the different inmates up there, I even asked the cops. They told me they were different. They told the social worker, made a phone call, called my house about three or four times. And I couldn't get anybody. They couldn't get anybody on the phone. So I was worried, I was scared. They couldn't get anybody at my house. They were calling at day, at night, in the afternoon, for three or four days, and they couldn't get anybody. But then I think they finally got my grandmother, and my mother was in the hospital, she had the operation. And my mother came up to see me, you know? I think she almost died from the operation, and she didn't want me to worry, you know? But she told me my grandmother did write the letter. You know, I'm not imagining this, this is true. She told me herself. You know, she didn't want me to worry, do anything to myself if something happened to her, anything like this. You know, I'd rather know right away if something happens. I think if she died, and I found out six months later, I don't know, I think it would make me go crazy.

56: All I know, I said, "My family's gone, I don't want to live." But I see the reverse now. They are gone because my mother put me here. See, all these things are reality now that I thought was make-believe. All is reality. . . . I thought it, you know, my mother tells me that I'm her favorite son, my sister tells me I'm her favorite brother. Like that. Now I ain't got nobody, when they put me here. . . . I thought my family loves me, they care about me, they send me this, they give me that. Even though they weren't visiting me, they didn't visit me.

In the self-destructive state, the content of delusions sometimes coincides—even to the patient—with key events in destructive family relationships:

1:   You hear your mother plus the echoes?

23:   Yeah, She told me, "go ahead and kill yourself, you're no son of mine." She said she don't care, and I was a bastard.

1:   Can you remember how you got along?

23:   She used to send me away all the time. She used to send me to juvenile court and have me locked up. 'Cause I wouldn't go to school sometimes. I'd stay out late sometimes.

M 46:   See, at one particular time, and hopefully it doesn't happen again, it may hit me, and it may say to me, like, "You're a black sheep." Or even better yet, like a sacrificial lamb. Now if I was to, like, eliminate myself, kill myself, do away with myself, I really do feel this, like in all honesty, like it would eliminate, like, all problems. And I have a very— my family life is very shaky. I used to always cry when I was a kid and stuff like that. A very, like, emotional thing if there was static between my mother and father, and there always was. And I feel, like, if I was to eliminate myself, it would bring the family all together.

The patient may sometimes thus see self-punishment as a "solution" to a family situation, and he may take the blame for the destructive acts of others as well as for his own:

I: You're saying that if they were rid of you they'd be a lot better off then?

M 46:   Yeah. It would make them, like, sort of see what's really happening. Or put it this way, maybe then they could appreciate me. . . . I believe it, it's just me. It's not that I'm an egomaniac, but it seems like everything is centered around me. And this is why if I was to really go, it would unite the entire family, like. . . . I don't like a separated house. I don't like no arguments in the family, and this is what is happening. I realize that I'm wrong, but I think myself that they shouldn't be harping on me like this . . . . rather than have somebody holler at me, I'd rather have somebody punch me in the face. 'Cause I know how to handle that. But if someone stands and hollers at me, I get very disturbed over it. And something like that could trigger me right off. Not violently, but if a guy hits me, I could become violent. But hollering and being chastised, I don't like that. . . . Their reasons are probably just, but still in all I say they're unjust because no family in my own opinion should go through any changes against another member of the family. It should be very interwoven. If they can do anything in their power to help you, they should do it. . . . My mother and father are very old. They are both seventy-one, and my sister had to get up for work. And I was causing a lot of friction. I was receiving phone calls at four in the morning, and I'm waiting for phone calls. And this here, you can't do this. I know that now. But when it was happening, there was no stopping me. . . . and I don't want this to continue. And I know that I'd probably do the same thing all over again. . . . That's why I usually try to do away with myself at a particular time. Because I am looking back, and I am looking ahead, and it don't look too good.

The crises of the self-alienated may originate in remote incidents. They are not independent, however, of settings which send their own double-messages. Prisons and other institutions, for instance, are "unreal" enough to accentuate confusions, stimulus-deprived enough to encourage fantasy, and crowded enough to spark vulnerability. Most important, they are impersonal enough to help a man suspect that others want him dead. In the self-alienated, this suspicion translates into self-hate and self-destruction:

M 46:   Yeah, well the first scene is I'm in the bull pen. I just come off the street, I'm used to being loose. Now I'm mobbed in the bull pen, and fifty guys in a bull pen made for ten people. And everybody's rapping, talking, and all this, and you're just sitting there, and you take all this, and there's nothing you can do about it, you just got to absorb it.

You're definitely not ready for that. And that bugs you. Especially bugs me. I ain't ready for no crowds. I usually don't like people, in general. I'm sort of antisocial. . . . And all this noise gets to me. And now I know that from here I got to go through the changes, going through the receiving room, getting searched, doing this, talking to the doctor, feeling sick from junk, and everything is going to just fall right on me. . . . Jail has the surroundings, they're not harmonious with good conduct and good thinking. It just brings on this state. Depressed state. And it's not something that you would do in the streets. In the streets something else might happen. In here, nothing even has to happen to you, you could just be taking the bag and there it is. . . . It's amplified. In the street I would need an incident, but in here I wouldn't necessarily even need an incident.

B. SELF-RELEASE

While self-hate bursts forth in the self-alienated in the shape of self-destructive urges, it may also boil over in the form of rage. The relationship between these two syndromes may be illustrated through the testimony of an inmate who set his cell on fire after attending his father's funeral. By way of explanation, the man noted that "I had a sensation that my father was there telling me to burn the cell up." In elaborating the experience, he recalls:

D 59: During my sleep I had a dream about my father, and I can't say that I was or wasn't close to him. But it seems like he's always in my mind. And in the dream he told me to burn everything up. This is when it actually came into my mind. This is where I didn't know if I was dreaming or awake. It was like a fog. This has happened to me many times where I do things in a fog. Like, if you talked to me one day, I would vaguely remember what happened a few days later. I can't say I really did it until you explain everything to me. And then I can't say, "Yes, I did it." But it wasn't really me doing it. It was like a pressure. You've got to get the pressure off you.

The "pressure" alluded to gives this incident a quality different from that of simple compliance with self-destructive urges. It refers to a buildup of accumulated negative feelings that demand release:

D 59: I got very upset, and my nerves were really shaking. I started yelling, and I got pains in my head, and I started yelling. It seemed like the more I yelled, it took the pressure off my mind. The next thing I knew I had the bedding in my hand, and I was sitting lighting it up with matches, and I was sitting on the bed. And everything started burning. So I just sat there until everything was burning pretty good. And I just sat there and watched the fire. And this was calming me down. By watching the fire, I had to do something, and I had to do something different besides yelling because yelling wasn't helping. This was taking pressure off my mind by watching the fire. And the next thing I knew, everything was burning. But before in the fire it wasn't real. It wasn't me that was burning. It had to be done. There was so much pain. . . . It's a throbbing in my head. I've got to do this. It's like there's no outlet other than doing this. Once it enters my mind to burn, I've got to do this. It's just like a solvent, and if I want to hurt I won't, and then I get this throbbing, and I go right at it.

The inmate can describe a process of struggling with feelings, or of being struggled with by feelings. He explains that he made efforts to channel feelings into acts, such as outbursts, but that at times—during crises—such efforts would prove ineffective:

D 59:   I've had these feelings a long time. But this time I really—when I felt it before I would sing loud or something, just to hear a voice. There would be my voice, and nobody else would be around. It didn't feel like it was me. You get that feeling that somebody is holding me down. I get dreams when I think somebody is trying to smother me. It's when you can't grasp them. . . . If nobody's around, it keeps building up and building up, until something has to be done. I had this feeling for instance in county jail. For instance here on my wrist, I chewed it just to get this pain out of my head. You're put into a box, and you can't move. You can't do nothing. It's just like here. You can't do nothing, and it just builds up and builds up.

The inmate reports that his explosion reduced tension and provided a means of obtaining peace of mind. Explosive self-injury reduces tension because it shocks and distracts and because it discharges physical energy. But it may also have this effect because of the content of the act, which responds to feelings of guilt and self-hate:

D 59:   It's like a punishment of me getting back at myself. Like my cramps and everything on my leg. Most of my cramps develop from hurting somebody to hurt myself. In other words, I know I've done wrong. I go into a place, and I've hurt somebody. Afterwards I know it's wrong, but at that time when I'm doing these things I don't really think it's wrong. I just feel like I'm relieving the pressure off me. And this is where I get in a lot of trouble. I think that's why a lot of people get in trouble. It's the pressure on them.

The inmate talks of "hurting somebody to hurt myself," and refers to guilt occasioned by past acts of hurting others. This issue is one that runs through much of Self-Release. Guilt converts to rage, and rage furnishes grist for new guilt. A tense man attacks others if they cross him while he is upset—particularly if they tread on guilt-related territory. In retrospect, explosions of this kind add to self-doubt because the man already sees himself as unpredictably unstable. Instead of reducing tension, aggression may thus serve to increase self-hate. An illustration of this process is furnished by a young inmate who attacked a friend for teasing him about his mother:

27: I was really very depressed. I was sitting in my cell, and I was thinking of home, you know, and a lot of things were on my mind. So I came down to dinner. I didn't really feel like eating, you know? I sat down to eat at the table, and they had these inmates sitting across from me, and they was all talking about each other's mothers, you know, and I don't like anybody to speak about my mother because she is something to me, you know—she's something very special, you know. I love her very much. Like, this kid happened to say something, you know? Somebody says something to him, and so he says to me—he told me my mother was a whore, you know? So I lost control of myself. I have a very quick temper, you know? I flew over the table. I wanted to kill the kid, you know. Like, the officers all grabbed me, and they held me back and everything. I couldn't get to him. I was really shaking because when I get excited I start to shake, you know, my whole body. I can't speak or nothing. I just lose complete control of myself, and I wanted to get my hands on this kid's throat so bad because I would have hurt him, you know. I know I could have hurt him because when I get mad I'm strong, you know?

In describing the incident, the young man tells us about his complete loss of control, and about the disproportionate character of his reaction. He also describes the episode, which parallels other incidents in his life, as alien to his self-image and as disturbing to him:

27: As soon as he said this, my whole mind went blank. The only thing I had on my mind was to kill him, you know? I wanted to hurt him so bad, you know? And I was so confused. I can handle a knife, you know. We had knives on the table, and forks. I could have stabbed him with anything. I pick a tray up. I was so angry, so lost, you know? All I wanted to do was put my hands on him. I didn't even want to use nothing, just only my hands. I wanted to take him around his neck. I wanted to—I had everything—it came to me real fast. I knew everything I was going to do as soon as I got my hand on him. I was going to choke him,

I was going to strangle him to death, you know? Make him beg me, you know? I wasn't going to forgive him—I was just going to hold him down there. . . . I wanted to hit the officer 'cause they wouldn't let me in at him, you know? I started to cry I was so mad, you know? I would've got a hold of him. I would've hurt him bad if someone hadn't broke it up. . . . I sit back there, and my whole body was shaking, you know—my insides—and I'll be all trembling inside because I don't like to fight, you know, because I don't like to hurt anybody, and I don't like anybody to hurt me, you know? I was sitting there trembling. . . . You see, I don't enjoy getting upset 'cause when I get upset I can't sleep, I can't think, I can't eat, I can't do nothing. My body just shakes all the time. My whole system is nothing, you know? I don't have nothing.

The loss of control and discomfort of persons subject to frustration-induced rage creates awe and anxiety among their associates. But it also creates sadism and exploitation. The predictability of heated reactions provides an arena for cheap demonstrations of power. It permits a man who is so inclined to easily prove that he can spark reactions in others and thus exert control. Our young inmate furnishes a second portrait of this strategy in action. Another inmate recalls a closely parallel—and similarly callous—encounter:

27:   People know how I am, you know, and, they aggravate me. They tease me. . . . They do this on purpose 'cause they know how frustrated and nervous I get, and they know I'll try to do something. I either want to harm myself or destroy something 'cause they know that's the way I am. . . . This guy gets me mostly upset. I mean he'll get me so I start to cry, you know, and I—right in front of everybody—I start. I hit the desk with my hands, you know. I want to smash things, so instead of breaking windows and things like that or doing something, I bang on the furniture, you know? I was out in the rec, you know. I started banging and kicking things up. I want to throw them. They call them tantrums, you know? . . . He started, you know, saying all kinds of things, you know? Things that weren't even true he'd be saying. Hollering in front of everybody, you know? Hollering things out on the tier, you know, about me, you know? And this got me really aggravated, and if I'd have been out of this cell I was so mad I wanted to take this guy, you know, my best friend, and I wanted to hurt him, you know? . . .
      Then he kept saying, he says, "Come on, you madman, smash up your cell. Here, want my razor? Come on, we'll cut up tonight," you know? He was saying all kinds of obscene things, you know, to me, 'cause he knows I will do this when I lose my head. He says, "Come on," he says, "here!" And he held the razor up for me. He says, "Here," he says "cut up." He says, "Smash! Come on," he says, "here!" He started kicking

things around in his cell. He says, "Do this, do this," you know? "Here is how you do it, come on, let's see you go. Come on, madman," you know? He said all kinds of things like that to get me aggravated.

That's when I started smashing the door, you know? I started beating on the door right there. I said to him if he'd come out of that cell I'd kill him, you know? So he kept laughing at me. That's when I went back to my cell, and I started thinking and everything. I couldn't do nothing to him 'cause he was locked in, you know? So that's when I started thinking what I could do, you know? I started thinking I want to smash things, but I realize I was only hurting myself. I says, "To hell with it, I am going to do something to myself tonight," you know?

M 19:   That one patient kept on bugging me about my mother being in another world. You know that school for retarded people, my mother's in there. And they kept on teasing me and saying that my mother was nothing but a retarded fish, and she's going to die. And I said, "Keep it up, and I'll bust everyone in the hallway." So they kept on teasing me, and that's when I did it. . . . This kid came up to me and said, "I heard about your mother. Is she retarded like you are?" And I said, "You keep your fucking mouth shut before I cut your fucking throat." And I broke the window because he didn't believe me, and that's where I got this. I broke the window, and I picked up a piece of glass, and I said, "What did you say about my mother, punk?" And he says, "Nothing." And I said, "I don't talk about your mother." I told the guard, and the guard said, "What do you want me to do about it? You can fight yourself." And I said, "Listen, motherfucker, if I fight myself I'll be placed in a straitjacket in three." And he said, "Tough, ain't it?" . . . When I was in the room I was thinking, "How can I pay this motherfucker back?" I said, "Maybe—." It was hard for me to do it. It was painful. I took the spoon and stabbed it back and that ripped the bandage off. And then I stabbed it again.

A factor that enters into the special susceptibility of explosive men is their mood or state of mind at the time pressures are applied. More often than not, the explosions of these men occur against a backdrop of preoccupation, depression, bitterness, and guilt. Thus, one victim tells of painful memories which obsess him and decrease his tolerance to pressure:

I: Both your hands, you've got a lot of scars from breaking windows and things. What do you feel like? Take an average day when you were breaking windows. What was going on, the kind of feelings you were having?

M 19:   I was letting my frustrations out.

I: Can you describe the things that frustrate you? Like, you wake up in the morning, and later on in that day you've broken out some windows, and what happened that day that made you do that?

M 19:   It's a tough thing to describe. I've been in an institution all my life and foster homes, and I was living with—we were in a Volkswagen, and we were on our way to a party, and my father was drunk. He had had too many martinis at the party, so he was driving away intoxicated. The speed limit is thirty mph, and we were going one hundred. And we hit a tractor trailer truck. And I watched the top of their heads get cut off. On some Volkswagens they have an ashtray in the back of the front seat, and I hit the ashtray.

I: You lost both your parents or your foster parents?

M 19:   Yeah.

I: In that accident?

M 19:   Yeah. It was something. I could see their brains come out of the top of their skull.

I: And these days that you're walking around, does this come back in your mind?

M 19:   Yeah.

Our other inmate is even more explicit about the relationship between his propensity to explode and preoccupations he brings to the situation:

27:   Even as of now you be talking to me, and that's why I had to ask you to repeat yourself, because I am thinking of something now, and this isn't the time to think of something, you know, when we're rapping. First of all, it's not polite, and I am not concentrating on what you're trying to tell me . . . . but I got something on my mind which I don't even really know what's up there right now. It's just something going around, and it's bugging me right now, you know?

I: Would you rather talk another time?

27:   No, we can continue to rap with our conversation. I just got to, you know, control myself a little more, you know? . . .
      I come in, and I rap to you, and I feel OK, but I know before the day is finished someone is going to say something or my mind is going to start drifting into thoughts about something that is really going to bug me, and before the day is over I am going to be very depressed. I won't even want to feel like locking in my cell. And then by me being depressed, somebody might come and say something to me which I might

not like, you know, and then I am going to think of something, you know?

This inmate's incident in the dining room did not result in his experiencing closure or peace of mind. It brought a temporary easing of tension, with a buildup of new feeling following transfer to a solitary cell. This second buildup terminated in another explosion, during which the man destroyed his solitary cell and injured himself. Although the episode is described as ending with a blackout, the man does not see himself as having been helplessly carried away. He talks of the process as one in which he experiences tension and then guides the tension to the exploding point (as did our friend Sam, in Chapter 1) by dwelling on hate—and on guilt-inducing memories:

27:   I think, to be truthful, I want to get upset, you know? I think I want to do this. I think I want to break wild, but I just can't break wild all by myself because I am not an animal. It is not my nature, so I sort of use it maybe as an excuse to break wild. I sometimes thought of this. I could sort of bring up all these things that I know bother me and get me excited just so I would break wild. . . . You see, maybe I really am upset, you know, about something, but I am not really upset enough to smash things, but I like to smash them, and I say I ain't got the courage to smash them, you know? . . . I just think of how people treat me all the time, you know? Go through the life I am living now, you know, and I just don't care no more, you know. I say the hell with it, you know? I just—I keep thinking everything over and over, you know, I just say to myself, "Smash it, smash it." I tell myself what I am going to do. I can almost picture—I can almost picture—I can almost picture what I want to do, you know? . . . 'Cause all I have to do is think of a few things, and after a few things I start to get excited and like it don't even bother me no more. My mind goes blank, you know? I'll still be thinking, but I don't remember anything I think about. I'll just, you know, I'll just look around, and, I'll see hatred. Everything I look at I want to destroy—pictures, letters, house, anything. . . . It kicks off by itself, and I have to help it on. I have to bring it on myself and help progress it, you know, and that's the way I do it. It's just like an airplane, you know, build up speed to fly. I build up the speed, and it takes off, you know?

The process is one that is designed to discharge accumulated feelings which are chiefly resentments directed at oneself and others. Unlike Self-Alienation, in which the mind is divided against itself, Self-Release is a syndrome of ambivalence. The individual is just as helpless and out of control, but he is still himself. He takes responsibility for his acts, though he defines himself as driven by hate. And he sees himself as a man who survives only by expressing hate, and who is thus an untrustworthy and unstable pawn of his own unconscious:

27:   In a way I feel good, in a way, but in a way, I don't because I don't like losing my temper, you know. But then after I smash everything I realize what I done, you know, so it scares me in a way 'cause I feel what'll I do if this was to a person or something, you know, or anybody —a child—anyone if I lost my temper, you know? But in a way I feel good because I lose all that tension, you know, all that buildup I had. All that hatred I had inside of me is all gone away. . . . To be truthful with you I don't think, I don't think I'm ever going to make it at all, period. . . . I really don't want to, you know, I really don't want to— really don't want to put no harm to myself or to anything, you know? It is just that I can't control myself.

The dilemma of Self-Release is poetically summarized by a young inmate whose life has been studded by efforts to kill himself through drug overdoses. The boy relates a dream in which he runs a frantic race, only to discover that the race has run him and that he has ended nowhere. He knows himself to be in the grip of compulsions and impulses that drive him against his best interests. He knows no way of escaping from his own impotence—from the fact that his actions are guided by blind urge. And he sees escape only in self-destruction—in Self-Release deployed to interrupt the cycle.

cx 20:   Then I have these weird—like, I have these dreams. Because I was watching this movie, and it was about running. And the guy was a coach, right? So it's pent up, the way I had this dream, the guy was coaching me. And it was half jail here, and half outside, and I was runing on the course, winning the race, but it was like going through doorways in the dream, and everything. And I was way ahead, and the next thing I'm going through the park, and then I'm going over the roofs. Like, what kind of race am I running in? But I was way ahead, but I made the wrong turn, went through the wrong doorway. And then at the end I found out that when I got there everybody else had already finished, and I was last. And the guy grabbed me, and he started shaking me—"All that hard work is down the drain." And the guy's shaking me and grabbing me. Like, this was that same coach that was in that movie over there with the guy, and he's shaking me and saying, "It's over, it's over, the wrong turn, all that hard work." And then I woke up. But that was a crazy dream. Like, you know, I was running over rooftops like these here, in fact this was them, in the back. And like this here, like I went in the jail, and then I was running on the outside, in a big, wide-open space like a golf course or something, and then we were going through doorways. Everything was mixed up. . . . In other words, I don't want to be depressed anymore. I don't want to have to go back to drugs and go downhill. Because if it ever did happen, I wouldn't want to come out. If I have to use it, may the first dope kill me, you know?

C. SELF-ESCAPE

Explosions can express feelings that break through efforts to suppress them. But they can also sound the alarm at an earlier stage, signaling the breakdown of internal controls.

Several of our interviewees recall the panic of free-floating anxiety, and describe a hopeless struggle to maintain sanity in the face of a developing delusion:

37: Well, I have a fear that I might lose my sanity. And ever since I've been here I've had a fear that I might lose my sanity. I thought if I lost my sanity I might get beat up. If I lost my sanity I might do something drastic, and there's no telling what they'll beat you up for. . . . I had imaginary fears. I'd see myself trying to harm myself. I could picture myself doing things to harm myself, and this would inspire fear in me. Fear that I would do these things. And I didn't want to do these things. But I'd picture myself doing these things.

MHDM 51: And then you come in. There's just too many things that don't fit, as if somebody upstairs is directing me towards a final conclusion. I don't know what it's going to be. . . . "Well," I'd say, "I've been in a mental institution. I've seen people who have really lost their minds. They weren't faking, they weren't trying to get out of anything. I don't want to be like that." And I just don't know how much my mind can take. I've got fear and, like I say, the disgust with people. . . . And I say now I don't want to walk around in some nuthouse for the rest of my life really with no mind.

The type of crisis described by these men, which the psychiatric literature calls preparanoid, consists of generalized, painful states of fear. A person enters this stage when he senses that unacceptable urges are close to breaking into his awareness and that he is helpless to deal with them. Some patients describe murderous or bizarre feelings which threaten to emerge and to engulf them:

MHDM 51: Sometimes I feel like a train heading for a wall. I know if I hit it I'm going to have trouble, but I go ahead and do it anyways. In the last ten years I've done it several times. This particular time here, something kept telling me to go to bed, go to sleep, get out of the bar, get off the street. I just had the feeling—maybe it's having had the feeling before. And I went out and, sure enough, something happened. And it happened again here. . . . I remember a flash from my pistol, I had a full clip in my gun—I fired one shot, two people fell, and then I just stood there more or less, and watched this gun, the flame coming out of it four or five times. But it doesn't seem real. I mean I've tried in my head to say this happened, and look at it objectively. "You were there, and these people were there." I can't see that. It's just weird.

D 53:   And it started out by making me hallucinate. By making me see myself as killing people. I see myself killing people or jumping off of buildings or shooting myself in the head or doing away with myself some kind of way. Or hurting people, taking advantage, you know? It was like it really made me see what I was like because I seen myself going berserk in the park, Central Park in the city. I saw myself sitting on a bench with a razor blade, and first I was cutting at my throat, and then I grabbed a little kid and threatened to hurt the kid. Then the next hallucination I saw myself running out of the park just cutting at everybody that came, that just happened to pass by. And I really got scared about these. . . . Like when I'm by myself, I may be sitting on the floor, just sitting there, and I'm not thinking, but it's like as though you can predict your mind. And my head was like a trapdoor. No matter where they come from, it was just a trapdoor. And I get all these different thoughts. And I sit there, and sometimes it makes me mad, and sometimes it don't make me mad. It all depends on what the course of the day has been and what the thought relates to. Actually now what I'm trying to do is remove myself from a sexual existence that I've been having for a long time. Like I'm craving for sex all the time, you know? I realize that it's not always me. Not the me that's doing it. It's the other force giving me feelings like this.

Because a patient senses dangerous impulses in himself, he suspects that other people must observe these feelings. This translates into what psychiatrists call "ideas of reference"—assumptions that one is being singled out for attention, or judged, or disapproved of, or suspected:

MHDM 48:   I used to have things coming from my head. Like I can feel it. I know I wasn't going crazy. I can come out of the cell, and I can sit down in the dayroom, and I can see everybody would look at the top of my head, you know? And like I go and ask them why they keep looking at the top of my head. There's nothing up there, you know, that's what I say to myself. And I used to feel it up there. And sometimes I put my hand up there, and I could touch it.

D 53: They was able to project into my mind and show me pictures of the incident that brought me to jail. And I said to myself, "Now, how would they know this? I didn't tell them." People come to me and ask me why I hate women, and I say I don't hate women. But they guess that I do because they can see what I see. Although they may interpret what they see their way, they can still see the things that I see.

Though ideas of reference are delusional, and occur even if the patient who suffers them is ignored by his peers, this does not mean that he experiences smooth interpersonal sailing. Bizarre behavior does attract attention, and if the patient is avoided, he may be studiously or guardedly avoided. If he is not avoided, he may arrange to be, by sharing his concerns with others who are likely to find his disclosures strange. This avoidance reaction of others is one that the patient, however confused he may be in other respects, is apt to sense:

MHDM 48: And like I had one fellow that always came and talked to me all the time. And mostly when he come out he'd stay with me the whole time. And rap, you know? And I'd sit down, and I'd tell him what I experienced. And he used to tell me, "You're kind of crazy." And I used to look at him, and I used to say, "I'm not crazy. Why do these things happen to me?" And he used to look at me and say, "You're too heavy for me, you got to get away from me." And, like, sometimes he'd scare me. Like, sometimes I used to tell him to keep to himself, and I used to get a feeling like he was going to tell it to somebody else. . . .

I used to like that, walk around, talking to people. Talking to people about the creation, God, whether he's real, and what man is doing. Things like that I liked to talk about.

I: When you started talking to people about that, how did they usually respond?

MHDM 48: They looked at me, you know, they looked at me kind of weird. They say, "I got to get away from him."

I: How did that make you feel?

MHDM 58: I feel like I'm not wanted, you know? Something they're escaping, and maybe something I'm escaping.

Interpersonal relations also bear on the issue of whether impulses can be controlled or suppressed. Patients may discover in their dealings with others that their capacity to keep themselves in emotional check is precarious when it is tested:

5: And there was this guy next door to me. I don't know what he was.

This guy used to jerk off about twenty times a day, and he used to bang against my wall. I couldn't get to sleep at night. Nothing. I hardly slept at all when I was in those cells, you know? I couldn't relax because this guy was over there jerking off, hitting the walls. . . . I just tried to reason with the guy. I said, "Look it, man, can't you give me some consideration?" I mean, I knew what he was doing because I heard all this hard breathing and shit. The guy was calling names and shit—like Mary and all this other. So I said to the guy, being polite, "I know you're doing time and your sex—is pretty high. I know you've got to get your rocks off, but can't you give me some consideration and let me get some sleep?" And he got all dignified. He took it the wrong way or something. And like I had my hand on my razor blade. It so happened a man was coming down to see what was happening. He was a friend of mine. So he must have known I had something in my pocket because I was coming on slow, you know? And he grabbed my hand, and he said, "You don't want to fight." And then, right there, I dug that I was losing control. I was getting ready to explode. And this is bad. Once you explode in jail—see a dude like me, when I start getting in trouble, I don't stop getting in trouble, I just keep on. It's like a chain reaction.

Preparanoid patients tend to toy with the notion that others wish to harm them. This notion, the core of the paranoid delusion, is one that the preparanoid patient may know to be subjective. But that knowledge does not eliminate the delusion. It simply increases the patient's discomfort and makes him more confused about how he is to act:

37:   I was so paranoid I couldn't even look a person in the eye. If I looked a person in the eye, I had a fear that that person might think I was staring at them and they would become aggressive toward me. And maybe a fight would break out, and then we'd go into the jackets. And then I had that fear of getting beat up again, by one of the strait-jackets. That's how paranoid I was. I couldn't look anyone in the eye.

5:   And when I first came in, this place scared the shit out of me. And I was scared shit, and I used to stand and watch people. I guess they used to think I was sick, the way I used to watch them. Always watching and looking behind. Because I thought one of these dudes may come up and try to attack me. So I was looking out for myself.

The key problem in the preparanoid state (and the reason for the theme of Self-Escape) is that the patient finds himself in a condition of disequilibrium that is disturbing to him. A man toys with insanity, moves in and out of psychotic solutions, sees no resting place in divorce from the real. Afraid of loss of control on the one hand, concerned with his own irrationality on the other, he may despair of the possibility of ever securing peace of mind:

MHDM 48: I walked around depressed, like there's nothing else. Like there's nobody I could turn to. I was down and out. I didn't have a thought, a clear thought in my mind for nothing. All I just wanted to do was just die. I was like that for about two months, two long months I was like that. . . . I think back on it, and I say to myself, "thirty-five days I ain't tried to do nothing. Is it going to come back?" That's what is constantly on my mind. Is it going to come back?"

5: Yeah, I was uptight. I was definitely uptight. My head was all in a fog. I didn't know what I was doing. I mean, I didn't know what I was doing, like I couldn't make my mind up about nothing. One minute I would hate my family, the next minute I would love them. One minute I was thinking about my kid, I was thinking about friends. You know, I was doing too much thinking. And like it just had me all mixed up and confused, you know? . . . Just recently the pressure came and went away. And now it comes back night or day, you know? Sometimes I'll be too uptight to eat. But I'll go off to myself somewheres, go and listen to records or something, and then I'll rap to myself. Not be holding a big conversation, but I'll be rapping to myself in my head. I'll say to myself, "Man, it's just about over, you've got to hang in there just a little while longer."

Within this painful cycle, breakdowns reflect a need to end the discomfort—and to end it at any price. Self-destruction is the functional alternative to insanity. It is also an effort to suppress urges that no longer respond to controls:

D: So I got a deep feeling that I didn't want to go to a hospital, I didn't want to have anything to do with crazy, so that rather than that I'd commit suicide. So one day when my mother was gone and my family was gone out of the house, I was staying there alone, and I took a razor blade, and I cut my throat. Tried to cut that vein that goes over here. I cut it three times.

37: I had a compulsion, an obsession and a compulsion. I used to do a lot of hunting, and every time I was out hunting I'd get this obsession and this compulsion to take a loaded gun and aim it at myself and cock the trigger and just cock it and touch the trigger but not pull it all the way. . . . I came to the conclusion that it would be the quickest and easiest way to escape from the pain I was in and the torment I was in.

D. SELF-PRESERVATION

Most psychoses are not crisis states. They represent, rather, resolutions of crises, and are relatively stable while they last. In paranoid psychoses, for instance, the patient does not struggle with his panic, as he does in the preparanoid state. He has externalized the threat, defined it carefully, and can avoid it by keeping to himself or by operating within zones of safety. He feels that the danger is objective; he sees himself as important and feels he deserves attention or esteem. His moods may be extreme (his controls are no longer operating), but modest medication may make such a man relatively comfortable.

But this equilibrium is a last-ditch equilibrium, and if it is upset the result may be more serious than any of the crises we have surveyed. It is also the type of breakdown most likely to be terminal. It is not accidental that all of the case histories of suicides in Part III of this book are sequences in which the paranoid equilibrium is upset.

It is also not accidental that such sequences are rare in mental hospitals but occur disproportionately in prisons. For prisons have built-in liabilities which make the paranoid solution unstable and difficult to sustain. For one, prisons furnish much raw material for the manufacture of fear. A fight that forces guards to intervene may convey an impression of brutality; or the mere existence of a custodial force may convey the feeling that prison is a physically dangerous place:

D 14:   I was scared of the police when I first went there, you know what I mean? I don't know why, I don't know what gave me that thought.
         But it's only natural to be scared of these people, because of their power. And you know that they can kill you, you understand? They can say that you attacked them or something like that. And besides this, you understand, things that you would hear from other guys, saying what they used to do with these guys, so they plant a seed in your mind, and put this in you.

47:    They kill people here. You may not believe it, they kill people. Five, six, seven thousand cops a year beating the shit out of you. Stepping on your chest. I seen these. . . . So I wanted them to kill me. All I had was a piece of stick. I cut it and said, "They're going to come after me, so they're going to come after me." I was like, how would you say, berserk.

More immediate than the climate of danger implicit in the power of guards and the violence of inmates may be firsthand experiences with physical threats. Paranoid inmates caught in a riot or subjected to a chance assault may be irreversibly and fatally traumatized:

A 4: The riot—that's the first time I've ever been in anything like that. Helicopters and gas, and people come out shooting at you and beating you up after the riot, and stripping you. That's the first time anything like this ever happened to me. So it affected my mind. . . . In other words, I started thinking all kinds of crazy thoughts. Like, in other words, the pressure of the riot made me think, you know—everything everybody was guessing, and whatnot. And I knew this was an imagination thing, because I wrote to the psychiatrist and asked for an interview. . . . It increased. In other words, like I was hearing things which wasn't there—like I was hearing people. I got very paranoid. You know, very paranoid. I mean, everybody's paranoid, but I mean very paranoid. And I started figuring that people's talking about me. I'm hearing voices, you know? And so I just couldn't take it no more. I bugged out.

D 7: Well, I was in Attica, I was there for the riot. And there was hallucinations. I thought people were killing my family, people were going to kill me. So I got real withdrawn. I couldn't eat; I couldn't sleep. . . . A Negro kept saying, "Hey, whitey, you're going to die." And this was an everyday thing for two weeks.

9: I remember I was stabbed while I was in prison by a guy who used to turn crazy. Upstairs, by a guy in prison. Ever since then I felt like I couldn't move around and associate with people like I used to, because I'd always be looking back over my shoulder all the time. . . . It was a case of mistaken identity. I don't know whether this made it any worse or not. . . . I had a pretty good program set up for myself. I used to lift weights, and I used to play softball, and it was something to keep myself occupied. And then, like I say, after I was stabbed, everything went out. I couldn't get myself back into _____, because I was always worrying about my back. . . . I had to go out in order to go to work. It just seemed like a daydream or a nightmare or something. I didn't even travel around the yard like I used to. I used to wait, just stand over by the door until it was time for my work gang to go in. . . . It seemed like everything that was done was done to aggravate me, that's the way it seemed. . . . The least little thing that I would normally pay no attention to seemed like "this is all against me too." It seemed like everything was turning against me. . . . It feels like you're all alone in the world. No one cares, no one listens, no one answers. Nothing, you're just by yourself.

The structured and regimented character of prison also lends itself to the premise of helplessness and the assumption of conspiratorial control. An inmate may thus conclude that his food or drugs are poisoned, or that lockups lead to executions:

D 48: I found that they were putting drugs in my food and stuff, and
I think everybody was against me, like my friends and everybody. So I
just bugged out, man. I was there for about three months, and I bugged
out. I wouldn't lock in my cell . . . . they told me to get back in, and I
was scared. I thought they were going to kill me or something. . . . So I
stayed in keep-lock for thirty-four days, and there I was really bugged
out. I really thought they was putting stuff in my food. I was going mad.

56:   Snatch me out of the cell at night, a lot of police. You know, they
put fear into you. They got a system, because they can do it. They can
put fear into you. I didn't think it then, I didn't know about it then, I
didn't know what fear was. I'd get a funny feeling, I didn't know what
it was. But I knowed that they could give it to you.

The interpersonal context of prison can play a destructive role. For
one, the impersonality of the yard encourages self-generated solutions and
secrecy. There is limited trust, and the inmate can find no one to give
credence to his fear, which he is thus unable to check against conventional, tangible danger cues. While the victim may feel a strong need to
be rescued from his fate, he soon sees his potential allies as unfriendly
and, worse, as threats:

47:   But this is also something that if you go up to the guard, and you
complain to the guard about this, he won't do nothing. They say this is
something you have to take care of yourself. . . . So my enemy now was
a hack.

A 4: Now I'm . . . paranoid, worse. I'm thinking the doctors and the
nurses and the porters here are talking about me. So this created more
hate in my heart, because I know they're supposed to be doing something for me, and they're doing nothing.

A critical interpersonal variable is the presence of large numbers of
fellow inmates whom one has no way to avoid. The sheer mass of this
human environment is something a man may find overpowering and
threatening. The interactions among strangers also give rise—in a man
suffering from ideas of reference—to the idea that there is a large-scale
conspiracy against him:

32:   But kids my age, like I feel they're all out to hurt me. And I feel I'm
trying to run away from everything around me. I was here, you know,
. . . oh, I don't know just how to explain it. I wish they could just put
me in a cell for the rest of my life, behind four walls, and give me a radio
and just let me be, you know? . . . I was always scared to go out with the

other guys, like in the rec room, out in the yard, you know? I feel like
they were all of a sudden gonna jump on me, you know? . . . I just
thought about going out there and having them guys—I thought about
myself going out there with a lot of guys in the rec room, and they're
all talking about me, and it just makes me want to be alone.

56: You know, like a group of guys could be over there, right? And they
could be rapping, right? And they could say something, and you get a
funny heartbeat. So you got a delusion, you think this guy is talking
about you.

A frequently exercised option of fearful inmates is to request segregation. Solitary confinement ("observation") is also a staff option for individuals with emotional problems, especially those with self-destructive
potential. But from a paranoid perspective isolation cells can be the most
threatening of all environments. For one, they close avenues of physical
escape. For another, by making it easier to concretize interpersonal
threats, they make such threats urgent and endemic. The effort to handle
panic by externalizing danger—the danger posed by one's own urges—can
thus backfire. The man may find himself in "square one"—in a new setting
for panic against which he has no further defenses:

8: I was walking around. I couldn't sleep. I was scared they might get in
my cell. I stood in my cell right over here. I just stood there. I was going
to keep watch and make sure that I knew whether they were coming
down or not.

M 19: After I'm put in there, I sit in the corner and think about what
I did. And then I lay on the mattress, and then after I sit there I feel the
walls coming in around me. And then when the guards come in and I'm
screaming, they say, "What the fuck is going on here?" And I say, "The
walls are closing in on me." And they say, "That's tough, you're going
to die anyway. We'll strangle you." . . . I was thinking that if I don't
get the hell out of there, they're going to kill me. And I don't feel like
fighting them.

There are other pressures in prison. There is the homosexual theme,
which is troublesome to inmates struggling with homosexual feelings of
their own. There is surveillance, which reinforces the psychotic sense of
vulnerability. And there is violence, which creates doubt about where
self-created danger ends and more tangible and unscheduled threats begin.

Prisons also spawn stimuli which bear superficial resemblances to the
delusions of inmates. This creates a problem for staff-inmate and inmate-
inmate dealings, because overdetermined and subjective complaints are

confused with standard dangers. The psychotic inmate may be reacted to inappropriately as a typical victim of inmate aggression. Real incidents may fuse with delusional concerns, and delusions may spark tangible, and sometimes fatal, conflicts.

Whatever the sequence of events, the psychotic inmate cannot depend on the reassuring flavor of his imagined fears. Instead of having a carefully controlled source of threat, he finds himself confronting a monster beyond taming or control. This creates survival problems, not only because a man faces far bigger threats than he can handle, but also because these threats mirror his unresolved internal problems. He is forced to cope with his own urges run wild, as they attack him from without. This onslaught is one for which no one is conceptually or emotionally equipped. It calls for survival without weapons, allies, or means of escape.

E. SELF-INTERVENTION

For the conflict-ridden patient, redemption is not a luxury to toy with but the alternative to continued domination by alien forces. He is plagued by the haunting memories of past dehumanization and the sensed presence of continued explosive potential. He knows himself to be a volcano with intolerably destructive rumblings; he doubts his power to suppress a threatening eruption; he feels the need for assistance in shoring up or cementing his powers of self-control.

A man can become obsessed with his own destructive propensities. He may oscillate between helplessness and the conviction that he can be helped to escape his fate:

D 49:   Like I said, I killed a person. And what keeps bugging my mind is, Will I kill again? 'Cause I got reasons to go out and kill again. I feel I have reasons. . . . Like I say, this is a hell of a thing. What am I going to do when I get out? And I'm more or less a coward trying to face this. 'Cause I know I need help. I know I'm not insane. I know I'm a very emotional person. And I know I'm a very dangerous person, especially when I'm in an emotional state. I just killed a man in cold blood. I looked for him, and I shot him twice in the head. And this bugs me, 'cause I did it, and the doctor said years ago I would do it. And this bugs me. Why did I? I know why I did it, but what made me pull the trigger? And I mean, this bugs me.

35:   I was real frantic. I'm trying to find out what am I doing here, what am I doing here? . . . People were telling me, "You're here for robbery, you're here for assault, you kidnapped somebody, you're pushing drugs." Everybody's got their opinion. Nobody knows exactly what I'm locked up for, but everybody's giving me an opinion on what I look like I'm in here locked up for. . . . This is not a first-time thing. This has been going on for a while, me messing up. This is my third time in Matteawan. And that's too many times to be in here. I tell myself for a while, "You ain't mad, you ain't out of your mind." But then I start getting in doubt, because I say, "Well, what am I doing here, again and again?" You know what I mean?

The patient may seek help in understanding acts he has disowned or in suppressing thoughts and feelings that take possession of his mind. In seeking help, he assumes that psychiatrists have the power to understand delusional thoughts and to manage impulses and feelings. The patient sees the need for this service as urgent but short-term. He is in crisis, and his goal is crisis management:

40:   I wanted to see this man to give me something because I felt funny. I don't just feel funny because it's raining out. . . . Well, to feel all fucked up, it's beyond describing. It's not like being someplace all alone or facing a hundred guys or nothing. It's not like jumping from one cliff to another. It's not like hanging off the edge of a cliff. It's like everything compressing all together. At one minute.

I: What do you think the psychiatrist can do for you?

40:   I just wanted him to give me something to relax with.

35:   It's starting to hassle me. I don't know what to do. So I'm sitting up in the cell, you know, late at night I'm sitting up in the cell, and I'm starting to hear things. I didn't know whether I was hallucinating or what, but I started to hear things, like loud voices, like me talking to myself, but out loud. And like I started banging on the walls, and an officer came down and told me to shut up or he's going to knock my brains out. You know, stuff like that. So what I do, I flood the whole cell, flood the whole tier. I figured, "Well, I'll get this guy to come in here, just to see somebody, talk to somebody. Maybe he can give me some answers. I'll flood the tier and get him down here."

A second crisis arises when the urgency of one's request for help is not communicated, and one feels increasingly un-self-sufficient. The patient may well resort to a dramatic act which defines him as an emergency case, and as thus entitled to crisis intervention:

D 49:   Like I say, I was in a state of depression that somebody that knew anything about therapy or anything they could have seen it and pulled me out of it, by just rapping. Maybe I would have cried my way out of it. But in the bathroom, being alone, I had nobody to rap to but myself. And the state my mind was in, I couldn't pull myself out of it. . . . I think a lot of it too was that I wanted help. Because I had asked for it because I was in a very bad nervous tension, like. And I asked the psychiatrist there for help, and he turned me down. He refused me two weeks before. He said there was nothing he could do for me. . . . And when this guy turned me down, who did I have to turn to? The doctor didn't want to do nothing. . . . And after I cut up, they put me in the bug cell. And then I seen this same doctor again, and he said, "Well, I'm gonna send you to the hospital." But I had to go through these changes to get to the hospital.

4:   How can I cope with this problem? What is the solution? There's got to be one available, you understand? And the only solution I see was the psychiatrist. Now he refuses to see me. So I tried the next official that I had, I asked the lieutenant. He wrote me back and told me some jive. So, like, I got to cope with this problem, this was the whole thing, you know. You know, there was a solution to this problem, and I couldn't find it. In fact, I'm locked up, I'm locked up twenty-four hours a day, I can't move around or do nothing, you know? And I wrote to some of my brothers in the population, and they told me to take it easy, don't bug out. I said, "Oh, man, this is nothing." . . . In other words, I was doing this for help. I wasn't doing this to kill myself. I needed help, and I figured the only way I could get help was by doing this. I said, "These people here, they don't understand my problem, they won't listen to my problem." So I said, "I need help."

40:   Well, I felt a little upset about my family. . . . And I just wanted to see the doctor, to give me something to calm me down. . . . I asked the man, and the man said, "Sorry, you can't see the doctor," and I said, "Why?" He said, "Unless you go crazy." I said, "You must be kidding with me." And he said, "No, that's the only way you're going to see the doctor." I said, "You mean I have to go crazy to see the doctor?" And he said yes. He said, "If you bang your head against the bars or hurt yourself in any way." So I said, "I understand." So I went in the back, and I cut myself. I came back and showed him and said, "Can I see the doctor now?" He said, "Yes, now you can see the doctor." And he sent me down. . . . The officer told me that was the only way I would see the doctor. If he told me I had to chop my arm, then I was going to do it. I just wanted to see him. And if that was the way he would open the gate for me, then I'm going to do it.

A third crisis may occur when mental health personnel prove not to have the power with which the patient has endowed them. At this juncture the patient may conclude that he is not taken seriously—that the psychiatrist doesn't care, or doesn't understand the genuineness or emergency of his need:

40:   He only wanted to know if I had suicidal tendencies.

I: Did he ask you just like that, "Do you have suicidal tendencies?"

40:   Yeah. "Did you ever try to kill yourself before?" And all this.

I: And he never asked about what was fucking you up?

40:   No. They just go over the surface, give you a fast runover to see if you want to kill yourself.

M 16:   Because all the people that work for these people sooner or later get so tired and so bored that it becomes a fucking routine, and I don't blame the people. You see these people all the time, and after a while, "Fuck you"; "Yeah, next." That's it. It's a joke.

Some patients must cope with repeated disappointments in their help-seeking efforts, while assuming that an aid formula is available but is being withheld. They may resort to extreme measures, including blackmail, to mobilize aid, and then conclude that even such moves are insufficient to secure available services. And when the next, disastrous breakdown occurs, the patient may feel that the mental health system is to be blamed for his acts or his fate. And though his logic has flaws, it points up a real and unresolved gap between human needs and human services:

M 16:   Now I'm sitting here once again, fucked up. I've asked the health and the parole department—I've asked numerous times to stop sending me around on a merry-go-round to institutions. It ain't going to do any good. That I need help, that I want help, that I won't get any help. . . . I'm just bypassed. And I'm tired of running around on a merry-go-round. Two thirds of my life in institutions. . . . And I told them I'm going to leave dead bodies from here to California in every fucking state. I called my PO and told him the same thing, but he wasn't home, so I told his supervisor. . . . Why do you have to be a weak individual or go to the doctor and cry about "I never had shoes when I was a kid" or "I never had this" or "I'm going to get twenty years"? Why do you have to cry to get help? Why can't they just give you help for being what you are? . . . All they can do is make out the silly report or recommend something which the guys don't give a fuck, don't mean a damn thing. To recommend a psychiatrist's help is the biggest joke when it goes before a judge. They recommend it to the judge, the judge sends you to jail, he recommends it to the prison. It just goes from one hand to another. It's a fucking joke all the way around, the whole circle. . . . I would just say that all my life, through every institution, I've hurt somebody, innocent people. It should be obvious that I've complained that I can't get help throughout my whole life, that I've asked for help and I never got it. And I would like to know to some conclusion why.

This patient (and others like him) may or may not deserve a reply. But the consequence of not answering such questions is that they are posed again—and posed in ways that make our inadequacy or impotence more obvious and costly.

II

The Effects of Predispositions and Settings

5

The Ingredients
of
Despair

To this point our survey has been omnivorous. We have ranged indiscriminately over our breakdown themes, without regard to their frequency or the time and place of their occurrence. We have not dealt with the questions of who experiences what type of crisis and where he experiences it.

We now turn our attention to these problems. We ask ourselves about risk (Who is likely to break down?) and examine differences among the dominant concerns of high-risk groups. Throughout we assume that self-injuries are characteristic reactions in detention settings because they provide an index of personal difficulties which are uniquely prevalent in jails and prisons. We have noted that there is no foolproof way of estimating self-injury rates in penal institutions. Records are incomplete, population data unreliable, and variations substantial. But with even the most conservatives figures we can show that the problem of self-mutilation is endemic and that nothing commensurate occurs in other settings. If a problem even remotely similar were to arise in the outside world, it would provoke outrage and emergency intervention.

In 1972 we surveyed an institution for youthful offenders with a population of 1,054 men. We learned from documented information that 57 of the inmates had injured themselves in detention. If we extrapolate this rate to the average stay in the institution (17 months), it becomes 7.7%. In the outside world, where such events are recorded at rates per 100,000, this would signify a self-mutilation rate of 7,700 per 100,000 persons. Attica provided us with 24 subjects out of a population of 2,277; given the average sentence at Attica, this means that an Attica inmate has a 2.2% chance of a self-destructive breakdown. The comparable rate for another major prison—Clinton—is 3.76%. And to these figures must be added the unrecorded incidents, which are of horrifying proportions. According to the data obtained from our control group, we can expect 3.2% of the prison population to have *unrecorded* self-destructive experiences in prison; and this figure rises to 6.5% if we include men who have injured themselves (without data to show the fact) somewhere in confinement.

But even these statistics are conservative when we compare them to the situation in high-risk settings. In a women's prison whose population totaled 297, we found 14 inmates who had injured themselves; in a random sample, the self-injury rate rose to 10.8%. We also interviewed at a mental hospital in a psychiatrically oriented prison. The hospital receives inmates with adjustment problems (primarily suspected schizophrenia) from anywhere in the prison system. We reviewed records of transfers into this facility over a nine-month period. These intake data showed that 38.4% of the daily population of the institution had a history of self-injury in detention and that 31.7% had injured themselves in prisons. In other words, though the institution's criterion of admission was psychotic breakdown, three or four out of every ten men admitted had mutilated themselves somewhere in the system. No such phenomenon is approximated in civil mental health settings.

How typical are inmates who injure themselves? In what way do they differ from their peers? Some indications are provided in Tables 5.1, 5.2, and 5.3, which compare inmates with recorded incidents to systematic random comparison samples drawn from the populations from which these inmates derive.[1]

Table 5.1 furnishes the picture for male prison inmates. It shows that younger inmates are more likely to break down than older ones. Whereas four out of ten men in the risk population are in the under-21 group, this group represents only 22% of the inmate population. The table also shows that the single inmate is more likely to break down than the married inmate.

Our findings with respect to ethnicity are consistent with those of other studies. Blacks are strikingly underrepresented in the crisis group: though they make up two thirds of the prison population, they constitute less than one quarter of the risk population. On the other hand, white and Latin inmates are overrepresented among our interview candidates. Addiction, strangely, proves to be a negative predictor of risk; of inmates for whom data are available, only 24% in the risk group have drug histories, compared to 49% of the entire prison population. However, men with a known history of violence are overrepresented in the crisis sample.[2]

TABLE 5.1 *Differences between Population of Male Prison Inmates with Recorded Incidents of Self-Destructive Breakdown (N = 357) and Systematic Random Sample of Prison Inmates (N = 601)*

	Proportion of	
	Risk Population	Prison Population*
Age		
Under 21	39.3%†	22.2%
21–35	41.3	61.4†
Over 35	19.4	16.4
Marital status		
Married	19.5	35.4†
Single	73.4†	54.7
Separated, divorced, widowed	7.1	9.9§
Ethnic background		
Black	23.9	57.8†
White	53.5†	28.3
Latin	21.9†	13.5
Drug involvement		
Drugs	23.9	48.6†
Nondrugs	76.1†	51.4
Personal Violence		
Record	34.8‡	28.3
No record	65.2	71.7‡

* The comparison sample proportions are considered estimates of the population proportions when population figures are available.
† Difference in proportions is significant at the .001 level.
‡ Difference in proportions is significant at the .01 level.
§ Difference in proportions is significant at the .05 level.

A similar picture emerges for the jail population (Table 5.2). But there are three interesting variations. Older inmates have more serious problems adjusting to jail, and marriage aggravates coping problems in detention. A third difference is the risk-enhancing role of drugs; whereas a history of drug use seems positively related to prison adjustment, it is a liability in the detention setting. We will return to these facts in Chapter 6. Meanwhile, it may help to recall that the transition from the free world to the prison environment takes place in jails.

Table 5.3 provides data for female detainees.[3] Again, youth is a powerful predictor of self-injury risk. Marital status, surprisingly, shows no significant impact. Black inmates are again underrepresented, and Latin inmates overrepresented, in the self-injury group. The data for drug history are striking among women. Fully eight out of ten of the risk group are

TABLE 5.2 *Differences between Population of Male Detention Inmates with Recorded Incidents of Self-Destructive Breakdowns (N = 415) and Systematic Random Sample of Jail Inmates (N = 1,674)*

	Proportion of	
	Risk Population	Jail Population*
Age		
Under 21	51.3%	59.5†
21–35	43.2†	31.8
Over 35	5.5	8.7
Marital Status		
Married	29.7†	22.1
Single	65.5	75.2†
Separated, divorced, widowed	4.8	2.7
Ethnic Background		
Black	35.3	59.1†
White	29.8†	16.0
Puerto Rican	34.9†	24.9
Drug Involvement		
Drugs	52.8†	40.0
Non-drugs	47.2	60.0
Personal Violence		
Record	19.0†	8.0
No record	81.0	92.0

* The comparison sample proportions are considered estimates of the population proportions.

†Difference in proportions is significant at the .001 level.

certified addicts, as opposed to 54% of the population for which data are available. Again, violent offenses prove predictive of risk.

Table 5.4 lists the marginals from our content analysis. It shows that the distribution of primary and secondary themes is similar, though some themes are more likely to occur as primary themes, and one or two themes

TABLE 5.3 *Differences between Female Inmates with Recorded Incidents of Self-Destruction on Rikers Island in 1972 (N = 56) and Systematic Random Sample of Female Inmates on Rikers Island in 1972 (N = 355)*

| | Proportion of Female | |
	Risk Sample	Random Sample*
Age		
Under 21	42.9%†	23.9%
21–30	48.2	56.1
Over 30	8.9	20.0§
Marital status		
Married	28.6	22.0
Single	58.9	61.4
Separated, divorced, widowed	12.5	16.6
Ethnic background		
Black	53.6	69.6‡
White	23.2	17.4
Latin	23.2§	13.0
Drug involvement		
Drugs	78.8†	54.1
Non-drugs	21.2	45.9†
Personal violence		
Record	35.7‡	21.7
No Record	64.3	78.3‡

* Comparison sample proportions are considered population parameters.
† Difference in proportions is significant at the .001 level.
‡ Difference in proportions is significant at the .01 level.
§ Difference in proportions is significant at the .05 level.

are apt to be non-primary. For instance, delusional schizophrenic breakdowns (Self-Alienation) occupy prominent roles in coded crises when these themes are present. Self-Victimization (a process theme) usually occurs in a secondary role; Self-Linking (the need for significant others) is a disproportionately secondary theme. The most frequent themes are Self-Linking and Fate Avoidance. This latter theme embodies problems of low self-esteem tied to fear of others. Self-esteem crises seem to be the most prevalent; coping problems occur less frequently than do problems in the two other categories, which involve more long-term motives.

Table 5.5 compares data obtained from jail and prison. It shows Self-Linking to be disproportionately a jail theme, a fact which (as we will see in Chapter 6) is related to the disruptive role of the jail in relation to the outside world. Detention facilities also disproportionately feature Aid-Seeking, the invoking of staff for the amelioration of personal problems.

TABLE 5.4   *Frequency Distribution of Crisis Themes for All Male Inmates in Crisis (N = 331)*

| Crisis Themes | Number of Occurrences as | | Total, Any Presence of Theme (N = 687) | Percent of Subjects Involved (N = 331): |
	Primary Themes (N = 331)	Nonprimary Themes (N = 356)		
Coping				
Sanctuary Search	4	8	12	4%
Self-Victimization	22	40	62	19
Isolation Panic	11	19	30	9
Self-Classification	13	17	30	9
Aid Seeking	11	5	16	5
Status				
Self-Deactivation	27	30	57	18
Self-Sentencing	22	26	48	15
Self-Retaliation	12	11	23	7
Fate Avoidance	39	44	83	25
Self-Linking	36	49	85	26
Self-Certification	36	24	60	18
Impulse control				
Self-Alienation	18	7	25	8
Self-Release	18	24	42	13
Self-Escape	23	20	43	13
Self-Preservation	28	19	47	14
Self-Intervention	11	13	24	7

Schizophrenic breakdowns (Self-Alienation) are more frequent in jails. This finding may arise in part from the fact that preconviction populations contain inmates who are eventually routed away from prison on mental health grounds.

Table 5.6 subdivides our sample along ethnic lines. It shows that black inmates suffer disproportionately from fear—in particular, from Isolation Panic and paranoid reactions. Inmates of Latin background show a sub-

TABLE 5.5 *Distributions of Crisis Themes among Men with Jail Events Interviewed in Jail (N = 103) and Men with Prison Events Interviewed in Prisons (N = 168)*

Crisis Themes	Number of Occurrences in		Proportion of Inmates in	
	Jails (N = 103)	Prisons (N = 168)	Jails	Prisons
Coping				
Sanctuary Search	2	7	1.9%	4.2%
Self-Victimization	17	32	16.5	19.0
Isolation Panic	7	19	6.8	11.3
Self-Classification	8	17	7.8	10.1
Aid Seeking	10†	2	9.7	1.2
Status				
Self-Deactivation	17	27	16.5	16.1
Self-Sentencing	15	22	14.6	13.1
Self-Retaliation	5	14	4.9	8.3
Fate Avoidance	23	48	22.3	28.6
Self-Linking	35‡	37	34.0	22.0
Self-Certification	15	31	14.6	81.5
Impulse Control				
Self-Alienation	14†	7	13.6	4.2
Self-Release	10	24	9.7	14.3
Self-Escape	13	20	12.6	11.9
Self-Preservation	11	27	10.7	16.1
Self-Intervention	11	10	10.7	6.0

† Chi-square significant at .01 level.
‡ Chi-square significant at .05 level.

stantial involvement in Self-Linking crises and a relative absence of prison fear. Whites seem prone to self-punishing breakdowns (Self-Retaliation) as well as prison fear. Chapter 7 will deal with black and Latin themes, and will examine them in the light of literature on ethnicity or subculture. We must recall that whereas Latin inmates are overrepresented among high risks, black inmates are not, so that "black" themes represent atypical (though consistent) concerns of deviant black men.

The theme which shows up most strongly among whites (Self-Retaliation) will not be discussed in Chapter 6. It is probably a neurotic reaction which—translated into cultural concerns—represents a distorted manifestation of middle-class upbringing.[4]

Table 5.7 breaks down the concerns of our sample by age. We see that the age groups are clearly separated on the fear themes. Whereas younger inmates seem prone to Isolation Panic and to ego-involved prison fear, older men are disproportionately represented among patients suffering

TABLE 5.6 *Relative Prevalence of Crisis Themes among Black Inmates, Inmates of Latin Extraction, and Non-Latin White Inmates (Male Inmates Only; N = 326)*

	Number of Occurrences of Theme among			Proportion of Occurrence as Percent of		
Crisis Themes	Blacks (N = 74)	Latins (N = 73)	Whites (N = 179)	Blacks	Latins	Whites
Coping						
Sanctuary Search	2	1	9	3%	1%	5%
Self-Victimization	19	15	27	26	21	15
Isolation Panic†	15	2	12	20	3	7
Self-Classification	3	6	21	4	8	12
Aid Seeking	3	4	9	4	6	5
Status						
Self-Deactivation	12	8	36	16	11	20
Self-Sentencing	7	12	27	10	17	15
Self-Retaliation‡	1	2	20	1	3	11
Fate Avoidance§	19	10	52	26	14	29
Self-Linking‡	17	30	37	23	41	21
Self-Certification	7	13	38	10	18	21
Impulse control						
Self-Alienation	5	7	11	7	10	6
Self-Release	8	9	26	11	12	15
Self-Escape‡	18	4	19	25	6	11
Self-Preservation‡	20	8	19	27	11	11
Self-Intervention	6	7	10	8	10	6

† Chi-square significant at the .001 level.
‡ Chi-square significant at the .01 level.
§ Chi-square significant at the .05 level.

from paranoid delusions. Younger inmates also show a greater tendency toward Self-Certification, a theme which refers to demonstrative or retaliatory reactions to degenerating interpersonal links.

Table 5.8 explores the relationship between violence propensity and personal breakdowns. Not surprisingly, there is a tendency for violence-prone inmates to experience tension-release breakdowns. There is also an indication that prison fear is most likely to occur among less violent inmates.

In Table 5.9, we compare data obtained for male inmates with those obtained for female inmates. Generally, female inmates seem overrepresented in coping themes, and particularly in Isolation Panic and Sanctu-

TABLE 5.7 *Relative Distribution of Crisis Themes among Younger and Older Male Inmates (N = 311)*

	Under 21		Over 21	
Crisis Themes	Frequency of Group	Percent (N = 143)	Frequency of Group	Percent (N = 168)
Coping				
Sanctuary Search	7	5%	5	3%
Self-Victimization	23	16	37	22
Isolation Panic	21	15‡	7	4
Self-Classification	17	12	13	8
Aid Seeking	6	4	9	5
Status				
Self-Deactivation	22	15	33	20
Self-Sentencing	17	12	29	17
Self-Retaliation	9	6	12	7
Fate Avoidance	47	33‡	33	20
Self-Linking	37	26	41	24
Self-Certification	36	25‡	20	12
Impulse Control				
Self-Alienation	6	4	11	7
Self-Release	20	14	19	11
Self-Escape	13	9	27	16
Self-Preservation	6	4	35†	21
Self-Intervention	10	7	12	7

† Chi-square significant at the .001 level.
‡ Chi-square significant at the .01 level.

ary Search (a theme which relates to psychological closure). Women are particularly likely to experience Self-Linking crises, which involve separation from significant others. The most striking finding for the female sample is the dramatic role of Self-Release. This theme (encountered among two thirds of the women inmates) relates to the propensity to explode whenever tension accumulates beyond a tolerable point. This process (and the others noted above) will be discussed in Chapter 8.

Themes that are not represented nearly as frequently among women as among men are the more serious fear themes and Self-Certification. The

TABLE 5.8 *Relative Prevalence of Crisis Themes among Inmates with Records of Violent Personal Offenses and Other Inmates for Whom Offenses are Known (Males Only)*

Crisis Themes	Inmates with Records of Violence (N = 85)		Inmates with No Violence in Record (N = 201)	
	Number	Percent of Group	Number	Percent of Group
Coping				
Sanctuary Search	3	3.5%	9	4.5%
Self-Victimization	20	23.5	35	17.4
Isolation Panic	11	12.9	15	7.5
Self-Classification	6	7.1	20	10.0
Aid Seeking	5	5.9	8	4.0
Status				
Self-Deactivation	10	11.8	41	20.4
Self-Sentencing	16	18.8	27	13.4
Self-Retaliation	7	8.2	14	7.0
Fate Avoidance	15	17.6	59‡	29.4
Self-Linking	21	24.7	49	24.4
Self-Certification	9	10.6	38	18.9
Impulse Control				
Self-Alienation	4	4.7	11	5.5
Self-Release	16†	18.8	18	9.0
Self-Escape	15	17.6	24	11.9
Self-Preservation	13	15.3	26	12.9
Self-Intervention	4	4.7	14	7.0

† Chi-square significant at the .01 level.
‡ Chi-square significant at the .05 level.

former are particularly interesting, given the concern with fear, or the presumed absence of it, in the male normative model. Self-Certification (retaliatory self injury) seems to be common among some younger men when they are frustrated in interpersonal relations.

Given the small size of the female sample, statistical differences within the group are hard to come by. However, Table 5.10, which breaks down the sample by settings, demonstrates that significant variations do occur even within this small group. We note that coping themes are more com-

TABLE 5.9   *Distribution of Themes among Female Inmates Compared to the Distribution of Themes for Male Inmates*

Crisis Themes	Total Females (N = 52)	Percent of Total Females	Total Males (N = 331)	Percent of Total Males
Coping				
Sanctuary Search	14†	27%	12	4%
Self-Victimization	19‡	37	60	19
Isolation Panic	17†	33	28	9
Self-Classification	7	14	30	10
Aid Seeking	7‡	14	15	5
Status				
Self-Deactivation	6	12	55	18
Self-Sentencing	7	14	46	15
Self-Retaliation	3	6	21	7
Fate Avoidance	6	12	80§	26
Self-Linking	26†	50	78	25
Self-Certification	2	4	56§	18
Impulse Control				
Self-Alienation	2	4	17	6
Self-Release	33†	64	39	13
Self-Escape	2	4	40	13
Self-Preservation	1	2	41§	13
Self-Intervention	1	2	22	7

† Chi-square significant at the .001 level.
‡ Chi-square significant at the .01 level.
§ Chi-square significant at the .05 level.

mon in jails, while the main female crisis theme (Self-Release) achieves disproportionate prominence in prison. Out of 29 female prison inmates, twenty-three (8 out of 10) talked of breakdowns that featured release of pent-up emotions. No similar peak is found elsewhere in our data.

Tables 5.11 and 5.12 provide data about the methods of self-injury used by inmates in our male and female samples. As might be expected, cutting is the procedure employed most commonly by both groups. In men, the second-ranking method is hanging, which (considering the chances of death) is used with alarming frequency—especially in jails.

TABLE 5.10 *Relative Prevalence of Crisis Themes in Detention Settings and Prisons among Female Inmates (N = 52)*

| Crisis Themes | Number of Occurrences in | | Proportion of Subjects in | |
	Jails (N = 23)	Prisons (N = 29)	Jails	Prisons
Coping				
Sanctuary Search	10‡	4	43.4%	13.8%
Self-Victimization	13†	6	56.5	20.6
Isolation Panic	7	10	30.4	34.5
Self-Classification	2	5	8.7	17.2
Aid Seeking	3	4	13.0	13.8
Status				
Self-Deactivation	3	3	13.0	10.3
Self-Sentencing	2	5	8.7	17.2
Self-Retaliation	2	1	8.7	3.4
Fate Avoidance	1	5	4.3	17.2
Self-Linking	12	14	52.8	48.3
Self-Certification	2	—	8.7	—
Impulse Control				
Self-Alienation	—	2	—	6.9
Self-Release	10	23†	43.4	79.3
Self-Escape	1	2	4.3	6.9
Self-Preservation	1	—	4.3	—
Self-Intervention	—	1	—	3.4

† Differences significant at the .01 level.
‡ Differences significant at the .05 level.

The second-ranking method of females, and the third-ranking method of males, self-injury combined with property destruction—usually, with smashing windows. Table 5.11 shows that this syndrome occurs frequently in prisons but rarely in jails. Table 5.12 suggests that female inmates repeat the use of this method more often than they repeat other procedures.

Self-administered drug overdoses, the next-ranking method for both groups, frequently occur in prison. This may be because addicts undergo supervised withdrawal in jail but are under less control in prison settings.

Methods of self-injury are not randomly distributed among our themes. Though the Ns become small, some differences stand out. Among coping themes for male inmates, we find Aid Seeking associated with cutting; among ego-related themes, Self-Certification—which carries interpersonal

TABLE 5.11 *Method of Self-Injury: Number of Times Method Employed in each Setting by Male Inmates* (N = 267)*

Self-Injury	Total Number of Times Method Employed	Incident Proportion, %	Jail vs. Prison Number of Times Method Used	
			in Jails	in Prisons
Self-Cutting	316	60%	130	186
Hanging	105	20	70†	35
Injury Incidental to Property Destruction	46	9	2	44†
Overdose of Drugs	15	3	1	14‡
Fire	17	3	3	14
Swallowing Foreign Objects	15	3	9	6
Jumping from Height	6	1	1	5
Other	1	—	0	1
Unknown	7	1	0	7
Total incidents	528		217	311

* This table includes only prison inmates whose incidents occurred in prisons; this reduces the N by 61 men.
† Differences significant at the .001 level.
‡ Difference significant at the .05 level.

messages—features drug overdoses with disproportionate frequency. A psychotic theme (Self-Alienation) accounts for six of the eleven self-immolations. Among women, property destruction is associated with Self-Release and Self-Linking crises. These differences are all significant beyond the .01 level.

The two bottom lines of Table 5.12 show that recidivistic self-injury among women inmates is very high—comprising two thirds of the sample. Startling as these figures are, they understate the actual extent of recidivism. One out of four women in our sample (28%) reported three or more self-injury incidents, and 6 of our 53 interviewees recorded six or more such incidents.

TABLE 5.12 *Method of Self-Injury Employed by Female Inmates in Sample (N = 53)*

Method	Employed in One Incident	Employed More Than Once	Number of Inmates Employing Method	Proportion of Sample, %
Self-Cutting	25	11	36	68%
Injury Incidental to Property Destruction	10	11	21	40
Hanging	12	2	14	26
Overdose of Drugs	8	3	11	21
Swallowing Foreign Objects	8	0	8	15
Jumping from Height	2	0	2	4
Any method, once	20			37
Any method, repeatedly		33		63

The recidivism figures for men (Table 5.13) are not as dramatic as those for women, but the numbers are large enough to permit breakdowns. These suggest that jail inmates who injure themselves have a higher probability of being recidivists than do prison inmates. In other words, there is a greater likelihood that a jail inmate who breaks down will do so on more than one occasion.

TABLE 5.13 *Proportions of Jail and Prison Inmates with Single Recorded Incident of Self-Injury and Multiple Incidents of Self-Injury (Male Only; N = 328)**

	Jail Inmates		Prison Inmates		Total	
	Frequency	Proportion	Frequency	Proportion	Frequency	Proportion
Inmates with Single Incident of Self-Injury	60	58%	168	75%	227	69%
Inmates with Two or More Incidents	44	42%	57	25%	101	31%

* Difference in proportions is significant beyond the .01 level.

Table 5.14 explores the relationship between recidivism and the content of crises. It suggests that coping themes are most likely to be associated with one-time self-injuries, while injuries related to impulse control themes show the highest recidivism. Closer inspection confirms the con-

TABLE 5.14 *Proportion of Male Inmates with Single Recorded Incident of Self-Injury and Proportion with Multiple Incidents in Each Thematic Category and in Selected Themes (N = 338)*

Category of Primary Themes*	Number of Inmates with Single Incident of Self-Injury	Proportion, %	Number of Inmates with Two or More Incidents of Self-Injury	Proportion, %
Situational Coping	47	77%	14	23%
Career, Social, and Self-Esteem	121	72	48	28
Impulse Control	59	60	39	40
Primary Themes				
Self-Release (discharge of aggressive tension)	8	44	10	56
Self-Escape (preparanoid syndrome)	11	48	12	52
Self-Retaliation (self-hate or self-punishment)	6	50	6	50
Self-Victimization (resentment, perceived injustice)	19	86	3	14
Self-Deactivation (inventory and hopelessness)	22	85	4	15
Self-Preservation (paranoid syndrome)	22	79	6	21
Proportions for Total Sample (all themes)		69		31

* The proportions in this section of the table are significantly different at precisely the .05 level ($x^2 = 5.93$, df $= 2$).

clusion that self-injuries associated with coping tend to be one-time events; in other categories, we find more variation. The second section of Table 5.14, which lists three "high" and three "low" themes, points to high recidivism for preparanoia but not for paranoid crises. The data also

TABLE 5.15 *Relative Prevalence of Crisis Themes among Self-Injury Group (N = 331) and Systematic Random Control Group (N = 154)*

Crisis Themes	Percentage Distribution in Control Group	Percentage Distribution in Self-Injury Sample
Coping		
Sanctuary Search	8%	4
Self-Victimization	33†	19
Isolation Panic	1	9†
Self-Classification	3	9‡
Aid Seeking	3	5
Status		
Self-Deactivation	10	18
Self-Sentencing	18	15
Self-Retaliation	8	7
Fate Avoidance	26	25
Self-Linking	50†	26
Self-Certification	8	18‡
Impulse Control		
Self-Alienation	1	8†
Self-Release	26†	13
Self-Escape	7	13§
Self-Preservation	4	14†
Self-Intervention	2	7†

† Difference in proportions is significant at the .001 level.
‡ Difference in proportions is significant at the .01 level.
§ Difference in proportions is significant at the .05 level.

show a difference between two inventory themes. Whereas Self-Retaliation (a relatively pathological self-assessment) is associated with high recidivism, Self-Deactivation (which borders on coping) is not.

The final table in this chapter (Table 5.15) compares themes in our male self-injury sample with those obtained in interviews with randomly selected male inmates. Though some inmates in the control group indicated that they had experienced no difficulties in confinement, the vast majority recalled incidents or occasions of serious stress. These experiences yield a distribution in which Self-Linking difficulties (problems involving abandonment by loved ones) stand out very prominently. Another disproportionate theme is Self-Victimization, which refers to the feeling of impotence produced by perceived inequity. Although impulse control themes (psychotic themes) are comparatively rare in the control group, nonpsychotic Self-Release (tension management) problems are fairly common.

The present chapter has presented gross statistical distributions of crisis themes. In the remainder of Part II we will expand on the themes that stand out in our tables. Chapter 6 deals with the jail versus the prison, and it illustrates the ways in which different stress settings affect susceptible men. Chapter 7 focuses on the crisis themes of black and Latin inmates, and explores ways in which culture-linked past experiences can affect personal responses to stress. This problem is also dealt with in Chapter 8, which takes up the concerns of female inmates.

Part III will permit us to take a more clinical view of the forces we have surfaced. Here, we shall pursue the careers of inmates who committed suicide, and trace the contributions of expectations, stresses, reactions, and counterreactions to their tragic fates. We shall thus see how the variables we have outlined can lead to irreversible crises and breakdowns.

NOTES

1. Though our distributions show valid systematic differences, they cannot describe a "real" risk population. It is unsafe to assume that incidents noted on inmate records are representative of incidents about which information has decayed. Moreover, our interview samples were not perfectly matched with incident samples on all key demographic variables.

2. For the purpose of this breakdown, violence was defined as one or more convictions for offenses against the person, such as assault or homicide. Robbery was not included because of the property motive in this crime.

3. We are not showing female prison data because the size of the incident sample makes statistical tests impossible.

4. We have noted elsewhere that working-class socialization converts a number of middle-class institutions into stress settings, but that the middle-class person encounters fewer "test situations" for which he is ill-prepared. The prison, like the concentration camp, may be an exception to this rule. (Cf. H. Toch, "The Delinquent as a Poor Loser," *Seminars in Psychiatry*, 1971, *3*, 386–99).

6

Jailing
and
Stress

In this chapter, we will examine the differential manifestations of our crisis themes in jails and prisons. We will show that presentence detention institutions and prisons pose different problems for the men they confine and that the two types of settings require their inmates to invoke different resources and to employ different strategies for psychological survival.

We do not mean to imply in this chapter that the crises experienced by men in jails are entirely different from those experienced by men in prisons. The problems represented in our typology are general difficulties of men in confinement, and we would expect them to arise in both types of penal institutions. However, we noted in Chapter 5 that there are some thematic differences between jail and prison. And we will show in this chapter that there are equivalent types of crises that have unique connotations and intensities for jail inmates.

The differences between jails and prisons are apparent from the very beginning. Entry into prison is gradual as compared with entry into jail. Prior to being assigned to a particular state prison, an inmate is usually sent to a reception center for classification and orientation. This gives him some time to ponder and test out the coping strategies he will employ in his future environment and to devote some attention to his psychological

Chapter contributed by John J. Gibbs.

144

links with the outside community. The initial concern upon entry into prison is "how to make it" or "how to do the time"; the focus is predominantly on the inside.

Shortly after being sentenced to five years in a state prison, one interviewee told us:

MHDM 3: I'm taking it a step at a time. Looking like right now, I'm learning all the things I'm going to need to survive in the penitentiary. Because I know now that I'm going to the penitentiary. This will be my first trip, but I'm going. I know that now. So I'm getting all the things that I need to live in the penitentiary.

We are not suggesting that the jail-prison transition is accomplished with the ease with which the average person's life changes are made. John Irwin tells us that "passing from the county jail to prison is [a] disorganizing event. . . . the daily routine is shattered, and [the inmate] is thrust into totally new surroundings. A new process of being moved like a pawn begins."[1]

However, the disruption is mild if we compare prison reception to Morton Hunt's description of the intake agency for pretrial detention, the arraignment court:

The judge, brusque and quick, impassive and hardened to the endless stream of unrepentant thieves, whores, addicts, pushers, muggers, armed robbers, knife-wielders, and rapists, would listen, occasionally interrupt with a question or two, then snap out his orders, and ask the clerk for the next one. But he could do nothing else: nearly a hundred prisoners were still waiting, and all had to be arraigned and either released or turned over to Department of Correction officers by mid-afternoon. There could be no let-up for an instant, and so the accused came up one after another to stand before him, hearing a smattering of phrases fly back and forth, and being led away almost before they knew what he had said, most of them disappearing through the door back to the pens.[2]

The scene at the reception room of the jail is equally discordant. Men shuffle and stumble from institutional vans to reception pens. Here they await processing, some immobilized by withdrawal pains, sweating, shuddering, and vomiting; others loudly protesting the legality of their incarceration; and the majority staring into space in a state of disbelief or depression. In the background, reception officers bark their inquires, and the machine that prints the inmate identification tags clicks its incessant click.

Initial reactions to jailing may include disbelief followed by some sort of effort to gain release.[3] The first worries are about the length of confinement and the seriousness of the charges. At the stage when the prison inmate is asking himself, "How do I make it in this joint?" the newly arrived detainee is pondering the questions, "How did I get into this spot and when do I get out?"

Once sentenced to imprisonment, a man must concern himself with his capacity to survive in a restricted, exclusively male world for at least one year. As we have seen, the coping strategy par excellence is to assume the stance of the Manly Man. This posture requires self-control in the face of danger and a working knowledge of the inmate and staff worlds. Prison populations are more homogeneous than the population of variegated offenders incarcerated in jails; it is this homogeneity that necessitates prudent awareness of the moves and motives of fellow inmates. "It is a situation which can prove to be anxiety-provoking even for the hardened recidivist, and it is in this light that we can understand the comment of an inmate . . . who said, 'The worst thing about prison is you have to live with other prisoners.' "[4]

In prison, the potential threat of fellow inmates is well recognized; thus the conditions of long-term confinement compel a man to direct his attention and energies to the prison world itself. Although some men adapt to prison by conceiving "of the prison experience as a temporary break in their outside career,"[5] even these fringers, who mark the boundaries of the inmate social world, are acutely aware of potential threats from other inmates and cognizant of the need to follow the inmate code.

Although the traditional Manly survival strategy is not ruled out in the detention setting, rigorous adherence to the precepts of the Manly model does not appear to have the same efficacy in jail as in prison despite the predominant presence in jails of working class men.[6] True, Irwin isolates a small group of "jailers" who seem to adjust to any confinement setting by assuming traditional prison roles. These men, says Irwin, "who do not retain or who never acquired any commitment to outside social worlds, tend to make a world out of prison."[7] But a jail inmate must deal with a larger universe of controllers than a man in prison. Decisions made by judges, parents, wives, prosecutors, jailers, psychiatrists, bail bondsmen, and jurors may affect his fate, and it would be unrealistic for him to view such decisions with the "imperviousness" of the Manly Man.

The dominant concerns of most prison inmates—personal security, reducing the rigors of imprisonment, and "doing time"—require a clear definition of the boundaries between the prison world and the outside community. The "doing your own time" precept of the inmate code implies that self-reliance should be maintained in relation both to custodians and to members of the free community. The structure and location of most prisons limits the inmates' view and facilitates demarcation.

Unlike the prison inmate, the jail inmate is in close physical and psychological proximity to the outside community. This factor, combined with certain characteristic elements of pretrial detention, engenders a distinct set of "real world" problems for most men incarcerated in jails.

Primary concerns promoted by pretrial detention include: (1) maintenance of a sense of control in the face of uncertainty and reduced resources; (2) securing support and assistance from significant others in the community; and (3) sustaining psychological integrity despite reduced status, the threat of further difficulties, the demeaning implications of incarceration, and the loss of valued or familiar social roles.

In a rather lengthy passage of *The Felon,* Irwin vividly describes the prisoner's jail experiences and his reactions to them:

These experiences—arrest, trial, and conviction—threaten the structure of his personal life in two separate ways. First, the disjointed experience of being suddenly extracted from a relatively orderly and familiar routine and cast into a completely unfamiliar and seemingly chaotic one where the ordering of events is completely out of his control has a shattering impact upon his personality structure. One's identity, one's personality system, one's coherent thinking about himself depend upon a relatively familiar, continuous, and predictable stream of events. In the Kafkaesque world of the booking room, the jail cell, the interrogation room, and the visiting room, the boundaries of the self collapse.

While this collapse is occurring, the prisoner's network of social relations is being torn apart. The insulation between social worlds, an insulation necessary for the orderly maintenance of his social life, is punctured. Many persons learn about facets of his life that were previously unknown to them. Their "business is in the streets." Furthermore, a multitude of minor exigencies that must be met to maintain social relationships go unattended. Bills are not paid, friends are not befriended, families are not fed, consoled, advised, disciplined; businesses go unattended; obligations and duties cannot be fulfilled—in other words, *roles* cannot be performed. Unattended, the structure of the prisoner's social relations collapse.

During this collapse a typical thought pattern often occurs. The arrested person usually reviews his immediate past and has second thoughts about the crime or crimes, or about the complex of behavior related to the crime. Facing the collapse of his personal world, the eventuality of conviction of a felony and a long prison term, he is very prone to express extreme regret. "Why did I do it?" "If only I hadn't done that." "Why did I get into this mess?" "If only I had another chance." All these typify his thinking. Regret and remorse probably reach the greatest intensity in the first few days when the impact of the disjointed experience is the greatest, but this type of reflection on his past continues throughout the presentencing phase.[8]

Some of the resources needed for psychological survival in the detention setting must be supplied by significant others in the community. The jail inmate must be concerned with two worlds, although physically confined to one. When the boundaries between the inside and outside environments are not clearly defined, and the two worlds are not perceived as remote from each other, the chances are that events in one environment will trigger inappropriate and dysfunctional responses in the other. A classic ethological example illustrates this point. Nikolass Tinbergen and his students noticed that sticklebacks would smash themselves against the glass walls of their fish tank each time a red truck passed by. The behavior was explained by the fact that sticklebacks instinctively attack when they see red, the color of a rival. "Their behavior was a senseless response, no longer functional; it had 'misfired.' "[9] If these fish had feelings and thoughts and could communicate them to us, we might expect them to report experiences of frustration, helplessness, confusion, and uncertainty and to express a need for information and assistance.

The detention setting contains many elements that confirm doubts a man may have regarding his adequacy and his ability to govern himself. Proximity to the streets, unoccupied time, and lack of diversion establish propitious conditions for dwelling on one's problems. A man physically confined in jail does not at first perceive himself as totally removed from the outside community. He has not experienced "psychological arrival."[10] As the new environment impinges increasingly on his awareness, thoughts concerning the outside emphasize the significance of his discovery of confinement. And the memories of the street which fill the mental vacuum created by the detention setting translate into recapitulations of the prisoner's loss of freedom.

In the words of two jail inmates:

ARS A: It does hurt, being in a cell and just looking outside and seeing things. I can see the Empire State Building. Just look outside and see the Empire State Building. That puts my mind around. The pressure gets too great, just by looking at the Empire State Building. You think them people out there are allowed to walk around free as much as possible. And you can't get out there to make love to somebody, have your wife, have your children. You can't do this. There's too much pressure on the mind.

ARS B: You're in the cell most of the day. You're locked in. And you have nothing to do but think. You get tired of playing cards. That's all they got here is cards. You get tired of that after a while. You get sick of that. And you got to think. And what do you think about? You think about home, girl friends, things that you'd be doing, like if it was Friday night or Thursday night, what you'd be doing. And, like, when I lay down, I think of things like that. I try not to, but I can't help it. And I see things that I would be doing. I know what I'd be doing, and I can see this. . . . I just couldn't take it.

For the detention prisoner the courts represent a pervasive source of uncertainty. Questions regarding bail, plea bargaining, availability of and eligibility for programs, probability of conviction, disposition, and quality of legal representation may be anxiety producing. Unexplained postpone-ments and adjournments, with shuttling between jail cell and court deten-tion pen, may add to feelings of helplessness.

The jail is a warehouse with a high turnover. This makes control diffi-cult, and limits the quantity and quality of assistance and support obtain-able from fellow inmates and staff to alleviate the psychological difficulties of detention. A man with a negative self-conception may find little help in this environment. Attempts to secure relief generally bring only in-creased frustration, which reinforces the impact of incarceration.

With impotence verified, alternatives exhausted, control over outside events waning, a tainted past, an accusing present, and an uncertain future, it is small wonder that jails breed personal crises among the men they confine.

The Shapes of Psychological Breakdowns in Jail

As we saw in Chapter 5, psychological breakdowns which occur in a deten-tion setting are more substantial for some people and some theme clusters than are prison breakdowns. The remainder of this chapter will describe the most common forms of jail breakdowns and their relationship to the conditions of detention. It will also explore the ingredients which distin-guish the climate of jail from that of prison, and which contribute to the unique flavor of jail breakdowns.

SUPPORT AND INVENTORY

Kurt Lewin notes that a primary requisite for human need satisfaction and psychological survival is the maintenance of a balance in relation to the forces that shape one's environment.[11] As these forces fluctuate, an in-dividual must adjust his behavior to establish a new level of psychological balance. Rapid, forceful changes in environmental conditions test one's capacity to cope. If the individual does not possess or acquire emergency resources to assist him in maintaining psychological balance when facing such abruptly changing situations, he may ultimately break down.

Few men exist entirely independent of significant others, and particu-larly when under stress most men will look to a circle of close familiars for support. Initial reactions to the stress and disorganization created by natural disaster are usually family oriented.[12] If a family is together when such catastrophes strike, the chances of physical and psychological dam-age to its members are generally reduced.[13]

It has also been noted that in environmental abruption—a condition clearly characteristic of detention—people suffer from feelings of lack of control and that those who make such rapid transitions most smoothly are characterized by "stability zones" or "certain enduring relationships that are carefully maintained despite all kinds of other changes."[14] In addition, as many observers have noted, during times of physical threat a "shrinking phenomenon"[15] occurs; that is, the new situation comes to be perceived exclusively or predominantly in terms of the special adjustment difficulties it poses.

The stress created by incarceration results in the reallocation of the import and meaning attached to various elements in an individual's "free world" perspective. A nagging wife or an overprotective mother may appear to be one's last link with survival, and a brother in a distant city may be expected to act as if he lived next door. The first telephone call is overwhelmingly important, and all conversations with those still in the community are major events. Waiting for a visit may be an excruciating eternity. A man may be dependent on individuals in the community for many important functions—procuring funds for bail, obtaining a defense attorney, providing information concerning his case, communicating with significant others, commissary money, clothing, and the like. At this stage, support in the community may be a "stability zone" which softens the psychological impact of confinement. Rejection or the threat of rejection can be devastating, and an individual may become acutely sensitive to abandonment cues. The data presented in Chapter 5 documents the importance of support for jail prisoners;—significantly more jail inmates than prison inmates were involved in crises that featured themes of Self-Linking and Aid Seeking.

Jail also poses the problem of rapid role transition. It changes a number of civil role relationships which have implications for the way a man views and values himself. Arrest and detention seldom enhance a man's self-image, and few jail prisoners perceive themselves as powerful or potent figures in their new world.

Increased dependency on others mirrors a man's reduced status, and the transition may diminish his sense of competence or his "feeling of being able to make some change in the environment, of being able to control the world, and by implication, of being sure that the world will satisfy [his] needs."[16] In this situation, maintaining control and a sense of competence—having the resources to take a manly stance—runs headlong into one's dependence on community ties. This means that one coping requirement mobilized by jail (the need for significant others) contributes to the genesis of coping problems in another sphere (self-esteem in a dependency situation).

The jailing process generates other negative feedback with regard to a man's self-image. The actions and decisions of criminal justice agents during the process can be interpreted as attacks on a man's credibility. Information from criminal justice sources can be viewed as implying that one is a social or societal liability.

Assessing one's worth includes viewing oneself from the perspective of significant others. This is the process of taking a personal inventory in which liabilities suggested by the situation are compared to one's contributions to the world, and a determination of self-worth is made. Inventory-taking may be especially prevalent among men who live in terms of very shortsighted perspectives or follow retreatist life-styles between stints in jail. In the external world, pleasure-seeking or escape coupled with support, supply, and arrest possibilities engenders a frenetic pace in which personal introspection is not afforded much time and importance. For men with such experience, the "reality" of detention may become evidence that exposes their lack of control and invalidates the routine of their street roles.

We have seen in Chapter 3 that as a man reviews his past he may recall guilt-inducing incidents involving family, friends, and victims; ponder irreparable damage to personal relationships; or become overwhelmed by thoughts of wasted potential. As the inventory of life situations which can be translated into personal liabilities expands, some men have difficulty in discovering mitigating assets that will help them to sustain a viable self-image. Lydia Rapoport observes, with regard to crisis situations in general, that "previous failure may act as an additional burden in the present crisis. . . . memories of old problems which are linked symbolically to the present are stimulated and may emerge into consciousness spontaneously."[17] Such an inventory is both diagnosis and prognosis. A man not only judges his previous conduct but also predicts how much support he can expect and how well he is likely to deal with the problems posed by confinement. He is also likely (as our data and the "shrinking phenomenon" suggest) to skew his inventory in ways likely to discourage him.

As shown in Chapter 5, *support* was an issue for a large proportion of the men who experienced psychological breakdowns in jail. Breakdown descriptions by our jail inmates contain implicit and explicit material regarding the need for support as a counterbalance to inimical forces inherent in the jailing process. A key excerpt from one of our interviews documents the importance a trial prisoner attaches to the services performed by family members in the community:

27: I'm a drug addict. Now I was in the process of kicking the habit when I was in the street. My wife and I were trying to get it together. We were trying to rent an apartment and everything else. I spent the money we were supposed to rent the apartment with on drugs. And I got myself in such a situation that we were desperate. We had absolutely no place to live, and I had to go out on the streets every day and steal in order to support my habit and in order so that we could eat. . . . You feel very lost. You feel like there's nobody that you can turn to and that there's nobody there to help you anymore. See, I was depending on my wife quite a bit with the attorney and with mail and just general things to try and make things more pleasant. And then, when that stopped, I just felt that I was completely lost. Like I was on an island by myself. There was just no communication with anybody.

This quote emphasizes not only the significance of the functions families perform for the incapacitated jail inmate but also the fact that the failure of significant others to provide needed services can result in a review of one's past social role. The withdrawal of support initiates a self-inventory that sparks guilt and shame, highlights inadequacies, and accentuates helplessness.

For some men, the very process of assessing the strength of their support can trigger anxiety and guilt:

ARS R: Sometimes, you know, I say to myself, "I wonder, does my mother believe that I done this crime, or what?" But I know my mother loves me. If she loves me, she won't believe that I done this crime. Because I never lied to my mother before, and I don't intend to lie now. And I told her the truth. Sometimes I wonder, and say to myself, "Does she believe what I tell her, or is it a lie she thinks I'm telling her?" I feel all depressed in different ways, thinking that she don't believe me or she does. That's the way I feel all the time.

ARS Z: I wasn't going along, you know, I was suffering a lot. You know, thinking about what's going to happen with my cases, what my parents were thinking about, if they're going to help me or not. You know, I just kept thinking. . . . things like I'm ashamed of myself, like what am I doing here when I should be out there doing something for myself or for my parents, my family.

For such men, inquiries concerning support can emphasize their dependent situation and their role in creating it.

Men with drug histories seem especially prone to Self-Deactivation and Self-Sentencing crises. They tell us that while they are on the street the necessity of obtaining drugs and the drugs themselves reduce their chance of seeing the implications of their actions:

MHDM 10:   When an addict hits the streets, his mind forgets about jail and all the hard parts. . . . And if I do think I think about, "Oh, yeah, we goofed over there, we done this over there." The good parts. You don't think about the bad parts. He phases this out and goes right back to the needle, not thinking about the consequences. What's going to happen to him. You see, he's thinking of that high, the relief, and then when he comes out, subconsciously he's seeking the heroin to take out all that hatred in him and all that hostility and pressure he built up in jail and all them changes he went through. He finds the release through the needle, you understand?

MHDM 27: Sometimes I had feelings of guilt, but the drugs usually took the guilt away.

It is upon reincarceration that the theme of impotence begins to take shape. As a man begins to register the fact of his reconfinement, it becomes evidence of his past transgressions and lack of control. Confinement produces physical and psychological imbalances for addicts as they face their return to a world without drugs:

MHDM 10: The process in the Tombs, every time I hear that click-click-click of that machine that makes up the tag for ya, I feel sick. I say, "Oh, no, not this shit again—the dope, if I didn't do this, if I didn't do that," and the process starts again with the arrest, you know, the court procedure. It's amazing how the mind will work just to blot it out. And my mother used to say, you know, ". . . how can you forget all these things . . . ," you know, but ya do.

MHDM 3: The hardest part of the bust, man, is when you first get busted, you know, and like if I walked out of jail today, by tonight I would have forgotten it, you see, but when I would start to remember this again is when I got busted again—that's when the tears would come to my eyes, that's when I would be hurt and crying and all upset because I realize—all of it comes back to me then.

With his "free world" chemical quest suspended, a man is left in limbo in the cell to reflect on the roles he played in the past and to extrapolate repeat performances in the future:

MHDM 19: It's like this saying, "You can get but so high, but you can't reach the sky." And eventually you come face to face with all that you've been running away from anyway.

MHDM 25: That's the whole thing in a nutshell. I'm not staying sober. When I'm in the street, then I'm drunk all the time. But when I'm in jail I have all this insight and guilt.

Many alcohol- and drug-dependent men see their fate as inevitable because they view their addiction (which they stipulate) as fully responsible for their past and future conduct:

MHDM 27:   When I started out with my marriage, I had a good job and we lived like two ordinary people. If it hadn't been for the drugs, our lives wouldn't have changed.

MHDM 10:   Like I knew I shouldn't be shooting dope, and I knew I was heading for trouble. And I would say, "Why didn't I stop when I knew it? What kept me going?"

These men regard addiction as the tragic flow that causes their downfall. They see the process in retrospect as a single fatal error or a wrong turn taken at a critical life juncture. Their self-admission of dependency is the base upon which other personal liabilities are reviewed and self-condemnation occurs:

MHDM 30:   And I spent the whole thing on drugs, sixteen hundred dollars. And after the check was gone, it didn't even dawn on me then that what I had did was wrong. I mentioned that I had a woman and three kids too, you know? And it didn't even dawn on me about them. And even to this day, right now, it bothers me every day. I feel very guilty, and it's something that I can't get out of my mind, that I can't run away from. . . . And I try to tell myself, "The money's gone, you've done it, it's over. So just forget it." But I can't forget it. Every time I think of it, my woman comes back in my mind, the kids come back in my mind. The fact that there were so many things that I needed with the money, that I needed to do with the money, so many constructive things that I needed to do, material things that I needed to do. I just threw it away.

ARS L: You start thinking of the way you used to get your money. The way innocent people used to get their feelings hurt, for you, for your habit. For something that you didn't really need, but it was all in your mind, thinking that you did need this, you know? And you start thinking of this type of stuff. You start thinking, "Wow, man, why did I do this? It wasn't necessary. I could have got it some other how." But the harm was done already.

ARS 1:   I mean, I'm ashamed to say that, but it was Christmas, and the Christmas tree was up, and it was Christmas Eve. And the presents were all under the tree. . . . I took everything and sold it, and didn't come back to my house for about two months. . . . That's when I was hooked on drugs.

From the man's jail cell view, he was worthless in the past, he is impotent now, and he faces doom in the future. Detention is a shift that is sufficiently abrupt and disequilibrating to jolt a man into believing that he is just discovering his "real self," that for the first time he is seeing his life as it really is:

MHDM 3: It's a hell of a thing if you come to the realization that you're nobody, or that you're nothing, or that you can never be nobody. And you start thinking that, "OK, I belong here, this is the right place for me. Because if I'm out there I'm liable to hurt somebody or shoot some dope." You really don't want to hurt nobody, and you really don't want to shoot no dope, but you got to do that. You can't do nothing else. I can't go nowhere, I ain't got no job. . . . Just one thing right after another, man. And you get here, and you start thinking it ain't no more good, it's useless. . . . I was trying to get away from me, because what I was thinking was me, and it was the truth. And you don't want to face the truth. Facing the truth is a lot harder than just facing what you want to, you know? I can tell myself I'm happy, I'll be all right. I'm going to be back out, I'm going to shoot some more dope. I'm going to do this, and I'm going to do that. That's bullshit. I know what's going to happen. I knew last time I was here, when they gave me the probation, I was scared stiff to go out, because I knew what was going to happen. I knew what was going to happen. What can I do, man? I can go back home to my people? I'm twenty-three years old now. What would I look like living at home? Pimping on my mother. Plus I've got a son. Little shit like that. If I'm not going to do right, or not able to, then I'm not going to go around that way.

A personal breakdown in this context signifies the stipulation of lack of control over one's free world life and a desire to interrupt the uncontrollable cycle, to provide relief to those who await one's return, or to punish oneself for one's transgressions and their consequences. Here breakdowns fall under our categories signifying psychological bankruptcy, recognition of overwhelming impotence, appeals for support from significant others, and statements of intolerable abandonment.

OPPORTUNITY COSTING

We noted in Chapter 2 that considering oneself a victim is a method of externalizing blame for the unpleasant abruption of being jailed. In addition, perceiving the blame as external can assist in sustaining one's self-image. "External threat tends to make men 'stand up to the occasion,' whereas internal threat has a tendency to undermine man's self-image and resistance, causing it to crumble."[18]

A man may cope with jail by viewing himself as the victim of an ignominious criminal justice system (Self-Victimization), Rancor inspired by the system's intrusion into one's life may escalate as a man computes the opportunity costs of his confinement. If such a man can undermine the credibility of those who judge him, his self-image may be salvaged.

But this strategy has problems. For if incarceration is an overwhelming and irremediable loss of opportunity, the criminal justice system becomes an organization designed to capriciously interfere with the promise of life, and the world a place where the potential fruits of honest intentions are habitually withheld. With this interpretation of confinement a man may develop a "billiard ball self-conception,"[19] and his sense of competence may be severely reduced. Computations of the cost of confinement in terms of lost hypothetical opportunities may change a man's self-image from that of a provider to that of an emasculated victim whose dreams have been arbitrarily shattered. This change may be incorporated into his retrospective and prospective world view. He may experience regret, despair, cynicism, and hopelessness as he views the world from his jail perspective. Moreover, incarceration may have erased any marks he may have made in the past: he may have lost his job, house, automobile, money, and wife while confined, and his chances to recoup his losses may appear slim through cell bars.

On the basis of popularized notions of criminality, most men explain their incarceration in terms of such factors as ethnicity, income, and family background. In an attempt to maintain psychological integrity in the face of an accusing present, they assume the posture of self-defined victims of systematic police harassment. When this perspective, whatever its validity, translates into a world view, the perils of the hopelessness and helplessness it implies become evident:

MHDM 14: My problem, I go out on the streets, right? I only stay out there a week. The same police officer, he bust me four times. This time I didn't do nothing. But every time we go to court, he lies, every time. So he knows they're going to offer me a cop-out, so I take the cop-out.

MHDM 30: Man, for the last year I've been cool. As a matter of fact, if you look at my record, man, the last six arrests, four of them were by the same officer. Four of them by the same officer. So that, right there, man, tells you something. So all of this here I was holding in, unable to do anything about the situation where the individual like this has the power just to snatch me at will.

ARS F: Like I said, I feel that I'm in here for something that I didn't do, and this officer, if I take this year, this officer's going to just laugh at me, you know? When I get out there on the street, he'll arrest me on my block. When I get out there again, he'll see me on the street and say, "This guy's a sucker. I can arrest him for something he didn't do, and he'll take a cop-out. I'll have me a promotion again."

MHDM 19: It was a sense of being defeated at my own purposes, or you know, like even in trying there was no sense in it. Like it was hopeless, because regardless of what you do, the establishment is going to make sure that you don't win anyway. Whether you go about it legally, or fight for it, or what have you.

In order to designate oneself as a victim, total harm must be demonstrated. Here a man interprets his confinement in terms of the devastating impact it has wrought upon his life chances. Although in some instances the retrospective view entails overly pessimistic thinking, and the diagnosis involves externalization of blame, there are clearly cases in which the reaction appears proportionate. And in all cases, the end-of-the-road feelings described are real enough.

MHDM 18: I lost all these opportunities I had of going to college. This was a lucky break for me, because I'm from the ghettos. I never thought that I would go to college. They didn't consider anything, you know? They just threw me back, and I did two more years, you know? I came out and tried, kept trying. Every time I go to get a job, as soon as they find out I've got a record, it's impossible. I lose the job.

RIH 8: And everything I had been working for for the last seven years was completely destroyed, see? So there was nothing left, see? There was nothing to go on for. Everything I had strove to accomplish was obliterated that one Sunday afternoon. And on top of that they were trying to take my kids, and I felt this pain—since they weren't going to do anything for it, I was going to die in jail. So what the hell, I had nothing left, so—what was there left?

MHDM 28: Emptiness. It was like being put into a hole, and slowly the dirt is coming in on you, and there's no way you can push the dirt out. That's the way I saw it. When they brought me upstairs and closed that door behind me, I could just see my dream like it was being pushed out of my head. And slowly as it got past my nose and past my eyes, the dream was gone. . . . And now it's all gone. It's sitting in here and rotting. I'm rotting. I'm actually rotting. For these past days that went by, I could have been out there—like I'm working for Savarin, washing dishes, making $84 a week, and for those days that went by I could have come home and said, "Hey, babe, I made $84 this week, and here's money." Where's my paycheck? Where's the money? So I'm rotting in here. . . . So what do you do? You sit here, and you wait and you rot.

In these instances, breakdowns take the shape of recognition of impotence, advertisement of the intolerable position of being a victim, and statements of hopelessness; here, a Self-Victimization crisis culminates in Self-Deactivation or Self-Sentencing.

DEALING WITH UNCERTAINTY

For most men predictability is necessary for need satisfaction and survival. Jailing can produce an unsettling amount of uncertainty in a man's life, and the unpredictability of abrupt change may result in confusion, distortions of reality testing, withdrawal, apathy, and ultimately, psychological breakdown.

The programmed personal decisions employed on the street to cope with social and survival situations may not be efficacious in the detention setting, and the information necessary to make decisions appropriate to the new situation may not be available. For example, while in the community a man may have found economic power effective in maintaining a waning love relationship. However, economic threats from an obviously unemployed prisoner can hardly have the same impact. In jail, the man may also be forced to ponder the strength of his appeal to the significant other with little feedback from her.

In the ennui of the cell, a man's demand for information and stimulation may become acute and urgent. The chaos of the court detention pen, the confusion of the courtroom, and the pandemonium of tiers and dayrooms present a paradoxical difficulty. A man may experience understimulation and information deprivation in one sense and overstimulation and information overload in another.

Hunt presents the following description of one New York City detention facility:

> Nothing, really, but 800-odd tiny cages for the captives, plus barren, tile-walled day-rooms in which, a few hours a day, they could play cards or watch television, and two gymnasiums in which, once or twice a week, they could get some exercise. Most of the time they spent here, however, was heavy, smothering, useless time, waiting hour after hour, through endless days and interminable weeks and months, for their cases to come up in court.[20]

In such institutions, inmates languish in cells expressing such concerns as, "What's happening with my case?" or "Where's my old lady?" When a court date arrives, the inmate is placed in an institutional van early in the morning and transported to the courthouse. There he is confined in a court detention pen until his case is reached on the court docket. He may wait in the pen for an entire day only to find that he will not see a judge; or he may enter the court only to hear the judge grant a postponement to a prosecutor or to his defense attorney. When the inmate does witness a judicial hearing, the language and purpose of the proceedings may be incomprehensible to him. All this can exacerbate his difficulties in making sense of his environment.

An inmate may attempt to maintain equilibrium in the face of unpredictability by assuming that his information needs will be satisfied in court. However, his day in court may simply confirm his impotence. At this point, his ability to make rational choices is, in theory, essential. He must make decisions related to plea bargaining, the probability of conviction or release, and the dispositional alternatives if he is convicted or his opportunities in the community if he is released. However, his decision-making proficiency may have been seriously impaired by the information overload and deprivation of the jail setting. Studies have shown that increasing the quantity of decision inputs by applying time pressure severely reduces the quality of decision performance and produces schizophrenic responses in normal individuals.[21] Experiments have also suggested that reactions to extreme understimulation are similar to those resulting from overstimulation.[22]

One strategy for dealing with uncertainty and decision demands is denial. For example, a man charged with murder may deny the seriousness of his situation and respond inadequately to feedback on his case and to other matters. By employing self-deception at this juncture, the inmate sets the stage for personal catastrophe. As the reality of his situation impinges increasingly on his senses, he may be subjected to a single massive assault of overpowering forces which shatter his personal equilibrium, rather than a sequence of simpler problems which, if recognized earlier, might have been manageable. For example, it may suddenly dawn on a man that he is very likely to be convicted of murder, that his defense is inadequate, and that his wife has left him at the very point when he is most unequipped to deal with such issues.

The long nights in jail limit activities and mobility. Men endure enforced insularity and fight sleeplessness and worry. Some anxiously pace in their cells or blankly stare at the ceiling from their bunks. Others sleep restlessly. Periodically, guards shuffle up and down the tiers, making their rounds. Sporadic groans and shouts pierce the muffled silence. Morning arrives. A loud metallic clanging resounds throughout the jail. The sound of hundreds of flushing toilets heralds the dawn. The new day in jail begins (as it will end) with the count. The tiers erupt into a world of discordant sounds ricocheting between steel and concrete.

In jail there are no sanctuaries, no quiet corners in which one may find temporary refuge. The man who remains in his cell is the captive of cacophony. He finds concentration important but impossible. Thus Sanctuary Search ensues:

RIH 8: It just added to it. I couldn't think straight. I lost all powers of concentration. Simple things I couldn't think of, little things. I can't recall the exact things—they were insignificant things compared to ordinary circumstances, but I just couldn't concentrate on them and figure them out. My mind was just like a blur. I was like a robot. I would move, move, move, move. And I was like a vegetable more or less. I couldn't do anything. And the things that were right in front of my nose, the answers were right there. I couldn't figure things out, I couldn't concentrate on anything.

MHDM 31:   It feels like it's sitting on a part of my head, and it's blocking my thinking. Holding it back. And I can't distinguish right from wrong, I can't get a hold of the environment that I'm in, or get the realization of what's actually going on. So like in a sense it's almost like I'm on the outside looking in at myself, and I can't get the hang of what's going on.

One of the most compelling concerns voiced by jail inmates relates to the status of their cases. While subjected to the confusing jangle of detention, a man's information needs concerning his case may spiral. Confusion and uncertainty may reach a climax—a court appearance (the finale) verifies the fact that his problem is unsolved:

RIH 4:   See, I'll tell you the truth about that thing. I don't know nothing about what happened in court. They say I pleaded guilty and this and that. My mother was telling me. I asked her what happened—she say I pleaded guilty and everything. I couldn't understand a word they were saying. I don't really think they should have convicted me, you know? I didn't understand a word they were saying. My lawyer was telling me, "Go ahead and say yeah, go ahead and say no." I didn't understand anything. I don't know, it was a bad thing.

MHDM 47:   And like I really don't know the meanings of like different charges. Like this time, I know now, like misdemeanor, felony, this here. And when I go up, and they explain this to me, I don't know, I haven't got a chance to ask the lawyer. All he do is call you, read it off to you, and now you come back. Like I figure like, the other guys that hear the charges, he don't have time to discuss with you, and I'll just have to sit and wait. And by waiting, trying to find out information and figure it out, builds up pressure.

The jail world is filled with noise, uncertainty, and confusion. In this environment, breakdowns may feature declarations of confusion and helplessness and attempts to attain closure when uncertainty appears overwhelming.

EXTERNAL AUDIT AND CONTROL

Gross psychological disturbances are not uncommon responses to abrupt shifts in life conditions. And where psychotic conditions or preconditions already exist, the setting in which even psychologically stable individuals have difficulty separating what is real from what is not can mobilize and aggravate schizophrenic delusions.

"Street voices" may make the transition to jail with their hosts, and some inmates rediscover long-dormant psychotic symptoms in response to their cell environment. These men deal with the shattering impact of jailing by assigning opportunity costing and self-inventory functions to self-created external forces. However, these reviews are even harsher than their nonpsychotic equivalents and are likely to result in Self-Alienation.

Since the voices externalize sources of conflicts, they can be virulently blatant in their self-castigation, self-judgement, and self-condemnation. They direct a man's attention unavoidably and sharply to the hopelessness of his situation, to his worthlessness, to his destructiveness to others, and to the senselessness of his life:

MHDM 12:   Telling me that my mother didn't love me no more and that I was going to stay in jail for the rest of my life. And I was a killer.

MHDM 13:   "You've got nothing worth living for." I felt that way too. Like I say, I have two kids, and I have my woman, and I blew that. And I lost a whole lot of opportunity. I fucked up at school. I had two more years to go in high school, and I blew that. My people was all out for me to make something out of myself. And I fucked up in everything. I just thought there was nothing to live for. I didn't give a fuck if I had nothing to show for myself after twenty-six years.

MHDM 32:   Well, they always say to me "there's only one thing that you could do. Get rid of yourself, and then you don't have to suffer no more, you don't have to make nobody else suffer."

Such delusional statements, in addition to serving the dynamic functions we described in Chapter 4, are responses to the jail setting. They are the psychotic versions of the standard dilemmas facing susceptible men in jail.

NOTES

1. J. Irwin, *The Felon* (Englewood Cliffs, N.J.: Prentice-Hall, 1970), p. 41.
2. M. Hunt, *The Mugging* (New York: Signet, 1972), p. 139.
3. F. Wilderson, "Considerations of Suicidal Trauma in a Detention Facility," in *Jail House Blues: Studies of Suicidal Behavior in Jail and Prison*, ed. B. L. Danto (Orchard Lake, Mich.: Epic, 1973), pp. 121–22.

4. G. M. Sykes, *The Society of Captives: A Study of a Maximum Security Prison* (Princeton, N.J.: Princeton University Press, 1958) p. 77.

5. Irwin, *The Felon*, p. 69.

6. W. B. Miller includes "Toughness," an acute awareness of the need to maintain a manly stance, as a "focal concern" of lower-class males (see "Lower Class Culture as a Generating Milieu of Gang Delinquency," *Journal of Social Issues*, 1958), *14*, pp. 5–19).

7. Irwin, *The Felon*, p. 74.

8. Ibid., pp. 39–40.

9. P. Ferris, "Nikolass Tinbergen Seagull," *New York Times Magazine*, 7 April, 1974, p. 26.

10. J. S. Tyurst, "The Role of Transition States—Including Disaster—in Mental Illness," in *Symposium on Preventive and Social Psychiatry* (Washington, D.C.: Walter Reed Army Institute of Research, 1957), pp. 149–72.

11. K. Lewin, *Field Theory In Social Science*, ed. D. Cartwright (New York: Harper, 1951).

12. E. S. Marks and C. E. Fritz, "Human Reactions in Disaster Situations," unpublished report, National Opinion Research Center, University of Chicago, 1954.

13. F. Hocking, "Extreme Environmental Stress and Its Significance for Psychopathology," *American Journal of Psychotherapy*, 1970, *4*, p. 9.

14. A. Toffler, *Future Shock* (New York: Random House, 1970), p. 374.

15. C. B. Bahnson, "Emotional Reactions to Internally and Externally Derived Threat of Annihilation," in *The Threat Of Impending Disaster*, ed. G. H. Grosser, H. Wechsler, and M. Greenblatt (Cambridge, Mass.: M.I.T. Press, 1964), pp. 251–80.

16. G. Lester and D. Lester, *Suicide: The Gamble with Death* (Englewood Cliffs, N.J.: Prentice-Hall, 1971) p. 44. The notion of "sense of competence" as the foundation of human motivation was originally postulated by Robert White.

17. L. Rapoport, "The State of Crisis: Some Theoretical Considerations," in *Crisis Intervention: Selected Readings*, ed. Howard J. Parad (New York: Family Service Association, 1965), p. 25.

18. Bahnson, "Emotional Reactions," p. 252.

19. D. Matza, *Delinquency and Drift*. (New York: Wiley, 1964).

20. Hunt, *The Mugging*, pp. 141–42.

21. G. Usdansky and J. H. Chapman, "Schizophrenic-like Responses in Normal Subjects under Time Pressure," *J. Abnor. Soc. Psych.*, 1960, *60*, pp. 143–46.

22. C. A. Brownfield, *Isolation: Clinical and Experimental Approaches* (New York: Random House, 1965): D. P. Schultz, *Sensory Restriction: Effects on Behavior* (New York: Academic Press, 1965); P. Solomon, P. E. Leiderman, P. H. Mendelson, J. H. Trumbull, and R. D. Wexler, *Sensory Deprivation* (Cambridge, Mass.: Harvard University, 1961).

7

Another Man's
Poison

A number of statistical studies (including ours) show that relatively few
black inmates break down in confinement, whereas many Latin inmates
find incarceration to be crisis-promoting.[1] Of course, not all black inmates
are equally well prepared to deal with prison pressure, nor are Latin inmates uniformly ill equipped to cope with the problems of confinement.
However, the differences in the breakdown rates of the two groups are
substantial enough to suggest that the free world experience of black and
Latin inmates may be differentially relevant to the problems posed in
penal institutions.

The explanations that have been advanced to account for ethnic differences in prison conduct seem either too limited or too broad. For example, Beto and Claghorn suggest that Latin inmates are prone to break
down because of their unique sense of individual worth and singularity.
These authors see the black inmate as less crisis-prone because "he has
never thought of himself as an individual; he has always been part of a
group."[2] Such observations have a stereotyped, all-or-none character.
More plausible explanations may require closer review of the historical
and sociological background of ethnic subcultures.

Chapter contributed by Robert Johnson.

163

Making It in a Dangerous World

Survival techniques developed in response to slave and caste status include the maintenance of a defensive, self-protectively vigilant posture, coupled with the concealment of feelings (particularly anger and fear) behind a facade of obsequiousness or serenity.[3]

Residues of such concerns and techniques have been described by various students of modern-day lower-class black culture. Grier and Cobbs tell us that "a Black norm has developed—a suspiciousness of one's environment which is necessary for survival,"[4] and similar observations have been made by a number of other authors.[5]

Mood-masking strategies—the norm of "playing it cool"—differ from the strategy of not showing feelings that could earn serious punishment. Whereas the "Uncle Tom" pose was directed at whites and was meant to convey servility or harmlessness, the cool role of the ghetto is directed primarily to peers, and conveys the image of someone who is smooth, easy, and "together," yet hard, cold, and potentially dangerous.[6] But both facades are meant to put people off, to avoid victimization, and to hide self-revealing ("uncool") feelings of anger or fear.

Many observers have dealt with the constant uncertainty under which many urban, lower-income blacks live. Their high-risk settings require a continuous posture of self-defense. The ability to avoid or escape unnecessary and unmanageable situations must be complemented by the readiness to deal with such situations when they arise. "I walk my walk and talk my talk" (I mind my own business) and "shucking and jiving" (talking your way out of trouble) are means of avoiding danger.[7] These strategies require considerable skill. If they are not carried off with aplomb, they may backfire by signaling lameness, weakness, or cowardice.

A ghetto background may give a man a coping edge in confinement because ghetto and prison share a number of important characteristics. For one, both settings are peer-centered, unpredictable and dangerous, and explicitly attuned to the issue of survival. Both settings reward an image of manliness which features traits of strength, forbearance, and courage. And because conventional indices of status and manliness are scarce in both settings, both place a premium on supportive peer groups and on formalized procedures for the stigmatizing of susceptible men. Moreover, in both the ghetto and the prison, survival concerns are reinforced by the presence of social control agents who sometimes pose substantial challenges and threats.

However, the problem of living in a hostile and unpredictable world is more salient in confinement than in the ghetto. As we have observed in Chapter 3, games of peer emasculation are particularly prevalent and insidious in prison, and these games may require more finesse and "cool" than their ghetto counterparts. And in confinement men are more directly subject to official control and to potential abuse by officials than they are in the ghetto. Such conditions are crisis-promotive for some few blacks because their ghetto experience, unlike that of other black inmates, has left them doubtful and afraid, hypersensitive to hints of violence and threat. Prisons amplify such doubts and fears, while making it difficult or impossible to avoid danger.

For self-destructive black inmates, the survival game has been played—and lost—in the free world. These men bring to confinement problems which are products of their traumas. Their attempts to put on a brave facade are unsuccessful because the prevalence of violent behavior in prison makes fear and resentment more difficult to control. Peers, rather than providing support, present a multiple dilemma: their aggressive behavior aggravates tension, and their norms condemn open bids for shelter—bids which arise, in part, because of the threat posed by peers.

Traumatized by experiences of failure and danger in the free world, a small group of susceptible black inmates experience breakdowns in confinement which are among the most extreme we have observed. Prisons are dangerous enough to inspire fear in even the manliest of Manly Men; when prior experiences have forged a link between self-doubt and vulnerability—as is the case for a few black inmates—confined settings can pose excessive threats.

Cells That Close In

Segregation, which is prison within prison, isolates men both from the outside world and from each other. Confinement is absolute and unqualified. A segregated man is very much alone. He is also paralyzed and shut in. The most vulnerable among black inmates tell us that these conditions create substantial personal risk. As they see it, the remoteness of the segregated setting and the helplessness of its inmates invite potential abuse. For some of them, segregation takes on the connotations of a trap:

c 7: It's the fact that they can do what they want to you.

d 34: The officers can beat you up, spit in your room, and all this kind of shit.

msh 5: To be in the maximum security unit was like the end of the line in terms of you being able to control the situation to any degree. . . . you're vulnerable.

GH 4:   Say you're up in segregation, and a riot jumps off the next day. Now the riot is not going to get up on the third floor. But the officers can always slam the door and come up there.

An enhanced sense of risk reflects and reinforces exaggerated survival concerns. In segregation, hypersensitivity to threat is particularly self-defeating because it alerts men to dangers which they can neither combat nor avoid, thus increasing their sense of personal vulnerability. Feeling trapped and resourceless, the inmate becomes a prisoner of terror, a victim of Isolation Panic:

CX 17:   If I started thinking I might get that same feeling that this whole fucking room is just closing in on me. I've seen pictures, spy pictures and old Roman pictures, where you see people trapped and shit and the whole room closes in on them. That's how that feels. . . . It's like solitary there. I didn't like being up there. I wanted to get from out of there. So I was willing to do anything I can to get from out of there. . . . All I know was I wanted out of there, man.

GH 4:   It was like Siberia. An empty gallery. You don't even hear nothing. So I had to get out of there. That was the only thing. I knew if I did this I would get out of there. . . . Right then and there. I couldn't wait until I got out. It had to be done right then and there. I couldn't put it off.

CORNERED AND ALONE

In prison it is difficult or impossible to implement avoidance strategies. Minding your own business presupposes the ability to steer clear of someone else's business. This strategy is of little value if you can't avoid the other person or if another person is trying to mind your business for you. Similarly, "shucking and jiving," essentially a stalling strategy, is of limited value over time. The aim of this strategy is to gracefully remove oneself from a situation and to judiciously avoid it in the future. But in prison you can't "shuck and jive" all day, every day, and expect to get away with it. Such a retreat option is precluded both by the physical structure and by the social norms of prison; it implies weakness and invites trouble but doesn't get you far enough away from potential antagonists.

Thus face-to-face confrontations occur more frequently in prison than on the street. Such confrontations—a variant of our Fate Avoidance syndrome—are particularly troublesome for fearful black inmates because their low self-esteem makes it difficult for them to appear unconcerned, to smooth over the difficulty, or to engineer a face-saving truce. Oversensitive to danger and prone to exaggerate the potential of other men for

violence, frightened black inmates often imbue personal threats with
life-and-death connotations, and perceive their opponents as insurmountable and implacable:

M 62:   They put a note in my cell and say they're going to come and
        kill me, they're going to hang me. So I showed the note to the police and
        told them I didn't know what was going on. Because I had heard that
        they will kill you in the Tombs, people have told me that on the out-
        side . . . . and the day before that they tried to kill another guy. They
        stabbed him with a piece of wire. . . . So nothing couldn't tell me that
        they wasn't going to do the same to me.

D 31:   I'm not a great fighter. I don't like getting into fights. And I
        really hate violence, as it is. And the thought of me getting involved
        with these guys, and no one helping me at all, really shook me up. I got
        an impression of guys really out to get you, you know? . . . the bad
        point of it all was that I didn't have it in my mind that I was going to
        get beat up. I had it in my mind that somebody was actually trying to
        kill me.

Perceptions of this kind—seeing oneself as weak and helpless and the
world as hostile and dangerous—can make it difficult to distinguish between subjectively felt vulnerability and objective danger, and can lead
to delusional fear. Selective perceptions of danger, however, may do
more than substantiate personal fears and feed self-doubt; because potent
threats are frustrating and degrading, they may also create overpowering,
helpless rage.

Engulfed from Within

Attempts to "cool" anger develop initially in response to a sense of one's
helplessness in the face of external threat. However, if the conditions
which intimidate persist, resentment may swell to rage, and this may
make the person fearful of his own feelings. Herbert Hendin suggests that
this is the critical juncture for young black suicides: unable to control
their feelings of anger, they panic and turn their violence against themselves.[8]

Some of the men we interviewed fit Hendin's description. These men
may feel hemmed in by cell walls or aggressive inmates, but what they are
really afraid of is the tension they feel, which threatens to explode and to
invite retaliation. As we have observed in Chapter 4, attempts to suppress
(and thereby escape) destructive urges can lead to the feeling that one is
surrounded by danger, pressures, and threat:

MHDM 4: I begin to have all these negative thoughts about what happened in the past. About officers' harassment, that brutality thing I went through in '69, this guy that shot my brother up and put him in the hospital. . . . I sit on the bed, and these thoughts are hitting me. . . . This is when all this shit starts going through my mind. And, you know, like I may get up to the point where, you know, the least little thing might send me overboard. . . . I feel that I have too much anger and frustration within me, and I feel that sooner or later it has to come out some way. . . . I feel if I let it go too long, then I will become violent, and I don't want to become violent.

Some frightened black inmates doubt their ability to maintain an appearance of calm, and feel that their resentments are readily observable by others. To "play it cool" they are forced to use Self-Escape as a control strategy. When they do, they can neither identify their feelings as their own, in any intimate or personal sense, nor fully accept a paranoid hypothesis. They feel frightened, confused, and helpless, and seek escape from this subjective condition:

M 43: I have no kind of control over myself at all. I get emotional. I get so upset that I just go off. And it's bad enough when your mind is with you. You don't know what you're going to do or what is liable to happen to you. I have no control over myself or my emotions. . . . I sense something happening, but I can't really pinpoint it. It's something there, but I can't really figure out what it is or where it's coming from. Or what is it trying to do to me. But it's there. . . . I just want to go off.

D 26: It's out of my control. It just takes control. . . . it just comes on—wham. Takes its time. I observe it. I guess whatever it is in me just tries to be righteous to itself. Still I have some problem adjusting to myself because I'm afraid of something. And what it is I'm afraid of, I don't know.

These men frequently demand protection for fear of what they might do to others or for fear of what others might do to them. They are therefore placed in isolated settings. But, as we have noted, isolation offers them no protection. It leaves fearful men walled in, feeling more vulnerable than ever.

A Caricature of a World View Come Home to Roost

Suspicious, self-protective vigilance may become excessive, or it may become functionally autonomous.[9] One surrounds oneself with threatening figures to escape not only from external dangers whose source is unknown but also from one's own feelings. In Self-Preservation we see a last line of defense erected by a fragile and flagging self seeking to find a concrete and manageable external enemy or threat. Prison, harboring numerous cues to violence and threat, fits the paranoid model all too well.

The conditions which generate suspicion and fear among self-destructive black inmates in the real world are emphasized in jails and prisons. Although in some ways less dangerous than the rural South or the urban ghetto, prison pressures can be continuous and unavoidable. The routine preoccupations of staff and inmates with power and coercion contribute to an environment permeated with danger. We have already noted (Chapter 3) that riots and violent personal encounters highlight and lend credence to danger cues.

Viewed with self-doubt and a sense of one's own potential for violence, the violence-toned situations of the prison setting are generalized, and feed emerging paranoid suspicions:

A 4: The riot was over, and I was a little nervous after it was over, but if we didn't discuss it so much, it would have just been one of those things. But we kept talking about it every day and every night. That kept penetrating in my mind.

M 1: Everything is said undercurrently. You know, like one dude whispers in another dude's ear. But you know what's happening, you can feel it. You know, like people don't have to open their mouth, you can feel it. . . . It was scaring me to the point that I knew that I had to hurt somebody. You understand? And that's fear.

D 14: I think they were trying to do something to me, that's what I think. And it ain't no joke. See, I'm not scared of one man, but when it comes to all five and ten and twenty, I can't handle them.

Penal institutions, with their dead-end situations and their concern for violence, require documentation for claims of manliness and demand virtuoso performances of the "cool" role. Some men, burdened with self-doubt and denied the support of peers, feel deficient under these conditions. They become afraid because they feel that life's games are played for keeps and that men who are weak and alone are prey to the strong. These men cannot, and probably never will, survive without external support. Prisons—and settings like prisons—present challenges with which such men cannot cope unaided.

Sons and Mothers

Fitzpatrick points out that "the world to a Latin consists of a pattern of intimate personal relationships, and the basic relationships are those of his family. His confidence, his sense of security and identity are perceived in his relationship to . . . his family."[10]

Latin men live in warm, supportive, family-centered worlds.[11] The prominence of the "emotionally supportive, martyrlike but controlling mother and a tyrannical but dependent son" has been noted by various investigators.[12] In this paradigm, "the mother assumes two general attitudes toward her son: she relegates him to a superior role by viewing him as a 'Machito' (a diminutive 'macho'), and she views him as subordinate and defenseless, needing care, protection and sympathy."[13]

The Puerto Rican family can be extremely protective of its men. Volatility, expressivity, and even unseemly emotional symptoms may be accorded family sympathy.[14] During periods of crisis, family members may make a self-conscious effort to find "external causes for [a man's] inability to fulfill the male sex role."[15] Such promiscuous family support and collusion, especially from mothers and wives, may perpetuate a "curious childish quality of adult manhood,"[16] which can conflict with norms (such as the norm of Manliness) prevalent in some non-Latin settings.

Although the Puerto Rican family may create problems with respect to some non-Latin versions of manhood, it is responsive to the demands of its environment. Crises which arise in the Latin world may be successfully reinterpreted or endured with the comforting support of the family. Moreover, the Latin tendency to view ideals—such as love, justice, and loyalty—abstractly rather than operationally may be comforting, though it may lead to flagrantly selective perception. Propositions rarely tested tend to become increasingly troublesome working assumptions. Looking the other way may save face, insure tranquillity, and ward off nagging feelings of insecurity. But it does so only as long as the supports that sustain the fiction are operative.

Incarceration can pose unavoidable tests of the Latin man's world view, his family status, and his self-image. Such tests can prove disturbing and crisis-promotive.

The Crisis of Abandonment

One of the most pressing problems for men in confinement is coming to terms with the interruption of their outside lives. As we have observed in Chapter 6, family concerns often take the forefront in jail, though they may become less salient in prison. For Puerto Ricans, however, family ties are a dominant concern in both settings.

In Chapter 5 we saw that over 40 percent of the Puerto Ricans inmates we interviewed experienced Self-Linking crises. These men see their survival in confinement as a direct corollary of their family ties:

ARS H: I ain't got nobody to go to but them, my mother and my family. What's the sense of me living if they don't want me? If they don't want me around, what can I do? I can't wander the world alone, so why not kill myself?

M 20: I was thinking if a doctor or someone could get my mother to come up here, I could stop this suicide. But if they don't come, I will kill myself, 'cause there's nothing. So I just figure, go ahead and kill myself and I'll be better off.

In explaining suicide attempts, Latin men often tell us that they have found their family lifelines too suddenly and arbitrarily cut off after they have been incarcerated:

ARS 4: My case went to Supreme Court, and my wife didn't appear, my mother didn't appear. They didn't care for me, so what's the sense of me living? . . . So I came back to my cell, and I sat down and started thinking. Tears started running down my eyes. So I said, "Nobody cares for me on the outside, what's the sense of me living?"

E 2: All I wanted was someone to help me out, and that was my mother. And she turned me down. . . . what was the use of me keep on living without nothing to fight for, without any family? Like there was nothing left for me, nothing else to do.

The passage of time guarantees that families will grow away from imprisoned men. Puerto Rican inmates undergoing long sentences deplore this consequence of imprisonment:

D 16: My young brother was just seven years old when I first went to prison. I turn around, and he's in the army now. My younger sister was fifteen, and she's married now and has a son of her own, four years old. And right after me, is nothing. There's nothing really there. So before I knew it I was putting lighter fluid all over the cell, myself. And I set myself on fire.

For the more brittle and dependent Puerto Ricans, the simple fact of separation from family can promote intolerable loneliness or preoccupation with the fragility of family links. It can also undermine internal controls because it removes the sources of personal stability:

I: When you were in here, were you thinking about your brothers and sisters and your mother and how much you missed them?

R 5: Yeah, right. That's what really killed me. It hurt me, it burns me.

It like burns my heart when I think about something like this, it burns my heart. And that's what makes me go explode and go crazy.

ARSH: The only thing, when I be inside this cell eighteen hours doing nothing, and you be thinking about home, you think about what's happening, or somebody come up to visit you and say, "Oh, your mother is sick," or something happened to her, or something like that, your mind get confused, it goes blank, you do anything.

Family covers a wide range of concerns for many Puerto Ricans. The cases which reflect the family's significance most forcefully do not involve real crises but only the remote possibility of a crisis. A Latin man may fear abandonment after one day without contact from loved ones; may feel profound discomfort at the prospect of being alone with thoughts of family; may become morbidly preoccupied with the possibility that harm will befall his family. The frequent statement of suicidal intent in the hypothetical event of the mother's death is forceful testimony to the centrality and ambivalence of Puerto Rican mother-son relationships.

D 2:   Like let's say, for instance, today I got a letter. And if I was in prison, and if I was disgusted like I was before, and I was to get a letter that my mother died, and that's the only thing that I care for, I have made up my mind that this is what I'm going to do. Because after her I won't have nobody to turn to.

Puerto Rican inmates invest so much of themselves in their families that the family becomes the background against which they review their life histories. The family is almost always intimately involved in their personal problems. For them, to be lonely is to be abandoned by family; to doubt one's worth is to question family commitments. To some extent this reflects the actual mechanics of family involvements. A man who fails often does hurt his family. But some Latin men find family connotations in what others tend to see as purely personal dilemmas.

The Pains of Familial Imprisonment

For some Puerto Rican men, incarceration represents the culmination of a history of dependency. This dependency is troublesome because it is one-way. Continued family support and concern after incarceration, particularly from mothers, make some Latin men feel impotent; so much has been and is being done for them while they have brought only shame upon their benefactors:

MSH 54:   I think of the suffering I would put them through. Like they would bail me out, maybe I would jump bail and get arrested for another charge. They would tell me, "it's best for you to stay there and get everything over with," and they would bail me out anyway, you know?

DSH 54:   On Friday I was convicted and sentenced. My family came in the courtroom and was crying. I couldn't stand seeing them suffer for something I'd done.

57:   My mother's the only person. Every time I get arrested, she tries to bail me out. She do that much, whatever she has, she bails me out. She bailed me out two times before, and I didn't go back to court because I was too depressed after coming in and out before then. And everywhere I go, my mother comes and visits, and she starts crying.

Considerable ambivalence can result from the perception of one's dependency. Some men characterize themselves as victims of benevolent tyrants. They question whether the world—especially the prison or jail world—is one for which their family experience has adequately prepared them:

MSH 54:   The idea of me being a man, and I'm still living with them, and I'm like a baby, and still dependent on them for a lot of things, and this kind of gets to me.

D 54:   Well, in the cell you wake up. You think about the good and the bad parts. And your family and what they've done for you. You justify some of the things they did for you, and at the same time you disagree with some of the things because you feel that you fell through for them sometimes because they didn't give you restrictions. You've waken up.

In the extreme, the disjunction between the family and prison can appear stark and unbridgeable, leading to the conviction that one is utterly ill-equipped for survival in confinement:

ARS: Most all of my life I was with my family. We went places and did stuff together. If I was outside with my friends, my brother was with me, or I was with his friends—we always stuck together. I was never too far from home. . . . I just feel that I'm in here, I could be doing time, [but] I'm so used to living with my family, you know? This will make me bug out, and I'm going to try to kill myself, that's how I feel.

Routine Institutional Problems: A Puerto Rican Dilemma

A recurrent concern of some Latin inmates is an intense irritation with the day-to-day abrasions of prison life: slow and censored mail, bad food, "arbitrary" decisions and actions by staff, lack of interpersonal warmth between inmates and staff.

This phenomenon may relate to the issue of family. For one, we infer that some Puerto Rican inmates cannot endure what differs too sharply in prison from that which is available in the Latin family. These Latin inmates may be saying to staff that if their family experience is not replicated, if they are not nurtured unconditionally, all of the time and on demand (as at home), their milieu justifies a tantrumlike explosion:

ARS H: You got any problem or anything about an officer, or if an officer don't want to let me do something, you cut up. . . . when you want something you get it.

z: Like it's their job, I feel it's their job, and it's my privilege to get what I'm supposed to get. And when I don't get it I get excited. If I could get to the person who don't give me what I'm supposed to get or what I need, if I could get to him I'd just break wild on him, you understand?

Aid Seeking may have special connotations for Puerto Ricans. They tend to define themselves as volatile, hot-blooded, and lacking in self-control, and may feel that in asking for medication they are asking for something that will help manage emotions and feelings which they feel are built into their makeup.

10:   I was thinking too much. When they don't give me medication, I think too much.

D 54:   And when I get uptight I bring my attention to an officer or a nurse or somebody, and I tell them I'm uptight, and I ask for help with some medication. And usually sometimes they tell me, "Wait for the doctor" or "You're all right." And they check me with a thing and say I'm all right. But I tell them it's not physical, it's my nerves.

In their interactions with Latin inmates, staff frequently respond in routine fashion to what they see as routine requests. However, the counter-response indicates that these inmates view their demands as nonroutine. For example:

D 54:   He was telling me that I couldn't see a doctor until he came in, and there was nothing wrong with me, to leave him alone. So I told him I was going to do one of my stupid things, and he said, "That's your thing." And I went and did one of my stupid things.

The guard here simply stated the obvious. No medication can be given without the doctor's approval. This answer proves difficult for this Puerto Rican inmate to accept, given his assumption that stated needs must be met. The inmate underscores his premise by threatening to harm himself and by doing so.

It may be argued that there is an element of coercion and revenge in such situations. The inmates see themselves as humiliated and abused, and their actions obviously cause embarrassment to staff, who must explain, if only to themselves, how routine situations are transformed into crises. Staff are also forced to respond, so that the inmate may see himself as having "won." However, Latin men who injure themselves may not be primarily interested in revenge. They may feel that this is the only way to gain some response from their environment.

To the officer, some Latin inmates are ready-made irritants. They shamelessly express unmanly needs. They are a constant source of requests that transcend staff purview. Their requests are illegitimate. A man demanding medication looks as healthy as the next to the officer. A man overly concerned with mail, visits, or assorted personal whims may appear childish. There is no way to communicate that love and nurturance are really at issue.

A 1: They said, "Why did you cut up?" I said I wanted to do a sweet bit. I don't want to say, "Lookee here, I'm lonely, I'm homesick." I'm a man, you know, I'm not a kid. I didn't want them to get on me, so I didn't bring it out.

C 51: And you don't feel wanted. The officer gave it to the other guy. *The officer don't want you.*

Z: Sometimes I think that nobody cares about me. They just throw me in the cell and forget and throw the keys away, you know?

In Puerto Rican culture a request denied is an insult. The culture assumes that a man does not make a request unless his need is real and the person to whom he addresses the request is able and likely to comply,[17] that the act of stretching out an empty hand precludes refusal. Many Latin relationships founder on denials of such requests. Puerto Rican inmates may therefore be outraged when they belittle themselves by making requests and are then further belittled by cavalier refusals to comply. Such inmates pose an unusual problem. They make nonnegotiable demands for care and love—then, if these overtures are rejected, they take a "super-manly" stance and defy their keepers:

D 54: An officer put his finger on me, and I said, "You better leave me alone" and pushed him off. And I said, "I'm just as much a man as you. Because you have a uniform don't mean anything." And he pushed the issue, and he put some handcuffs on, and on impulse I broke a piece of glass and cut myself. And I said, "You better leave me alone," and he said, "OK."

GM 9: I feel hurt, because if you would talk to me not in front of the population and say, "Give me what you've got," I would give it to you. . . . The way he did it, he just walked up to me and put it in his pocket. He didn't even ask me for it or anything. He just put it in his pocket. . . . He was trying to show that he was more a man than I was.

These men vacillate from plaintive requests for special assistance to volatile hypersensitivity to incursions on their integrity. This combination of anger and of requests for warmth, which are reminiscent of family conflicts, confronts staff with alien dilemmas.

Some Latin inmates make an issue out of what guards and other inmates consider the givens (admittedly unpleasant) of prison life. A frequent complaint is that there is no communication with respect to the irritants of confinement. In fact, very specific and accurate information about prison routine is given out daily. Some Puerto Ricans apparently cannot accept the reality of impersonal prison life. For one, they do not see the real issues, such as warmth, to be covered by neutral definitions. Second, they feel that they are not taken seriously, which is probably true, considering the questions they consider compelling. Third, they may see the language problem as one-way, failing to recognize their own contributions to it. They may communicate less clearly than they are able to, then feel slighted when the message is lost. This takes an ironic turn when a man claims not to understand English, and then testifies to having heard crude remarks about himself or his family.

But it is equally true that prison staff do not appreciate the connotations of mail, visits, and medication to many Puerto Ricans. These inmates cannot broach their real needs, their requests for warmth and consideration. And the style of their demands promotes degenerating sequences. The men may push because they feel cornered or abused, and this engenders staff responses that corner and abuse.

Puerto Rican prison conflicts often stem from a need to personalize an impersonal environment; minor encounters become critical junctures: slights of one's manhood, arbitrary tampering with the necessities of life, failures to attend to advertised needs. Virtually every Puerto Rican in crisis will list such issues as open wounds that require nursing. When he tries to sew nursing stripes on his guards he discovers an obdurate (hence malevolent) system.

Some Puerto Ricans do experience problems which are real by prison standards—for example, trouble with other inmates. Puerto Ricans, however, rarely have problems with inmates which are not fraught with family connotations. When guards face inmate conflicts involving Puerto Ricans, their assigned role may be that of parent-surrogates or adjudicators of sibling rivalries.

Often, inmates are resentful of staff not for having intervened in inmate affairs but for *not having intervened* on their behalf. Staff—these inmates feel—have authority. Therefore, injury could not occur without staff consent and it is staff who must be blamed for it.

With an abiding, culturally inbred distrust of impersonal organizations, Puerto Rican inmates engage in futile attempts to hold staff responsible for systemic properties. Failure to take "appropriate" action is seen as lack of personal concern. An aggrieved Puerto Rican inmate may feel personally victimized by the refusal of staff to transcend organizational limits on his behalf. Such treatment suggests an unloving parent. "They" don't act, or don't act equitably, because "they" don't care.

Demands on Prison

Penal institutions present unique problems to many Puerto Rican inmates. Latins often extol the warmth and feeling that characterize their families, and they may wilt in prison because there is little warmth there and because prisons equate feelings with personal weakness. The Manliness Myth hits Puerto Ricans hardest not only because they may bring with them sensitive problems in this area (the "machismo" syndrome), but also because Puerto Ricans are men with roots. The Puerto Rican does not stand alone, while the Manly Man is a rock that thrives on arid soil.

Many Latin inmates feel the need to be nurtured, cared for, accepted. Armed with interpersonal resources, they can endure. Lacking such resources, they may embark on quixotic ventures for symbolic rewards —approaching staff for warmth and understanding at one point, insisting on respect at the next, and often intermingling these seemingly contradictory demands in confusing sequences. In so doing, they may help to create further conditions which they cannot accept.

Some Latin inmates mesh peculiarly badly with the psychology of prisons. Their areas of central concern, dependency and authority, are dimensions around which the prison is purposefully skewed. These men find themselves in a world which encourages dependency (and thereby raises painful questions of personal adequacy) while surrounding its clients with blatantly unsympathetic (and very unlikely) parental surrogates.

Latin inmates often form supportive groups, but in prison such groups do not seem appropriate. These inmates therefore seek out staff instead, those with authority, those who can help.

Seeking out benevolent intermediaries is a tradition ingrained in Puerto Rican culture. The weak and the poor sought out "padrinos," men who would intercede on their behalf in a harsh economic world and who were available for personal consultation and advice.[18] A padrino could never be a fellow sufferer. He had to be secure, warm, and interested in his protégé because of the protégé's inner uniqueness. If a man fumbled, his padrino would carry the ball. Responsibility ultimately rested with the padrino. The man with a padrino had found a mother away from home.

Guards, doctors and psychiatrists are only remotely analogous to padrinos. Nevertheless, it is clear that Latin inmates often approach guards for human services they consider essential; they make unabashed bids for special consideration, and see staff as conduits to psychological ease. They may use breakdowns to punish and embarrass the negligent benefactor, or to secure special benefits from otherwise unresponsive sources. These inmates proclaim that staff have something which they need, which they are entitled to, and which they will go to extremes to secure. If guards fail to meet their expectations, the inmates may feel free to explode with rage and despair.

We have seen that the Puerto Rican family may simultaneously support and suffocate. Those Puerto Ricans who link prison survival with family ties or who seek a family model in prison may find incarceration cold and lonely. Those who feel smothered by the unresponsive prison milieu may develop guilt or be tortured by doubts about their adequacy. Without outside emotional support, such conflicts become unmanageable.

Conclusion

Differences in susceptibility to breakdowns in confinement may partly reflect differences in the degree of fit between the free world experiences of various ethnic groups and the survival model called for in penal institutions. Thus, most black inmates seem to be relatively resilient to the stresses of prisons, because their manly, peer-centered free world posture is compatible with coping strategies that effectively address the prevalent survival requirement of prison, and because many black men are familiar with the threats posed in dangerous, male-centered worlds. Conversely, Latin inmates seem more susceptible to breakdowns in confinement because their family-centered free world experience is incompatible with the roles that must be played to survive in penal institutions.

Because black and Latin men approach confinement with different frames of reference, confinement appears to be a qualitatively different experience for some inmates in these groups. When a few black inmates break down in confinement, their breakdowns reveal special susceptibilities created by specialized past experiences. This group of black inmates breaks down in confinement because penal institutions offer threats to which they have become oversensitive in the ghetto. On the other hand, the breakdowns of Latin inmates pinpoint problems for which prior experiences do not prepare them. These Latin inmates suffer because they cannot survive without family support, or because their dependency needs make it particularly difficult for them to deal with an impersonal environment.

NOTES

1. Marked ethnic differences in rates of self-destructive conduct in both jails and prisons have been consistently reported. Almost invariably, blacks are underrepresented in the self-injury or suicide group. (See T. Allen, "Patterns of Escape and Self-Destructive Behavior in a Correctional Institution," *Corrective Psychiatry and Journal of Social Therapy*, 1969, *15* (2), pp. 50–58; D. L. Beto and J. Claghorn, "Factors Associated with Self-Mutilation within the Texas Department of Correction, *American Journal of Corrections*, 1968, Jan/Feb, pp. 25–27; B. L. Danto "Suicide at Wayne County Jail: 1967–1970," in *Jail House Blues: Studies of Suicidal Behavior in Jail and Prison* ed. B. L. Danto [Orchard Lake, Mich.: Epic, 1973]], pp. 3–16; R. Espera, "Attempted and Committed Suicide in County Jails," in *Jail House Blues*, pp. 27–46; S. Heilig, "Suicide in Jails," in *Jail House Blues*, pp. 47–50; J. Fawcett and E. Marrs, "Suicide at the County Jail," in *Jail House Blues*, pp. 83–106; W. Reiger, "Suicide Attempts in a Federal Prison," *Archives of General Psychiatry*, 1971, *24*, pp. 532–35.) Latin inmates, on the other hand, are overrepresented. (See Beto and Claghorn, "Self-Mutilation"; A. Beigel and H. Russell, "Suicidal Behavior in Jail: Prognostic Considerations," in *Jail House Blues*, pp. 107–117; Fawcett and Marrs, "Suicide at County Jail.") Some of these authors erroneously assume that their findings reflect a disproportionate rate of suicide among incarcerated blacks either because they ignore the high percentage of blacks in the institutional population (Danto) or because they compare institutional rates to outside rates without controlling for age (Espera).

2. Beto and Claghorn, "Self-Mutilation," p. 26.

3. A. Pettigrew, *A Profile of the Negro American* (Princeton, N.J.: Van Nostrand, 1964); H. Finestone, "Cats, Kicks and Color," *Social Problems*, 1957, *5*, pp. 3–14; W. H. Grier and P. Cobbs, *Black Rage* (New York: Basic Books, 1968).

4. Grier and Cobbs, *Black Rage*, p. 172.

5. A. Kardiner, and L. Ovesey, *The Mark of Oppression: Explorations in the Personality of the American Nego* (New York: Norton, 1951); G. Suttles, *The Social Order of the Slum* (Chicago: University of Chicago Press, 1968); E. Baughman, *Black Americans* (New York: Academic Press, 1971; Pettigrew, *Profile of Negro American;* H. R. Cayton, "The Psychology of the Negro under Discrimination, in *Race Prejudice and Discrimination*, ed. A. Rose (New York: Knopf, 1951), pp. 276–90; B. Karon, *The Negro Personality (A Rigorous Investigation of the Effects of Culture)* (New York: Springer, 1958).

6. U. Hannerz, *Soulside* (New York: Columbia University Press, 1969); Suttles, *Social Order of Slum.*

7. Hannerz, *Soulside;* E. Liebow, *Tally's Corner* (Boston: Little, Brown, 1967).

8. H. Hendin, *Black Suicide* (New York: Basic Books, 1969).

9. A. B. Sclare, "Cultural Determinants in the Neurotic Negro, *British Journal of Medical Psychology*, 1953, *26*, pp. 279–88; E. Brody, Social Conflict and Schizophrenic Behavior in Young Adult Negro Males, *Psychiatry*, 1961, *24*, pp. 337–46.

10. J. Fitzpatrick, *Puerto Rican Americans* (Englewood Cliffs, N.J.: Prentice-Hall, 1971), p. 78. See also J. Gillin, "Ethos Components in Modern Latin American Culture," *American Anthropologist*, 1955, *68*(1), pp. 488–500; W. Madsen, "Mexican-Americans and Anglo-Americans: A Comparative Study of Mental Health in Texas," in *Changing Perspectives in Mental Illness*, ed. S. Plog and R. Edgerton (New York: Holt, Rinehart and Winston, 1969, pp. 217–251.

11. Only those aspects of Latin culture reflected in lower-class Puerto Rican culture are considered here, as Puerto Ricans constitute the vast majority of Latin inmates in New York State jails and prisons.

12. L. H. Rogler and A. B. Hollingshead, *Trapped: Families and Schizophrenia* (New York: Wiley, 1965), p. 312. The same observation has been made by others. See K. Wolf, "Growing Up and Its Price in Three Puerto Rican Sub-Cultures," *Psychiatry*, 1952, *15*(4), pp. 401–433; S. Mintz, "An Essay in the Definition of National Culture," in *The Puerto Rican Experience*, ed. F. Cordasco and E. Bricchione (Totowa, N.J.: Rowman and Littlefield, 26-90; O. Lewis, *La Vida* (New York: Vintage Books, 1965); D. Guerrero, "Neurosis and the Mexican Family Structure," *American Journal of Psychiatry*, 1955, *112*, pp. 411–17; R. Fernandez-Marina, E. Maldonado-Sierra, and R. Trent, "Three Basic Themes in Mexican and Puerto Rican Family Values," *Journal of Social Psychology*, 1958, *48*, 167–81.

13. Rogler and Hollingshead, *Trapped*, p. 312.

14. A. J. Rubel, "Concepts of Disease in Mexican-American Culture, *American Anthropologist*, 1960, *62*, pp. 795–814; A. J. Rubel, "The Epidemiology of a Folk Illness: Susto in Hispanic America," *Ethnology*, 1964, *3*, pp. 268–83.

15. Madsen, "Mexican-Americans and Anglo-Americans," p. 239.

16. Mintz, "Definitions of National Culture," p. 75.

17. Fitzpatrick, *Puerto Rican Americans*, p. 82.

18. Fitzpatrick, ibid., p. 91.

8

Women in Crisis

Is the prison experience a more difficult one for women than for men? Are there specific adjustment problems for women in prison? Setting such value questions aside, we might pose the more general query: Is the prison experience a *different* one for women than for men? Since the setting and the routines of prisons for males and prisons for females are similar, the physical deprivations of imprisonment (e.g., loss of liberty, isolation from the community, lack of heterosexual contact) can be assumed to be equivalent in both. The same assumption cannot be made about the "pains of imprisonment" which arise from deprivations. For just as black and Latin males react differently to the stresses of prison because of differences in their backgrounds, so should men and women who are products of different patterns of socialization and cultural expectations.[1] However, the varying extent to which these culturally conditioned needs and adjustments are carried into prison and the varying degree to which an emerging social system embodies them in prison makes it difficult to speak of a homogeneous female inmate "subculture."

The data presented in this chapter were collected from three correctional institutions in New York State in which adult women are incarcerated.[2] The three institutions contained both detention (pretrial) and

Chapter contributed by James G. Fox.

prison (postconviction) facilities. The women described in this chapter represent those women who have failed to evolve solutions to prison pressures.

We have referred in earlier chapters to studies of male prisons which suggest that an inmate social system emerges as a response to the frustrations and deprivations of imprisonment. According to this view, the inmate cannot completely eliminate the pains of imprisonment, but he may obtain relief from such pressures by creating a cohesive social system which provides compensating satisfaction.

The structure and function of the inmate social system has also been related to lower-class cultural concerns.[3] Lower-class male values, such as strength, status, and toughness, are pursued in prison. While the official prison system may not reward these concerns, the inmate social system can provide a group setting in which members may achieve male lower-class versions of status and recognition.

Several studies have examined the women's prison.[4] Most of these have focused on its social organization. The studies, like those of male prisons, suggest that cultural concerns brought into the prison by female inmates evolve into "solutions" to prison-related deprivation. While the values of lower-class women prisoners differ from those of their male counterparts, the *dynamics* involved in the development of an inmate social system would be similar for men and women.

Most studies of women in prison have identified a "family" group as the primary element of the social system.[5] There are several aspects to the prison "kinship" system. On one hand, it expresses individual sexuality through sex roles. On the other, it provides links consonant with those valued among lower-class women outside the prison. Inmates can turn to the family as a resource when interpersonal problems arise. The family, however, does not always alleviate inmates' problem. Problems arising around events tied to the outside world are beyond the kinship group's scope. But the prison famliy does help women to endure the frustrations of imprisonment. According to Giallombardo, the social system of female inmates is an attempt "to resist the destructive effects of imprisonment by creating a substitute universe—a world in which the inmates preserve an identity which is relevant to life outside the prison."[6] Thus, the prison kinship system may help to ward off the depersonalizing effects of confinement.

Close personal relationships are formed within the prison family. Unlike the male inmate who adjusts to prison by prizing isolation or insulation, the female inmate seems to find that her needs are better served by interaction with another inmate. Gagnon and Simon tell us that homosexuality among women in prison "offers protection from the exigencies of the environment and the physical homosexual contacts are less sought for the physical release that they can afford than for the validation of emotional binding and significant relationships."[7]

Ward and Kassebaum assert that

> the kind of experiences women have had prior to prison have ill prepared them
> to cope with pains of imprisonment, which include indefinite loss of affectional
> and interpersonal support, role dispossession, and status degradation. Many
> women who have been supported and protected by parents, husbands, and
> lovers in the free world find in the homosexual affair the answer to the prob-
> lems of adjusting to the lonely and frightening atmosphere of the prison.[8]

Prison relationships often do create a greater problem than they are
intended to solve. They may also foster a level of dependency beyond that
normally arising from inmate-staff relations within the prison. Prolonged
role playing in the inmate family may also produce marked changes in
self-image. Burkhart explains that female inmates sometimes "become
what they pretend to be," including make-believe men.[9]

Giallombardo points to several dimensions which distinguish female
roles in prison. These include women's "acceptability of public expressions of affection displayed toward a member of the same sex. . . . and
perception of a member of the same sex with respect to the popular culture."[10] Because women's primary goals are centered around the family
and homemaking, and because women are "more emotional and dependent; and are more orientated toward the marriage market,"[11] the homosexual social relationships formed by women take on a "calculated" family pattern.

A major concern of women in prison is the status of motherhood. Ward
and Kassebaum assert that imprisonment is more severe for women than
for men because of women's "closer link to the care and upbringing of
children."[12] Women in confinement experience anxiety because confinement separates them from their families and renders them unable to fulfill
the role of motherhood. This separation anxiety does not arise solely from
the physical absence of their children. The continuing care and upbringing of children is a role intricately interwoven with that of motherhood.
Ward and Kassebaum write:

> The confined mother's concern is not only with separation from her children
> but also with how they will be cared for while the husband works; moreover,
> the husband may look for another female to take over the maternal role. The
> distinction between male and female prisoners here is that the father in prison
> is presuming that his wife will, despite economic hardship, continue to play her
> role as mother.[13]

Another frequent observation is that the prison experience infantilizes
many women. The extent and amount of control over the lives of grown
women prisoners forces many of them into a childlike behavioral syndrome.[14]

An important issue regarding the differential coping strategies of male
and female prisoners is tied to an aspect of adjustment which both Sykes[15]

and Giallombardo identify. This is a "loss of security," which is Sykes's characterization for an attack on the Manly self-image. The male focal concern of strength and courage apparently does not transfer to women in prison. Giallombardo posits that "the loss of security evokes quite the same degree of anxiety"[16] for women as for men but seeks its compensation through interpersonal feedback.[17]

The female inmate's ideal self-image may be *a pattern of advertised weakness* rather than the ideal self-image of strength and ability to withstand the frustrations of prison life as dictated by the Manliness Myth. This ideal pattern may selectively reinforce expressions of emotionality rather than of stolidity in periods of crisis.

Lester and Lester[18] and Stengel[19] believe that the suppression of experienced rage may play a role in female suicidal behavior. Stengel suggests that

> women appear to use suicidal acts as appeals to the environment more frequently than men. . . . Women seem more inclined to use the suicidal act as an aggressive and defensive weapon and as a manipulator of relationships than men, probably because other means of exerting pressure . . . are not at their disposal to the same degree as they are to men.[20]

Where open and free expression of aggression by women is sometimes accepted in the free world, the denial of all such expression in prison may produce situations resulting in outbreaks of violence. Where status among female peers is obtained by the ability to fulfill the role of competent mother in the free world, the denial of such status in prison may produce social adjustment difficulties. Where the unrestricted sharing of love, concern, and recognition is commonplace in the free world, a radical inhibition of such expression may result in breakdowns (intentionally or unintentionally) designed to demand minimum standards for prison survival.

Our interviews partially illustrate many of these dilemmas. They suggest that for some women in prison the denial of previously expressed needs and concerns, coupled with the deprivations of imprisonment, may produce responses which are clearly intended to be last-ditch efforts to survive with dignity.

A Self-Definition of Low Frustration Tolerance

One female interviewee told us, "you get to a point where a person is capable of withstanding only so much and after a while even the little bit of defense that you have left is broke down."

In fact, by far the most salient theme revealed in our interviews with women has been that of self-defined vulnerability; the interviewees have reached a point in their institutional experience at which they declare themselves unable to cope with some continuing feature of prison living. As shown in Chapter 5, the over-representation of coping themes, especially Self-Victimization, Isolation Panic, and Sanctuary Search, reveal postures of victimization and helplessness. The inmates tell us that they have become engulfed or overwhelmed by day-to-day frustrations inherent in the prison environment. The referents vary from one inmate to another. Some women consider other inmates to be the source of their anguish, while others point to specific facets of prison existence, such as correctional officers' discretion or regulations and restrictions governing their lives. For still others the difficulty may be a composite of the negative aspects of imprisonment. What remains clear is the consistency with which the interviews illustrate declarations of personal defeat.

One inmate points to her difficulty in relating to correctional officers. She claims that officers are unresponsive to her, and that they force her into tantrums:

I: When are you most tense or frustrated?

BH 5: Like when I ask the officers to do something, and they just stand there and look at me. Like the morning officer, she just stands there and looks at you, and you have to ask her twenty times to do something, and she still stands there. Then you have to wait for the afternoon officer, and she says, "I don't know if I can do it. I have to call so-and-so." And then when she calls and they say no, that's when I get upset. And everything goes flying. And they say I act like a spoiled child. And I'm not acting like a spoiled child, but they don't want to hear it no more.

The same woman posits an endemic system of monitoring and sanctions, which she regards as unsupportable to her:

BH 5: Every little move you make, they are ready to write you up and they are ready to put you in punishment. And if you don't wear a uniform top, they are ready to put you in punishment. Any little error you do at all, they put you in punishment. And that makes me nervous and upset.

An inmate transferred to Matteawan State Hospital as a result of her emotional crises complains of exploitative peers whom she feels unable to tolerate. She describes herself as so constituted that she is left without resources:

M 1: Being in a place with all one sex, there's a lot of tension. There's a lot of lying and stealing and tension going on. Out of all the institutions I've been in, I'm still not used to it. And people are always telling you what to do, and I hate that. This is a major thing that goes on and on and on in Bedford. So I said, "OK, if you don't want to remove me, if you don't want to bend a little for me, then why should I bend for you? Why should I be like a rubber band and stretch, and you've got to be like a chair put together and can't stretch? It don't make sense."

Another woman considers "mental torture" to be the price of confinement. She defines "torture" as over-stimulation, in the form of interpersonal pressures, demands, and impositions:

M 7:   You could take somebody punching you in the jaw. Your jaw swells up and goes away. But when it's mentally on your mind, that's the worst torture that anybody can ever indulge on another man. And this was where it was at. I had a hang-up over my family, not knowing if they was all right. They hadn't wrote me anything. Then I was aggravated by two broads, one in the middle of both of them. One's pulling me this way, and the other's pulling me that way, and I'm saying, "I don't want to be bothered with nothing. Leave me alone." And they wouldn't leave me alone, they were driving me crazy. So I said, "Oh, wow." They made me want to get rid of them too. I wanted to get rid of everybody. And then the people on the corridors, at six o'clock in the morning they're yelling and screaming, they're singing, and you're trying to sleep.

Another inmate similarly complains of the suffocating omnipresence of others:

M 9:   There's always some kind of shit going on. It's nerve-racking. I just want to try and do my time and get out. But if you be good and stay to yourself, then they say goody-goody, or you do this or do that. They always have something no matter what you do. And you try to get away from them so you don't have to fight or go to seg or anything like that. They don't have no feelings for nobody.

A seventy-one-year-old inmate who leaped from a third-story window of the Bedford Hills prison hospital on Christmas Eve catalogs a series of incursions she defines as cumulatively transcending her threshold of tolerability:

BH 6:   From kneeling down I used to have hemorrhages through my nose. And the nurse sent me upstairs for punishment because she said I refused to work. I scrubbed, and it was hard, but I finished it. And then for some other things. They had me high up to clean something, and I couldn't climb anymore. I said, "I'm going to fall down. I feel dizzy." So the nurse came downstairs and said, "If you don't want to do the

work, you're going to learn a lesson." . . . It was 1970, the day before
Christmas Eve. I was sitting on a little stool and doing the ironing because it had to be done before Christmas, and I sang Christmas songs.
An officer played the piano, and I sang. And an officer came over to me
and grabbed me and made me stand up. She said I had to iron standing
up. And then we had a little window open for fresh air. It was stuffy.
And the officer came and said, "Shut the window. And don't open it up
again, or I'll lock you up." And she said, "You'll sing upstairs for Christmas." . . . So I finished my work and went to my room, and I said, "I
can't stand it no more." . . . And then I thought my suffering would be
all over.

The most simplistic division occurs between excess "interpersonal"
stimuli (problems centering on disputes with inmates or officers) and "environmental" irritants (problems centering on the physical makeup of
the prison—e.g., type of confinement or segregation).
One can multiply statements which illustrate the extremity of images
generated by interpersonal conflicts in the institution. Thus, one woman
defines herself as a perennial victim or scapegoat for inmate disputes. She
sees herself as blameless and passive:

BH 2:   I've been in here since '68. It never fails, my name is in everything.
And when something comes up, and I do something to myself, they find
out that I really didn't do it. My name is always in something, and I
really don't do it.

I: Can you describe some of those situations that bother you like that?

BH 2:   They tried to take my girl friend away from me, and then they
went in my room and took my stuff. I can't stand this and never have.

Another woman arrives at a similar inference from a theft incident:

BH 10:   Every day it's something new. This girl in reformatory, her watch
is missing. This other girl had it and put it under another girl's mattress. So the girl was going through my stuff first. She went under the
mattress and busted the watch right there. So they blamed it on me. And
I went in the room and started packing up, and I saw a pin lying there,
and I picked it up and scratched real hard.

Sometimes the focus is on a catalytic issue. One inmate, for instance, attributed her nemesis to a defective haircut and ridicule from peers,
though she later added more substantial contributing concerns:

M 3:   The first time I wanted my hair cut. It was too long for the summer, and I couldn't stand it. I asked if I could get my hair cut, and she said yes. I went to the place and watched the girls cut. Because the inmates do it, and if they don't like somebody they'll do an awful job on it. But I watched, and then when they cut it, this one end side was so much shorter than the other. I looked terrible. So I was all upset. I went back to quarantine, and I took a tin can, and I cut my arm. . . . Well, see the girls laughed after I got my hair cut. The way it was so uneven, they used to go around making fun of me saying it was like a boy's haircut. Just poking fun at me. And then I was upset because I hadn't heard from home.

Interpersonal disputes are by no means limited to peers. One woman, confined for the first time, saw herself as abused by inmates and officers alike. She tells us of the self-defined limits of her tolerability:

BH 17:   Being that this is the first time that I've been locked up, it was very hard for me with the officers and the inmates. Because they push you around. You get pushed by officers and pushed by inmates. And I'm the kind of person that I have a very bad temper, and once I get scolded two or three times, that's about as far as I can go. I can't take too much scolding or too much pushing. At Rikers Island it was constantly this sort of pestering with me.

Another woman talks of accumulating tension resulting from failure of the officers to relate to her as an individual. She perceives a social barrier between herself and the officers which offends her need to be personally recognized:

NYC 9:   Well, a lot of things started piling up. Like I don't generally like to rebuke authority. Because a lot of these officers in here, they can really cause a whole lot of shit, in plain English. If I was in the street, it would drive me to drink, and I don't drink. I try to relate to them as people. You know, I try to pass the badge, even though I know it's there. But I try to come through as people, "Hey, I'm human, you're human." But they come, some of them, they'll come up to you and throw the badge dead in your face. You know, you're not going past this. They think the number that's there stands for God in code. And it drives me up a wall, and I'm trying to relate to them as people, and they got to come at me with this badge shit.

Even these few examples illustrate that the definition of intolerable pressure may focus on minor interactions with others. The complaints also suggest that specific interactions with others may be interpreted in terms of predefined thresholds to make a case for being overwhelmed by malevolent persons and unbearable events.

The following statements relate to feelings arising from specific environmental concerns. Generally, these are concerns generated by facets of prison structure. Many women cite environmental over-control as the primary source of their frustration. However, here again a closer examination reveals prior expectations or feelings which may contribute to define crisis.

A Rikers Island detainee describes her concerns about being made into an object of circumscription and public exhibition:

NYC 1:   I felt like I was being caged in like an animal. They let you out certain times of the day, but the rest of the time you've got to be locked up. You have the cell door closed on you, and you have people looking in on you. You feel like you're under observation or something, and that you're different than everybody else.

Another detainee explains her difficulty in coping with the uncertainty surrounding her case. She describes how a family visit triggered feelings of helplessness and isolation:

NYC 12:   I had a visit in the morning. My mother came. I was asking her to find out about my court case and speak to my lawyer. And she calls him up and gets no answer, or he's never in. I've been in here seven months, and I don't know nothing about my case. I get depressed just sitting here for nothing. After I got the visit from my mother, I started talking about my case, and every time I start talking about my case I get depressed. And this is what brought on my cutting myself, because nobody is find out nothing for me.

Complaints about overwhelming environmental pressures are not necessarily overdetermined or illegitimate. In some instances, the context of universal "wolf-crying" may make staff in a women's prison unresponsive to objective needs. A dramatic instance is provided by a twenty-seven-year-old black woman who, after an apparently conventional appeal for medical attention, was committed to Matteawan State Hospital, where she was eventually diagnosed as having a malignant tumor in the lower portion of her brain. She describes her ordeal as follows:

M 2:   I had pains for three days, and I begged those people to do something for me because I couldn't stand the pains. And they kept giving me the runaround that there was nothing they could do. And I couldn't take it no more. And I said, "If I do something, then they'll do something for me." So I took a jar, and I broke it. I didn't really intend to hurt myself. I was just going to show them blood and make them scared. But I was in so much pain that when I did it, I just went like that. And then they come. I was just crying, and I told them about my neck and my head. . . . I never had that before, the pains started shooting up in my head. Instead of getting better, it got worse. So I went to see the doctor and told him about it. He said put a towel brace on my neck twenty-four hours, and that still didn't help it. It got so bad that I couldn't sleep. I couldn't lay down. By this time I was so exhausted that I was crying. I wanted to sleep. I was begging them that they would do something for me, take me to the hospital or something. But they kept on giving me the runaround. Finally, I told them I couldn't take it no more, they had to help me. I stood there and cried and begged, and I saw I wasn't getting anywhere. I said, "OK," and that's when I went to my room and did that.

Another woman who had received medication for a physical ailment was confronted by the shortcomings of the prison's records system. She describes her discomfort and her inability to postpone the assistance she felt she needed:

BH 13:   I had a very bad backache, and I went to see the doctor, and they gave me some medication for it. They put the medication on a card, but they couldn't find my name. My back was in pain. And they told me they couldn't do anything for me, I had to wait for morning. That set me off, and I broke the window. All these things, like not hearing from home and that, built up, and that one thing, like not finding my card, set me off. They said I had to wait for morning because they couldn't find my card.

For men and women alike, one of the most difficult environments within the prison is solitary confinement. This may mean either segregation, which is used as a form of punishment for violation of an institutional rule, or observation, which is used to temporarily remove an allegedly disturbed or self-destructive inmate from the rest of the prison population. Regardless of the purpose, solitary confinement can pose a special threat to inmates who have limited resources for coping with frustration. Women in crisis report a variety of reactions ranging from situational anxiety to panic and terror. They also tell us of difficulties in managing a flood of emotions seeking immediate release.

One woman explains her reaction as follows:

NYC 9:   It was just that I had been in there for five days. And there's nothing to do. You can't read. And you can't sit down and smoke a cigarette if you want to. Because you're not allowed anything. Because a lot of girls set things on fire. And I happened to be looking out the window, and all of a sudden I just felt, "Bam, what's wrong with you?"

And a lot of tension came down on me. And I usually don't get like that, but just at that particular time everything flooded in. And I went "Damn," and I cracked it. Not thinking that it was a window—it was just something to pound my fist against.

Another inmate describes an accumulation of tension arising, in part, from feeling herself to be a victim of arbitrary punishment. She speaks of being engulfed with thoughts of significant others during her attempts to fill the void of stimuli in her setting:

NYC 1: When I broke out the window in the bing I was in there two days, and the tension was building up then. But I said the bing is for punishment, and I didn't do anything wrong, but they forgot to examine me. A lot of other girls feel the same way about it, and they do the same thing. But they kept me in there another four days, and during those days I was thinking about my girl friend, and that's all there is to do in there, because they don't give you anything to do in there. No books or magazines to read. You just lay around all day. The only thing you do is think. So I was thinking about my girl friend again.

Another woman describes how solitary confinement produced a pre-emptory need for human contact or response:

NYC 18: Down here it's supposed to be solitary confinement, and a lot of girls holler for the officers, but they don't really want anything. So sometimes the officer is tired of walking down there because the girls don't want anything. So sometimes when you're in solitary confinement you have to holler for the officer and keep hollering until she sees that there's something you really want. I felt helpless. As soon as I smashed the light, they came. That's when they came. Not even five minutes later they were there, and they took me out to see the doctor. That's the only way I got some response.

Not all aspects of difficulties in imprisonment can be attributed to a direct conflict between the inmate and the institution. Often, the special handicaps encountered by women in prison serve to aggravate an already difficult adjustment situation. Questioned about the most difficult aspect of imprisonment as such, many women point to feelings of insecurity and thoughts of rejection produced by separation from their children. Thus, one woman talks of painful feelings arising from separation from her son. She tells us of her difficulty in parting from him after a long-awaited visit:

M 3: The hardest thing is that I know I can't be home and that I have a son there. He was up to see me in May and asked me when I was coming home, and I just cried. I didn't know what to say to him. And he said he wanted to stay with me. And that bothered me a lot.

Another woman, who is uninformed of the whereabouts of her infant daughter, speaks of runaway fantasies and culminating panic:

M 6:   Like I stated before, it was Mother's Day, May 14, and I was away from her, and I wanted to be with her because I was her mother. So the tension just built up. In the beginning, I started crying and I got excited, and the next thing I know I had broken a piece of glass and swallowed it, several pieces of it. And I just wanted to escape, that's the whole point. Escape, that was the only thing that came to my mind, escaping. That my baby was dead, over and over and over, I was screaming and telling myself, "She's dead, she's dead, and I'll never see her anymore." That was all I could see, "she's dead. I'll never see her." I didn't want to kill myself. I just wanted to get away, get away from it. I didn't want to face reality, that's the whole point.

One of the most painful problems confronting mothers in prison is the possibility of gradual loss of their children:

NYC 14:   I worry that something might happen to them since I'm not at home. And I worry that when I go back home they might not recognize me as their mother, and they won't want to have nothing to do with me because I was a drug addict or because their mommy was in prison. This is going through my mind. And it's a really bad feeling to be thinking that way.

There is also the feeling of helplessness arising from concern for the welfare of children:

NYC 14:   I had seen my mother-in-law around a day before. And she had told me that the shelter was going to take the kids away from her. And she said she would try not to give them up. She wanted to keep them. And I told her, whatever she did, not to give them up. She promised that she wouldn't. But I knew they had more power than her and that by law they could take them away. And that worried me. So I tried to talk to one of the officers to see if she could help me or send me some-place in the institution that they would help me. But I didn't know where to go for help. But every time I would call to her for help she was busy and she would tell me to wait, but she never came to me. She had 130 girls on the floor, and she said she couldn't help me. I talked to the girls then, but they didn't come up with no answer at all. So I felt it was no use worrying anymore. I'd rather be dead than be in here with all these problems.

Such feelings may escalate to tangible terror, generated by fears about a child's physical safety:

BH 16: Being I had a baby, I could hear the baby crying, and all night long I would hear it, whether I was sleeping or not. And I would get scared. And then I have this feeling that somebody is going to do something to my son. And that's why I always ask her about the baby when she comes. And when she don't come, it scares me. I think if they don't come, something happened to my son, or he's sick.

Women who break down in prison often perceive themselves as pawns of fate, martyrs, pariahs. They see a cold, unresponsive universe, prone to injustice. And they dwell on the arbitrariness and malevolence of Men (and Women) who Persecute or Abandon.

These inmates feel that their sensibilities have been exploited. They diagnose a state of complete extremity in themselves. A switching point is reached for them—a line between the barely tolerable and the unbearable. They feel that too much is demanded of their coping skills and resources.

Their response follows automatically, as they see it. It is dictated, built in, or given. It is pressure *as such* which breaks them down. Their stance is passive, and their hand is forced. They feel backed up against the wall, hemmed in, immobilized.

There are no grays in this picture, no problems in minor key. There are no irritants, inconveniences, frustrations that pass. There is never an option to act until one is pressed to react.

The themes are overwhelming pressure and stipulated weakness. Each inmate sees herself as sensitive and brittle, and each ascribes to others the burden (which they never shoulder) of treating her with extra-special care. Each seems to herself a finely tuned instrument on which malignant forces insist on playing cacophonous tunes—until the delicate strings must break. The stance toward the institution is that of a flower expecting to be crushed.

A Perceived Requirement of Interpersonal Closeness

In Chapter 5 we indicated that our women were overrepresented in the Self-Linking category. When we compare the female sample with the male sample,[21] it becomes apparent that the concern for support from significant others during moments of personal crisis is more commonly found among female prisoners than among male prisoners. This response to personal crisis, unlike most of the other responses involved in our themes, does not seem to vary with the type of confinement setting.[22]

This section describes a variation on the dependency theme, that of a hunger for interpersonal closeness, intimacy, nurturance, and concern. These needs poses built-in problems within such settings as prisons. They originate demands which are hard to satisfy in institutional contexts. The result is accumulated concern over the alleged coldness and uncaring quality of the environment. Women in crisis tend to view themselves as sensitive beings seeking love, trust, and respect, as opposed to the male stance of being locked into combat with the environment. Women in prison suffer not so much from the frustrations of physical deprivation as from an inability to play appropriate and meaningful social roles. They bemoan the absence of demonstrations of care, warmth, concern:

M 1:   You feel like they don't care. They don't care about nothing. The only thing these people do here, is they come here and they get their eight hours of work and out the door they go. And they come the next day, and it's the same thing.

BH 4:   They disrespect feeling. Like you try to be all right. You try to be somebody's friend and be nice to them and give them something they don't have. They take kindness for weakness and abuse you. And then they tell everybody how they can use you. It's terrible. . . . Then you have a lot that show they don't care. The way they talk to you, and the way they treat you. . . . They don't care nothing about you.

An inmate may blame staff and peers for coldness, callousness, manipulativeness, or sadism. Or she may blame herself. Feelings of worthlessness arise if the inmate sees her situation as a product of personal unattractiveness or a lack of social skills:

M 1:   The only thing that comes into my mind when I'll be hurting myself is, "Why can't I be like other people?" I want people to treat me human. And why can't I have friends? Why can't I associate with people? Everyplace I go I never have any friends. When I first go there I have friends, but after everybody gets to know me I don't have friendship no more because I don't have money to buy things and share with them. They're not friends of mine no more. So it's a feeling that I really need someone to love. Someone to care so I can feel human again. Because without this there is nothing. There is no hope for me.

This type of syndrome is frequently compounded by preconfinement experiences. The inmate may feel herself rejected by the world and then snubbed by the institution:

BH 11: I figured my family didn't care because I didn't hear from them that much, so why should I live? My old man wrote to me once when I was there, and that was to tell me he didn't want anything to do with me. That I wasn't no good.

I: What do you mean by saying that life has no meaning? It's not worth living?

BH 11: I thought I didn't have anybody. No one really cared, and they were just being nice to me because they felt sorry for me. That's what my old man told me. That's what he married me off for, to keep me from being sent away to reform school when I was fifteen.

Separation from significant others may evoke feelings of abandonment and betrayal. One woman, whose communication with her family had been interrupted, tells us of deep feelings of rejection:

BH 13: I just wasn't hearing from home. And I got the impression that just because I wasn't there anymore, she didn't care. It's like saying they don't have the time or they don't care anymore.

Confinement may amplify the processing of sorrow when a loved one is lost. Inmates may feel unable to manage both grief and their reaction to an (allegedly) unconcerned prison staff. The prison's resources are not always available when the women experience their greatest need. The professional staff, whose skills may enable them to respond to inmates during moments of personal crisis, are not generally present during the evening or early morning hours when inmates are most likely to reflect on their situation. Even during hours when trained staff are available, they are often so overburdened with administrative tasks that their services have to be rationed.

Most women in prison describe attempts to establish rapport with at least one other person so as to communicate on a feeling level. Usually the selected person is another inmate who experiences parallel needs for warmth, understanding, and intimacy. The similarity of needs and experiences, coupled with the almost constant availability of companionship, may promote a deep personal relationship.

One woman discusses the supportive role another inmate can play during moments of depression. She adds that prison policy against close interpersonal contact may produce feelings of impotence or anger:

BH 13: If you have a close friend in the prison, and you get very depressed, like I might want to break out a window, and I might warn her I feel this way, and I might break out a window if I don't talk to somebody. That friend might be the only person I want to talk to, and they say I can't talk to her, I have to talk to somebody else. And they can't understand that since I can't talk to who I want to, I'm going to go off and break a window.

Several factors may operate to inhibit another inmate's responsiveness. For one, the other person may be too wrapped up in her own problems. For another, the institution prohibits physical contact which, although not requisite for intimacy, serves as a vehicle of inmate-inmate expressions of warmth and compassion. Still another inhibiting factor is the absence of the element of trust necessary to engage in meaningful interaction. In many cases, women are fearful of being exploited in their "weaknesses." They sometimes feel that they must choose between exploitation and indifference:

M 1:   It builds up in me, because I've been wanting to tell somebody so bad, somebody that I can trust. But I can't find anyone to trust, anyone that will lend me a helping hand. I try to talk to the girls, but they don't listen to me.

When an inmate invests most of her emotional needs in one other person, she may discover that she is virtually helpless when confronted with the possibility of a separation. Another reaction may emerge in degenerating relationships. Many times the emotionally vested contact becomes so involved that one woman may react to the frustrations and pressures of the other. An inmate illustrates how an attempt to share her concerns led to reciprocal self-destructive behavior:

BH 16:   Me and her were close. We were like mother and daughter. She had been depressed earlier, and that's when I got depressed. But when I got depressed I started thinking about home. And I got to thinking that nobody cared. And so I did it. And when she saw it she went and did it too. She was ready because she already had the attitude.

The search for a friend becomes a difficult task given the prescribed interpersonal distances of an institutional social system. As a result, women socialized into self-assessments based on themes of love, trust, and affection come to feel insecure and unfulfilled. And from their unrewarded search for love and trust, they may conclude that they are unworthy and worthless:

NYC 14:   Yeah, I was looking all around trying to figure out a way which I could get rid of myself. I was trying to help myself, but no one would help me. It seems that nobody really cares. And being that I never had a mother and a father when I was young, and my grandmother was the one that brought me up, I never had anyone to help me. I was always on my own. So sometimes I feel real uptight, because I see I never really had a person that could help me when I need help. And this gets me into a bag.

Confinement for women may serve to elicit dependency needs which the institution is not able to satisfy. In many cases, women possessing strong needs for reassurance, respect, and significant human interaction may conclude that they are incapable either of maintaining an already existing relationship or of developing new outlets for their needs. In their efforts to communicate demands for recognition and love, they may turn against themselves with disdain or self-hate.

Management of Feelings

There is little basis for asserting that female inmates are different from other persons under pressure. But what women in prison may illustrate is a process by which accumulated pressure and tension are released through a self-sanctioned outburst. This Self-Release process is described in detail by the women we interviewed. They posit a sequence in which they experience a "building up" of tension which they relate to their situation in a general manner. A stage follows in which these women dwell on a specific condition or event affecting their lives. Finally, they feel overwhelmed and entitled to seek some form of release. One inmate thus attributes tantrums to a series of casual triggering remarks:

M 4:   Well, it can start with a very small thing. Someone can say, "Go to hell." And I'll say, "Why did you say, 'go to hell'?" And she'll say, "I was only kidding." And then I wonder, "Was she kidding or not?" And it builds up, and it just doesn't set right. But I'll just let it ride, and it builds up and builds up. And I have to let loose and let it all out.

It is difficult to locate the exact point at which tension reaches its explosion point. One woman views herself as unable to maintain control over her behavior once a given quantum of tension is permitted to accumulate:

NYC 1:   At times I'll try to lay down, and I can't sleep, and I'll be laying there, and everything will be building up. It takes a while though before anything happens. If someone talks to me first, then I might come out of it. . . . But if tension really builds up, then I just start swinging. When it gets to a point.

Another woman describes attempts to block out painful thoughts during a period in isolation. She tells us of being finally reconciled to overwhelming tension:

BH 17:   You would just be in that room all by yourself. And there's nothing in there but a bed, a toilet, and a sink. You'd have nothing else to occupy your mind. You can't look out the window, you can't go out in the hall, nothing. You're just thinking about the same problem. You get to thinking about it, and then it takes over your whole body. There's no way you can sit there and relax unless you were really doped up.

Many women place blame on the unavailability of significant others with whom they can resolve their feelings and defuse their tensions:

M 8:   I would say the only time that I become really, really depressed is when I get into my cell where I can think. This is when the problem starts. And when you're laying down in bed, your problem starts. When I'm by myself in my cell, there's no way out because there's no one to turn to.

I: Then you can't block it out? It keeps coming in?

M 8:   It keeps coming in. Now if I had someone that I could discuss it with daily or whatever, or three times a week, maybe I wouldn't have such a problem. I could discuss the problem and once and for all get it out of me. But when it's shut up inside of me with no way of getting it out, then what am I supposed to do?

It appears that once the female inmate defines herself as under pressure, she sees herself as in need of meaningful interaction with someone who can demonstrate empathy and compassion with respect to her problems. The unavailability of this type of contact is regarded as a precipitant of breakdown:

M 2:   The best thing when I get like that is, don't let me be by myself because I start thinking about it more and more. And it gets worse. But when I get like that, and if I have people around me, to talk to me, change the subject, keep my mind occupied on something else, I'm much better off. If I stay by myself—no.

I: What happens when you or somebody else like that stays by themselves?

M 2:   They get worse and think about it and magnify it. It's much worse. You ask yourself, "How could I do it?" This is what I was saying. I can't do it. There ain't no way. You're thinking all kinds of things. The only thing that kept me going was that I said, "If I do anything foolish, kill myself, then my son won't have a mother."

Women in crisis may describe themselves as un-self-sufficient, and thus may ascribe their breakdowns to failures of the milieu to provide vital problem-sharing services:

M 8: Right, you deal with it yourself. Because it seemed like no one could relate to me. Everyone was being objective rather than subjective. And from that there was no one to talk to. So having no one to talk to, I had no way out.

Efforts at achieving reduction of tension by crying or screaming may occur, but these tend to be viewed as ineffective. Such expressions are seen instead as signaling a state of helplessness and a proposed abandonment to despair. They announce the point at which the inmate voices her resourcelessness and loses control over her emotions.

Self-Sanctioned Catharsis

When women in prison break down, they tend to do so explosively, with a considerable display of randomly aggressive behavior. It is as if these inmates carry about ready-made tantrums which are set to "go off" whenever they encounter frustrating situations they define as intolerable. When the "fuse" is ignited, the surrounding environment may be the target of uncontrolled, abandoned, promiscuously destructive acts:

M 4: I feel tight, and a lot of times I feel like I could just explode. One night I got so upset for coming here and having her come here that it all piled up. I went into the kitchen on the ward and threw the chair out. The officer asked me what was wrong. I said, "Nothing. If you want to come near me, go ahead." I just kept throwing tables and chairs and pots and pans.

Such reactions may be viewed as expressive behavior, considering the extent of emotional involvement in them. Only rarely, however, are they directed against other persons. The behavior involves destroying objects, such as personal property, windows, and furniture. The sequence may continue until, in despair, the inmate turns her rage against herself.

The quick, sharp response relates to the intensity of feeling invested in the behavior. The initial release may have a catalytic effect which further releases emotion. Under these conditions aggressive/expressive behavior may actually serve to heighten frustration and despair.

What is illustrated appears to be an inability or unwillingness to react to frustration with less drastic and active responses. Once a point of susceptibility is defined, the women appear to demand instant reduction of pressures. In addition, they appear to assume that "acting-out" behavior is their only appropriate option, that strong feelings must be translated into action or full expression:

M 7:   It feels good when you get it off, it do. Because I tore up some windows because I was frustrated. I was so aggravated, and everything seemed like it—I just wanted to break something, I had to hit something. But I tried to control myself from hitting another human being. So I mopped the floor in the morning. I took my bucket, went to the bathroom and got water, and proceeded to go up to the corridor and to all the glass windows and tore them all out. I felt so good, because I was getting this thing off. Something has to come out, there has to be some kind of release. If you have no release, it's not good.

Once feelings are expressed, the matter may be viewed as closed, if not resolved:

M 7:   And I just sat there, and tears started coming to my eyes, and I started crying because I was so angry and frustrated. Because I was aggravated from the woman. And she didn't make matters any better for other things that was on my mind. And it was just like I said, "Well, I just don't give a damn." And then I just got mad and took the bottle and threw it up against the wall. And then after I cut myself, I was sitting on the floor near the door and they came running. She said, "What's wrong with you?" And she saw the glass and she said, "Open the door." She tried to talk to me. I just didn't even want to rap with her. I didn't want to say nothing to her. And they finally brought me outside, and I just went through a thing where I didn't want to be bothered.

One factor which sometimes enters the picture is a final precipitating event which activates the aggressive or explosive response. This precipitant may arise from virtually any situation within the prison which is related to the inmate's frustrations. The large number of stimuli which can finally trigger aggressive and subsequent self-destructive responses are illustrated in numerous interview excerpts. The following is a simple sequence:

BH 18:   And I went to the game room. And two officers came and said I was locked, and I asked them for what, and they didn't tell me. I was very angry, and I got excited. So they finally told me that I had been written up by the supervisor for kissing this girl. And that really hurt me. Usually they tell you if they're going to write you up or something, and I didn't think it was right that they let me go to work, and then when I was going to recreation they wanted to lock me. If she was there, I probably would have hit her. But instead I broke out the windows.

Sometimes, several precipitants may trigger a series of tantrum episodes:

BH 5: Now look at me, I'm upset. And she tried to take me to my room. And I said, "Don't touch me. If you put your hands on me, I'm going to hit you." So she said, "All right," and got me some medication. I went to my room. I hit an officer in the face with some food. I threw my tray and broke it, and I tried cutting myself. . . . So she put me under observation for about two weeks. I asked the doctor if I could come out, because I felt better. They weren't giving me any medication, so why should I stay in observation? So they let me out, and I still had time to do, so I got upset and went off again and busted up my room.

NYC 10: Like, I asked the doctors to let me out of the hospital because, like, I had no habit and I wasn't sick. And they kept me up there for two weeks, and they wouldn't let me out. So I got so uptight about it, I took the chairs and busted out all the glasses and cut my wrists. So they took me to the bing. And, like, in the bing I started thinking about I thought it was stupid, and it just made me madder. So I broke out the windows in there, and I cut my wrists. And, like, I stayed in the bing for around a week, and they had came and told me that I was coming out. The captain had came and told me that I was coming out. But they said they couldn't let me out because I had to see a psychiatrist. . . . So they told me I had to stay in there till I seen one, and I got mad again, and I busted out the windows and cut up my arm.

The self-definitions of episodes like these often feature self-images of abandon and loss of control. The acts are viewed as natural and unavoidable:

M 5: Tearing up everything, that's all. Sometimes this would be an impulse, sometimes I feel it, sometimes I don't. Like one day I cut my wrists, and I didn't even know I did it. I didn't even know I had did it. . . . It was impulses. Most things I do are because of impulses. I never think about what I'm doing.

M 4: Sometimes I don't realize I'm doing it until after it's done. . . . It's a fast impulse at the last minute. It will come to me, and I'll throw something, and the next thing I know I find myself throwing a lot of things.

The key theme in the definition of these acts is the self-image of irrationality, impulsivity, and the built-in necessity of total emotional expression. This self-characterization is more than a diagnosis. It is a norm. And it is this legitimation of expressiveness which constitutes the sharpest difference between the subcultures of male and female inmates. As one interviewee put it:

M 7:   A woman is very, how would I say, you know how they made tor-
nadoes, storms, boats and everything they name after a woman. A
woman is violent. A woman inside I think is more violent than a man.
And with a man, he's going to try to be structured, not to go off on
everybody, just one definite thing. With a woman, she wants everything
out of her way, everything goes, there's no mother, no father, no sister.
Everything goes. And I think this is because a woman is highly emotional. . . . I'll tell you what it is. Maybe too it's come to a time when
they're supposed to recognize women as being able to do anything out
there. For the woman that has so many inner feelings that have been
kept in for so long, from generation to generation, has kept them down,
that you never really knew how furious a woman could be. It's just like
if they had a war, and they sent women, I believe women would kill
faster than men. . . . And if they think they're right, you know what I
mean, if I think I'm right, then she'll fight for it, no matter what it is, no
matter who goes down with her, she's going to fight. Where a man might
think rational about it, and say, "Well, it doesn't make much sense for
me to mess up everybody, I'll just get this son of a bitch right here," a
woman doesn't care.

We stated in Chapter 5 that Self-Release is more prominent in prison
among women. Given the type of adjustments required for long-term confinement, it is not surprising that prison is more likely than detention
to produce Self-Release. What is surprising is that this particular response
is far more frequent among women. The data reveal what when women
succumb to pressure in prison they tend to do so explosively.[23]

We have seen several other themes revealed in our interviews. We
have surfaced resentment that is harbored, nurtured, and documented.
We have seen such resentment characterized as disappointment with a
callous world. We have seen a peremptory, unqualified demand for love,
with one's survival as the only weapon.

Though breakdowns may be a reaction to environmental unresponsiveness, the process is not blackmail, nor is it directly manipulative. When
women with pent-up feelings explode, they do so more in protest than in
vengefulness. They permit themselves to explode where they would not
permit themselves to be aggressive or counteraggressive. In fact, they con-
fer on themselves the duty of translating feelings into expressive uncontrolled action. This promiscuous violence is both frustration-centered and
nonaggressive. It says, "Look what you have driven me to" and "See how
much I resent you," while simultaneously declaring, "I am helpless" and
"I'm at the end of my rope."

It is probable that in this context prison is more injurious to women
than to men. Whereas men can defend themselves against pain through
variations on their manly stance, women have no such recourse. The cop-

ing tools of mature women—their interpersonal concerns and skills—presuppose security and responsiveness in others. Where these requisites do not exist, there is a forced regression to earlier options. Thus, prison may promote among its women inmates extreme and primitive modes of adaptation which mirror their complete resourcelessness.

NOTES

1. Differential patterns of socialization have been generously documented in the literature. See for example: T. Cadè, *The Black Woman*, New York: Signet, 1970; P. Chesler, *Women and Madness*, New York: Avon, 1972; J. Dollard, *Caste and Class in a Southern Town*, New Haven: Yale Univ. Press, 1937; H. Gans, *The Urban Villagers*, Glencoe: The Free Press, 1962; H. Hacker, "Women as a Minority Group," *Social Forces*, XXX (October 1959), pp. 60–69; M. Horner, et al., *The Feminine Personality in Conflict*, Belmont, Calif.: Brooks-Cole, 1970; V. Klein, *The Feminine Character*, Chicago: Univ. of Chicago Press, 1972; M. Komarovsky, "Functional Analysis of Sex Roles," *American Sociological Review* (August 1950); E. Maccoby, ed., *The Development of Sex Differences*, Stanford: Stanford Univ. Press, 1966; J. Lifton, ed., *The Woman in America*, Boston: Beacon Press, 1967; M. Mead, *Male and Female*, New York: Morrow, 1943; M. Mead, *Sex and Temperament in Three Primitive Societies*, New York: Peter Smith, 1935; E. Neisser, *Mothers and Daughters*, New York: Harper and Row, 1967; T. Parsons, "Age and Sex in the Social Structure of the United States," in *Essays in Sociological Theory*, Glencoe: The Free Press, 1949; L. Rainwater, R. Coleman, and G. Handel, *Workingman's Wife*, New York: Oceana, 1959; G. Seward, *Sex and the Social Order*, New York: McGraw-Hill, 1946; W. I. Thomas, *Sex and Society*, Chicago: Univ. of Chicago Press, 1906.

2. These institutions were: the New York State Correctional Facility for Women at Bedford Hills; the New York City Correctional Institution for Women at Riker's Island; and the Women's Division of Matteawan State Hospital at Beacon. During 1972, incarcerated female offenders comprised 3.0 percent of the total New York State incarcerated offender population (*Characteristics of Inmates under Custody*, Department of Correctional Services, Office of Program Planning, Evaluation, and Research, Vol. VIII, No. 3), and 5.3 percent of the total New York City incarcerated offender population (*Highlights, 1972*, New York City Department of Corrections).

The New York State Correctional Facility for Women at Bedford Hills had an average daily census of 297 women for the period of May 1, 1971 to June 31, 1972. Of these 297 women, 239 were serving prison sentences and 58 were serving reformatory sentences which are generally given to youthful offenders. The New York City Correctional Institution for Women at Riker's Island had an average daily census of 679 women for 1972. Of these 678 women, 298 were serving sentences under the New York City Penal Code and 380 were in detention awaiting various stages of disposition.

3. See: W. B. Miller, "Lower Class Culture as a Generating Milieu of Gang Delinquency," *Journal of Social Issues*, 14 (1958), pp. 5–19; O. Lewis, *La Vida*, New York: Vintage Books, 1965; W. Whyte, *Street Corner Society*, Chicago: Univ. of Chicago Press, 1955.

4. See: K. Burkhart, *Women in Prison*, Garden City, New York: Doubleday, 1973; R. Giallombardo, *Society of Women: A Study of a Woman's Prison*, New York: Wiley, 1966; E. Heffernan, *Making It in Prison: The Square, the Cool, and the Life*, New York: Wiley, 1972; D. Ward and G. Kassebaum, *Women's Prison: Sex and Social Structure*, Chicago: Aldine, 1965.

For prisoners' perspectives see: B. Deming, *Prison Notes*, Boston: Beacon Press, 1966; E. Flynn, *The Alderson Story: My Life as a Political Prisoner*, New York: International Publishers, 1963.

5. Giallombardo, op. cit.; Heffernan, op. cit.; Ward and Kassebaum, op. cit., M. Nagle, "Play Families," unpublished master's dissertation, Catholic University of America, 1958; L. Selling, "The Pseudo-Family," *American Journal of Sociology*, 1931, *37*, pp. 247–53; L. Le Shanna, "Family Participation: Functional Response of Incarcerated Females," unpublished master's thesis, Bowling Green University, 1960; S. Halleck and M. Hersko, "Homosexual Behavior in a Correctional Institution for Adolescent Girls," *American Journal of Orthopsychiatry*, 1962, *32*, pp. 911–17; S. Kosofsky and A. Ellis, "Illegal Communications among Institutionalized Female Delinquents," *Journal of Social Psychology*, 1958, *48*, pp. 155–60; A. Taylor, "The Significance of 'Darls' or Special Relationships among Borstal Girls," *British Journal of Criminology*, 1965, *5*, pp. 406–18; A. Taylor, "A Search among Borstal Girls for the Psychological and Social Significance of Their Tattoos," *British Journal of Criminology*, 1968, *8*, pp. 170–85.

6. Giallombardo, op. cit., p. 103.

7. J. Gagnon and W. Simon, "The Social Meaning of Prison Homosexuality," *Federal Probation*, 1968, *23*, p. 25. See also W. Simon and J. Gagnon, "Homosexuality: The Formulation of a Sociological Perspective," *Journal of Health and Social Behavior*, 1967, *8*, pp. 177–85. It is unlikely that the adaptive styles of women prisoners arise primarily from sexual deprivation. The deprivation of emotionally satisfying relations, within and outside of prison, is more likely to play a major role in the type of prison adjustment made by women. The concern for closeness and intimacy among women is largely a result of socialization into sex roles and expectations which, unlike those of most men, are generally satisfied through a community of stable and predictable relationships.

8. Ward and Kassebaum, op. cit., p. 74.

9. Burkhart, op. cit., p. 371.

10. Giallombardo, op. cit., p. 17.

11. Ibid., p. 15.

12. Ward and Kassebaum, op. cit., p. 14.

13. Ibid., p. 15.

14. Burkhart, op. cit., p. 129.

15. G. Sykes, *The Society of Captives: A Study of a Maximum Security Prison* (Princeton, N.J.: Princeton University Press, 1958).

16. Giallombardo, op. cit., p. 99.

17. Ibid., p. 102.

18. G. Lester and D. Lester, *Suicide: The Gamble with Death* (Englewood Cliffs, N.J.: Prentice-Hall, 1971), especially pp. 47, 71, 92. See also H. Hendin, *Black Suicide* (New York: Harper and Row, 1969), especially chap. 5.

19. E. Stengel, *Suicide and Attempted Suicide* (Middlesex, England: Penguin Books, 1964).

20. Ibid., p. 135.

21. With the exception of the Puerto Rican males discussed in Chapter 7, women, more than men, appear to draw on existing ties in an attempt to deal with personal crisis.

22. The data presented in Table 5.10 indicate that women demonstrating the Self-Linking theme are as likely to do so in jail as in prison. Setting appears to have little influence on this particular response to personal crisis.

23. The data presented in Table 5.9 reveal that women demonstrate the Self-Release theme far more frequently than men. In addition, the Self-Release responses shown by our sample of women appear to be unique to women prisoners. That is, none of our male Self-Release responses display the degree of explosiveness or the promiscuous violence that is associated with the female sample.

III
Psychological Autopsies

The approach we have employed thus far has relied on a classification which permits a survey view, highlighting features of the terrain and tracing links among them. But except for occasional glimpses furnished by a turn of phrase or a chronological vignette, it has left us unacquainted with the individual man in crisis.

Nor has our approach permitted us to trace the sequences of events and experiences—the causal chains—that produce the crises we describe. We know that for some persons—at some junctures—the lines of survival are drawn. Some of these persons pass through the gates of prison bearing the seeds of self-destruction within them. Others bend and break under the threats and pressures posed by situations that arise in prison. Demands too heavy for even the strongest to bear may arise in the lives of inmates who are far from strong.

Can we trace the concrete relationship between susceptibility and pressure, between conduct and context? How do guards and cellmates, rules and routines, enter into a man's decline? What roles do peer mores and staff habits play? How are links in the destructive chain forged?

We shall address these questions through a review in depth of four prison suicides. Such tragedies pose the most obvious practical problems and the most urgent existential questions. For these are sequences we would all give anything to undo. We must understand these lives better now because we did not understand them well enough at a time when our understanding could have made possible helping relationships and ameliorative acts. The urgency of this realization, shared by custodial officers and inmates alike, is reflected in these pages.

The approach we have taken is in the tradition of Allport, of Murray, and—most particularly—of R. W. White.[1] Our procedures adapt the work of Shneidman and his colleagues, who originated the "psychological autopsy" of suicides.[2] This device was used by Los Angeles Suicide Teams "to clarify . . . questionable suicide cases . . . by obtaining a great deal of information from a number of persons (spouse, friends, etc.) who knew the victim, and then reconstructing the life-style of the deceased and extrapolating over the last days of his life."[3] A more immediate precursor of our effort is the procedure employed by the New York Board of Corrections, which interviews institutional acquaintances of detainees who have committed suicide in city facilities.

Our approach is probably different from that of suicidologists (and more in line with White's) in its emphasis on the sequence or development of difficulties. Whereas the Los Angeles autopsies focus on the degree to which men intend their death (lethality of motive), and the New York inquiries seek clues to carelessness, we search for psychological changes and turning points.[4] As is our practice elsewhere in this book, we seek information about the core concerns of our subjects. Our partners in this search are a large group of bereaved men who watched helplessly as the data took increasingly tragic turns. It is through the sensitive, retrospective eyes of these informants that we try to recreate the nightmarish worlds of our subjects.

In terms of our typology, all four cases exemplify the familiar paranoid syndrome—Self-Escape turning into Self-Preservation. The evolution of the syndrome, however, differs markedly for each of the four men. Though three of the suicides were blacks, they were three very different individuals. At the time of their arrival in prison, the four men differed markedly in their outlooks, their resources, their susceptibilities, their modes of adjustment, and their stance toward incarceration. They differed too, in the extent to which they had managed, or failed to manage, outside. The precipitants as well as the motives of breakdown also differ in each of the four cases.

There are commonalities, to be sure. In all four cases, we will see self-insulation, swinging moods, and ultimately, bizarre behavior. We see worried, involved staff. We also see the limited, inadequate, and at times counterproductive character of the available options for help.

Though we will explore the import of these facts in our last chapter, we must disclaim one dangerous inference. Our stories are history. We know much more than anyone could have known before these deaths took place. Suicides are infrequent events. Some fifty men in our sample had experienced crises of Self-Preservation; countless more similarly afflicted inmates roam our prison yards or huddle in cells, fearful of their lives. Every symptom of our suicides has been replicated in hundreds of other men. No one could have known—nor can anyone be blamed for not knowing—what we know now. Though the tragic climaxes will seem inevitable in the telling, this is so only because they have happened—not because they had to happen. The moral is not the scapegoating formula of retrospective prediction. It is rather the knowledge that similar crises are evolving in other men and that, irrespective of the probability of completed suicides, these men deserve the most imaginative and strenuous measures we can devise to ameliorate their sufferings.

The four men we describe died during the course of our work in the state system. Through our incident report forms, we were apprised of their deaths within hours.[5] We proceeded to the site of each suicide as soon as we could, and interviewed staff and inmates who had known the victims personally. In each instance the interviews were conducted by a team of three interviewers, and took place over a two- or three-day period. On the average, each psychological autopsy entailed twenty in-depth interviews, as well as the contacts necessary to locate key informants. For the most part, the persons we talked to were helpful, thoughtful, and eager to share their views and impressions with our teams.

The interview schedule comprised queries dealing with perceptions of the victim's conduct and state of mind. The questions centered principally on conversations and other first-hand contacts. The interviews also explored each informant's opinions relative to the motives of the victim, the pressures operating on the victim, and the resources available to the victim.

We combined interview data with information in the institutional folder and constructed a chronological sequence. We were able to include our own impressions in one of the autopsies. This autopsy was particularly painful for us because at the time of our contact with the victim he had been mildly psychotic and had told us of the fears that ultimately engulfed him.

Each autopsy begins with a factual chronology. This is followed by a reconstruction of interpersonal impressions. The autopsy includes the speculations of our informants and our own psychological summary. It also presents data concerning crisis intervention efforts directed at the victim.

Throughout these chapters we try, as best we can, to dispassionately record what we have learned. Insofar as inferences can be drawn, we feel that these must be plausible and fair. Our portraits are too tragic to be reduced to caricatures. The lessons to be learned must be documented and relevant; the recommended changes must be realistic and feasible. We owe this much not only to the dead and their survivors, but also to the prospective victims now in our prisons.

NOTES

1. H. A. Murray, *et al, Explorations in Personality* (New York: Oxford University Press, 1938); G. W. Allport, *Letters from Jenny* (New York: Harcourt, Brace and World, 1965); Allport, *Pattern and Growth in Personality* (New York: Holt, Rinehart and Winston, 1961). R. W. White, *Lives in Progress: A Study of the Natural Growth in Personality* (New York: Dryden Press, 1952; White, ed., *The Study of Lives* (Englewood Cliffs, N.J.: Prentice-Hall, 1963).

2. The Los Angeles group originated the term "psychological autopsy" and pioneered the procedure of interviewing survivors with specialized teams. Efforts to reconstruct the motives of suicide victims have more remote historical precedents. M. Fuller, for instance, claims that Jean Pierre Falret performed "psychological autopsies" in the early 1900s ("Suicide Past and Present: A Note of Jean Pierre Falret," *Life-Threatening Behavior,* 1973, *3,* 58–65).

3. E. S. Shneidman, N. L. Farberow and R. E. Litman, "The Suicide Prevention Center," in *The Cry for Help,* ed. by N. L. Farberow and E. S. Shneidman (New York, McGraw-Hill, 1965), p. 12.

4. Though the New York City autopsies are not intended as psychological reconstructions, they sometimes contain relevant material. We have illustrated this fact in H. Toch, "Two Autopsies: A General Impression," in *Jail House Blues: Studies of Suicidal Behavior in Jail and Prison,* ed. B. L. Danto (Orchard Lake, Mich.: Epic, 1973). Pp. 187–202.

5. Though four incidents were reported to us, other suicides took place in the same period for which no project forms were submitted. We were precluded from conducting autopsies in New York City because this function is assigned to the Prison Mortality Board and the Board of Correction.

9

Trauma
and
Breakdown

The inmate we call Dave Barnard died before dawn, on a late-summer day in a protective segregation cell in Attica. A guard found him hanging by a twisted sheet. A sleeply coroner certified him dead.

At the time of his fatal crisis, Barnard was thirty-one years old. He was a black laborer from a medium-sized city in upstate New York, stocky (weight: 190 pounds) and of medium height (five feet eight inches tall). He had left school at sixteen, after completing the ninth grade. His family was very large (thirteen siblings), and Dave himself, though unmarried, had five children. In prison, he had received regular visits as well as periodic packages from his family. He maintained a correspondence, and the prison records show that he had mail-ordered a book and a tobacco pouch some months before his death.

When Dave Barnard entered prison, he brought with him $6.38 in cash and a knife. Fifteen months later, his institutional account totaled $7.00, and his possessions still included the knife. They also included an assortment of the kind of items that make up the world of the inmate—toilet articles, condiments, writing equipment, tobacco, photographs, greeting cards, a heater, a plastic pail, legal papers, and a crucifix.

Dave Barnard's contacts with the law date from his teens. Most of his early arrests were for larceny. Later there were charges of vagrancy and possession of dangerous weapons. During the last decade of his life, he was often arrested for intoxication. There were also incidents of petit larceny and assault. His final commitment arrest was for first degree assault, reduced (through negotiation and plea) to a conviction for second-degree assault. The circumstances are described as "shot and wounded man with shotgun-street-daytime," and the act is attributed to "self-defense." Barnard was sentenced to four years in prison, and at the time of his death had served almost half his term.

We have no information about the first two months of Barnard's prison stay. We know that after ten weeks he was subjected to a painful, frightening, harrowing experience. The event occurred during the final night of the Attica riot, in the early hours of the morning. For unknown reasons an inmate, or a group of inmates, slit Barnard's throat while he slept.

Barnard recovered, but never completely. Four weeks after the riot, he was admitted to the infirmary with a bad swelling and an infection. The wound healed, but Barnard developed new and different problems. These came to a head five months later, in March 1972. At that time Barnard wrote an urgent note to the superintendent of Attica. This note reads:

I have to see you right away, before lunch, please. Call me out, I'm going to be killed if I don't get out of this cell now. Please let me talk to you.

Barnard was interviewed by a sergeant of the custodial force, and segregated at his own request. The sergeant notes:

[Barnard] was extremely nervous, was biting his fingernails constantly, and stated that he would be killed [by other inmates] if "I don't get out of this cell now." . . . Inmate claims that he has been feeling this way for the past week with growing intensity.

In response to a question dealing with speech and ideas "different from normal," the sergeant notes:

[Barnard] claims that he hears other inmates talking about him. Such talk centers around threats to his life. On at least one occasion he thought an officer was talking about him, although [Barnard] did not hear what was being said by the officer.

Six weeks after arriving in the observation area, Barnard was interviewed by a prison psychiatrist to complete his file for the parole board. The psychiatrist reports that

according to the officers, this inmate's behavior and attitude are unpredictable. Generally he would be cooperative, then all of a sudden he would become uncooperative and defiant and also expressing exaggerated fear that somebody is going to harm him.

The psychiatrist found Barnard in an "uncooperative" mood. He describes his reception as follows:

This morning at first inmate refused to leave his cell in order to come out and talk to the undersigned and when I appeared in the front of the cell with the officer and explained to the inmate who I was and asked him if he would like to have an interview, the inmate answered in very rude fashion, and he was verbally abusive towards the officer who was standing at my side. Finally he decided to leave his cell and to come to the outside area but it was obvious from the start that interview would not be very fruitful.

The interview—from the interviewer's standpoint—did prove "not . . . very fruitful." Barnard was "not interested" in talking about his "past life"; he "acknowledged" previous incarceration and "admitted that he used to drink a great deal." He also confessed his commitment offense, but again claimed self-defense. He talked more volubly about recent experiences:

He stated that he came to Observation on his own request because somebody threatened to kill him. He claims that during the prison riot his throat was cut by other inmates. He was asked how does he spend his day at the present time and if he goes in the yard. He answered that he does not go out and when asked why, he answered "because I don't want to."

The psychiatrist characterized Barnard's responses as "negativistic and uncooperative." He notes that "most of the time [Barnard] exhibited a slight smile, but at times his facial expression showed annoyance and irritation." These interview impressions, and Barnard's record, produced a negative bias. The psychiatrist wrote that

perusal of [Barnard's] folder indicates that he has spent most of his life hedonistic and antisocial. Basically he presents characteristics of psychopathic personality. . . . His present reaction is probably just expression of his personality, but it cannot be ruled out entirely that his behavior might reflect some more serious mental disturbance.

The psychiatrist made no comments relating to Barnard's fears. His emphasis on Barnard's past history relegated Barnard's more immediate concerns to insignificance.

But these concerns would not die. A week after Barnard's psychiatric interview, he committed the only disciplinary violation of his prison stay. The Infraction Slip reads, "Using obscene language to the doctor on sick call. Told him to fuck himself!"

The incident resulted in an investigation which involved interviews with another sergeant. In these interviews Barnard touched on the Attica riot and its aftermath:

> He explained to me that he was in D Yard during the riot, at which time his throat was cut by unknown persons. He further explained that during the months following the riot he was in fear for his life. He was moved to several different companies. In all of these areas he claims to have overheard threats on his life.

Barnard also told the sergeant that his problems were not solved with his transfer:

> On 3/11/72 he was moved to Reception B-53 for his own protection. Now he claims that he is hearing threats from those inmates locking on Rec B and also from Rec C upstairs. He refuses to name anyone. It appears that he knows who some of them are but that he does not want to "rat." He claims that he is too nervous to eat or sleep. He says that he does not want medication because he is afraid to sleep. I could not convince him that he was safe in his cell. He says that he is afraid to take recreation because that is the logical spot for him to get "hit."

Later that day the sergeant returned and asked Barnard for the names of inmates who had threatened him. Barnard replied "that he did not know who [these inmates] are." The sergeant was alarmed. He made an entry noting that Barnard "appears quite disturbed and should be seen by a psychiatrist."

There is no mention of another formal psychiatric interview. We know that six weeks prior to Barnard's death he claimed to be suffering from a hernia and that physicians classified the claim as spurious. We know that Barnard was upset by this incident. A final item appears in the folder, the day immediately preceding Barnard's suicide. On this day—a Sunday—an officer requested Special (psychiatric) Observation. He stated:

> [Barnard] sits on the far end of bed with sheet over his head for hours at a time. Also has mattress pulled up against bars. When spoken to fails to acknowledge your presence. . . . He has been doing this for about a week.

The request was persuasive, but too late. Hours later, the distraught Barnard had taken his life.

Sequence of Decay

It is ironic that while Barnard was alive, he impressed those around him by his inconspicuousness and noninvolvement. Inmates and staff who knew the man stressed that he took pains to isolate himself from others, and to limit his human contacts to unavoidable essentials. As one of his cell neighbors put it:

> I think the things that impressed me the most were, he rarely ever talked. If he ever talked, it was to answer a question. . . . He rarely ever joined in conversation, or else it was to say yes to a question. My main impression is that the only time he talked was when you asked him a question or when you said something directly to him. He wouldn't volunteer anything by himself. If he was asked a question, he would answer it. And a lot of the questions were like, "Will you pass this from one cell to the next?" "Yeah." "Thank you."

An officer acquainted with Barnard made the same observation:

> When he was talking to you, it wasn't actually a conversation. You couldn't carry on a conversation with him, because he'd button up. But if he wanted something, or if he was having problems with something, well, then he would explain it to you, but that was it. There would be no carrying on a conversation. And I never really heard him carry on a conversation with maybe somebody next to him either.

Inmates and staff stressed that Barnard kept his physical contacts and movements as restricted as possible. He went out of his way to remain in his cell, to the point of refusing the relative safety of the exercise yard:

> He wouldn't come out of protection. As a matter of fact, to my knowledge he never even took avail of his privileges to go to the yard. Just that little yard that was over there. He wouldn't ever leave his cell at all, for any reason.

Barnard showed concern for personal cleanliness but performed even hygienic functions in the most circumspect way, so as to avoid contact with others:

> When it was shower time, he always took showers. Most of the guys, when they take a shower they stop at the cells of guys they know and rap, and then the man tells them they've got to lock in. He never did. He used to take his shower, come back, and lock in the cell, and never say anything.

Barnard's caution did not seem to bring him peace of mind. A porter tells us that during periods of inactivity and isolation Barnard showed signs of strain and depression:

Sometimes he would come out for a shower, and he would ask for underwear, things like that. "I need a T-shirt, towel," whatever it was. And he'd act normal at that time. . . . But once he was in that cell he was really depressed.

A guard notes that Barnard sometimes refused to leave his cell for any reason, and that he often showed no interest in food:

Some days he wouldn't shave, and then other days he would come out and he would shave. He seemed to be off and on. Some days he seemed to be going along OK, and then the next day you'd ask him if he wanted to shave, and he didn't want to come out. I can faintly remember when he first came up here, you'd get him out to get a haircut or something, and he'd be very reluctant to come out.

And when I went up with the food, some days he would take food and other days he wouldn't. He'd just be like withdrawing. He would know that you're there, but pretend that he didn't know.

There were marked variations in Barnard's mood and disposition. One guard describes the cycle as follows:

He could talk as lucidly as you and I in a conversation on the nineteenth, and then on the twentieth he'd be disorganized, unable to carry out a conversation, or he'd withdraw. Either if he did talk to you he'd be disorganized or he wouldn't talk at all. Or maybe the next day he'd be mad. He'd take a real defensive attitude, really be mad at you, "Get away from my cell!" he didn't want to talk to you. And this went on as long as I knew him. . . . The changes were changeable. I mean, there didn't seem to be any set pattern to it. Like I say, from day to day he would change, or he would remain in good shape for a couple of weeks, three weeks, everything would be nice, and then the next day you'd walk in and say "good morning," and he was ready to throw something at you. Just that quick.

The inmates noted the same mood variations, and one reports that these moods excited peer curiosity but no alarm:

Before they moved us downstairs, he would go through these stages of depression. A guy would go by my cell and say, "Is there anything wrong with Barnard?" And I would say, "No, not that I know of. Whatever is going on in there is his business." And I didn't figure that it was serious anyway. I just figured that he didn't feel good. This place is enough to make you depressed.

This inmate (among others) records that Barnard's dark mood lifted two months before his death, after relocation, but reimposed itself quickly:

So they move us downstairs. Now he comes out of his depression. It must be the change of cells, from one to another, another floor. He comes out of the depression, and he's all right for about a month. So then he started going back into another one, and I just figured, "Well, the guy goes through stages like this, what the hell do I know?"

From comments Barnard made to others, it appears that he had restricted his activities because of fear of harm. Some informants claimed that Barnard lived in dread of other inmates; some told us that he feared guards:

He would never come out when we were let out for the hour rec period. He didn't come out. He was afraid of the inmates. He thought maybe the inmates would try to kill him.

He was never where anybody could harm him, except when he went to take a shower and nobody else is out there anyways. He figured the guards were going to erase him.

When discussing his problems with guards, Barnard took care to talk exclusively of enemies among inmates. However, inmates often cite guards as the object of Barnard's apprehensions:

I called him up and talked to him, and he told me that people, other people in that particular building, were making threats toward his life and just constantly bugging him. . . . In that building we had a lot of protective custody inmates that were considered involved in the riot. But he not only felt that they were bothering him, he felt that everybody else was bothering him. . . . He was afraid of everybody.

I: Would that be officers too?

No, he didn't express any fear of officers. He expressed fear of other inmates.

He expressed these various beliefs about how the officers were listening to everything he was saying, and that when he heard the officers talking out where they sit, or whatever they do in there, he would think they were talking about him.

Several weeks before the final tragedy Barnard's fears took a turn for the worse. He felt himself under observation from cameras and recorders, and showed apprehension when faced with anyone's approach:

He always thought that they were spying on him, you know? From the hospital. If he was looking out the window, he'd say "Well, I don't want to be looking out the window," and he'd turn his back on it, because he thought that they had some kind of high-powered camera and they were looking on him.

You know, he was under the impression that they had a camera on him twenty-four hours a day. He'd say, "I can't go to the bathroom without them looking at me."

He would say, "Every time you turn around, there'll be somebody there, or the intercom will be on." Shit like this. . . . And he wouldn't say anything to me when I would talk to him. He would just back away.

Men who had observed Barnard over time report dramatic changes in his conduct over the last weeks. They describe complete and total withdrawal and an impermeable self-insulation:

He had changed a lot. He had got where he wouldn't even talk to me. He didn't trust me . . . and he started withdrawing from everyone, you know? Like first he put notes up on his wall: "Fuck the pig"; "Just bring it, don't give no rap or anything—what you have to give me, just bring it, the necessities." And then it got where he didn't even want anything. Like they used to pass out snacks here. And the snacks would sit on his bars for three or four days at a time, you know? And I'd say, "Hey, you want this stuff, you going to eat it?" And he wouldn't give up any kind of a rap, you know? . . . Like guys he locked right next to, he wouldn't communicate with them at all. He stopped rapping completely. Not that he rapped a lot, but every now and then you could get the guy to talk, and wherever the hell his mind was, get it away from it for a while so he could find some comfort. But when he came downstairs he was shot.

The three weeks preceding his death he would not talk at all unless you talked to him first, and then not say too much. I would call it total apathy.

I think most of the time he was just staring, because on library days he wouldn't turn in any books or ask for any books from the library. As far as I know, he just sat there and stared.

Barnard's self-exile became complete, and included silence, immobility, and refusals to eat. There were also occasional outbursts—some bizarre and some angry:

> Quite often he would refuse to eat for maybe two meals. He'd have just maybe the coffee and nothing else. Or he'd only have, let's say, the po- tatoes, and he'd refuse the rest of the meat and the vegetables and that. And then sometimes he'd say, "Give me some more potatoes, I'd like some more potatoes." You'd give him some more potatoes, and then he'd complain you gave him too much. And he'd throw the whole bowl, whatever it was, in the john. Rather than just take what he didn't want, he'd throw everything away and say, "Well, I'm not going to eat." Then he wouldn't accept anything else.

> Well, usually his body was just there, just his body. He never asked for anything. Once in a while, like at mealtimes, he might get a little nasty or something and say, "Get away from here with that shit," in a kind of nasty voice, but a low—not a screaming voice.

> He graduated down to this thing, because before he wouldn't say any- thing and then towards the end, constantly, at night when everybody was sleeping, you could hear him over there saying, "Watch me, you fuckers, watch me wipe my ass. Watch me every time I wipe my ass."

During the last days of his life, Barnard climaxed his withdrawal by sitting on his bunk facing the wall, with a blanket over his head and a mattress drawn about him. His response to people varied from minimal to rejecting:

> And then there was sometimes when he'd face the back part of the cell, wouldn't even face the front. And he wouldn't turn around for any- thing. You'd come with the tray, ask him if he wanted something to eat, and he'd just shake his head, wouldn't say a word.

> He would sit at the end of the bed with a blanket or a sheet wrapped around his whole body, facing the wall, staring at that wall. Now I would go down and ask him, "Do you want tea?" . . . And sometimes he would just say no. Most of the times he never said nothing.

The day preceding Barnard's suicide, even recognition of stimulation seems to have been missing. This was noted and recorded by the guard who referred Barnard for a psychiatric contact:

I: This particular time that you wrote up the observation, was that very unusual behavior for him, just to sit there and refuse to eat?

Yeah, he would at least look at you. He may give you the blank stare like a lot of people will. But this day he just faced the wall, and I believe that he did have his earphones on, and he had like a towel or a sheet over his head. And he just kept facing the wall. . . . I know that night I put the referral on him he was sitting on the end of his bunk facing the wall, and we'd ask him if he wanted anything, and he wouldn't answer. . . . That day he was really different, that's why I put it in. He was acting a lot different than he had ever acted before. . . . I put the referral in, and then the next day I came in and found out that he had hung himself.

Alibis and Caveats

The guard who referred Barnard tells us that the cell block was not conducive to differential diagnoses and careful personal assessments. He also stressed that on the surface Barnard's usual self-insulation was not out of the ordinary:

Other than things like, "What do you want to eat?" or "Do you want to go to rec?" or if he had a visit or something, other than that you really don't have the time to just stand and talk to anyone. Because you have so many up there, it's pretty difficult. . . . there were about three or four others down there that very seldom went to the yard. It wasn't that he was the only one. There was quite a few of them that didn't want to go to the yard.

Guards agreed that within the range of prison conduct, particularly in protective segregation, Barnard's pattern could be regarded as normal:

The fact of the matter is we have quite a few strange-acting people up there. Not necessarily violent-acting people, but they are very strange. Possibly the officers that worked with him, or the doctors, were so accustomed to seeing these people that they accept it. A certain type. He's a certain man that does certain things and responds certain ways, and this is it. Where if a stranger walked in on a situation like that he might be shocked or appalled or concerned, after a while you begin to realize that this is just a man and this is the way he reacts.

Every once in a while we do get an individual in observation or protection where he won't associate with nobody and don't want to have anything to do with nobody. And he was one of them. . . . Of course, if he misses so many meals in a row you report it. But he'd only miss maybe one meal, and then he'd eat part of another. And it never went beyond maybe two or three or four meals at the most he'd ever refuse. And he'd usually take a liquid, coffee or tea or whatever it might be, that was being served.

The guards and some inmates also argued that Barnard's conduct discouraged contacts and intervention. For one, his pattern precluded communication. At minimum, it made the task of approaching him hard and thankless:

I did at one time ask a psychiatrist to see him, because at this time he had been quiet for quite a number of days. He didn't say anything, and he'd been looking at the back of the cell continually. Sitting on the bed, looking at the back of the cell. He'd eat maybe once every day or something like that. And the doctor couldn't get anything out of him either. He wouldn't even talk to the doctor. No matter who went to the cell and tried to talk to him, even a friend of his, an inmate buddy that somehow had talked to him a little bit, he was clammed up at this particular time, he clammed up on him too. . . . [the psychiatrist] came out and said, "He isn't even going to talk to me. He just won't say nothing." Sergeant M——————— the same way, he tried to talk to him, and he didn't want to talk to Sergeant M———————. This inmate porter tried to talk to him, and he had talked to him before. He just didn't want anybody.

Others, particularly among the inmates, stressed the element of danger in approaching Barnard. They attributed risk both to Barnard's stance and to his ambiguous status among peers:

I wouldn't say they were afraid of the guy, but the state that the guy was in, everybody knew you don't know what he's going to do. . . . He always had a mean look on his face, didn't look like he wanted to contribute to anything or participate in anything. And it seemed like if you said the wrong thing, he'd catch an attitude. And he didn't look the kind of guy who'd stand up and say "Fuck you" and punch somebody. But he'd wait, you know? Until his time comes, then he'd get even. This is how he appear to me.

I: What about the doctor and the psychiatrist?

He didn't seek it. He didn't want it. In fact they would have had to do something to give it to him.

Among those who viewed Barnard with alarm, the majority adjudged him a psychiatric problem, falling within the province of professionals:

But something like that, I don't see where we could do anything for them here, and they should shoot them up to Dannemora or Beacon. We can't do nothing for them here. . . . But I think you could see this guy needed some help, at least that's the way I felt. I told the doctor this, this is why I called him. . . . I told him, "As long as you're up here, why don't you go down and see this guy?" This is when he was facing the back of the cell and not speaking to anybody. So I said, "Maybe you can reach him, maybe you can help him."

Well, I think he would have to be considered a mental case by the people that were working with him because of his attitude. But he had psychiatric interviews and stuff like that, and they didn't feel that he was mentally ill or they would have put him in an institution. But you'd almost have to consider him some kind of mental case because his actions weren't normal among inmates. A lot of inmates are scared, but not to a point where they will refuse to leave their cells at anytime.

In line with this assumption, the guards not only made efforts to have Barnard observed but also showed special concern in some of their own dealings with him:

The officers on the third floor asked me, 'cause they noticed that I was talking to him, and they said, "Well, try."

I always make it a habit that when I approach a man like that or one that has his back turned to me that he hears me coming. I don't all of a sudden be there, and a voice breaks through his subconscious.

I tried to explain to him where he was that he had no fears. And that he would be under observation by an officer at all times. And if he was out working he would probably come into contact with only two or three others that were out.

A Retrospective View

Barnard's death left staff and peers frustrated about the inadequacy of their helping efforts, but with little consensus about where to place the blame for failure:

So he sits there and he sits there for about a week and doesn't eat nothing. So the doctor comes by, and the guards are coming by, and they can see this guy back there. . . . The doctors come by, and they act like they don't even see him. They don't even see him. They just keep going on. So finally the guards say something to a psychiatrist, and the psychiatrist tries to come and talk to him. But Dave don't talk to him. He don't say nothing. So the psychiatrist just goes on. Nobody tries to pull him out of his cell, take the stuff out of his cell, nothing like that.

He was more or less ignored except by a couple of us gentlemen that were locked in near him.

To me, there's just too much involved in order to get a man where he can get some help. Either that or give us [officers] some help, where we can help them a little bit there.

Barnard had obviously received little by way of intervention and treatment. He did receive thought, most of it after his death, of a painstaking and sometimes sensitive kind. Most staff and inmates who reviewed Barnard's conduct empathetically traced his increasingly omnivorous suspicion and consuming fear.

Several of Barnard's acquaintances pointed to what they saw as an inescapable dilemma: whereas Barnard required isolation to protect him from danger, isolation left him with a feeling of vulnerability, and the stimulus deprivation obviously depressed him. A guard sergeant pointed out (with acumen) that in this context suicide represents the ultimate search for safety:

I: What do you think finally did it to this guy?

He felt that this was an escape.

He needed protection. But he couldn't really do the time very well because he wanted to be with other guys. . . . he didn't read much and he didn't have anything to do but sit in his cell and draw and listen to the radio.

Most of our informants attributed the key role in Barnard's panic to his trauma during the Attica uprising, which, some maintained, had sexual overtones. Several inmates noted that the fact that Barnard did not know who had attacked him or why it left him in the position of suspecting everyone:

He wouldn't talk about his experiences in the yard at all. It was something he tried to keep shielded from everybody, I think. I almost think it might have been a sexual deal involved there too, which kind of shattered him. Now that's just a personal opinion. . . . I think he was all right up until the time of the riot. So something pretty shattering happened to him personally in the yard. And I think it was a pretty bad experience. You know, the best of situations out in the yard was a bad deal. But I think something also happened to him in particular, and that pushed him over the brink. He lived with it from then until March of '72. So he stayed with it quite a while, but apparently it just got to him finally.

The man's been cut before. He's faced the guns before, and he's been cut before, and he's got scars all over him. The only thing that might affect him like that is that he didn't know who did it, and he was sleeping, and to wake up in the morning with blood running down your chest and realize that you're lucky you woke up. That would be the effect that did it. . . . That's why he came in protection, because somebody wanted to cut his throat and he didn't know who it was. And he got shocked.

Several guards and inmates told us that Barnard had been convinced that his victimization in the riot was based on a "rat" rumor. There was consensus that such a reputation would be difficult or impossible to neutralize:

That's just the thing that he couldn't face, that people thought he was a rat. . . . this rat thing here, it actually hurt him. His feelings were actually hurt. He never did nothing and he couldn't understand: "Why do these guys think I'm a rat?" This way he wasn't calloused over, he had a lot of feelings about that.

But since they labeled him a rat, I guess it more or less put a bind in his mind that he didn't know when somebody might come up and try to shiv him or try to cut his throat again. And all of this mounting up, I guess he figured more or less it would be better for him to take his own life than to wait around for somebody to kill him.

Some theorized that Barnard's fears of being labeled might have arisen because he had been questioned by investigation officials after the riot:

If they call you down, first thing that comes into the inmate's head is you're giving somebody up to save your own ass. Because there were so many men involved in that riot, and it seemed like the only stories you heard were guys breaking and guys giving other guys up, guys going to protection now. And it just looks bad, you know? And then a lot of the inmates wouldn't give them a chance to explain why they were down

there. They were already marked, the wire went out that they were rats.
They were down there giving somebody up.

I'd also bet that a great deal of that depression is due to the fact that
he was conversing with the Fischer Commission. And he wasn't liked by
any person in here, any of the inmates that were fearing an indictment.
And also, I heard—this is scuttlebutt, of course—that there was a contract for him out on the streets.

Several inmates asserted that Barnard's fears, though out of hand, were
objectively based. The grapevine had at some juncture labeled Barnard an
informer:

Well, I know there's a lot of rumors here, but these are things I hear
a lot of times. When I heard rumors from a lot of different people that
aren't related to each other, I basically consider it almost a truth. For
instance, if I met you, and you told me something, and I had never met
you, you weren't associated with him, and you told me the same thing,
then to me it's no more a goddamn rumor, it's the truth.

i: How about how much general information, the rumor kind of thing,
     was going around about him being a rat?

Oh, everybody knew it. Every inmate knew it.

Inmates also theorized that Barnard's environment provided him with
clues which, given strong enough fear, could lend plausibility to delusions:

And, like, he was worried about cameras taking pictures of him all the
time. And when I walked over there I could see, occasionally, certain
lights where I could see how a person would presume that there were
cameras there or something.

He was telling me that he was locking next to some other guys, and he
thought they were pretty tight and this, that, and the other, and he
figures that they taped him. So here's the thing, when you face reality,
they could have been taping him. Chances are they were. But then
again, equal, the chances are they weren't. It's hard to convince yourself
that somebody didn't if you know that they want you for something.

In a more general vein, some argued that the atmosphere of distrust of
prisons promotes the development of exaggerated fears:

Of course, in an environment like this it's not hard to see why a person
would not trust anyone, not place any confidence in anyone. And why

a person would be filled with fear. Because this environment here breeds all sorts of emotions. So it's my opinion that Barnard's thinking to a certain degree was delusional, to a certain degree was not delusional. . . . There's much hostility here, and hatred, aggression, every conceivable negative emotion or combination of emotions that you can think of.

Finally, both guards and inmates discussed the role of prolonged confinement. A custodial official argued that when Barnard completely insolated himself he sealed his own fate:

I don't know any inmates that could stay all that time in one cell, without leaving. It must do something. . . . On occasion I know he would get a little loud in his cell, not conversing with other inmates, actions that were irrational. But I can understand that because he never left his cell. . . .

I: Do you think that was from being locked up too much?

Something like that—oh sure, I would say. I would imagine that if you were in the same cell for twenty-four hours a day—and it's not that he couldn't leave. He wouldn't leave.

Several interviewees raised the possibility of social support for Barnard's suicide. Barnard had witnessed an attempt resembling his own, under closely parallel circumstances:

Now the gentleman locking next to him while he was in population had attempted to hang himself. Which was why he was brought up to the observation yard. And this gentleman believed that there was a camera on us, taking pictures of him. And he was afraid to come out of his cell and take a shower, he was afraid he was going to get killed. I guess you would call it delusional thinking and hallucinatory. And then later on Barnard seemed to develop the same type of delusions. He thought that there were cameras on him at all times. It seemed to be more or less like a contagious psychosis. Or maybe Barnard was already a potential psychotic, and this gentlemen just helped bring it out.

Barnard had also participated in prison bull sessions which glamorized death by postulating reincarnation:

Two nights before he did it, me and this other gentleman that was locking right next to Barnard were discussing death. And we were giving different philosophies on how death might be an illusion or death might be the only reality, death was nothingness. This might have affected

Barnard's thinking to a certain extent, and we were talking about how the philosophy of life and death are one, the same, two masks hiding the same reality. That death is nothing but a transition from one plane to another. This and that. That was two nights before the tragedy. . . . No, he did not join in the conversation, but I know he must have heard it. Let me mention one more thing—this was two nights before his death that we discussed it. Now one night before his death, that night we were discussing Gibran's book *The Prophet*. And we were reading sections in there on death. And I read it out loud, and also I read the last chapter in that book. As a matter of fact, the last sentence expresses a belief in reincarnation. Now this might have affected Barnard's thinking too.

He usually would get into this discussion with those two guys that came down with him. And the main thing that I can recall is one thing in particular. . . . There was no such thing as real death. You only die—your body dies, but you will recycle. You come back. So death was no problem and fear—it was just something that happened.

ı: Did he really believe that?

Yes, I'm almost positive he did.

In addition, Barnard was exposed to the delusions of fellow inmates as well as to rumors pertaining to his own fate:

Every day this gentleman, and every night, was discussing how the cameras were on him and how they were going to pay him $100,000 for the movie they were making of him while he was in his cell, and all this and that kind of stuff. Barnard was deeply influenced by this thing.

And I told him one time, "You don't have to worry about anything if you're in this building here as long as you don't go in population." And I said, "It's not because you did anything but because of this rumor. The guards were going around saying that you did this and that. And you didn't do it, you understand?" . . . A few days before he committed suicide, I told him that I was outside and I heard a couple of guards talking about him. And they were talking about harassment and taking him to court. The next thing I knew when I was upstairs, he had committed suicide.

The Inner Circle of Fear

When he entered Attica, Dave Barnard excited—and deserved—little attention. He had no eccentricities and an undistinguished past. He was neither a novice nor a hardened veteran. After his fashion, he had a life of his own and ties to others.

To be sure, Barnard was not strong, or impressive. He had taken to drink and to petty crimes. His use of violence showed difficulties in coping with others. He had approached maturity with few promises and fewer prospects.

Barnard was not slated for prominence among his peers. His were not status crimes—he was not a fighter, nor a manipulator, nor a tower of strength. But his scarred face cautioned tact, and sometimes respect.

What would have happened to Dave Barnard had it not been for the Attica riot? One would assign him a modest fate—a prison career as a fringer or an isolate; an occasional fight; ineffective, minor outbursts.

The brutal assault on September 12 changed all of this. The terrifying experience shook Barnard to the core. The obscure motives for the act and its cryptic intent overtaxed Barnard's capacity to understand or conceptualize; nor did he know how to cope with enemies who acted in this way. Barnard lived out his life in fearful expectation of new unannounced violence.

We know that several months saw the blossoming of Barnard's terror. Surrounded by strangers, alert to danger, he found promiscuous cues to threat. The line between possible and certain danger, vulnerability and resourcelessness, thinned and disappeared. There was no check, reassurance, balance. And there was no means of escape.

This pattern is familiar to us from Chapter 4. There we noted that in the real world externalized danger becomes manageable. The fearful man —even the paranoiac—can find peace of mind. Such a man has friends and allies, means of evasion, lines of regress.

But we also saw that in prison the way out leads to confinement. Self-protection entails self-imprisonment, immobilization, restraint. Escape makes the cycle narrower, more intimate, more immediate. From a cell, there is nowhere else to turn. If danger is not left outside the gate, it pursues into the cell. Ultimately, it may surround the man in his retreat, permeate the remotest corner of his sanctuary.

In Barnard's case, there is the cumulating logic of his fear. In the eyes of peers, escape denotes culpability and feeds rumor. Barnard's status as a riot figure subjected him to curiosity and concern, spawned theories premised on guilt. The object of fear thus becomes a subject of fear, suspected and shunned. There is also the larger context. Tape recorders and cameras observe Barnard in crisis; officials approach him later. Ultimately, he feels violated, believes himself monitored even in his ablutions.

Barnard retreats. He avoids contacts, reveals little, observes warily. Prison knows such conduct, and accepts it. Barnard is alone with concerns which preoccupy and isolate, depress and feed on themselves. There is some sympathy, but there is no one to reach out and console, to reassure and restore. The psychiatrist bent on retrospection lends a deaf ear to panic. The guards—some wise and humane—have their restricted, unavailing tasks. Barnard's ever more restrictive cycle moves on to a concentric climax.

There is no culpability here, no negligence, no blame. But prison—with its restricted options and its constricted roles, its apprehensions, suspicions, and defenses—reinforces and accelerates a tragic cycle. Emasculated staff and warped peers, rigidity and routine, are factors in Barnard's equation.

The system had, in a sense, done its best with Barnard. Concerned cellmates and guards, medical observers, protective transfers responded to him. But none of this was to the point. For what Dave Barnard needed was an ally in a desperate search for meaning and safety. He had to make sense of the senseless, to cope with his night of threat and terror. He needed, but failed to obtain, help in a task he could not achieve unaided. This task was to work through a traumatic past—to lay it to rest—so that he could proceed with the business of life.

10

A Facade
and
Its Message

It was a routine Saturday afternoon in the hospital at Attica. Dinner had been served; dusk was settling. The man we call Greg Johnson tapped on his cell door; the inmate nurse responded. At Johnson's request, the nurse shut off the cell radiator. Later a guard passed by. Another guard and nurse began the round of evening medication.

When the pill cart reached Greg Johnson's door, his cell was dark. Alarmed, the guard pushed the door and found it blocked. The nurse peered through the darkness:

> When I looked in it appeared that inmate [Johnson] was leaning against the radiator with his head cocked to the side watching us. Then I noticed that he was hanging. Officer B—————— went to call for help. When we went back again we were finally able to force the door open. I went over and cut him down.

The life that thus ended had been a stormy one. It had been a life of hate and obsession, of battle, defiance, and bluff. It had been a bloody campaign, awkward and doomed. While the campaign raged, it challenged odds and strained credulity. It sought salience, fear, respect; it fought doubt, impotence, despair. And it lost. For too much was claimed too loudly and too often. And the facade caved in, revealing the void beneath.

Prison had played a role in Johnson's end. But the role was lawful and constant. It was that of arena and proving ground. The sources of Johnson's own contribution lay elsewhere, in the outside world, in Johnson's past.

We know too much about Inmate Johnson, too little about his life prior to imprisonment. Greg Johnson was born in Columbia, South Carolina. He left school from the sixth grade, at age thirteen. Almost at once he became involved with the law. At age seventeen, he graduated to adult crime, and to arrests for armed robbery, auto theft, and possession of weapons. He served time in prison, and took up truck driving after his release. But his freedom was short-lived. In 1969, at the age of twenty-one, Johnson was arrested for shooting two men during a quarrel; one of the men died.

At the time of his imprisonment, Greg Johnson was twenty-two, six feet tall, and weighed 186 pounds. He had remained close to his family, who lived in Philadelphia. He had three children, was widowed, and was living with a common-law wife. His maximum sentence was fifteen years.

Johnson served his first six months at Ossining, a hilltop institution on the Hudson. Soon after his arrival he filed a transfer request. When this was denied, he filed others. Following one such denial (three months after his arrival), Johnson made his opening move in a private War against Prison. A guard tells us that during a march to the dining hall Johnson erupted in strongly worded terms. According to the guard:

> [Johnson] said that he would slap the shit out of me, also that he was a five percenter (5%)[1] and that he was going to get my ass no matter what the outcome of the report may be.

This incident had peculiar features which we meet over and over again. Johnson reacts disproportionately to apparently routine instructions; he advertises his toughness and fierceness in the presence of peers. He threatens violence and retribution.

On the day of his outburst Johnson had filed a rejoinder to his denied request. In this note he named inmates as enemies and claimed other enemies elsewhere—many enemies in most prisons, a few in others. He talked of "problems from various people—practically daily confrontations of victimization."

Ten days later Johnson was transferred to Great Meadows. In this setting (not of his choice) he embarked on an impressively checkered career. Illustrative incidents emerge in staff reports. These incidents range from passive noncompliance to challenges, outbursts, and overt threats. Orders are ignored or are reacted to angrily. A guard reports that in an early incident

Inmate Johnson delayed count by refusing to get into his cell. When I asked him why, he said, "I don't have to run to my cell, and it don't make no difference to me." He became arrogant and I told him no one expected him to run and he said, "Fuck it, I ain't going to do it, go ahead and put a sign on me. Fuck it."

Two weeks later an officer complained that

Inmate Johnson called us all "white pig mother fuckers" as we went through the rotunda leading to the mess hall. He began yelling very loudly—"pigs—mother fuckers—lock me up and fuck you." He almost created a riot condition.

Even the infirmary filed a disciplinary form. The nurse contended that Johnson

demanded that I give him medication without telling me what his difficulty was. I refused under these conditions. As he turned, he called me "homo assed old mother fucker."

On occasions, guards seem partly at fault. Petty orders spark and feed Johnson's need for confrontations. One such incident starts when "Johnson decided he would use a radiator as a bench and sat down." The guard relates:

I informed Johnson the radiator was not for that use and ordered him to stand up. He complied to the order, but in doing so stated that all blue shirts were suck ass punks. I informed Johnson if he didn't shut his mouth he would go back to his cell without seeing the notary. Subject belligerently threw his papers down and assumed an aggressive stance and stated nobody would prevent him from seeing the notary.

Through incidents such as these, Johnson's tarnished reputation among staff rapidly cemented. Had that not been the case, a week in July—seven months after his arrival at the prison—would have established it firmly. The week started with the now familiar dialogue of order and rejoinder. The report notes:

Subject did refuse outright to march in line and in pairs. He was told several times to do so and one of his retorts was "What kind of a tin god are you?"

As Johnson was led back to his cell, he continued to offer comments along the way:

[He] was boisterous and made claims to "get even." Inmate Johnson called C.O.R. a stupid old mother fucker and he should be dead any day now.

Other inmates gathered; one joined in verbal attacks on guards. The guards claimed that Johnson played to the audience:

He stated "I'm a man and these stupid sucking officers treat me like a kid. I'm not going to take it. You'll see." By this time approximately five inmates were gathered around his cell and inmate Johnson said "You people are stupid if you don't do something."

In this incident, Johnson had staked a claim to his version of Manliness. For guards, he had become a focal, infectious figure, promotive of threat and riot.

This view of Johnson was consolidated by subsequent incidents. An inmate fight provoked sideline comments from Johnson. He began whistling in the midst of the melee and refused to stop. He also loudly characterized guards as pigs. The next day, after midnight, Johnson shouted loudly and refused to subside. The strongly irritating nature of this conduct was not happenstance. A friend of Johnson's recalls:

They had some fat police officer, and every time he used to come around we would call him pig. Harass him just like he harassed us, right? So every day. And he really had a complex about his fat. Like if you called him pig, he would blow up. So at night we'd just make fun of him. We didn't do nothing all day but rap in our cell, so we could stay up all night. So we'd stay up all night squealing "Pig, pig, pig." All night.

During this time, Johnson reacted to another order by physically threatening a guard:

While returning inmate Johnson to his cell he refused to fold his arms and asked me if I was going to make him. Just upon entering his cell he picked up a feed up rack and said again, "Are you going to make me fold my arms?" I feel this inmate was ready to use the feed up rack in an act of violence. He put it down just before the cell door opened.

For two days, guards expressed fear and frustration in reports on Johnson. One guard wrote:

Inmate Johnson's actions are becoming more and more direct, vicious and belligerent. . . . As he gets away with this he is accumulating more followers to join in his domain of verbal attacks.

Another complained:

He has been calling me and other officers pigs, mother fuckers and making verbal threats.

A physical confrontation occurred that same day. Several guards reported that Johnson had assaulted them; Johnson claimed a deliberate beating. The exact details of the incident cannot be established. We do know that when it occurred Johnson had become an extreme irritant to the guards, and it has been reported that during the confrontation six officers came to one another's aid. It can be assumed that in the charged atmosphere that existed at the time, minimal provocation by Johnson could spark retribution. It is possible that Greg Johnson did make the first move. It is equally possible that the guards' response was more substantial than safety considerations required.

Be that as it may, Johnson's reaction was characteristic. He had been spending time composing requests, protests, rejoinders, writs and appeals. He now set to work charging brutality and suing the institution. A cellmate described the period after the incident as follows:

So he laid down and rested for a while, and as soon as he got up, the first thing he said was, "Who's got a pencil and paper?" That's all he wants to know, "Who's got a pencil and a paper?" We know Greg is going to start writing writs. So we give him the pencil and paper, and he starts writing. Then he wants an affidavit from everybody, and they would give it to him, because he really believes in the law. The nurse comes and asks him if he's all right, and he said he didn't want to talk to no nurse. He ain't going to let them talk to him or touch him. He don't want anybody to touch him. He don't want to sign no papers. He wants to go right to court. So he started writing and writing and writing.

Johnson succeeded in producing at least one inquiry from the United States Congress and in having a summons served on the warden. His efforts sparked inquiries relating to thefts of his mail and neglect of his medical problems. He fought—and won—when the institution attempted to certify and commit him.

He continued throughout to exercise his penchant for challenging guards. Two weeks after his fight with the officers, a report notes that

Inmate Johnson started calling Officer C——————— and me pig mother fuckers, and said that we sucked cocks. He said that he was going to get us when he got out. Neither Officer C——————— nor I said anything to Johnson to receive this verbal abuse.

At this point Johnson made his first—and only recorded—suicide threat. A report refers to a search of Johnson's cell, in which he was informed "that his mother had told Deputy B_____ that he threatened to hang up." The report goes on to note Johnson's denial:

At this he went into a tantrum and shouted that we were all mother-fucking, lying cocksuckers and were trying to bug him.

Subsequent incidents trace a picture of increasingly erratic, more fever-ishly pitched, conduct. On September 16, Johnson reached out of his cell with a broom and attempted to strike an officer with it. The next day he claimed a campaign to starve him to death. Three weeks later he was read-ing a book in his cell when an officer walked by. The latter reports:

I didn't say anything to him. He jumped up and said "I'm reading. What in fuck do you think I'm doing?" I told him to take it easy. He then said, "Are you going to make me, you mother fucker?" I left, saying nothing to him.

During the next few days there were other broom-striking incidents and other charges that mail was being withheld. A quiet two-month interval followed, marred only by an outburst in the dentist's office:

After pulling Inmate Johnson's tooth, Dr. S_____ told John-son there was nothing else he could do for him today. Johnson de-manded that more work be done on his teeth. Johnson became abusive in his language. Leaving the dentist's office, Johnson turned to Dr. S_____ and said, "You will get yours, you slimy ass mother fucker."

In subsequent weeks, reports again speak of challenges, threats, and profanity. But such encounters seemed to leave Johnson unsatisfied: in late March he began to attack guards more directly. In one twenty-four-hour period, Johnson threw shoes at one guard and tossed a book at an-other. The following week he fired a tray at a passing officer. In late April, Johnson took to spitting at the guards:

This man asked to have a letter back that he had sent in. I didn't know if it was still on the desk. When I told him this, he spit at me. His letter was still here and returned to him.

As I was feeding this inmate, I handed him his tray and he spit in my face twice and took a swing at me. This inmate threatened me and told me he was going to kill me. Also, as I turned away from him, he spit on Officer K————————— and threatened him.

While feeding Johnson his breakfast he called me a "punk mother fucker" and spit in my face.

Not surprisingly, an officer filed a psychiatric report, characterizing Johnson as "unstable," "crazy" and "violent." The officer records one of the spitting incidents, and notes:

I realize this kind of harassment we have to put up with, but this is very annoying and degrading. . . . I'm hoping that something can be done about this.

During this period Great Meadows received several letters sparked by complaints from Johnson. Johnson had also filed a series of strongly worded transfer requests. In June he was transferred to Attica.

Johnson spent four months at Attica before he attempted suicide for the first time. This period is marked by two verbal attacks on guards and several threats to inmates. A weapon is discovered, and a guard notes that "Inmate Johnson has been acting strangely."

Inmates who had known Greg Johnson previously report that he had undergone a change of character. Two men who knew him well at Great Meadows characterized him as having become blatantly psychotic:

When he came up here, after he left Auburn, he was sick. I don't even know the dude no more. . . . When he came there he was a big dude, weighed 200 pounds. I don't think he weighed over 160 pounds when I see him here. . . . He was acting as strange as a motherfucker. He was looking all around. You can see when a dude is acting strange. So this dude that used to come to me all the time, he said, "Where do you know this strange dude from?" I said, "I don't know, the dude was all right when I knew him. He's crazy now." Man, you could see it. I've seen crazy people before. The dude was crazy. You could see it. Somebody said he would go in the cell at night and start cussing dudes out. Nobody would be talking to him, and he would just start cussing dudes out. Telling dudes, "I know you think I'm a punk, but I ain't no punk." . . . And different dudes that knew him said he would say that. He was stark raving mad.

When Greg came in here he was uncommunicative. He didn't say nothing to you or rap to you. If he said something, it was like, "Give me a roll of toilet paper" or "Give me this or that," and that was it. He was losing his mind. And if he talked, it was a whole lot of gibberish and shit that didn't amount to nothing. So there was nobody that could know Greg when he was in Attica. Greg was crazy when he came here. Greg needed to be in the nuthouse when he came here.

Despite Greg Johnson's custodial record, studded with his rebellious outbursts, the staff at Attica viewed him as a psychiatric rather than as a disciplinary problem. Two weeks after he arrived at Attica, Johnson tossed a shoe at a porter, insulted the guards, and threw water all over his cell. In response, staff tried to talk with him and found him "uncommunicative." They referred him for clinical observation. Several weeks later, Johnson swore at, threatened, and offered to fight a guard who had never seen him before. The guard completed a form requesting psychiatric intervention.

The psychiatrist noted that Johnson was "responding to stress at the present time in a paranoid fashion" and expressed the hope that the condition would improve in a protected environment. A week later the psychiatrist recorded:

There is essentially nothing to add—He is not psychotic and is well aware of his interaction with other people, all of which is on a voluntary basis. In my discussion with him today he seemed in fact a little more agreeable or perhaps a little less disagreeable than he was previously.

Johnson made mention of suicide to staff, but the psychiatrist quoted him as saying, "I don't wish to hurt myself. If I said anything like that, I was just making a lot of noise." Another psychiatrist, who saw Johnson two weeks before his suicide attempt, wrote, "There is apparently no danger of self-injury."

In the interim, a number of persons had become concerned about Johnson. A guard who befriended him reports:

I always tried to be on the good side of him. I mean somebody has to be on the good side of these inmates so they can talk to someone or rely on someone that if they want something they can get it. So he was never anything else but good with me. He knew that I was the one that if he was going to get something, I would be the one that would get it. That if he had problems he would call me down.

The guard noted that Johnson's conduct tended to move in cycles of aggressiveness and fear:

I: When he first came, how would you describe his behavior?

Sarcastic.

I: Belligerent? Hostile towards the officers?

Yeah. And the inmates.

I: And was that a persistent thing, or did it change back and forth?

Yes, it would change. He would seem to be like this for a while, and then he would go what you might call almost the complete opposite, like he was scared. He always had the idea that someone was talking about him. In other words, if he could look through his window and see two people talking or something like this, he'd call me right down there to the wing and want to know why the officers were talking about him. And of course they weren't.

Johnson's fear took the form of ideas of reference and persecution. These delusions emerged, according to the guard, whenever Johnson had contact with other inmates or with staff:

Well, of course, this would happen on shower days, because on shower days he would get a chance to see more people than he would normally. So when he'd take showers, we'd be right around the corner. And if he'd be taking a shower and he'd look out the windows, of course you can see out them, and if he'd see two officers talking and they'd be looking this way, then this would start this thing off. He'd carry this with him all day long until I got in in the morning. Then he'd give a note to the breakfast man and say, "I want to talk to you right away." So I'd tell him I'd be right down when I finished. And I'd go down, and he would say, "You've got to stop these guys from talking about me." I said, "What are you talking about?" He said, "I seen them. They were right down there in the corner talking about me. I seen them and I heard them. . . . Like he was taking a shave, for instance, during the daytime. Now he could hear the men in the west gallery talking. Now, whether they were talking about him or not, it wouldn't make any difference. He would get to his door and rattle his door and call them all kinds of names. He'd say, "You guys are doing it, I know it." Why he thought this, I don't know. These people would holler down. Of course, these people here, contact to them is a big thing. A guy in the west gallery would holler to somebody on the second floor. Now, he would hear this, and he would take off on it.

One problem Johnson encountered increasingly was the fear his erratic conduct inspired among other inmates. A friend complains:

He walked around and stared at everybody. And dudes would be nervous and shit. He would stare at dudes, and it wouldn't bother me 'cause I know him and shit, but other dudes would be really nervous.

Johnson had become persona non grata in the recreation yard. A guard tells us that "they were all afraid of him. . . . As a matter of fact, they all complained that we should have an observation man recreating with them." The officer reports that Johnson

> came out here for recreation one day, and he started waving his arms in the air and looking at twenty or thirty inmates out here, and he started saying, "They're all a bunch of fags, they're all a bunch of fags."

One of the inmates who had encountered Johnson in the yard told us:

> The guy might have been a schizophrenic, because sometimes he might be sitting outside there watching a card game and then other times he'd be walking around like this, calling out, "You motherfuckers" and "Fuck you nigger." And he was going to blow up. . . . Sometimes the guy was very quiet. You looked at him, and you didn't think he was the same guy. You could look at him sitting there. And then for no reason at all he would start walking up and down and start pacing and talking to himself, sometimes under his breath. Or sometimes he would come right over to you and call you. He would say, "You nigger fucker, say something to my face now." But other times he would sit there, and you could hold an intelligent conversation with the guy, and you would wonder, "Why is this guy in the fucking nut gallery?"

October 11, the day Johnson attempted suicide, he assaulted another inmate on the yard. Johnson's friend describes the morning as follows:

> So he was walking around one day, and he had a habit of talking loud when he was talking to himself, and everybody could hear him. About "those dudes up there, they was pulling shit, and they were looking for me to fuck them over" and "Why don't they try and get themselves together?" Something about "sitting around and playing cards all day." So anytime you walked by him you'd flinch. You see a dude looking like that, you're scared. What of, I don't know, but that's what happened. I seen Greg hit him first, and he fell on his face, and then he got up, and they started fighting. They didn't do nothing to each other, but I'm saying the dude didn't do nothing, and he couldn't believe it.

Following the incident, Johnson was locked in his cell. A guard describes his reaction as pleasant and congenial:

> When we separated him, he gave us no trouble at all. No resistance. We put him in his cell, and the nurse came up and gave him a physical to see if he had been injured. And then he said, "Well, Mr.

B——————, I guess I'm keep-locked." And I said, "Yes, I'm going to háve to write a report on you. You know you can't be fighting out there." "Well, that guy was talking about me." Then he said, "Will this interfere with my going to school?" And I said, "It shouldn't. But certainly you've got to recognize that this type of behavior isn't going to help you get off the observation floor." He said, "That's right." And this was probably before dinner, before noon that day. Now when I went home at three o'clock, nothing was further from my mind than that he would attempt to harm himself.

Johnson's mind, however, was filled with suspicions of affronts, denigration, and conspiracy. As he later described the incident to us:

A 7:   I had trouble with some guys, some inmates also. They take up the words, you understand what I'm talking about? This verbal harassment, you understand—they won't do it in my face, they do it behind my back. So I caught them out, you understand? I caught them red-handed, and we had a little rumble. . . . If I happen to catch someone, you understand, red-handed, we is going to have a rumble out there. I'm speaking about some of the inmates, because some of the officers, you understand, they were enticing them, the inmates, to harass me down there. . . . It was just calling me all types of names, you know? Motherfucker and this and that and the other, and all this. Things of this nature. When you would get out, when you're out in the recreation area, you know? And they'd say these things while you're on the other side or something of that nature. . . . I mean there were other guys also, but he just so happened to be one, you understand, that I caught. . . . And I was standing in my cell, and this guy so happened to be out there. And I heard him make this statement. I was looking right at him. And so when I came out for rec I asked him, "Who are you making these statements about?" And he denied making any meaning about me, but I knew better, and I asked him why. And he still denied, you understand, he wasn't making them. And he made some smart remark out of his mouth, and so that started the rumble right there.

After the fight, Greg Johnson arrived at the conclusion that he was to be punished by being burned alive by guards. He complained to staff that he had overheard discussions of the projected lynching:

A 7:   And some officers that worked on the floor, you understand what I'm talking about, they went down to see the deputy superintendent. So the words that they were speaking, the deputy superintendent had given his consent, you understand? They said they would burn me alive for what had happened. They said they were going to do it that night. So I tried, you understand what I'm talking about, to talk to the lieutenant. As a matter of fact, I seen one of the lieutenants this morning, to find out what is all this about. Why are they continuing to harass me? And so he said, you understand what I'm talking about, that nothing was going to happen to me. But actually I heard him myself, you know what I mean? Speaking on this matter. But he denied knowing anything about it. Which I expected, you know what I mean, anyway. But these things that I'm telling you, you know, I mean they're not illusions— these things really happened.

As the officers arrived for the evening shift, Johnson watched their movements apprehensively, and thought he saw preparations for his impending immolation:

A 7: Anyway, that night, the shift had changed and everything, and night had fallen. And it was rather late. I would say around eleven, eleven-thirty, something like that. And so officers were coming in the block, more than usual—they had a larger amount than usual. So what happened, I heard the officers pouring gasoline in cans, or whatever they had. As a matter of fact, I seen them from the cell that I was in. They got a yard that's fenced, it's steel-constructed on part of the yard. Anyway, I seen them down there with the gasoline, and they said they were going to take me out and cremate me, you understand what I'm talking about? They made threats against my family, and they were saying, "He's from the South," and so-and-so, and this and that and the other. You know what I mean? And you understand what I'm talking about, I wouldn't question that they would really—this was not being done for nothing, you understand, to try to put in the fear or nothing, you understand?

He considered, but dismissed, the possibility that the intent of the acts was to upset him or to drive him insane:

A 7: I also took into consideration the fact that they could say they were going to kill me and do the preparations, which I saw myself. And do something with you, do you understand what I'm talking about— bullshitting, you understand what I'm talking about?

I: That would come in your mind?

A 7: Yeah, I seen these things being done. I don't know, maybe whether they were trying to drive me crazy or something, you understand, make me stop, or whatever have you. I don't know, I wasn't thinking in this manner. In a way I was thinking in this manner also, but I wasn't going to let them do this, you understand? But I seen these things, gasoline and what have you, and naturally I took it like that this thing was going to be conducted.

Johnson intended to commit suicide. He tried to hang himself. When he did not succeed, he sliced his throat and cut his arm badly enough to expose bone. The purpose of suicide, as he saw it, was to forestall a painful execution and to make himself the agent of his own death:

A 7: I came to the conclusion myself, you understand? Why should I wait, you understand, and let them cremate me alive? I should, you understand, go on and do it my own self. And so this is what happened. . . . I said, "I've got to die, I'm going to die anyway, you understand, I shouldn't wait on them to do it. I can do it myself." Pretty wild thoughts started running through my mind and what have you. I mean I had this razor blade, so I start cutting on my wrists.

As soon as guards had been alerted to Johnson's suicide attempt, they arranged for emergency first aid and transportation to a hospital. This effort proved very costly. Johnson, still convinced that guards were trying to kill him, resisted fiercely. He sliced two guards—one in the face—and he bit a senior industrial officer.

Five weeks after this incident Johnson took his own life. In the interim, he committed another self-destructive act. Again he talks of fears relating to conspiracies and self-immolation:

A 7: The same thing was happening. My family was being threatened, and they were talking about coming to get me, burning me again. They were doing the same thing. . . . The deputy sheriffs were doing this. Things started running through my mind again. I mean, what would be done to me.

A note written by Johnson during this period certifies to the magnitude of his fears. Intended for one of the nurses, it reads:

Sister! Please get in touch with Assemblyman E——————— Tell Mr. E——————, the officers at *Attica Prison* are going to kill Inmate Greg Johnson tonight or tomorrow. Tell Mr. E——————, they have already killed his mother, sister and brother, and threatens to kill his wife and child. Tell Mr. E——————, Greg is in Meyer Memorial Hospital now. That's me. Thank you very much, black sister.

The incident occurred at Meyer Memorial Hospital in Buffalo. In this hospital, Johnson roomed with a sympathetic fellow inmate. He was heavily medicated and also received four electroconvulsive shocks. He was transferred back to Attica hospital with a notation certifying that "he appears to have made a good psychiatric recovery."

At Attica hospital, Johnson was placed in a solitary cell, under "medical keeplock." He spent much time brooding. The inmate across the hall reports:

I used to be up all night, and he would just lay in bed. He would just lay there. He wouldn't read or nothing. One time he asked me for some matches, and I didn't want to give it to him. I told him that I didn't have none. But he just laid up there like this, straight. Like he was dead.

I: Would he lay there for a long period of time?

Yeah, all day. He would just lay there.

Staff describe Johnson as reticent and uncommunicative. A guard tells us:

He was quiet. He would answer your questions, but that would be about it. He wouldn't carry on a conversation. If you talked to him about the weather or "How's things going today?" he'd say "OK," but that was it.

According to the guard, Johnson appeared normal while working (typing legal papers) but tended to get depressed when unoccupied. The same observation was made by an inmate:

Well, this time that he had all these writs going, he seemed very content. He was kept busy. Every time we went by the cell, he was either working on these writs or writing letters. He wrote a few letters home. Let's say he was busy. He was doing something. And as long as he was busy like that, then I figured that he was all right. But once he got all his writs taken care of, and then he wrote a few letters and that stopped, and he had been doing all right, then he started pacing around and wanting to come out in the corridor. That's when we got him a bunch of books, but this didn't seem to help. The writs seemed to keep him occupied. He seemed to be all right then. But once he got them out of the way, he started slowing down.

When his legal work was over, and they took his typewriter back, I imagine from that point on. 'Cause he wasn't no bother, and as long as he was occupied and he had something to do he didn't harass no one or "Hey, could you get this?" or none of that. He was just quiet and kept to himself. Feet up on the bed and working, or stretched out on the floor working. Or at his desk. So I imagine from that point on, I would guess.

Johnson's preoccupations seemed to take the form of guilt and ideas of reference. According to one staff member:

He was just worried about people talking about him. Talking about what he did to his family or something of that nature. He burnt them up or did something like that. And people were talking about this. He said, "Even at night I hear them in the mess hall." At first I thought that he was gone, but then it dawned on me that at night we have a rec in the mess hall and he might hear the noise and this might disturb him. . . . He said he kept hearing somebody calling his name, and he didn't know what they were talking about. I tried to reassure him. . . . And he would see the point for a while and would go off and do something else. And then a few seconds later he'd come back and say, "I think there's a couple of guys that are talking about me." This was the main thing that he was concerned about.

It was during this period that we interviewed Johnson. He described himself to us as watchfully awaiting new developments. He also expressed a resolve to fight new threat as it arose:

A 7:   I'm up here in this hospital now, I'm on keep-lock. So I don't know what they're going to do. What's going to be their next step. But one thing I know for sure, you understand what I'm talking about, I've gotten in contact with some people—some people know about this and whatever happens. I won't endeavor to take my life, you know what I mean, regardless of what the circumstances be. If they're going to do something, you understand, they're just going to have to do it to me. But there is people that know about this in advance, you know? Like I say, as far as me doing something to myself again, it won't be. . . . If I'm attacked I'm just going to defend myself, you understand, to the extent that I can, you understand, till I can't defend myself no more. That's all there is to it. But I'm not going to do anything to myself. I made a very bad mistake, you understand what I'm talking about, by doing it from the beginning, but the position that I was put in—I was never in a position like this before.

During the last days of his life, Johnson's fearful watchfulness became a chronic state. He spent much time standing at his cell door furtively monitoring the guards:

He was right there at that window—for the eight hours that I'm there, he would be there at that window seven hours. Because he was constantly there looking out the window to see what we were doing. And as I say, other inmates have told me that he thought people were talking about him. This is why he was always looking out, peeking out the win-

dows, to see if we were talking about him. According to these other inmates, he just had the idea that we were all talking about him. So as I
say, we didn't have nothing to worry about really. We didn't have to
walk down as often as we did, because he was always at the window
watching us. He walked up to the window and over to the wall and
right back to the window, and then he would stop and look up. See
what we was up to. Then he'd walk back and forth again.

Johnson wrote requests for interviews with a psychiatrist, noting that
"there [are] some matters of importance I would like to discuss." An interview took place two days before his suicide. The psychiatrist reported that,
according to Johnson, "the other inmates and some guards have been talking about him behind his back, accusing him of many unreal things." The
psychiatrist prescribed medication, and advised psychotherapy.

Two days later, Johnson's fears came to a climax. A guard coming on
duty was told that Johnson had complained of being talked about; hours
later, the guard reassured Johnson that his fears were groundless:

I was told by the guards when I came on duty, the day shift guards, that
Johnson was upset, and he believed that they were talking about him
and his mother and his family and things like this. . . . He wanted to
know something that I had said to another inmate that was locking
right next door to him. He seemed a little hostile, and he just misunder-
stood something I had said. He thought I was talking about him. But I
cleared it up with him.

I: Did he feel better after that?

Yeah. And then he asked me a couple of times what time will I pass
medication, what time will the medication pass, and I told him what
time, at five. And that's about it.

Another guard noted that Johnson was extremely restless and that he
seemed anxious to escape from his cell:

And Officer E——————, that same day, we both of us noticed that
he was getting a little uptight. So we gave him a bunch of magazines
and books and took them down to him. We asked him if he would like
to read some. And he said "OK." So we took them down and he'd look
through them a few times and then put them aside. He was constantly at
the window, looking out. . . . Everytime I walked down back, he was
right at the door. He'd want a drink of water. I'd take him out, and he
would go get a drink of water. I could have just took the thing itself,
but I figured the guy is in this room. And when you're in there constantly—well, it would get to me after a while too. So I figured that he
was probably better off if I let him out and walked around with him

and that would give him a chance to get the hell out of his room for a few minutes. I'd take him out and he'd go and get water. We probably made about four trips to get water. I knew damn well he couldn't drink it all. But he got it. But I thought if this relieved him a little bit, OK. And the same way with the bathroom. He was down there a hundred times that day. Go to the bathroom, or he was reading a journal, which he had never done before.

Shortly before his death, Johnson contacted an inmate who celled across the hall from him and asked to see another inmate who worked in the kitchen. The two men returned to Johnson's cell door for a brief conversation:

So he said would I go get him because he wanted to talk with him. So I went to the kitchen, and me and C——————— went back to the window, and then he said that everybody up in the hospital was talking about him. He seemed like he was spaced out, you know? He was saying a whole lot of stuff you couldn't really make nothing out of. It didn't seem like it had no value to what he was saying. And he accused everybody of saying that he broke up his family or something. He was talking in riddles, couldn't make nothing out of it. C——————— got mad. He said, "Man, this guy's crazy—fuck this guy," and he walked away. Well, then, after a while he was talking. Like I said, I couldn't make nothing out of it. Finally I told him, "OK brother," and I left too. So we went back, and we were sitting there watching TV. No more than about five minutes later a guy came, and he said, "You know that guy in there, Johnson, they just cut him down off the window." I said, "What, we just got through talking to him." So I went in the kitchen. I said, "C——————, that dude just hung up." He said, "Who?" I said, "That guy we were just talking to."

The two men, who did not know Johnson, found themselves cryptically accused by Johnson of conspiring against him and his family:

He didn't show no emotion at all, his facial expressions. His voice was soft, he was talking real low, and he didn't get excited or nothing, you know? That's why I say it seemed like he was spaced out, you know? He was talking real quiet and smooth. . . . He said everybody there was talking about him. And accused him of burning up his family or something. . . . I guess he meant fire, I don't know. . . . He started talking about everybody in the hospital was talking about him, and he thinks that we accuse him of burning up his family. So I asked him what makes him think like that? He shook his head, and he didn't say nothing. Like I said, he's spaced out. He's quiet. And then I said, "I don't even know you, man. This is the first time I ever spoke to you. Except that day that you came out of the bathroom, and so was I." And I said, "I don't even know you. Why should we have any reason to say anything like that about you?"

Convinced that his life was in danger, Greg Johnson hanged himself in his cell that same afternoon.

A Message of Vulnerability

When Greg Johnson entered prison he advertised himself as a Man to Be Reckoned With, as a fearless figure for whom guards were no match and rules no obstacle, a tower of strength who could—and would—do exactly as he pleased. He made challenges and expressed contempt, and he claimed resources that could keep overwhelming odds helplessly at bay.

Such postures cannot be lived up to. They are face-saving poses, designed to mask feelings of dependency and inadequacy. They are bids for undeserved respect, unearned awe, unwarranted impact, entered by men uncertain of their autonomy and impressiveness. They tend to be peremptory bids because they are based on doubt; they gain urgency from fear of contempt or dread of defeat.

Opponents faced with such strategies are hard put to rejoin appropriately. Engaged at face value, the poses magnify themselves and reach (as with Johnson) caricaturelike proportions. If deflated, the pretense often collapses, exposing (as with Johnson) the unprotected helplessness beneath.

Johnson's tragedy is magnified by the fact that prison is attuned to challenges of power. In a prison context, Johnson's bluff was inevitably noted, and called. It was inevitable that he would be tested and found wanting. He could thus be left without resources for survival with honor.

We have seen that staff were trapped by Johnson's goading. Motivated by concerns for safety, order, and inmate morale—and personally affronted —they dignified his claims to notoriety, violence potential, and militance. They quartered him among the elite of inmate toughs. They give him new and more rewarding arenas for boisterous aggressivity.

They also played his game. They singled Johnson out, punished him, ordered him about. In front of his peers, they challenged him to tests of strength. They knew—or should have known—what his response would be. For Johnson played a well-worn role. He stood fast, roared, threatened. He spewed obscenities, proclaimed himself inviolable and dangerous. He could afford no less. The guards, too, were trapped. If they backed off, the field was Johnson's. If they stood fast, they dignified his claim. And they tended to stand fast.

Ultimately, neither the guards nor Johnson won. The guards played scenes not of their own choosing, on burlesquelike stages. Their perspective was tarnished; they invoked disproportionate resources to counter paper tigers, and at times became unprofessionally engaged. Johnson's fate was more damaging. He was sidetracked from his studies, controlled and monitored, tested and goaded. And ultimately he was keep-locked and impotent, alone with his doubts.

While Johnson's reputation grew among guards, his image solidified for inmates. Some saw him as a legal scholar and a resource. Others classed him as Manly. Still others viewed him as threateningly unpredictable or unstable:

> All I can say is that Johnson, even when he was first transferred back here, he would spit on you, he would throw water on you when you come by his cell. So to me, you can't call him a militant. He was just irrational, that's the word I'd use. It seemed like he don't have no feeling or nothing . . . he's that type of person that you can't trust.

Although most of Johnson's time was spent in segregation, he developed problems with inmates while still in population. One such conflict grew out of his loud demonstrations after hours:

> Due to the fact that they locked up twenty-four hours a day, they rack off according to conditions about them. Sometimes if you want to nap, the inmates upstairs, they want them to shut up. If one of the brothers is protesting against something, trying to get something for themselves, those upstairs can't understand this here.

Johnson also initiated confrontations by insisting in his dealings with other inmates on his model of prison adjustment:

> Anybody that was prepared to blend into the conditions that were required for them to blend in in order to remain out there in population, he had a big animosity against them.

> Whenever anyone was talking about anything, he would say, "Oh shut up, creeps." Or, "If you was a man you wouldn't be here." That's the way he felt. . . . The guys on the side would be talking about the revolution or so on, and he would holler, "You guys ain't no revolutionists. If you were, you wouldn't be here."

In segregation, Johnson had friends who shared his militant views and stance. He also had enemies who knew—and exploited—his threshold for anger:

> Well, they had porters working there, trustee inmates—they call them goons—who were under the same status that we would be down there

for, as far as just segregation. Their case may have been for protection or what have you, some voluntary thing. But I've seen inmates throw water on Greg, seen them throw bottles of water on him. I've seen inmates throw other articles in the cell, such as soap, food, curse him and agitate him from a distance. And misinform the officers that were working there of his activities in the cell.

So we're in there, and the guys were saying, "Oh, you're a punk, Greg. You let them beat you up. You can't even fight, man. You let the hunkies beat you up." And they were making a joke, but it's not a joke for Greg. Greg is a full-grown man, and this isn't no joke to him. He feels bad about it. And this is everyday action. It don't come out of your mouth no more because everybody thinks you're a punk and you can't fight. So you just shut up. And this is every day. . . . All you can hear is them voices from the other cells. Now, can you picture looking like that? Twenty-four hours a day, every day, for months, with dudes fucking with you all day long. Understand?

Johnson himself characterized inmates at Great Meadows as immature and as contemptuous of a Manly reaction to prison:

A 7:   I was at Comstock, and down there, you understand what I'm talking about, I had problems down there. It seems as though, you understand, if you don't run around and act like a kid, you understand what I'm talking about, people despise you. If you're taking care of yourself in a quietlike manner, carry yourself like a man, this is something to despise. They'd rather see you running around like a kid. But I refused to do this, you know what I mean?

If Johnson's "Manly" stance was designed to impress his fellow inmates, it failed to do so. Johnson's response to the discovery consisted of categorizing nonadmirers as "punks." He created a dichotomous world, in which guards and inmate-collaborators stood arrayed against him and his kind. This process of dichotomization was facilitated by the atmosphere in the observation or segregation wing. Close cohabitation promoted outgrouping and suspiciousness among the inmates:

It was drawing us together, it was also splitting us up. . . . It seems like you couldn't hardly trust nobody around there. . . . And when somebody new came down, we was all suspicious because of that Attica incident. There was a whole lot of dudes that were ratting on the other inmates that participated in the Attica thing that were being sent down there. So we had no way of checking nobody out, so we had to accept everybody at face value.

Immobilization produced experiences which confirmed Johnson's feelings of vulnerability. Any unpopular man could find himself a caged target for the aggression of the uncaged. In Johnson's case, the situation was aggravated by his Self-Release syndrome, which (as we noted in Chapter 4) invites badgering and a cycle of confrontations:

> Oh, he would vociferously express his disapproval of the treatment. You know, he would use profanity and use various epithets there as far as name-calling goes, and stuff like that. And that's the only possible retaliation. I mean, he's behind bars, and he can't move over six feet in any direction, water's being thrown on him, hot, cold food, soap, sticks being poked at him.

The staff's impression of Johnson's career at Great Meadows focused on his overt conduct; it emphasized intensified challenges to them, culminating in arbitrary attacks on passing guards. Fellow inmates noted Johnson's increased vulnerability and cornered status.

Attica received Johnson and his bulging disciplinary file. Attica staff became aware of Johnson's record but could not confirm their colleagues' stereotype of Militance. Johnson was too transparently vulnerable at this point in his life. The guards came to regard him as a fear-obsessed man rather than as a fear-inspiring figure:

> The first time he was here on the west gallery he had a very, very belligerent attitude about everything and everybody. Very suspicious and very uncooperative. And he had this incident over his cell. When he came up here in observation he was pretty quiet for the first day or so, but he was so reasonable I couldn't believe it. His attitude had changed so. He was a lot different. And I said to him, "Regardless of what happened in the past, if you want to start off from scratch, this is fine." And I'm telling you that aside from the fact that he was on that side, he behaved himself good. . . . See, he might have had a turning point that we weren't even aware of. Certainly there was things going on his mind that we didn't even know about.

Johnson himself rejected the cues to this new image. He saw himself as a perceived threat, surrounded by retaliatory forces—like Custer with a Last Stand overdue. Throughout his life, Johnson had invoked and relied on outside support. His writs and letters, his interminable petitions, were designed to reinforce a campaign to escape prison and reassert his integrity. They helped him discharge his cumulating tension. Several inmates saw Johnson's Aid-seeking efforts as insuring his sanity and survival:

> Well, he was constantly in this law bag, trying to get home. I notice that he was always running to his law books. He was quiet. And when I say he was a nut, it doesn't mean that he was out of his head. . . . He was scared. He didn't want to do his time.

His outlet was law, and he didn't have it anymore. You see dudes in here doing twenty to life, that's all they do is fuck with the law. Because if they lose hope with the sight of law, what else do they have? Are they waiting for parole when they're fifty years old and shit? So you notice that all the dudes with big time, they are always sitting with their typewriters typing out law and shit. . . . If you don't have no role, that's when you go off in there.

The image is that of a man afraid of prison and doubtful of his ability to survive there. He overlays fear with a facade of bravado, and embarks on an effort to escape through appeals, requests, and writs. Early clashes center on staff interferences with writ-writing or on rejections of requests. The obdurate walls of confinement do not yield to Johnson's trumpet. On the contrary, challenges produce increased pain, humiliation, and demonstrations of impotence. Ultimately, there is prison within prison, creating more adjustment problems and greater fear.

As fear grows into the Self-Escape syndrome, so does the wildness of the reaction. Eventually, climactic tantrums fizzle into outbursts; writs become paranoid delusions. Ultimately, there is stark paranoid panic. Attica, as Johnson sees it, is the personification of what he fears. He has heard, we know, of plans for a "maxi-maxi" institution. He has heard Tales of Attica, borne by riot figures. And he cannot muster, for Attica, his pretense of bravery and his trapping of strength. He is spent, naked, past reassuring.

The dangers he feels are those he has feared too long. He is exposed, surrounded, outmatched. There are omnipotent staff, and pliable inmate-allies, able—on whim—to squash him and his. The knowledge brings pain, insulation, tense watching. No one can help; fear has made Johnson a pariah, a threat to peers. Staff invoke psychiatrists, who can drug, imprison, or exile. An occasional kindly person speaks of reality, but cues to danger drown out these feeble voices.

And inevitably, there is the omnipresent isolation cell, with its emptiness and silence, its cold, suffocating vacuum. For it remains a tragic fact that our ultimate tool for dealing with fear-obsessed men defies and defeats their regeneration: we isolate such men, and seal their fate. We place those who are their own worst enemies face to face with themselves, alone, in a void.

Note

1. The "five percenters" are a black militant group composed of youths who view themselves as a divinely ordained army of liberation.

11

The Price
of
Conformity

In the preceding chapter we described the collapse of a frantic challenge
to the prison system. We reviewed the end of a stormy, troublesome, stri-
dent campaign for recognition and autonomy. We now turn to the story
of a self-effacing, model inmate. It is the portrait of a man responsive
to staff, admired by peers—a man who "did his time" quietly and with dignity, a man who was program-centered and mindful of his work and
personal adjustment.

We shall see that Militant and Con can meet similar fates. We shall see
that two streams—one turbulant and one quiet—can converge in the end.
That they can merge in a dark pool of fear, fed by shared undercurrents
of panic and doubt.

The man we shall call Duke Anderson was convicted at twenty-two of
second degree murder. In company with four others, he held up a neighborhood card game in 1963. One of his companions—startled and nervous
—shot the host. The man died of his wounds.

Anderson talked to the police of his participation in the tragedy. He
said that he had "gone along" with a plan he viewed as make-believe. He
had wielded a knife, with a fierceness born of heavy drinking. He had witnessed the shooting. His assessment of the event was fraught with fatalism.
"I didn't want to see the dude get shot," he said, "but he's dead now, and
there's nothing I can do about it." His view of prison was similar. The

250

district attorney records "that he expects to be imprisoned for at least 15 years and sees no reason to engage in any maneuvering or denials of his implications in the affair." Duke also explained that he had no fear of going to prison.

After almost a year in jail, Duke Anderson was sentenced to a minimum of twenty-five years, a maximum of life. This sentence is a very substantial one. It was partially based on Anderson's youthful record, "particularly with assault." In these "assaults" a young Anderson, in company with others, took lunch money from schoolmates and threw "snowballs and pieces of ice" at a teacher. These events did not produce serious immediate repercussions. Ultimately, they proved fateful. They were invoked as grounds for stiff sentencing and gave Anderson a reputation for "assaultiveness" which permeates his file.

Duke Anderson's social history is a standard account of slum life. He grew up among fourteen siblings under deprived circumstances. His father, a barber, eked out a marginal existence. Both of his parents were black, southern-born, and uneducated. When Duke left school after the tenth grade, he was classified as a slow learner, performing at seventh-grade level. He took a barbering course at the Elmira Reception Center and helped his father as an apprentice. In his spare time—according to the probation report, Duke engaged in "drinking, carousing, and general idleness."

Psychiatrists who interviewed Duke and read his arrest sheets took a dim view of his mental health. They diagnosed him as a "Schizoid Personality–Sociopathic Personality Disturbance–Anti-Social Personality." They cryptically noted "some evidence of thought distortion during the psychological test [which] could not be confirmed clinically." They concluded that Duke's "personality impresses as that of a schizoid, aggressive, impulsive, easily suggestible individual with anti-social tendencies."

Duke Anderson entered Sing Sing on January 31, 1964; he died nine years later at the Green Haven Correctional Facility. The intervening years were marked by growth and ambition, maturation and activity.

In Sing Sing, Duke was assigned to the barber shop, where he was rated "excellent." He continued functioning as a barber after being transferred to Clinton and Attica, until he requested work in a textile shop. Wherever he worked, Duke was ranked highly by supervisors. Except for some self-requested keep-lock, his first years in prison show no disciplinary reports. His correspondence with staff is studded with the needs of a man involved in the affairs of an active inmate. In 1965, Duke asked and was granted permission to (1) make a box of matchsticks for his mother, (2) buy boots and gloves, (3) order a pair of slippers, and (4) replace a broken frame for his eyeglasses.

The following two years show continued evidence of constructive leisure-time concerns. Anderson was intensely involved in sports (his warden's correspondence deals with requests for sneakers and basketball shoes). He played a guitar, talked of reading textbooks, and showed interest in study courses. He requested permission to try oil painting (which he received, "providing . . . you will not paint any nude or suggestive pictures"). He inquired into the cancellation of a music program on the inmate radio station.

The first disturbing note in an otherwise placid picture was struck in mid-1967 by plaintive correspondence relating to a knee injury that had come to preoccupy Anderson. From the start, Duke Anderson had been concerned with his physical fitness. He was active in weight lifting, football, running, and other sports. In late 1965, during one such activity, he had injured a knee. An X ray showed no abnormality, and the condition was treated with heat and withdrawal of fluid. In December, Duke complained of pain but refused to have fluid withdrawn. He continued to complain, and late in 1966 he demanded an operation. The physician found no grounds for surgery and refused to honor the request.

An Aid Seeking problem (of the kind described in Chapter 2) cumulated. In June 1967, Anderson appealed to the warden. He wrote of pain and loss of weight in the injured leg. He expressed fear of an amputation and demanded surgery. The request prompted another X ray, with negative results. Anderson wrote to the warden again (and to the commissioner), complaining of pain, asking for another physician, and requesting an interview. The warden spoke to Anderson. Duke yielded, and accepted treatment for a diagnosed arthritis condition.

In September 1967, Duke Anderson had his first prison fight—a serious conflict featuring home-made weapons. A guard reported that he discovered Anderson and another inmate (Smith) slicing at each other in the latter's cell:

> They were both on the floor in back of the bed doing combat. . . . I ordered them to break, but Anderson said, "Let me kill him, I can finish him right now." . . . I raised my stick and said, "If either of you make another advance toward each other, I will have to forcibly stop you." . . . I ejected Anderson from the cell and saw that he had two weapons in his hands. I told him to give them to me, and he did.

Though Anderson had initiated the fight, he was the more seriously injured. On his way to the hospital, amid jeers from Smith, he declared, "If I ever get a chance to get to him, I'll kill him." Anderson claimed that the quarrel had started the previous evening, when he asked Smith a friendly question about another inmate. According to Anderson, Smith had called him a "punk" and had cast aspersions on his mother. Smith's story had it that Anderson "was parading up and down the gallery like an Indian, taunting [Smith] ever since [Smith] had been on the company."

No further confrontation between the two inmates occurred. Anderson's situation appears to have normalized again. In October he talked of drafting an appeal of his case. He became concerned about appearing in court, and requested plastic surgery to remove his recently inflicted scars. He also complained of pains in his knee, and worried about losing his leg. Anderson underwent a cycle of plastic surgery. The scars were repaired, and at Anderson's request, a lip was narrowed. His knee was also treated, though Anderson continued to be concerned about it. He had also developed a new affliction—hemorrhoids—and this condition was also attended to.

Throughout this period, Anderson continued to work in the tailor shop. His entry sheet describes him as "satisfied with his assignment" and notes that "progress reports indicate that he works in a steady, cooperative, courteous and skilled manner and qualifies for outside employment in this area." On two occasions, Anderson embarked on Self-Classification. In mid-1968, he wrote to the warden, telling him,

> I am now in Tailoring Shop—been in about four months trying to get use to it. But I can't get use to my surrounding. I feel I may get into a little difficulty if I don't get out. I ask for the yard, so my surrounding wouldn't be so close. If you please transfer me to the yard gang—I will give you no more complaining. Thank you, sir.

In January 1969, Anderson asked to be returned to the barber shop, claiming that his barbering needed "sharpening up." He expressed hope of release, indicating his desire "to work out in society with my father if all goes well in court." Two weeks later, Anderson explained to the warden that

> I am not refusing to work—I just can't work in those kinds of shops very long. I ask you for the barbershop job—maybe that a mistake too. So I am asking you for a job working out in the yard—any yard gang or yard job.
> Another reason for this is that I would like to stay in this institution, I think I can serve better time here, I wouldn't want to be transfer to another prison.

In this period, Anderson was routinely seen by a psychiatrist, who diagnosed him as an "Anti-social personality—severe habitual excessive drinking—severe." By contrast, Anderson's supervisors continued to submit glowing reports. At year's end, these ratings were summarized as follows:

> He is a willing, interested and satisfied worker who has a cooperative and courteous behavior on assignment. Subject learns easily, is quick

and does his best. He does not ask for higher jobs, but is able to do them. Anderson gets along well with others . . . is qualified for outside employment in garment manufacturing. Very cooperative worker and keeps busy at all time. Very dependable—should have no problems. His personal conduct is indifferent, and he's calm, courteous, and with other inmates he adjusts easily. . . . Has neither gripes nor problems . . . is resigned to encarceration . . . adjusts to new situations easily and requires no extra supervision. Good worker, keeps out of trouble.

These ratings were unaffected by a fist-fight in the garment shop between Anderson and a fellow inmate. The other inmate was described as a troublemaker and transferred. Anderson declared that "the guy pushed me. I can't take that." He testified that he had made every effort to avoid the confrontation. A fight had been precipitated when Anderson's opponent "went by his machine and brushed a bundle of clothes against him."

In 1970, two tragedies occurred in Anderson's family. In February, one of his sisters died suddenly. Duke was escorted to New York to attend the funeral, and spent a night at the Tombs. In the following weeks, there were visits from members of his family for the first time in six years. On one such occasion, Anderson produced two portraits of his dead sister.

In July, one of Duke's brothers met a violent end. He was mugged, thrown onto a subway track, and run over by a train. Duke was spared the details, but he somehow ascertained them later.

In December, Duke Anderson showed concrete signs of tension. In one outburst, he attacked a deserted ski jump. Two weeks later, he had his third fight, over priorities in the inmate Christmas show. Witnesses saw Anderson as the aggressor, and they testified that he had been generally "uptight." The theory was that Anderson's problem "had something to do with [having] lost three brothers." A staff member recommended to the warden "that Anderson have a meeting with a professional medical person to uncover what the trouble was." No such meeting was scheduled.

At this time, Anderson continued to perform at work, underwent cosmetic surgery, was active in sports, and enrolled in a high school equivalency study program.

Anderson showed his stress in other ways. He renewed complaints about his knee and was X-rayed. In May 1970, he developed a very large peptic ulcer. In November, he requested a transfer to Green Haven. He complained that

the city inmates are making my time hard for me, and I am afraid something will occur when push comes to shove. I just can't do my time here any more. I will appreciate if I can go where there is more state men. I chose Green Haven prison because it is closer for my family to visit me.

On January 4, 1971, Anderson was transferred to Green Haven. After his arrival, he requested admission to the school program and began a course of study. He continued his regime of sports, and spent long hours playing his guitar.

For the next two years, Anderson functioned as a model inmate. He studied, played ball, lifted weights. Then in December 1972—for the first time in his prison career—he rebelled against the staff. During a search, he refused to hand over his belongings for examination. Instead, he stood in front of his cell and told the guards, "If you want it out, take it out."

In the next few weeks, Anderson requested assignment to the barber shop and then asked for work as a cell porter. He also pleaded for a transfer to Wallkill or Auburn. The assignment at Auburn, which would have permitted full time schooling, received strong staff endorsement. The superintendent's recommendation notes:

Checked with School and they say inmate is [an] excellent, well-motivated student, who has just taken GED, and they strongly recommend this inmate's transfer for educational purposes.

On February 15, Anderson showed clear signs of a Self-Escape syndrome. He asked for self-segregation. He wrote, "I would like to isolate myself from the messhall, so I can get myself together." A week later, Anderson had a fight with another inmate, James Hull. Anderson used a sharpened spoon, and Hull a garbage can cover. According to the guards, "Both inmates were threatening to kill each other." Anderson later maintained that Hull had been harassing him and had tried to induct him as a Black Muslim.

The fight brought assignment to isolation. During the following week, a guard noted that Anderson had become depressed. The guard requested psychiatric observation for Anderson, adding that "the inmate . . . said there is 'something wrong. I don't know what. I've lost all my friends. Something's going on and I don't know what it is. I'm worried.'" The guard also noted that Anderson talked in a "nervous voice, shakey . . . on the verge of crying."

The next day Anderson was assigned to another segregation unit, and four days later he electrocuted himself with a disassembled pair of earphones. He left notes to members of the staff (guards, teachers, physicians), fellow inmates, and relatives. In these messages, he conveyed blessings, affection, gratitude, and good wishes.

Anderson also wrote one or two general notes, addressed to no one in particular. In one of these, he observed

Through my mind going back, it's impossible for me to be innocent, where I am in reality and in any other way, innocent. . . . Confusion is not a part of me. It's more got to do with a something I don't know about, me outside and inside.

Elsewhere he wrote:

> You know, it's funny how the pattern of one's life turns out different
> from his own thinking and dreams. . . . Now it has turned out beyond
> his reach, and because of this his pattern of life is really not of his own.
> But behind it all he still wants *love* from the world.

These documents end the recorded career of Duke Anderson—the details that are furnished by his file. There is also an informal portrait, a
view of Anderson provided by his associates and his friends.

The most striking fact about Anderson's perception by his peers is his
reputation as a model of stability and self-control. The consensus among
inmates was that Duke Anderson had achieved a formula for doing his
time effectively:

> It's a hell of a thing, you know. I'm not trying to build him up at all,
> but everything I knew about the guy was positive. There was no nega-
> tive stuff. He was a real cool dude. He's the kind of dude you'd like to
> do a bit with because he don't mind nobody's business, he just did his
> thing. . . . The dude was just dynamite people. Now a lot of the old guys
> that have been around the joint before, they appreciate a guy like this
> because they know a guy like that ain't going to get out of line. Some
> of the others have to get involved in programs and groups and shit, but
> they're not going to hassle this guy because they know he's got his shit
> together already.

> I thought he was strong mentally. He had been down a whole lot of
> years. He wasn't the type of person to be complaining about doing time.
> Like crying about all this time, like some people would do. He knew he
> had to do it.

Some staff who knew Anderson also shared this favorable assessment:

> As a matter of fact, I would think that he would be stronger than the
> average inmate. That was my impression.

> He was the type of guy you always liked to go out of your way to help.
> And I always did go out of my way to help him because he was so nice.
> This guy here would only come in, he'd only want something when it
> was really necessary. I always went out of my way to give him a hand.
> Because of that reason. And he's really an exception as far as I was
> concerned.

Anderson was described as conquering imprisonment by being (1) independent, (2) reserved, and (3) active. His independence was defined as

self-sufficiency; he was seen as a nonjoiner—a man who had no need to involve himself with others:

> He was somewhat alone. There were only three or four people that he associated with, and he just liked to lift weights and run around and punch the bag and things like that. . . . we ended up in Attica together, and even there he was the same way. He played a lot of sports and minded his own business. . . . He didn't infringe on anybody else. He didn't bully anyone else. And he didn't like to see anyone bullying anybody either. He was that type of person.

> Duke always stayed to himself. The only time he'd be, like, with a crowd is in, like, football. And even when he plays football, he don't sell no tickets like what he going to do on the field or nothing like that. He goes out and does his thing.

Anderson was also described as noncommunicative, as a man who kept his problems and feelings to himself. Conversations with Anderson were characterized as sparse and unrevealing:

> If I seen him in the yard I'd say, "What's happening, Duke?" He'd say, "What's happening, Blood? What you doing?" "I'm going to football practice." In other words, the conversation always stayed on that sort of level. You know, like it never got personal. His never got personal to me, mine never got personal to him.

> Well, he's always been the same quiet dude. He don't let you know what's on his mind. You never know what he's thinking. You can't figure him out.

Anderson was seen as a man who discharged feelings through action rather than words. His activities—sports and music—were perceived as the means whereby he coped with the pains of incarceration:

> Dig this here, he had this program. See, like guys in here get in a certain program, you're going to lift weights, you're going to play football, you're going to play chess. That's your program, day after day. Like he had his, that was his program that I just outlined. In other words, it wasn't coming out in the yard, and like, "What am I going to do today?" You know, OK, today is iron day. When you finished with that, you play some chess or go to football practice or what have you. He had a program, you dig what I'm saying? Now a lot of guys don't have programs, you understand, they go out in the yard and, whatever happens. If they're going to do this they happen to do this, but it's not mapped out that way. But he had it, he had a program.

As far as I know, even when he would get a little mad he would go to the yard. He would run all day. If he'd be depressed or anything he would run the yard. Or play handball.

Staff views of Anderson also highlight his constant activity. Where inmates stress the extracurricular concerns, staff focus on work and study. In addition to supervisors' ratings, there are informal testimonials. We have, for instance, statements from Anderson's teachers about his extraordinary drive and dedication:

He always wanted extra homework. He did his homework and boom, hand it in the next day. And that, in this place, is extremely unusual. . . . And in this eighth-grade class he was dynamite as far as, not necessarily always getting the correct answer, but constantly working. He was a real hard worker.

To make a long story short, it was really very simple. He was the best student I had in that class. He was a straight A student as far as I was concerned. He would have made it in a special theory class. I remember he said very little. He sat still, very still and upright in his chair, sort of back in the middle. Very attentive. Apparently he had taken in everything.

Some inmates suggested that a man with Anderson's pattern of involvement needed activity to preserve sanity. They argued that in an isolation cell Anderson might have had no tools to cope with whatever problems he had:

Like I said, I felt he was as sane as anybody else I seen in here. And, like, it was a question of him being isolated and not having no one to rap his problems out. See, in other words when he was in the yard, right, he used to lift his weights and maybe play some chess, but he had, like, companionship, guys to talk to and whatnot. Now you take that away from him, right? In other words, if something did happen emotionally in his family, he got it off by being in the yard, playing chess, lifting weights. In other words, he didn't have time to think on that. But now, taken away from his friends, like I say, the yard, and just putting him on his own, he had time to, like, think. You dig what I'm saying? . . . He was put in a position where he had to think alone, about maybe his own problems. In other words, before he was active, and now his mind was laying dormant. He was in the cell, no one to talk to, nothing to do. And whatever problems he may have had, he may have just said, like, "Fuck it, I can't take it no more."

Now you're locking him in there with everything he has ever been thinking about and couldn't solve. So . . . that could bring the walls in on him. . . . He would have probably got out there and done pushups and sit-ups all day long. And no problems. But when you take a kid that's active like that and coop him up, it drugs him. I think this is one of the reasons he liked to work outside a lot too.

The problems attributed to Anderson were (1) concerns about the death of his brother, (2) concerns about the search of his cell, (3) fear of losing his program, and (4) fear of other inmates.

Concerns about family matters were seen as contributing motives for Anderson's breakdown. Anderson's fight with Hull, for instance, which led to worries about transfer possibilities, was attributed to suspicions connected with his brother's murder. Anderson's segregation, coming at a time when he was preoccupied with his family, was seen as amplifying his sorrow and helplessness:

Now somebody told me, I think, he lost his family . . . while he was doing his bit, somebody in his family had died. So, like, I still couldn't see where this would be the point where he'd start killing himself, right? But then I start thinking, "OK, he gets locked up during the shakedown. He comes out, gets in a fight, and gets locked up again. All this time he has no one to talk to. In other words, he's isolated. Now if he did have problems, like family problems, if he did have family problems or anything of this nature, he had no one to talk to. Both times, he's isolated, right?

The only thing I could think of, they said he had three deaths in his family. And maybe being locked up over there, it got to him a little bit.

Several inmates mentioned that Anderson's depression began—or became obvious—after the search of his cell. There was speculation that officers might have defaced or confiscated pictures of Anderson's family:

Just one thing might seem to bug the guy. When we had a shakedown in December or something like that, some officer mistreated his pictures or something personal like that. And this seemed to bug him a little bit.

He didn't have no trouble until they started his frisk. This frisk they have down there. He never had any trouble before that, but then he started. He was depressed. . . . like I said, the only trouble I know that he had was when they had the shakedown. And they took his family pictures, and that's what started it, and he got sent to E Block.

There was also a suggestion that Anderson might have been afraid that his involvement in the search and in the fight with Hull might impair his prospects for transfer:

> Like I said before, Duke, his whole style was to get that school so that he could get some kind of program so when he goes to the board he gets something going for him. He didn't want nothing interfering with that, you know?

> Another thing, he wanted to go to Auburn. He asked me, "Do you think I'll be able to go to Auburn?" To me, at this point it seemed that he wanted to get away from this.

The most prevalent view was that Anderson's difficulties centered on his fear of other inmates, including associates of Hull, and of staff. He was seen as having become extremely apprehensive about being abandoned, attacked, or stigmatized:

> Now my belief was that fear of the administration combined with fear that he had for the dude's comrades. 'Cause the guy that he stabbed was a follower of Elijah Muhammad. And they're closely knit, right? So this added on to the fear too.

> Well, he was saying I was causing him to lose his friends. And the officers and police think he's a Muslim and a revolutionary and this and that. . . . he goes up to the temple and tells my Muslim minister that I'm still jitterbugging. Right? And by him going up to the temple, he gets the impression that everybody stopped talking to him for this here. He said that the officers think that he's a Muslim now and a revolutionary. . . . There was another two fellows that is here, and he said they kept staring at him. And the little fellow, he's on the company, he would wash his underwear out and hung it up there, and he said, "Why is he doing this? Why is he hanging his underwear out in front of my cell?"

> When he was downstairs he seemed pretty uptight with the inmates that were down there. And the way he put it to me, he was having problems with the Muslims. That he was being forced to become a Muslim and he didn't want to. They just kept pushing him and pushing him. He tried to get around it, but he got put in a corner where he thought that the man might try something with him. . . . He was scared. The man was scared half to death.

Inmates and guards who knew Anderson during his final days claim that he expressed strong apprehensions and that he tried to protect and isolate himself from perceived danger:

I said, "What's the problem?" He was nervous as hell, and he looked ready to crack. I said, "What's the matter, Anderson?" Just like that, he said, "Something is going on, and I don't know what. I've lost all my friends. I'm worried." And that's just the way he said it.

When he came out of the box he looked scared, and as a matter of fact he told me, "They're trying to kill me." I said, "Who?" He said, "The administration." I said, "Why don't you get out and—?" He said, "Yeah, I'm trying to go to Auburn."

He'd done come out in the morning when there ain't nobody hardly in the yard. . . . In other words, he didn't want to break out in the open like he did that day. It was more or less like, you know, don't give a dude no excuse to mess with him. Go out early in the morning, just to get away from him.

How could Anderson's panic be reconciled with his reputation? If he was a model inmate, how could his resources fail? The dilemma bothered Anderson's friends, and few had a solution. Most saw a soft core under Anderson's shell or blamed situational pressures. But a few inmates saw in Anderson's facade some built-in or hidden liabilities. Consistent reticence, for instance, was not always viewed as an asset. Although some saw virtue in reserve, others talked about the price of suppressed feelings. Some traced Anderson's crisis to his unwillingness or inability to communicate:

Like me, I get pissed off, and I blow up verbally and then forget it five minutes later. But him, it looked like he was just holding it in.

He was, like, an introvert. He was one of those guys who would get it all, get it all, and he never really had anyone to let it out with. He didn't trust anybody. That's what it really came down to. And by not having anybody to talk to, all that stuff just piled up and piled up in him.

Another thing that comes to my mind is that he may not have had a good command of English, and how to communicate properly with people. And this is another drawback with people, is they can't communicate. I seen a good example in a picture they showed here some years ago called *Billy Budd*. And he committed an act because he didn't know how to express himself.

Several of the inmates advanced psychodynamic theories. One view centered on Anderson's concern with his appearance and physical fitness. This school of thought theorized that Anderson had self-doubts, and that he needed to fight so as not to be seen as homosexual or as weak:

Usually a small, little man, he does have a complex about his build, he has a complex believing that people are trying to take advantage of him. The person that he attacked was a big man. Tall. This alone would make him have some type of resentment to this person.

Someone called him a punk one time: "Get away from my cell, you little punk." Something like that. And he said, "What?" And the guy was keep-locked, and he went in the cage, opened the door to the guy's cell, and went down there, and went in there. Now the guy had a knife in there. This was the incident where they ended up cutting each other. I don't know if he took the knife from the guy or the guy took the knife from him, but I know that both of them got cut in there. So he definitely resented being called a punk. He would fight quick. Very quickly from being called a punk, or if you infringed on his manhood in any way, he would fight.

And there's no telling where he could have been coming from, like, "What are you, a homosexual or something? Are you trying to hit on me? Do you think that I'm a homosexual? Are you trying to just plain disrespect me and say that all this space is mine over here? You want to show the people that I'm weak and you know how to take advantage of me?" You really can't say where he was coming from unless he told you himself, and he didn't volunteer no information on that.

Others noted that when faced with pressure Anderson took great pains to avoid conflict. They suggested that his past, his assaultive reputation, was a problem to him. They argued that Anderson might have been troubled by the fact that his efforts at self-control were at times unable to prevent violence:

He had already established a rep that he was Big Duke. Strong. And so he felt that by people knowing this, they'd let him isolate himself. When he saw that even with this there are going to be people that will try to talk to him, communicate with him, try to say something to him, although he may be withdrawing from this, they make him come back out.

When I heard about his records from the counselors after the fact, sometime during this whole thing, it seemed really strange to hear that he had almost another personality. Because it was never shown.

No fluctuations. He was one way all the time. . . . I've only seen him upset one time, and that was the time he approached me about the underwear hanging in front of his cell. But I've never seen him upset.

There was also speculation that Anderson might have become depressed as a result of remorse, or on the assumption that he had let his family down:

> You see when he first came in he was a kid, a jitterbug. And possibly his people had been telling him things like, "Son, you should get this job, and you should help with the house." Or . . . "You've got to watch out for your sister and brother. We're depending on you." And he felt that he let them down by getting that bit. By getting involved in that club fighting incident and getting that bit. He felt that he had let them down considerably. Because, as I said, he matured in the penitentiary. . . .
>
> He was definitely remorseful. He definitely felt bad about it. I imagine the way his brother was killed brought that home to him. Because I imagine that this happened—that a group of dudes or one or two dudes killed his brother. But it was the same situation. He saw himself and his fellows attack whoever it was that they attacked and killed. He saw this in the event that took place that killed his brother. He knew what it did to him and what it did to his family. And he thought about what they had done to this other guy's family. So he felt that he paid for it by the electrocution. I don't know, I've never heard of anybody taking their life like that. This is unique. This is different. And then again, there he was. He was a unique and different kid. And he was doing it in a unique and different manner. Who would have expected him to do something like that? But I see that as a connection with the crime and with what the penalty was at the time. That's how deep he was.

There is a marked conflict between professional clinical assessments of Anderson and descriptions by those who knew him. Psychiatrists and institutional parole officers centered unfairly on Anderson's record and on his fights. They inferred that he was a dangerously assaultive man. Those who knew Anderson, by contrast, asserted (1) that he was painfully and successfully conquering his past and was engaged in a search for a new identity, and (2) that fights initiated by him resulted from pressure exerted on him by his opponent.

The descriptions add up to a portrait which seems consonant with facts. In light of that portrait the view of Anderson as assaulter becomes farcical. Prior to his imprisonment, Anderson was not at any time a dispenser of violence. He began as a follower of peers; the violent activities in which he was involved—including murder—were games designed by others. Though serious games, they were intended to pass the time.

Anderson's prison violence was a series of outbursts under pressure. We have described such reactions elsewhere. We have noted that a man like Anderson (whose violence is "pressure removing") is a person

> whose repertoire of available interpersonal strategies is limited, or at least insufficient to cope with some situations. Where others may be able to solve a problem through nonviolent techniques, such as verbal persuasion, the pressure remover feels himself smothered, walled-in, or subject to overwhelming odds. He may try to cope with this dilemma with brief, desperate, half-hearted, floundering moves, but it is usually clear that he had arrived at the bottom of his resources before he started. . . .

> The simplest version of pressure removing is the effort of verbally unskilled persons to terminate altercations in which they feel unable to respond. Here violence not only expresses frustration but also represents a brusque and inadequate summary of the argument the person cannot verbalize. In addition, it constitutes an effort to suspend the offending level of interaction.[1]

We first met Anderson as a congenial, suggestible young man—not overly bright—close to his family, associated with destructive peers.

We met him again in prison, saddled with a sentence whose length he did not grasp. The first years of imprisonment showed us Anderson superficially content, involved in his activities. Then we noted the first rumblings of tension and anxiety. We saw Anderson concerned to the point of panic over pain in his knee. His fear was such as to neutralize an almost subservient stance toward prison.

More hints appeared in the next months. There was a fight which showed Anderson afraid of seeming weak. And there was the request for plastic surgery—the need to present a more acceptable self to the world.

Anderson still worked hard, but now he found his surroundings oppressive. There are hints of a Fate Avoidance theme. Anderson had a fight, claiming he "couldn't take" being "pushed." The outside world pushed him, hard. In 1970, two members of his immediate family died, one under mysteriously threatening circumstances. For the first time, peers described Anderson as shaken. His distress exploded in psychosomatic symptoms; he became irritable with others; he saw familiar scenes as disturbing.

He requested transfer and got it. A new equilibrium was established, but a brittle one. Caught in a lock-in, Anderson became more seriously afraid. Peers point to his need for consuming work at this time. Anderson reacted to a search in unprecedented ways. Later he talked of reprisals.

Anderson's state became increasingly agitated. He made requests for transfers. He locked in, confessing that he must regroup. He failed to regain stability and had another fight. By now, his fear was obsessive.

Panic became overt and uncontrolled. What hold Anderson had over his feelings collapsed. He was in tears; he felt abandoned, endangered from an unknown source. He made a useless plea for help.

The paradox lies in his coping effort. The loyal gang boy becomes the model inmate, but the role is strained. Anderson is not cool, independent, or strong. He is dependent and concerned. He needs love, assurance, safety.

His sentence is disproportionate; it is a sentence for human wolves. Anderson, the lamb-man, is no match for prison. Touchingly, he makes the best of his fate. He keeps wolves at bay without exploding himself; he appeases keepers by working hard and well. He builds his world around sports and his guitar.

But the prison impinges. Anderson begins to suspect that he cannot control himself. His fights—far from being victories—cement his views of forces he cannot resist. The deaths of his brother and sister tell him of his uselessness, his failure, his impotence. They feed his shame.

Activity tides Anderson over, but not for long. He is locked in, and now knows the meagerness of his resources. He is stripped of a future to be worked for. He suspects that he has been taxed beyond his capacity to survive alone. And he knows he is "friendless"; he can lean on no one for support. He is surrounded by preoccupied men, and others able to destroy.

Acting on fear, he produces fear. The myth of his violence revives. He is segregated. He reaches out in death, with his love notes. The words belie his insulation, independence, reserve.

For Anderson is not—and never was—a "cool" inmate. He is not immune to the reality of an impersonal system. He is a gentle, simple soul, hungry for love, lost in a jungle.

NOTE

1. H. Toch, *Violent Men: An Inquiry into the Psychology of Violence* (Chicago: Aldine, 1969), p. 154.

12

A Question
of
Trust

Peter Slovat's mind started slipping on June 16, 1973. No one had any
doubts about the date. The event stuck in people's minds because it occurred on what for others was a happy occasion, and because Slovat's
reaction made no sense.

It rained on June 16, and in the rain Attica is stark and depressing. But
June 16 was also Father and Son Day at Attica, and the prison's large mess
hall—scene of a picnic—was filled with laughter and chatter.

Peter Slovat had spent the day with two of his children. He had cause
to enjoy the experience. Yet it marked the onset of a depression from
which he would never recover. The transformation, according to Slovat's
friends, was dramatic:

> I noticed this building up after Father and Son Day. He'd sit in his cell
> at night, look at the pictures of his family, you know? . . . After this
> Father-Son Day thing he just kept to himself all the time, you know? He
> was more or less in a fog.

> And he was all right until they had the open house on Father's Day. . . .
> I don't know what happened that day, at Father's Day, open house. He
> stayed down there all day. . . . Ever since then, he's been getting more
> and more nervous.

Peter Slovat had been arrested in April 1972 for killing a parking lot owner outside a nightclub, and injuring the victim's wife. He was sentenced in December to four consecutive terms totaling forty-seven years. The judge, in imposing this sentence, noted his reasons:

I'm going to very briefly recite a few things that don't—that were not directly involved in this case, solely for the purpose of indicating the basis of the sentence I am about to impose. One is that, according to the Probation Report record, there has been a long record of drinking and of violent behavior. This is not the first time that there has been violence involved, and it would seem that this increasing, mounting round of intoxication and violent behavior was going to lead ultimately to the kind of situation which led to the death of one person and what appears to be the permanant crippling of another. There have been assault charges and menacing charges and intoxication charges and at the time that this occurred there was an illegal possession of a weapon charge still pending going clear back to 1968, undisposed of.

Slovat's police record shows brushes with the law from 1955 through 1958, involving two property offenses, a motor vehicle charge, and a violation of probation. There is also the arrest for possession of a weapon referred to by the judge, which occurred in August, 1968. Slovat was hardly a seasoned felon: he had been confined three times in connection with the 1955–58 incidents; thereafter, he had ten trouble-free years to his credit.

At the time of his arrest in 1972, Peter Slovat was a self-employed cabdriver. He was thirty-four, twice-married, with six children. He was a heavyset man, with an alcohol problem and serious physical disabilities. His medical record discloses a daily consumption of one to two quarts of whiskey over a fifteen-year period. The record also describes a chronic thyroid condition and reveals a history of heart disease. Under medication, Slovat showed ungainly increments in weight; when unmedicated, he felt uncomfortable and anxious. Slovat also had had other problems: at three years of age he had been treated for congenital syphilis; his childhood included a term in a concentration camp with his mother; his father, who died in 1972, was a chronic alcoholic.

A psychiatric examination raised the question of suicide potential, but the psychiatrist saw Slovat as normal. He noted that

his wife, according to him, has been unduly concerned about his behavior, feeling that he was suffering essentially from a mental condition and that this condition may have been genetic, and that the children were in danger of inheriting some of his behavioral problems. Actually, his condition is essentially physical. . . . He is not considered to be a psychiatric patient.

Peter Slovat arrived at Attica in December 1972, and was assigned to work in the prison garage. There he performed occasional janitorial functions. After several months, he was promoted to driving a prison truck. A garage job is considered a choice inmate assignment; it carries relative freedom and provides access to extra food and occasional contraband.

In many respects, Slovat was—objectively speaking—a favored inmate. He spent a good deal of time playing chess and dominoes, activities he enjoyed. He corresponded assiduously with his wife and received frequent visits. He committed an inconsequential disciplinary violation in May 1973, but was not penalized for it.

Peter Slovat brought himself to staff attention on July 2, when he displayed a stove in his cell and destroyed a set of earphones. He was interviewed by staff and reprimanded. The same day, Slovat saw the Catholic chaplain. According to the chaplain's records, "He felt someone is going to kill him." The chaplain noted that he told Slovat that "precautions, according to his wishes, will be made for his welfare."

Two days later, the prison sponsored an Independence Day picnic. Peter Slovat refused to attend, remaining in his cell. The next day, after three days of self-segregation, he demanded protective isolation. He was transferred to the segregation floor, then moved to the Reception wing. The guard who had requested observation for Slovat wrote in his reports:

This man arrived on this floor in a nervous and emotional state of mind. . . . He broke down and started to cry. . . . He did not make much sense when talking, and kept insisting that we were trying to kill him. . . . When making my rounds at 7:00 A.M., I noticed he had tied his cell door closed with a piece of cloth from his bed sheet. . . . He indicated to me that there is a plot to kill him. . . . Over a four-hour period this man called me to his cell several times to tell me of the plot on his life. . . . He told me he knew he was supposed to die in this cell. He said his coffee was poisoned.

The record of Slovat's last six days is a log maintained by custodial officers in the Reception wing. The log notes that Slovat received 100 milligrams of Thorazine on July 5 and July 6; on July 8, the dose was doubled by a prison physician. The psychiatrist saw Slovat July 9, and continued medication; he also ordered a few privileges, to ease Slovat's confinement.

The log shows that Slovat refused breakfast on July 5 and 6. On July 10, he "was awake all night, crying and saying that someone was going to kill him before morning"; he asked to see the chaplain, who spent an hour with him during the afternoon. The log notes that on July 11 Slovat was "crying, [and] feared that someone was going to kill him." It also records that "Slovat had lengthy discussions with officers, [and] seemed to be reassured of his safety." At 3:55 the log certifies that Slovat had taken his life.

The last person to see Slovat alive was a guard who responded to his request for an officer at 2:45 P.M., July 11. The guard summarized the interview as follows:

The discussion we had lasted about fifteen minutes and centered around the fact that he feared for his life. Inmate Slovat was acting very nervous and was on the verge of crying; he had tears in his eyes throughout our discussion.

Inmate Slovat stated he had overheard several inmates say that he had "ratted out" Inmate I——————— about the cannibus crop discovered behind the garage. THEY (he would not or could not identify those people), said that Inmate I——————— or his friends were going to kill him for this.

I assured him that the officers on all shifts would give special attention to his safety. This had been done the previous night and he slept soundly for the first time that night. We agreed to talk the following morning. We shook hands and he said he felt much better. . . . At the end of our talk he looked better and acted calmer. He assured me that he felt much better.

On July 11, Slovat also started a letter to his wife. It reads in part:

A man makes many mistakes . . . some forced on him by circumstances. I have made that kind of mistake and it has been carried along by others and made into looking more than it was. . . . I have *never* hurt anyone since I've been here. . . . Since I've been here, my only mistake has been to try and do my time by myself. It seems a man is suspected when he doesn't mix much. Although I spoke to a lot of men when I was working, nobody can say I was unfriendly only that I wanted to be left alone. How all this started I don't know but now I wish I had never taken that job and instead tried to find something else; now it is too late, one way or another this has to be solved. I love you and the kids too much and my self-respect would have never allowed me to turn into an "informer" on men I had to live with for so many years. Darling you know that without my telling you that this is not the way I had ever been and that is not the way I am now. . . . Fr. G——————— told me yesterday you will be coming to see me. Ask when you decide to come ask my brother that way you'll save some money, maybe T——————— will watch the kids for you.

Although Slovat depicts himself as a social reject, some inmates considered him a friend, and many were on good terms with him. These inmates trace the progression of his difficulties in a warm, sympathetic fashion.

Almost all agree that during his first months at Attica Slovat spent a great deal of time in his cell and seemed wrapped up in his private concerns:

> I didn't see too many guys like that. Even the invalids come out and watch TV and talk to each other, because, let's face it, you have to talk to someone. If you stay in your cell the whole time up here, you're really going to start thinking.

> He wouldn't come out of his cell. He wouldn't ever go out in the yard. He would just sit and look at the picture of his wife.

Slovat's need for privacy was respected, and it was viewed as normal and routine. But at times Slovat was seen as antisocial or oversensitive:

> I don't know how you'd say it, but there were some days that he just didn't really feel like associating with anybody. Like, you'd talk to him, and he wouldn't really answer you, or he'd just kind of walk away or something. He'd just give out the impression that he kind of wanted to be left alone or something. I guess the guy had a lot on his mind or something.

> He had a complex there for a while, when he was first in the garage. He thought people didn't want to talk to him.

> I had heard him mention it before, that he thought that somebody didn't like him or people didn't like him, this sort of thing. I had heard him say that around the shop.

There is consensus that Slovat had a Self-Linking or Self-Certification problem. His preoccupations during this period revolved monomonia-cally around his family. He was obsessed with the subject, consumed with ambivalent sorts of family worries:

> He was always talking about his wife and kids. His wife always was good to him. He wrote her a lot, and he couldn't ask for a better wife than he had. Any time you talk to him, it's about his wife and kids.

> And I told him, "You can't think too much about these things in jail." I've got a family too. My mother died when I was in here and I lost my girl friend. But you can't live in here and go on living out there too.

You can if you've got a year or two to do, but if you've got forty-seven years you can't think about those things or they will drive you crazy.

He was always kidding about his wife. He was always talking about her and the marriage and things like that. I remember once he said she wrote him a letter using his institution number instead of his name. Maybe he did seem a little nervous about it. He wanted the kids to have a good opinion of him and everyone else. And if someone didn't, it upset him.

Slovat's friends report that he had asked other inmates to react to family photos, requesting feedback or reassurance of some kind:

He had a picture with his family on it, and he'd just look at it all the time. Anybody come by the cell, he'd stop and ask them, "What do you think of my family?" That's all he would say, he wouldn't go no further than that.

So I started talking to him, and he showed me a picture of the kid and said, "What do you think of him?" And I didn't know what he wanted from me. Tears were running down his eyes.

As Father's Day approached, Slovat told friends that he was looking forward to the occasion with eagerness. But sometime on June 16, Slovat's anticipated pleasure turned sour. Those closest to him recall that he had complained about his children's impressions of him and about their loss of appetite; the chaplain remembers that Slovat worried about some of his (the chaplain's) reactions:

He said he liked to see them, but in a way he didn't like them to come up and see him in jail. He said he's going to be in here for a long time, and his wife is fairly young, and his kids were all small. He said he didn't know what he was going to do.

He acted kind of down and depressed, you know? Like, I didn't know, he wished he could have had his kids here longer, or maybe it would have been better if they hadn't come up, or something.

I saw him there in the auditorium with his two children, and I thought he was nice to me that day with his two children, but he began to apologize to me for the way he acted. And I never got a chance to find out what he meant. I thought he was very nice to me, and cordial, and he introduced me to the boys, his sons. And that morning, that Monday morning, in the course of talking, conversation, he said, "And I want to apologize to you." He wants to apologize to me for the way he acted towards me, and I can't figure out. . . . I noticed nothing wrong with his conduct towards me, or his children's conduct towards me. I saw him down there, I think, both in the auditorium and in the mess hall, briefly, and talked with the boys and him. And I saw nothing that he would apologize for. I don't know what he meant.

Two inmates tell us that Slovat received bad news during the picnic—that one of his sons had mentioned the visit of a man, and that Slovat was consumed with jealousy. Slovat had intended to talk to his wife, but the weather—which caused the picnic to be moved indoors—precluded the meeting. Slovat's concerns were deemed aggravated by his wife's youth, and by the fact that she had written letters about her loneliness:

One of his sons said something about a man at the house or something while they was over to the thing. And he couldn't get back. Like when the Father and Son Day was over, the officers took the kids back, and he couldn't get back to see his wife. And he just started going off. And then he got a letter from her one day. And she was telling him in so many words that she needed a man, blah, blah, blah, you know?

I read the letter from his wife, one of them. . . . she must have told him . . . how she missed him and all that. And them kind of letters weren't just coming in once in a while. She would write him every day. And I guess the letters were all about the same. But I read that one, and it wasn't exactly filthy or nothing, but every third or fourth word was she needs him home.

Some of Slovat's worries after June 16 revolved about his wife and children. However, his main concerns seemed to lie elsewhere. He became obsessed with the idea that he had been labeled an informer. He intercepted other inmates, and he inquired plaintively whether they still viewed him as reliable:

And I went by and said, "How you doing? Are you having any beefs?" He asked me, he said, "Oh, you're still speaking to me, huh?" I said, "Yeah," and it puzzled me, because I didn't know what he was talking about. He said, "Well, everybody else thinks I'm a snitch."

Oh, maybe every other night he'd call me from his window. See, the windows are in the back of the cell. He'd say, "Hey B————————, you still want to rap with me?" I'd say, "Yeah, man, what's happening?"

He'd say, "Whenever anybody tells you that I'm a rat, don't believe them, because I'm not a rat."

He'd look at a picture of his wife he had, and he'd tell me, "That's my wife. She doesn't think I'm a rat. She thinks I'm a good guy." I said, "I don't think you're a rat either."

On July 4, Slovat asked one of his friends to circulate a manifesto disclaiming his presumed status as informer:

So one of the men in the morning came up to me and handed me a note. He said, "Here's a letter that Slovat wants everybody in the garage to read." So I took it. And it was about five pages, written on both sides. And it was kind of, like, how in the beginning he had made a home in the garage and he wanted everybody to like him. And then he said he didn't see why people should start bringing up things about him that happened in Rochester, that didn't have anything to do with him now. And he mentioned about the eggs, and he kept repeating that he wasn't a rat and he didn't want them to believe that he was a rat. Things of that sort. . . .

I walked out of the cell and down to his, and I brought the letter with me. I gave it to him. The reason I didn't pass it along any further [was] because the Attica prison is full of young men, and this kind of thing could be used to ridicule a man. So I decided to take it back and talk to him.

Slovat saw several reasons why other inmates suspected him of informing: (1) he had obtained his assignment as truck driver at the expense of another man; (2) the garage had been the target of sanctions—one inmate had been captured with fermenting juice; another had been caught growing marijuana plants; (3) men working with Slovat had been subjected to search; (4) Slovat had been intercepted with food, but the guard had overlooked the infraction.

Inmates recall that these incidents had occurred and that selectively perceived they might have falsely incriminated Slovat:

See, the guy who was threatened, he lost his job, and Slovat had taken it over. So that could have started something.

Evidently he had passed a note out of his cell among the officers requesting to see the priest. And I don't know whether someone saw him hand this note out or not, but he kept returning to this. He seemed to think that someone saw him pass the note, maybe information, to an officer. But that's common knowledge, that that's the only way you can get on

sick call or whatever, by passing a regular form—or one of your own—
to the officer that is making count.

A couple of the other workers were busted, I guess, were caught with
something in their locker, and they got keep-lock for a few days. And
it all pointed in the direction of this Slovat and this S——————
guy.

Although some inmates knew that Slovat could not be an informer,
others confirm that he received communications in which he was accused
and threatened. According to Slovat's friends, some of these threats were
made on July 2:

The secretary of the liaison committee works around that area, and he
said that there was, and he had seen them, a couple of threatening
letters.

I do know for a fact that he got one note, because I seen one note that
he had gotten maybe two months ago. The note said, "Watch your ass
when you come out in the morning." He asked me if I'd watch his back.
I said, "Sure I'll watch your back." The doors open, and I'd come out
and stood by his door till he come out, and then we went up for chow.
I don't know why somebody was bothering him or why somebody had
something against him, but it seemed that somebody was messing with
his mind.

Then they got busted with the booze, and they right away thought
Slovat was ratting them out. And they went down there and threatened
him. . . . somehow or other somebody overheard him talking to somebody else, and they thought he was a rat. So this other guy got pissed
and thought that he had ratted him out. . . . on the way back to the
cell he stopped, threatened the guy. . . . a matter of two or three days
later he just went to protection, and they took him out of the population, and he stayed up there a week, and he hung himself.

Slovat reacted to danger with uncontrolled fear. He shared his panic
with other inmates, who recall that Slovat's conversations took an increasingly irrational turn:

When I come back, sometimes he'd call me to his cell, and he'd talk to
me, start crying. You couldn't make him out.

The words were plain enough, but they didn't make any sense. He acted
like he was really afraid. He was rattling. He wouldn't stick to any sub-

ject. He acted like he was real afraid that somebody was going to kill him. He kept saying, "If I go out there I'm a dead man."

Then he said, "I wrote to my wife," and at first he said he was going to die—"I know I'm going to die." Then he said, "I wrote to my wife, and I told her that I'm going to die." . . . And he said, "They're going to get me." And I said, "Who?" He said, "I don't know who, but they're going to get me." And he wrote to his wife and said he was going to die. And he was crying.

Several inmates recall that they made efforts to reassure Slovat. They mention attempts to restore his perspective and to suggest constructive courses of action:

So he was crying, and I said, "Listen, I think it's all in your mind. You're in this cell right from work, and you stay in there." And he said something about a note. I said, "Pete, if you found this note and whoever wrote this note, you don't have to worry about him. Because he don't have the heart to do anything. That's why he's dropping this note, to mess you up." I said, "If it was a man, and he was out to get you, he wouldn't talk about it." So the tears were coming out of his eyes, and he said, "Don't believe I'm a rat." So I said, "Listen, you've got to come out of that cell." I said, "Tomorrow is the Fourth of July, and the picnic is outside, and a bunch of us are getting together. Why don't you come out in the yard with us and not worry about anything?" He said, "No, no," and that was it.

I heard the guy tell him myself, "I don't care about the job. If they give it to you, well and good." The guy told him that himself. And I told Pete, I said, "See, you're getting all shook up for nothing." I said, "They hear you get in trouble, and he's one of the first ones down, 'Can I get you anything, do you need anything?' " I said, "If the guy was after you, he wouldn't say nothing to you." . . . I stood out there by the door, which I usually don't do, for about a half hour, running it down to him. I said, "Ever since Father's Day you've been shook up, you've been doing crazy things. Like this morning, leaving that right on your bed. This afternoon you lock in. That's crazy. You've got a good job, good connections, you're eating better than other people, you're getting hold of stuff, getting it fixed for you. You got outside help working on your case, you get your visits. You blow that, and you go up in observation or something, you ain't got nothing. If you can't make it down here, you damn sure can't make it in observation."

The prison staff—to whom Slovat turned for protection—report parallel reactions. Several officers had been impressed with the magnitude of the man's fear. They tried to provide whatever reassurance and support they could:

> I think he was on the verge of flipping out, yeah, very definitely. I only talked to the guy for two minutes, and I knew I had to write an observation report. You can get strange answers from an inmate or strange statements and still know that he's within his wits when he's talking to you, but this guy here was scared. It's that simple. . . . I told him, "You don't want to stay here. I know you don't." This is to the best of my recollection. I told him that I would do everything I could to get him out of here. He told me that he was in fear of his life, that they were going to kill him. When I said, "who?" he wouldn't tell me. Just that somebody was after him. He was generally scared, that's all. I told him that I would help him. I told him that we were here to help him. He alluded to the fact that I was here to kill him, that he was to die in that cell. And I told him that I was here to help him. I tried to use a little cheap ten-cent psychology on him. I told him that I was doing everything I could to get him out of here as soon as possible. To give him as much help as we could. That he didn't have anything to fear. He calmed down for that minute. I told him to calm down and try to relax, and so on and so forth.

> And he told me that the officers were looking in, I don't know how often, but they insisted, "Now you go to sleep and rest. It'll do you good, you need it." He told me that himself. Or eat, for instance. He missed his orange drink or some kind of drink, and they insisted that he drink it. And he wouldn't, you know? He was afraid, I think, that it would poison him.

After Slovat arrived in the reception area, his paranoia took a Self-Preservation turn. He became specific about the object of his fears. He asserted that hostile inmates would kill him, would burn him in his sleep or poison his food:

> He was scared to death that the other inmates were going to come up and kill him. He didn't seem to be fearful of any of the employees. The doctor was there. But on several occasions he asked us, would we see that nobody would make it down the gallery, and this and that. We have a couple of inmates that work on the floor with us, and he didn't see much of them. But he did talk to them sometimes, and he seemed to get along with them good. He didn't seem to be the least bit fearful of them. . . . He had pictures of his family out. And one night he had his blanket on the floor, and it was all wet because he told us that they were going to burn him up the night before. We tried to get him on other subjects, but it wouldn't work.

He was a little bit, like, let's say, emaciated. But he told me, "Father, I didn't sleep for nights. I just won't go to sleep, I don't want to sleep. The officers tell me to go to sleep. Everything's all right, but I just don't want to go to sleep." Fearing, I guess, that when he does fall asleep, something will happen to him. He had that paranoia that he was going to die. Then he, as I say, he looked emaciated, looked sleepy, and I guess also wouldn't eat. He told me that, that he wouldn't eat. He didn't want to eat because he was afraid that he was going to be killed. I said, "How can anybody kill you here, in protection? How can anybody get to you? I can't understand that." Well, he had some idea that somebody was going to be sent from some other part of the institution and get through the officers and either burn him or poison him. He had that idea. He thought that someone would get through, somebody would probably be sent into protection on some kind of made-up misdemeanor or act, and would be sent into the same block where he was and do the dirty work.

On the day before he died, Slovat told the chaplain he would be killed the next day. The chaplain expressed disbelief and thought he had dispelled Slovat's fear of the immediacy of the threat:

He came out first of all with his prayer book, and I asked him to sit down and talk to me first. And two, three, four times he said, "I'm willing to die, tomorrow I'll be dead." I saw him on Tuesday, and he said that "tomorrow I'll be dead." Once, two, or three times he said that. I said, "How can you die? Who's going to harm you here?" And then he brought out the idea somehow. His imagination was really, I think, running away with him. He said, "Somebody may be sent here and get through the officers and put my cell on fire or put some poison into my drink or food." . . .

And he went to holy confession and asked me to bring him Holy Communion Wednesday morning. In the back of my mind, I thought to shake him off from the fact that he was going to die during the night. I said, "I'm not going to bring you Holy Communion Wednesday, but I'll bring it, like, Thursday or Friday morning." So to show that I, by putting it off, didn't believe that he was going to die during the night. And after confession we talked, and I left him with a smile on his face. He smiled at me, and he agreed that I bring Holy Communion Thursday or Friday. And of course, as you know, Wednesday I was called in there about four o'clock, four-fifteen, and it was suicide.

The guards—who had also talked to Slovat—felt that they had eased his fears by assuring him of special protective measures:

I talked to him before I went home that afternoon, and another officer did. . . . The officer assured him that he and the other officers were going to keep an eye on him and make sure that nobody got down there. It was an assurance that we or the other shifts wouldn't let anyone down there to harm him. And that seemed to satisfy him on that occasion and other occasions previous to that. The officer said that when he left he felt better. They shook hands, and he really felt much better. . . . After he talked to him, he looked better and he was calmer. He settled right down. Now this was around quarter to three or five minutes to three. . . .

The only thing he asked for was that one of us would be with him almost all the time. And me and other supervising officers assured this man on previous days that they would let the officers on the night shift know that he was afraid that somebody was going to harm him, and we went out of our way, and the night men went out of their way to come in and tell the man, and the supervisor went in and told the man, "Don't worry, we're keeping a special watch so no one will get over here." And that seemed to satisfy him. But he just wasn't convinced that somebody wasn't going to get at him over there.

In the short run Slovat responded to reassurances, but invariably he returned to his fear. He had passed the point where safeguards could protect him. The threat he saw was implacable and pervasive. No physical barriers, no human actions, could keep danger from reaching him.

Self-Trust and Trust in Others

Nine days before Slovat's death, a disgruntled fellow inmate had threatened his life. The threat impressed Slovat deeply—more deeply than the circumstances justified. Though Slovat was no career inmate, he was not a prison novice. And he was not friendless, helpless, or physically weak.

But Slovat was very vulnerable. He had been afraid before. He had carried a gun out of fear. He had used it out of fear. And his vulnerability had matured over a week of self-torture, after years of self-doubt.

Fifteen years earlier, during Slovat's stay at Elmira, a prison official had observed that the then twenty-year-old inmate showed intense concern about peer and staff goodwill. He wrote:

Inmate is considered unusually helpful in programs, seems to be attempting to gain status and acquire leadership in the group situation. However, he is not too well accepted by others. He is inclined to be overbearing and bossy. This cagey aggressive individual appears to use others to impress staff.

Slovat's efforts appear to have been generally unsuccessful. His 1972 probation report relates:

When defendant was at reception center in 1958 he could not get along with the other inmates and was transferred to Naponoch. . . . it is interesting to note . . . that he is currently kept in isolation in Monroe County Jail because he cannot get along with the other inmates.

The same report also tells us that Slovat lost the first of his two wives during his 1958 incarceration:

In 1957 the defendant married one S_____ L. While he was institutionalized, the two were divorced in 1960. There was one child, B_____, who currently lives with her mother.

Slovat arrived in Attica with experiences involving severed relationships and failures to gain acceptance by others. He also arrived bereft of the intoxication that had for fifteen years deadened his awareness of social reality.

Reality, in Attica, included the fact that Slovat had lost his family. He had lost it physically through the length of his term. His projected confinement, well over thirty years, precluded reunion with his young wife and his young children. The family to which he would return—if he returned—would be inconceivably different from the one he had left.

During his first weeks in prison Slovat tried—unsuccessfully—to assimilate this reality and adapt to it. The reassurance he asked of others (which they could not understand or provide) was that of his continued hold on his family. The implication of his questions about his family—"What do you think of *my* wife? *my* children?"—was his realization that he had irredeemably lost both wife and children. The hours he spent in staring at their photographs could not rekindle the illusion that they were still part of his life.

Father's Day loomed as a critical test of his status. It brought the physical presence of Slovat's wife and children. But it also brought—inescapably—the realization of the evanescence of their presence. It did so because of the setting. The picnic was not a reunion of father and sons but a visit of uneasy and mystified children with a convict. The encounter was strained and artificial. Neither Slovat nor his sons could eat. Slovat felt—the chaplain tells us—embarrassed and clumsy.

A chance remark of a child gains significance from the fact that it dramatized Slovat's absence from home. New men could enter, would enter, and possibly had entered the lives of his loved ones. He might know nothing of them, could not dispute their claim and was impotent to compete with them. With loyalty and candor Slovat's wife assured him that she wanted and needed him. But Slovat was faced with the realization that he could not respond to this need. He had no alternative but to infer (1) that he had failed and betrayed a sacred trust; (2) that he would continue to leave legitimate demands unsatisfied; (3) that his wife could not and would not rely on him in the long run; (4) that she would lose trust in him and no longer see him as the object of her needs; and (5) that there were others more deserving of her trust and affection. It is probably significant that in his last hours, while convinced that he would die, Slovat arranged for an impending visit from his wife. He was still struggling to preserve a rapidly waning illusion.

Following June 16, Slovat redirected his need for love toward those with whom he would spend the rest of his life. He failed because he suspected his own motives and could not convince himself of his worthiness of trust and esteem. He had become imbued with the idea that he must betray trust and forfeit it. He was a deserter—a man to be seen as informer or rat.

Slovat was still dealing with his family. "That's my wife," he told a friend, "she doesn't believe I'm a rat." "I love you and the kids too much," he wrote home, "to turn into an informer." But the main test of Slovat's reliability was prison; it was inmates to whom Slovat turned, fearing rejection. And he had cause for fear, for nowhere does trust loom larger as an issue than it does behind bars. Slovat's friends could reassure him that he was no informer. They could never tell him that they liked him *if he was*. For prison is not a setting that can offer unconditional regard.

Slovat approached his peers with the propositions, "You cannot afford to trust me. You must perceive me as untrustworthy. I cannot reassure you of my reliability." He could not accept disclaimers because he knew them to be unfounded. He was convinced that even though he was innocent of informing on his peers, he was transparently blameworthy.

The threat on his life was real for Slovat because it confirmed his views. He saw himself as guilty, deserving death. No escape, no defense, no protection was possible. The men who tried to reassure Slovat could not help, because they could not see him as he saw himself. They did not know of his guilt, his untrustworthiness, his betrayal of love. They could not counter the essential truth that Peter Slovat was a traitor who deserved execution.

IV

Context
and
Implications

13

Problems
and
Crises

In the course of our control interviews, we were exploring one inmate's concerns about having been abandoned by his family. Were the feelings disabling? Could he deal with them? Was he tense? The inmate explained:

See, I don't view it as a *crisis:* I view it simply as a *problem.* So I try to deal with it within what I feel would be an intelligent manner. For instance, once I leave prison I know it will be pretty difficult for me to get a job, so I try to condition myself while here. . . . I realize also that my wife is the major support of my family now. It will be harder once I'm released—now if I go into the streets and I can't find a job, I become a drain or a strain on my wife and my children. . . . Either I will do something to relieve the strain, or I will remove myself from that family. But in any event it will cause a destructive attitude, and that is something I'm trying to condition myself for. So I'm taking educational courses that I feel are necessary, that might get me around that particular problem.

In general, the distinction between "problem" and "crisis" summarizes, for us, the difference between two thirds of the inmate population and the persons we have discussed in this book. A number of our controls had contemplated suicide, or had toyed with the idea. They mentioned self-

283

destructive thoughts as the index of extremity appropriate to the occasion. There were other clues to crises. Some controls had segregated themselves, or become hostile and explosive; some were acutely depressed at the time we saw them. But most of the control group had somehow experienced, and weathered, their psychological storms.

If a single fact emerges from our control interviews, it is the observation that almost no inmate's institutional career had been free of serious (and potentially disabling) stress. This fact highlights the question—with which this chapter deals—of how some inmates cope (or at least survive) while others do not.

We have seen in Chapter 5 that, on a group basis, there are differences in susceptibility to breakdown in such variables as age, marital status, ethnic background, or earlier violent involvements. There are forces (associated with such conditions as being young) which enhance for some the chances of being exposed to stress, or of succumbing to the experience. These forces are differentially deployed (even within a risk group) and add differentially to the tragic outcome they help to promote. Youthfulness, for instance, may lead to homosexual overtures; it may involve separation anxiety, or it may be associated with crippling inexperience.

The point holds with regard to cultural background, the variable we explored in Chapter 7. We have traced a sequence, for example, in which a sheltered family helps make prison a more alien and lonely experience. And we have seen fear feed on fear, so that trauma outside prison can lead to panic inside it. But such chains are shorthand abstractions. They exclude much which affects stress and breakdown among individual members of the same group. And they tell us nothing about why some individuals of similar background do and others do not survive comparable stress.

It is also obvious that key susceptibilities—most susceptibilities, in fact —are inaccessible through clues we can observe and count. *Some* men with dependency problems may be Puerto Rican, but most are not; *some* tense inmates may have records of explosiveness, but most do not. And vulnerability (or resilience) is the reverse of a coin. We know that when Inmate Jones breaks down, there is something within Jones which has given way to stress; but we also know that there are also forces within Jones which have *resisted* and *fought* and *lost*. Jones may have hung on a valiantly— even superhumanly—against insuperable odds, while Smith (his smiling cellmate) may be a hotbed of vulnerabilities that have not yet been tapped. When (after the fact) we classify Jones as vulnerable, we do so (1) on a statistical basis, because the chances *are* better that he, rather than Smith, is a noncoper, and (2) to pinpoint Jones's vulnerabilities, with the full knowledge that he also possesses strength and resilience.

When vulnerabilities are isolated, we know that they have been invoked, not that they had to be. A man can only tell us where he's been. We know the forks he's taken, and the streams he has (or hasn't) crossed.

Did he have a choice? By what hairbreadth? What could it take, or must it take, to turn his tide? Could we have predicted? early? late? Could we have helped? Before we address this question (in the next chapter) we must know about differences between those who cope and those who don't.

We know from the content of our interviews that a trend toward paranoia exists among our subjects. Some men enter prison with a perspective containing feelings and assumptions which—given certain stresses—will bloom into persecutory delusions. These men have a better chance than the average inmate of experiencing the most lethal breakdowns in incarceration.

But what are the seeds of panic? What cues do they offer? They differ, our autopsies tell us, from man to man. They blossom privately, and—most crucially—with no hint of their goal. They are not homunculi of psychosis, but predispositions to it. No one, intimate or pro, need sense their unfolding. Later they may take blatant shape, usually when the person has entered crisis.

The point holds, in reverse, for our controls. Our controls have known stress, and have, so far, survived it. Some even talk of fears. But these are men who have been skilled, or lucky, in finding ways or means of modulating stress. Their resources have been tested, but have not as yet broken down or given way. These men can talk about harnessing stress, rather than—as with our subjects—about being controlled by it. They can highlight for us the skills which they, like our subjects, possess, but which they, unlike our subjects, deploy.

Data Sources

Since our control sample was small, we took care that it fitted our needs, Though random—every *n*th name out of alphabetical rosters—the control group was stratified to mirror the composition of our subject group. It was younger than a random sample, skewed in ethnicity, and centered in the sites of our study.

The control interviews followed the form of our subject interviews, but we could not assume that the controls had had personal difficulties. Instead, we asked each control what (if any) problems he had had in prison. We also explored the area of coping strategies and supports. We introduced the survey as derivative, and the theme of the study as coping. The control interviews were, on the average, shorter than those with our crisis subjects. It proved harder to gain rapport, because the aim of the study carried less plausibility than did that of our crisis research.

Given the restricted aim of our control survey, the transcription of tapes was hard to justify. We evolved a compromise—listening to each interview, then coding and summarizing it. Though a few control interviews are available in raw form, the bulk of our control data consists of "Study Group Summaries" prepared after the auditioning of tapes. These highlight the content of each interview, and our impressions of the respondent.[1]

Coping and Solution

Our most salient finding relates to the prevalence of stress derived from perceived failure of support systems in the outside world. Fully half the sample reported problems having to do with abandonment, betrayal, doubts, jealousy, or grief relating to significant others outside the walls. The following is a summary of a jail interview dealing with a Self-Linking problem which has inventory and Self-Release overtones:

> The main difficulties he admits to are that he has acutely experienced a loss of contact with people he valued, and he also has had urges to hurt people, and this bothered him.
>
> Now he had a gambit he had attempted to exercise now and then of systematically thinking of pleasant things, like the wonderful people he robbed and the gains from these robberies. But unpleasant content does manage to intrude in unplanned ways. For instance, he finds himself leafing through a newspaper trying to pleasantly reminisce. There is a bolt out of nowhere, possibly sparked by an ad from Korvette or some such stimulus. And there vividly comes to his mind a camera from his brother-in-law which was lent to him and which he sold. And apparently those kinds of feelings fall under the heading of conflict.
>
> The remarkable thing about his discomfort is that on at least one occasion it has led him to consider jumping off a very high jail tier. And it seems to have been a fairly serious thought. Now, as he reconstructs the situation, this occurred right after the loss of a female companion—in the sense that his correspondence was returned "addressee unknown". And, incidentally, that's not the only loss of female companions that he has experienced. He is in the same predicament now. But a social network to which he belonged, his companionable cellmate and a crew with whom he hung out and who spent at least part of their time robbing cells—that sort of support system rescued him at the last minute from this contemplated act. In terms of his current perspective, he seems to feel that he has control now, at least in the sense that he is resigned. And you do get the feeling that being resigned includes not only being resigned to the fact that his impending marriage is no longer in the offing, but resigned to the fact that he will be spending time in prison which he thinks he can use constructively and then forge a new existence for himself when he ultimately does get out.

One point illustrated by this summary is that crisis avoidance does not preclude coping failure. We note that one strategy deployed by our subject—dwelling on past achievements—boomeranged for him, in that it led to self-doubt. We see the importance of the advantage enjoyed by this inmate through membership in a close—to him meaningful—group (which, incidentally, is delinquency-supportive, so that survival goes hand in hand with an increased probability of recidivism). Lastly, there is a long-term liability in the man's tendency to devalue his problem and to operate with possibly self-deluding resolves. A short-term solution is thus attained, and a crisis averted, at the possible expense of insight and change potential.

The contrast is explicated by another subject, who used the same strategy but recognized its liabilities:

It took away responsibility, because how could I do something for my kids? So it was easy for me at that point in jail to make promises. But as time went on, up till now I know I can make myself promises and I can also crawl out of a hole.

I: So in one sense you can make promises that seem to have no holes in jail because they're cheaper than on the outside—

They're easier than they are on the outside.

I: And they can help you get through this thing?

Yeah. You can use that as your reason for being, in a manner of speaking. You use this for your reason for weathering the storm.

I: Now in your own case this was one of your helps, these promises?

Yeah, but it got to the point where I wasn't using it for my help. I was using it for my reality. I took myself in hand and said, "What are you going to do? You've been in this before, and you bullshitted yourself, and then you went out and did the same sort of crap more or less." Change of time, change of circumstances, change of locale. I was still messed up. So I said, "What are you going to do? You're no kid no more. You can't convince anyone on the outside because you've got to show them."

For this inmate, a more self-searching inventory follows his self-consciously stopgap solution. This effort involves discomfort, but a crisis is avoided because the interim stage makes the painful inventory taking more manageable:

There's a whole lot going on inside of me and inside of my head, inside of me. But what it all boils down to is, I have to do something. I have to do something now that I have a choice. . . . There has to be more to it. There has to be more than just drugs or the momentary pleasure or the rush to life. The guy on drugs, myself included, looked at anybody who didn't use drugs as one category, a square. No, it's not true. Guys using drugs are the squares, in the truer sense of the word. A square, somebody who doesn't use drugs, parties 365 days a year. They get up in the morning, and it's a challenge, an experience, and they don't know what's going to happen to them. The drug user does. He knows when he gets up in the morning that he has to get that fix or else do what he has to do to get the money for it. . . . There's now a wall between me and what I did. I've constructed another kind of defense between it. The defense now is my family, my future, a wife, me. I want things for myself now that I never wanted before. I've always wanted it, but I never wanted to make the effort to get it. I sat down, and I got very cynical.

Coping Props and Coping Skills

Crisis management sometimes invokes an external support system, and sometimes rests on skills, and on personal ability. Contrasting examples, involving Self-Linking problems, may make this distinction clear.

Our first case involves serial rejection, aggravated by dependency and self-hate. We summarize the situation as follows:

This man tells us that most of his life he's been able to live with strong supports from his family and his wife. He sees himself as someone who was spoiled with support, and was given enough support that he could avoid looking at things he was doing to himself and to other people. When he gets confined, he says that with these supports behind him he was able to cope with confinement.

His crisis begins when he is rejected by his wife. He tells us that this is the first experience of that sort that he's had, and he's now forced to go in upon himself and look at himself, and what he sees he doesn't like. He begins to reassess his impact on other people and the extent to which he has been selfish and ecocentric and had made the lives of other people difficult and only thought of what he gained from his relationships.

In prison he tends to recreate a manipulative and a supportive relationship with a homosexual because he feels he needs this to go on. This relationship backfires. As he says, he's too intense with this man. His demands are too deep-seated and too important. And this homosexual turns his back on him. At this point he is pretty much left with no supports at all, and he contemplates taking his life.

At the culmination of this crisis (the man describes himself as "standing in front of a mirror with a razor blade and asking around for the location of the jugular vein"), a new option appears in the shape of an intervention by a fellow inmate:

> He is then approached by a Muslim who responds to his evident depression. He first was very hard to approach, because he had given up on people. He saw himself as unloved and unlovable. And he was mostly convinced of his own despicableness. He was goalless and had nothing left going for him. And he now saw the ideals of Muslimism and to some extent the social supports available as a way to submerge himself in something that he could portray as selfless. He could identify himself with a greater goal to help humanity and to help other black brothers and to submit to a higher principle. And by doing this he could revive himself, give himself some purpose.

Here, external stress—abandonment by persons on whom he had learned to depend—brings home to the man facts about himself which are hard for him to accept. These are crisis ingredients.

The difference consists in the fact that support becomes available to this man—first through a homosexual, later with Muslim membership. The man arranges for the first relationship. He is wooed and won in the second. Through his adherence to the Muslims he gains two types of resources. One is internal—work that defines him as a giving and mature person, instead of as dependent and selfish. The other is external—support that ties into his admitted dependency needs.

Impending crisis and proffered support characterize coping for many inmates. The confluence may look like an accidental juncture—a man in need happens to stumble across the resources that enable him to survive. For the juncture to appear, however, the person must share his problem; at the least, he must not retreat from contact. An example is provided by an inmate who has had feelings bordering on self-hate. He describes his difficulties, and their solution through contact with a friend:

> Well, mainly, when I first got here, when I got sentenced, my mother and father broke up. I had two foster brothers, and the home took them back. So, in other words, I blamed this all on myself. Because it was because of me that this happened. When I was on the street, the family stayed together. But when I got busted and sentenced, they just blew, went different ways.

I: And you felt that you were the cause of that?

> Yes, I did.

i: Do you still believe that?

No, I might be two thirds of the blame, but I'm not the whole thing.

i: Would you rap this to your friend?

Yeah. He explained that it's like if somebody dies of old age. When the time comes, the time comes. That's it. You can't be blaming yourself for your whole bit just because something happened to your family.

The same inmate also describes difficulties inside prison with which his friend proved of help. Again the support comes in the form of modulating advice:

He gave me an outlook. He said, "You have to abide by the rules and regulations of the prison." So I conformed myself. I ain't never had a keep-lock except last year. They were going to give me twenty minutes to decide whether I was going to move from the block because I had told them no. And during this twenty minutes Billy rapped to me. He said, "Man, you're still in prison, behind walls, and you're not going anywhere." So I went.

This man's crisis potential, as he himself sees it, includes runaway feelings—particularly feelings of anger and despair. The friend—whose disposition is more even—functions in a diagnostic and counseling role:

One or two times I seen guys commit suicide by doing this or that, and I've thought about it. Then again, I say, "This is a punk's way out—to commit suicide. Unless the man is really disturbed and off balance." And when Billy talked to me he said, "You've got an IQ of 122 and you can control yourself, but you get emotionally involved and that brings out the anxiety and all the frustrations." It's true.

Though the man finds his friend's message plausible, its content—exclusive of interpersonal aspects—would not suffice as support for him. Structure consists of allies, kinship, people who care. It supplements a man's deficits, without belaboring them, or without bringing them home.

Coping, however, need not involve aid from without. Many of our controls prize their own skill in facing up to problems, and in surmounting them. This skill begins at the stage of stress appraisal. We summarized the problem of one of our Self-Linking cases, for instance, as follows:

He goes home on furlough—to pleasantly surprise his wife, to whom he's been married for ten years. And he is understandably shocked to find that she's been living with someone else. He sees this as a hurting experience, as something that he had some trouble with, but he said he's come from the streets and he's learned in prison that these things are what he calls occupational hazards. In other words, he knew in advance that this kind of thing could happen. It was now a question of, Could he put into practice the principles that he felt he had learned?

One of the themes he tries to bring out, although he says that much of his learning is prison-specific, is that these kinds of things are happening all the time in his world, in the street world, and that this does give some insulation, in the sense that you can see it as a possible event. He says that this prior recognition nevertheless is not enough to get you through the crisis. When it hit, he had to find out if he could stay down with it.

The man's demeanor in the situation had all the earmarks of the prototypical English aristocrat ("Pardon me, Daphne, can I fix you a drink?") in parallel circumstances. But there are differences. For one, the incident contains elements, such as the connotation of unmanliness and disrespect, which make it a serious injury. Moreover, the man views the stress not only as a test of his cool, but as an opportunity. We summarize this general orientation as follows:

Briefly, these principles are that survival comes first, that no matter what happens life goes on and he has to go on with it, that in the long run it's his ability to be sharp, to be smart, that will overweigh any tough or blundering or stupid move that he might want to make, emotionally. He says that previous to his prison experience, when he was younger, he could never have pulled this off, that he would have blown it. As he sees it, he went out and was confronted with a situation which was radical and shocking, and he handled it in the best way possible and, in his terms, the only way possible. That, in effect, he demonstrated that he was true to himself, that the principles that he felt he had taught himself about survival served him well in this context, that he was, in other words, victorious. One of his continuing themes is that having experienced this crisis, he feels that he's stronger, that it's a growth experience, and it's another way of gaining more understanding of himself. His whole program in prison has been one of trying to build himself up, to get to know himself, to improve himself. And, as he sees it, this was a concrete example of the success of his endeavors, and a source of new learning which would help him through any future crisis which might arise. In his particular case, coping is a bit more of an active process than the way some others define it. Coping means manipulating and handling people who cause you difficulty so as to neutralize them. So that it isn't just a matter of, "Do they have an impact on you?" but a matter of effectively responding. And then the effectiveness of one's response gets added to the credit that one has in terms of being a good coper. And this man is almost obsessed with the idea of becoming an increasingly good coper, and would argue that prison, in the sense of containing a great many opportunities for coping and a great many sources of information about coping, would be a beneficial experience. And in terms of the one crisis he describes, which was the issue of being suddenly abandoned by one's only significant outside other, he definitely feels that he can enter this on his ledger of self-improving experiences, as an experience which has not only demonstrated that he is effective, and thereby has put to the test the proposition that prison has made him a better man, but that he has now come back from that experience being even more effective.

Situational coping, here, is part of a life plan, a self-conscious blueprint for growth. A man not only expects misfortune, but requires it to mold, and perfect, his skills. Ultimately—in theory—a person becomes a Perfect Coper, uniformly competent, cool, and impervious.

Cutting One's Losses

A more common—and passive—deployment of resources in Self-Linking situations is the de-cathexis of relationships. This strategy, which presupposes that strong dependency needs are absent, is part of the prison lore shared by inmate sophisticates. It holds that thoughts of the outside must be suppressed, and involvements with women, relatives, and friends minimized. The argument rests partly on the premise we have illustrated that abandonment is an everyday event, a likely contingency. Coping requires forearming, in the shape of an attitude that precludes surprise, or loosens emotional ties so as to make them less significant. Women are fickle, or have legitimate needs for companionship. Parents are old, and siblings prone to trouble. A man's head, to remain clear, must be "inside," exclusively concerned with prison coping, uninvolved with his loved ones. In the extreme, the prescription calls for physical distance (discontinuance of correspondence) or for a "shell" which blunts emotion and minimizes affect.

Although a number of our controls share such premises as a philosophical stance, they are not all equally able to translate them into action. The difficulty is that the strategy entails sacrifice of other coping options, which are those of support. The following inmate illustrates the dilemma dramatically:

I just tell her I want a divorce and I don't want her coming up here no more. In fact, I first went to jail to get away. She would come up once a month, and she had two nervous breakdowns. So I came back here. So now I get these visits twice a week, and I can't take it. Seeing her twice a week and going through the agony. I only do it for her. It's just one of those things, as far as I can see. . . . It's difficult to do time that way. If she came up here once in a while, maybe I could cope with it much better. But when she comes up she talks about the children and this and that. I can't do nothing to help her. . . . I tell her to go out and do things and that as time goes by maybe you can find somebody or something.

I: Do you think you really want this?

Do I want it? No. But I think this would be best for her. . . . See, I have a life bit, as you must know. Like, we talk about it, and she comes over with these new laws. I have something to look forward to. Like, to do ten years or fifteen years or whatever is involved. And this is hope for her. But I tell her maybe I'll have to do twenty-five. If she is discouraged at the beginning, I try to give her hope. But then I discourage her again. I keep going back and forth. I go out there and just start arguing with her to fight so that maybe she will walk out.

I: So it sounds like, if I'm not mistaken, that you're going back and forth on this yourself?

I am. I say, "Should I keep her or not, or should I let her go?" . . . And there's no way out. Even if I didn't have visits. Like, say, I didn't have visits. If I was up in Clinton the way I feel now, I believe that might even be worse, her not coming to see me. 'Cause now it would be a whole month before I would see her. I don't know—it's a circle.

Runaway Coping

The second most prevalent problem for our controls is that of Self-Victimization. This difficulty involves a "discovery" by the person that he is subject to inequity, harassment, or arbitrary treatment.

The problem of Self-Victimization highlights one of the biases in the stress literature. Though stress experts recognize the fact that stress must be *perceived* or *felt*,[2] their paradigm calls for the presence of an independently definable stimulus, such as an extreme environment or an abrupt impingement. We have seen in Self-Linking that the contribution of the subject (in the shape of dependency) to the definition of stress may be substantial, and that some persons require little "objective" data to feel stressed. It is not uncommon for an inmate to feel abandoned if one of his letters is slightly delayed, or is cautiously worded.

Self-Victimization points directly to the transactional relationship between man and environment,[3] where the victim creates his own stressful stimulus; at least, he interprets impersonal and routine events as deployed or designed to his detriment, or as insufficiently in his favor. He may do more than that. He may suppress or undersell his contribution to the sequence of interactions which produces the stress:

This man is a victim of destiny. And, incidentally, the destiny he's a victim of seems to encompass all of his brothers too. One of his brothers just came back from six years in the federal prison system, and another is in Dannemora. His parents, however, are currently vacationing in Hawaii, so they seem to be nonvictims of destiny. Now, the fate that he seems to be a victim of at the moment is that he is a drug addict who, when he loses a job, is faced with the need to maintain a $75-a-day habit, plus having to accommodate a respectable standard of living, and that, naturally, forces him to steal and commit other acts which technically violate the law. The law, taking insufficient notice of this fate, incarcerates him on some kind of technical reasons which are invariably transparently incorrect. He can deal with these technical reasons if he has support from various legal agencies and relatives, but, unfortunately, though at the moment he finds himself in some kind of dilemma, he also finds himself with his parents in Hawaii. And since he is reluctant to disturb his parents' vacation with the announcement of his current status, he finds himself operating with a more limited set of resources, and therefore he is facing a period in jail. What he does when he sits in jail is to ruminate on his fate, and he ruminates not only about the inequity of his confinement, but also about the fact that he is separated from his loved ones and that, when it comes right down to it, his loved ones have little to thank him for. And he dissolves that set of particularly discomforting thoughts by computing that there is not really terribly much that he can do about that problem in his present condition. Then he also is disturbed by the thought that all these agencies are not available to him at the moment, and this ends up with the feeling that there isn't terribly much hope at the moment. So the main feeling that he has to deal with is the feeling of hopelessness which seems to be derived from the absence of an adequate support structure and the inequity of the system which pushes him to violating the law and then unfairly pounces on him when he does something like steal.

Though the man's view is stressful, it is also functional. It precludes self-criticism, justifies dependence, and romanticizes failure. It also serves to prevent insight, to forestall inventory, and to postpone the discomfort of change:

The way he describes his situation definitely gives the impression that he stipulates his addiction, and the only negotiable elements that he sees have to do with whether enough provisions will be made for him to maintain his addiction with one type of financial support or another. He sees the availability of money to be the main variable in determining whether he is confined or not confined. Everything else seems to be given for him.

Self-Victimization problems are efforts to cope with other, potential stresses, which are more serious and threatening. For our crisis victims, the solution can be unstable. It can produce stress of its own, which must then be coped with. This stress consists of the fact that one sees oneself as helpless, powerless and alone.

The Care and Feeding of Resentment

For our controls, the Self-Victimization perspective is not usually one of complete helplessness. These men see options which are plausible, or even required. Unfortunately, the main option is to react angrily, which has drawbacks. For one, anger—since it is blind—has a way of claiming innocent victims. And if anger is not blind, it calls for retaliation against the sources of victimization. These sources (guards, courts, parole boards) tend either to be beyond reach or to have power. This fact produces new stress, in that (1) one can react angrily—as some of our controls did, when young —and find oneself more seriously victimized, or (2) one can store one's rage, which brings tension. This tension, beyond being uncomfortable, may tend to discharge in the wrong place—again, with consequences.

Coping with victimization thus translates, for most controls, into problems of tension management, or into control of hostility. This sequence— which is familiar from our discussion of ghetto coping—can produce a variety of resolutions, some more precarious than others. Our summaries contain descriptions in which the main theme is one of a battle for a detached stance. Among the coping strategies of our controls, some call for outside support, others for self-segregation; some rely on distraction, or on exertion, or on consuming work. There are also psychological sets, ranging from insulation and mood control to positive thinking. The following summary describes a person who copes by means of supports in the inmate culture:

His frustrations are the injustices which are committed against him in terms of being charged with things that he didn't do, at least not technically, things like the "it was really my brother-in-law's gun" theme. He also has some difficulty adjusting to the prison routine, since his life is really just supposed to start. Now, as he sees it, these kinds of experiences produce tension that requires violence. If the situation isn't controlled, he is going to go out into society and take revenge on it, thereby putting himself back in jail again, and while he's in jail he's likely to get into fights with people who happen to irritate him while his tension is high. As he sees it, he reacted in this fashion in the past, but he now is able to secrete himself and control himself. He sees himself as being relatively fortunate by being a streetwise black who almost by definition has resources in terms of his background, so that he makes do with just about anything. And he has also endowed himself with friends, particularly since he's back for the second time, and he has a network of acquaintances among the inmates. And still, as he sees it, there's a possible crisis in the fact that he's being shuttled back and forth to court and eventually sees himself railroaded into a prison sentence that he does not deserve.

The presence of peer support is a two-tailed variable: whereas friends can serve ego functions by pointing to the consequences of explosions, they can also push a man over the brink by egging him on. Some prison groups (whose prevalence is exaggerated) provide grist for Self-Victimization mills: they "document" cases for retaliation, and bring consensus to the man who is in doubt about the validity of his rage. The issue is posed by one of our controls, who feels that peers must help one to regain perspective, while permitting one to maintain one's dignity:

> He received rejection from the parole board and thinks he has to remain in prison for at least another year. He resents this very much and calls the parole board a farce, but he maintains his cool, and for him this is self-respect. But this time he does it with peer support. He's an old-time inmate, and he doesn't agree with the views of young militants, but thinks that men should be right guys who maintain the Manly stance, but yet have friends within the institution that they can talk to. . . .
>
> He describes some of the younger inmates getting extremely resentful about things, and he says this is sometimes seductive, but rather unhealthy. He doesn't advocate suppressing a sense of injustice, or passively taking what is dished out to you. The picture he provides of his own strategy is that when a situation becomes unfair and he has no way of operating within it, he goes off and permits his resentment to surface privately. Except that in some instances he shares it with his peers, who help him gain a sense of proportion, and he expresses it to himself, and then he has discovered that his case doesn't necessarily have to be lost, and he can go on to the next event.

The same inmate makes another point, which may not be obvious in thinking about peer group support. He points up the role of the supportee in the relationship, and shows that a man gets from his group the sort of support he wants. The type of commodity prized by a "mature" militant, as he sees it, is one that takes into account the need to avoid crises:

> He would describe himself as being aware, just as the younger people who feel all this resentment are aware, but yet in the sense of being more sophisticated, because he's not only aware of the grounds for resentment, but he's also aware of his own need to keep his cool so that he doesn't win battles and find himself losing the war of survival.

Other men talk of approaching their peers open-endedly, but hoping for tempering experience and mood-modulating advice:

> Well, there's always a certain person you go to. Like, you call him your main man. Like, you go to him when you got something on your mind, and you say, "Hey, man, this and that." And you get the rap, get the special opinion and whatnot. Like, he give you little things. Like, maybe it happened to him before. He'll say, "Hey, man, this is how you settle this." You dig where he's coming from.

i: Does that loosen things up?

> Yeah, it loosens things up a lot, you know. You done talked it over.

Irrespective of the inmate's stance, reactions to his bids for Self-Victimization support can make a difference to his survival. The presence of crisis-preventive or crisis-precipitative support is a variable of crucial consequence in crisis self-management.

Self-Management

In the absence of peer support, mood modulation is independently generated among many of our controls. In some cases, self-control has an all-or-none flavor, and even minor irritation is seen as a peril to stability. A man may talk of having to shut off negative affect, or of making himself impervious or oblivious to his environment:

> The shell he describes, he describes as a product of repeated injustices and unfair treatment that he has received in his life. He says, in effect, that he needs this shell to resist the impact that things might have on him otherwise. He tells us also that he was at one time and still is (although it's something that he hides) very emotional and nervous. And that in part he was very susceptible to overreacting to slights. Now his shell seems to be in part one of the ways he not only protects himself from encroachments from without, but from his own anger and resent-

ment, his own responses to situations when he is thwarted. . . . He's about to appear before his old enemy the parole board, and he says, in essence, I steel myself before I walk in there, and that way no one is going to get hurt. It's a kind of philosophy of life, as he sees it, and it's a very workable philosophy of life, and it's evolved in order to cope with a world that requires that sort of philosophy. In fact, he makes it quite clear that even when he walks out of prison he's going to be facing a world which is treacherous and where there is a lot of unpredictable crime going on, so he isn't going to be able to relinquish this stance.

The coping strategy is intimately related to the cycle involving Self-Victimization and Self-Release. Environmental stress cues—cues to injustice—are converted into a Self-Victimization view by increments. Expectations are partly shaped by resentments based on "experience", or previous Self-Victimization interpretations. Each stage adds to the probability of stress and to the appropriateness of crisis. The problem is one of breaking this cycle, and there are men who feel that they have achieved this by denial, almost through an act of volition.

Less radical options for breaking the Self-Victimization cycle have to do with efforts to change one's frame of reference to ameliorate the connotations of stress. One of our controls, for instance, attempts a future perspective in which he sees justice restored:

He endorses a set of maxims which relate to the issue of having to keep cool and also to the system ultimately presenting you with an opportunity to confront justice in court. And this comes in particularly handy at this juncture, where he is facing what he characterizes as his only problem, which is that he is being held on what he characterizes as a "meatball charge." He does admit that this upsets him, and he indicates that the criminal justice system would be better deployed against individuals who snatch babies or who jump at old ladies out of trees, and when the system does come down on people like himself, he feels that it ought to come down on them in such a way as to minimally inconvenience them. He admits not only that he has come to that realization intellectually, but that he is miffed by his fate. But then he gets rescued from being obsessed by an outlook which presents him with premises that virtually assure him the probability of being exonerated.

In other instances, the interpretation of reality remains unchanged, but the person defines himself as nonpowerless, and thus as a nonvictim. He may feel, for example, that mind-over-matter capabilities can reduce stress to the level of petty annoyance:

Well, on my father's side, he was very stern, and he always knew how to cope with his problems, and he always managed to provide for the family somehow. And I think I have this type of character. It's very, very strong. No matter how bad the situation was, he always showed a very strong character. And sometimes I don't have something, but my appearance and my character show these people that I don't need anything. I'm qualified to cope with anything they give me, and I don't need anything. . . . Sometimes for relaxation I would just play handball for five or six days straight. Constantly. And the tension would be relieved. Whereas I've seen other people that had tension, and they would walk into the mess hall, and they would hold their hands together, and somebody would say something, and before you know it, they were fighting. And I used to look at them and say, "I wouldn't do that." And if they have problems out in the population, imagine the problems they're going to have twenty-four hours a day in a cell by themselves after getting locked up.

More sophisticated and effective strategies involve readjustments of interpersonal perceptions or dealings. They may include efforts to see the victimizer's point of view. There may also be attempts to constructively relate to victimizers, to make future contacts less conflict-laden. At minimum, a man may explore his own contributions—if any—to his victimization:

His self-control problems have to do with reacting disproportionately to situations and thereby making them more serious. Now, he is perceptive enough to see what he is doing, and he's perceptive enough to see this as a loss of control, and he's perceptive enough to see himself in a state of equilibrium and to count on his not making social interactions more serious than they already are. And he is aware enough of himself to know that he approaches authority figures with a negative set, particular authority figures with a more negative set than others. So that in a sense he's set the groundwork. He's done the groundwork for understanding his confrontation. And he can't see himself anymore being a pawn of violence or being completely blind, or acting in defiance of consequences.

The inmate to whom we have referred as the mature militant makes almost a game of seeing the guards' perspective of any interactions he has with them. This sometimes provides him with the opportunity to defuse possible confrontations:

He talks in particular about one guard who was traumatized by Attica. His position with this guy is a sympathetic one, saying, "Gee, I can see why he might think that way. But what I can't understand is what he's still doing here." . . . And our man doesn't hold back. He'll usually tell the person that he's dealing with, the authority figure, that he wants to

break down roles and wants to be treated as human being to human
being. Yet he knows enough not to push beyond a certain limit.

In readjusting interpersonal orientations, some inmates not only see
change in themselves, but report an easing of their tension, particularly if
erstwhile victimizers become allies in self-control efforts:

> Myself, lately, in the past few months. I find myself able to get along
> better with the doctors. And I find situations that I can ask the doctor
> for something, and he'll give me something to rest. And I can sleep it
> off for a few days.

I: So that's one of the ways that you would try to get this pressure down?

Right.

Coping Resources

Though a man may shoulder the burden of retaining his sanity, he needs
some help from his environment. Coping requires tools; at minimum, it
requires tolerance for a man's moods, and constructive responses to his
self-interventions. One of our controls, concerned about marital problems,
cites tolerance and empathy among custodial staff and from his cellmate:

> And I'd be locked up in the cell, and I'd have a lot of pictures, and I
> used to think about the family a lot. And waiting for her to make a deci-
> sion was really hard, so I spoke to a couple of sergeants, a captain, that
> I would like, instead of being locked up, to get on a house gang, work,
> do something, you know? So, like they understand my situation. So
> they ended up saying I was getting, like, paranoid, plus I'm very quick-
> tempered anyway. Because I have exploded before, but never as far as
> hurting myself or hurting anyone. But I used to get paranoid from
> being locked up, period, anyway. But, like, they put me on the house
> gang, and I was able to work, do tiers, help feed-up—it took a lot off
> my mind. . . . Whenever I was locked in and it was on my mind, I just
> had to get it off some way. I used to just holler down the tier, and every-
> body'd ask me, "What's wrong with you, man?" I'd say, "There ain't
> nothing wrong with me. Everybody got to get their thing off some kind
> of way, so I want to holler. So I'm going to holler." So I'd get to holler-
> ing, and an officer would come up and ask me, "What's wrong?" I'd say,
> "You got to let me out of here. I can't stay in here no more." He'd say,
> "You know I can't let you out of here." So I'd say, "All right." So I'd sit
> down and I'd smoke. This was in the city jail, there's two in a cell. So
> my partner, he might say, "You want to play some cards?" So we'd play
> some cards, and we'd get to arguing about some card. But one thing I

could never understand: it would never get to the point where we would fight or anything like that. It would never come to that point. We would argue, call each other names, but it would never get to the point where we would fight. . . . So then one of us would say, "I feel like writing my woman," and I'd say, "I feel like writing too." So I'd get up on my bunk, and he'd get on his bunk. I'd let him read mine, he'd let me read his, and we'd say, "This ought to do it," and send them out. . . . I don't think that during that period of time I could have stayed in a cell by myself. I mean, as far as hurting myself or anything like that, I don't think it would have been that serious. But, like, it's, like, lonely. I mean, there's always somebody next door that you can talk to, or something like that. But, like, with someone in your cell, you never really get enough time to do too much thinking.

This inmate dealt with his problem in part by convincing his wife of his respect for her feelings, his concern for her welfare, and his serious plans. The constructiveness of this stance was made possible because prison absorbed the impact of his jealousy, and cushioned—rather than magnified—his despair. Given different staff and other peers, the same individual could have reacted with bitterness and fear, and frightened off his source of long-term support.

A milieu which is stressful can minimize its crisis potential by making allowance for human problems. It must tolerate irrationality, provide activity and outlets for tension, modulate solitude, and permit social support. Men who are in crisis require *crisis* intervention, which we shall deal with below. But men with problems—which includes almost all inmates—require coping resources. A guard who classifies himself as purely custodial, or an inmate who disclaims responsibility for his fellows, is abrogating elementary social obligations. In the case of inmates, that abrogation spawns a system which deprives even insensitive men of the coping tools they need.

If our penal administrators are serious about having incarceration do no damage beyond the intrinsic discomfort it involves—as I believe most are—they must take a broad view of mental health. They must seek information about the difficulties and concerns of each inmate. They must consider such data in classification decisions, and in deploying resources.

Our control interviews suggest that reducing the most elementary pains of imprisonment entails two minimal responsibilities. One is to cement links between inmates and their loved ones, to help the inmates cope with the rupture of supports. The other, more difficult, responsibility is to personally relate to inmate concerns about inequity and powerlessness.

If humanitarian considerations do not suffice as reasons for reform, there is one fact to add: stress is unfreezing, and *potentially* regenerating. A man who has a problem is more apt than he would otherwise be to delve into the "why" of his fate.[4] But he is not thereby provided with constructive resolutions or the skill to change. If he is not to unfreeze further, or to break down—or if he is not to refreeze in undesirable ways, problem-solving resources must be available to him. Once a man's equilibrium is restored, his change potential is minimal. And the unchanged man is likely to recidivate, which is neither in our best interest nor in his own.

To be sure, the relationship between coping and constructive change is imperfect. For one, a man may solve a problem in a way that reduces his ability to deal with future difficulties. This occurs most obviously where extreme defenses are deployed. Such defenses affect a person's capacity to process information or to react to it freely. Building an emotional "shell" to deal with anxiety produced by separation, for example, can result in impoverished relationships; more remotely, it can create a psychotic world view. And using stopgap suppression to control affects can fuel eruptions in the future.

And where more substantial resolutions occur, it is not clear that their impact need be regenerating. A man can become more effective without becoming a more socialized person. He may profit from experience, for instance, by sharpening his skills as con man or exploiter. He may become more cynical, more isolated, or more helplessly linked to destructive peers.

If the amelioration of personal problems is to run hand in hand with reform, it must aim at the improvement of coping competence. A man must be supported when he needs support, but he must also have the chance, when he is able, to play a more responsible role. One way he can both receive and give support is by being involved in a program of human service relationships in which he acts both in a helpee and a helping capacity. Human service relationships—freely participated in—are important for other reasons. If the proving ground for coping competence is society, it helps to address a man's problems in a social frame. And prison can be a community, of sorts. Stress in prison is prevalent enough to make most inmates candidates for services such as empathy, brokerage, and support. Inmates have an interest in building a system in which such commodities are available, and stressed inmates have a stake in providing such services, because reciprocity reduces the stigma of dependence. A lifer assigned as tutor to a new inmate, for instance, can gain status and self-confidence; a sadder-but-wiser divorced inmate can take a more mature view of his experience if he can share it, in a monitored group, with an aggrieved husband.

Noninmates have equally pressing interest in playing helping roles. Stress sources—staff and outsiders—do not enjoy their assigned roles as inmate bugaboos. If wives, mothers, guards, administrators, and parole boards can increase constructive communication and reduce their level of conflict with inmates, their lots are eased. A supervised furlough, a seminar about prison rules with a guard, a brief session with a prosecutor or ombudsman can go a long way toward reducing discomfort. More important, it can ease tension and initiate shifts in attitudes.

As yet, the potential for the development of community in prison, and of links between prison and the broader community, remains comparatively unexplored. But the prospects for imaginative innovation in this area are a challenge for progressive penal administrators.

NOTES

1. This procedure was adapted from the study group method used in our research on violence (Toch, H., *Violent Men*, Chicago: Aldine, 1969, pp. 24 ff.). The process involves review of the interview in toto, group discussion, and the recording (by a summarizer) of the central themes in the interview content. The group process is designed to enhance reliability in the recording of interview impressions.

2. Lazarus, R. *Psychological Stress and the Coping Process.* New York: McGraw-Hill, 1966.

3. Ittelson, W. H. et al., *An Introduction to Environmental Psychology.* New York: Holt, Rinehart and Winston, 1974.

4. Toch, H. and Cantril, H. A preliminary inquiry into the learning of values, *Journal of Educational Psychology,* 1957, *48,* 145–156. A classic statement of this issue with regard to extreme situations is Frankl, V. E., *From Death Camp to Existentialism: A Psychiatrist's Path to New Therapy,* Boston: Beacon Press, 1959.

14

Crisis
Intervention

′Crisis intervention started with ministrations directed at persons who had been overwhelmed by natural disasters.[1] The approach is based on the premise that otherwise normal persons can be faced with situations that temporarily paralyze them, that suspend or undermine their customary frames of reference, and that produce dysfunctional perspectives. The interventionist's role is to help restore men's equilibrium, to moderate or modulate their moods, and to increase the effectiveness of their adjustment modes. A closely related approach, exemplified by the peacekeeping activities of police, emphasizes the defusing of interpersonal tensions and the restoring of communication among persons in conflict.[2]

By far the most popular connotation of crisis intervention is that of breakdown prevention—the type of service rendered by the soothing voice (on the telephone or rooftop) that seeks to keep distraught men from completing tragic and desperate acts. This model, which is given wide currency by suicide-prevention programs and drug clinics, shifts the focus from here-and-now despair to the future consequences of despair. It seeks to break a cycle which is expected to culminate in extreme acts of self-destruction.

The breakdown-prevention approach poses a number of difficult problems, and the more exclusively it is relied on, the more difficult these problems can become. One delicate issue rests in the fact that in order to qualify for intervention the man in crisis must demonstrate that he is likely to break down. Time and effort are expended, for instance, in distinctions between "suicide," "suicide gestures," and "self-injuries."[3] Training revolves around predictive indices, such as insomnia or suicide notes, which identify candidates worthy of help.[4] The breakdown-prevention approach not only carries the burden of proving its questionable premise—that qualitative differences exist between lethal and nonlethal crises—but also restricts the range of clients to persons who seem least willing to survive.

Aside from the potential violation of civil rights implicit in this approach,[5] it defines its target in a nontherapeutic fashion. If death rather than human suffering is the enemy, the change agent becomes the equivalent of a physician who is solely concerned with terminal diseases. The functional progression of personal disorders over time makes such an approach shortsighted, *even on its own terms.* Pouring medical resources into the treatment of metastases would be an obviously irrational strategy in the war on cancer deaths, because such a strategy assumes that cancer arises full-blown, and because the strategy calls for the use of the most expensive resources on those least amenable to cure. If limited tools are available, intervention is best deployed where it is most effective; and no one argues for the proposition that last-minute surgery can address disorders at their most strategic junctures.

It is also questionable whether the prevention approach to crisis management achieves its own goals, particularly in closed institutions. Many suicides, for instance, occur in settings where people are segregated for preventive observation.[6] While this in itself proves nothing, because the persons involved have been identified as high-risk to begin with, it raises the possibility that our practices have run ahead of our knowledge. We have seen that segregation often escalates or compounds a man's despair. Moreover, an emphasis on the physical aspects of prevention can have antitherapeutic consequences. Men who have been deprived of light bulbs, sheets, and electric cords have committed suicide by such ingenious techniques as fatal concussions. The physically safe environment—the perennially illuminated padded cell—is, among other things, the most stimulus-deprived and amenities-free setting; it is hardly the sort of milieu one selects for remedial therapeutic work. Surveillance presents additional difficulties. Unless it is continuous or randomized, the most seriously disturbed man can deduce enough of a pattern in the rounds of his guards to act on his strongly motivated resolves. Even if the interventionist is concerned with institutional rather than therapeutic goals, these goals can hardly be achieved by a procedure which implies that suicides represent failures of safeguards. At best, this permits scapegoating, by enabling the suicide of patients to be tied to the negligence of staff.

It is true that prevention may be therapeutically oriented, and may involve concern with the here-and-now problems of men in crisis. Like other intervention models, it can dovetail with efforts to deal with noncrisis problems. Through referrals, intervention agents may operate in a network of strategies that address different client concerns in different, tailor-made ways. The division of labor can be one in which the crisis interventionist deals with "emergency" problems while longer-term concerns are delegated to other agents.

The network model for the human services industry may be required in the free world, where fragmented agencies and competing interests preclude a more systemic approach. But closed institutions that use a multi-strategy model can employ greater flexibility. It is not really necessary for institutions to shuttle an inmate, or a patient, from specialist to specialist, like an incomplete assembly line product. Staff are centrally employed and can, in principle, be deployed in combinations that make the best sense in terms of client needs. A prison, or a hospital, can be a multiservice center, and the shape of staffing can be changed to accommodate variations in function.

The physical and social environments of institutions are also alterable. Men in crisis have different susceptibilities and requirements. While some need a stuctured milieu, others need meaningful activity, or reduced stimulation, or social support. Even within the narrow range of settings of the prison system, the social-ecological dimensions of different prisons vary significantly, and a single prison may contain a variety of subenvironments that differ significantly. Some prisons, for instance, provide more work opportunities or more companionship than others; some are less crowded, less formal, or less violent than others. If we know what a man's milieu requirements are, we can use crisis-relevant dimensions to place him in a "matched" setting. Such placement requires knowledge about the properties of environments which can ameliorate or aggravate crises. It requires ecological mapping of tiers, wards, public rooms, and living accommodations. It requires a detailed breakdown of available options. Human ecology, which studies such problems, is a burgeoning field in social science.[7] The institutional practitioner could easily find experts to help him plot the range of environments available to him, and to develop ways of improving relevant environmental attributes.

Once the properties of institutional settings are known, classification calls for a mapping of the needs of clients. Our typology is a prototype of such mapping. It also suggests that the relevant facts can be obtained by disinterested fact gatherers who can show concern for the self-defined difficulties of classification subjects. Traditionally, prisons have seen inmate biographies in management terms. A gruesome offense, for instance, translates into longevity or psychiatric status. To the offender, the same action may have different connotations. He may feel that his offense earns him the disdain of peers, or merits guilt, or presages a future of compulsive predations. Traditional approaches not only fail to ascertain such feelings but give us no way of discovering them.

At present, prison is always a zero-sum game. The inmate must talk about his crime in such a way as to cast doubts on the legitimacy of prison or the length of his sentence. He must proclaim his innocence, deny circumstances, discuss lack of evidence, or claim bias.

Investments cover facts. Staff classification decisions are generally dispensations of rewards and punishments. The inmate presents a case by exaggerating or minimizing the social or psychological connotations of the available environments. Staff obliges by exaggerating or overlooking key features of subenvironments. Such matters as intolerance for isolation or crowding are rarely ventilated by inmates or addressed by staff.

Psychiatric or counseling interviews—which are presumably free of investment—are games with very tangible stakes. To win, inmates must present themselves as sicker or healthier than they feel. Their aim must be to "bug" or "de-bug," to invest or divest themselves of "bags." Ease of life in institutions, length or indefiniteness of assignment, career and social implications, make up the hidden agendas of psychiatric fact gathering and fact supplying. In this context, the shape of inmate concerns cannot emerge. I am reminded—as I am sure some readers will be—of contrasts presented by prison patients at different stages of their careers. At Stage One, inmate-patient Jones may conclude that prison is intolerable, and may regale the prison psychiatrist with a lurid account of his tribulations; at a later stage, he may wish to flee hospital confinement and confess himself an ex-malingerer; still later, struggling with consistency, he may revert to his sick stance because prison pressures mount.

The solution may be a fact-gathering and evaluation procedure applied to *all* inmates and devoid of direct administrative links. Such monitoring must operate under the assumption that every inmate has private concerns, though these may not be incapacitating. The queries must stress presumptive human problems, such as relations with loved ones, aversions or predilections in peer relationships, orientations toward physical settings, attitudes toward offenses, view of self, and career perspectives. Although the facts obtained in this way must not translate into classificatory acts, the emerging profiles can be fed to treatment staff and decision-makers to permit more sensitivity to the personal consequences of institutional dispositions. This does not neutralize hidden agendas; it merely creates a setting in which openness is not foreclosed.

The final ingredient of systemic intervention is the issue of Who Intervenes. Ideally, crisis intervention agents should be whatever persons may prove effective in addressing the client's problems. They should be deployed so that the qualities and skills of intervention agents are matched with the different needs of clients.[8] And they should be selected without regard to tangential criteria, such as professional status or academic degrees. If we take a functional view of intervention, there is no reason why a shop foreman may not help a particular inmate as effectively or more effectively than a psychiatrist.

Increasingly, therapeutic professionals have accepted the premise that human services cannot be rendered monopolistically by a group of licensed experts. Task forces of psychiatrists, psychologists, and social workers have produced well-received working papers that not only endorse the use of therapeutic aides in principle, but prescribe their use in community settings and in various other contexts.[9]

The roots of this new development are hard to trace, but at least one factor contributing to the trend has been the refocus of goals from the treatment of individual patients to the provision of broader services to larger, more diffuse target groups. For example, "Community Mental Health Centers," may be established, designed to offer such "helping services" as brokerage, material aid, human contact, or crisis intervention.[10] Profiting from experiences like those of Maxwell Jones,[11] therapeutic institutions have redefined their role from the intensive treatment of select patients to the creation of regenerative climates in which each staff member or patient can exert constructive impact. Parenthetically, crisis intervention becomes a component concern of this model, because Jones highlighted personal crises as events which could be used to benefit not only the individual in crisis, but other members of the community as well.

A third development of relevance has been the evolution of behaviorally based therapies which stress the role of "natural" sources of personal influence. In such therapies, housewives, mothers, teachers, and friends are trained to be front-line interventionists,[12] and crisis management means pointedly ignoring dysfunctional reactions and "reinforcing" constructive moves and solutions.

The behavioral sciences have also exerted a more general impact by pointing to the peer group as a prime source of personal influence. Particularly with strongly dependent individuals, therapeutic approaches which stress the use of "peer pressure" have proved effective where more traditional (professional-centered) interventions seemed relatively ineffective.[13] It follows from such approaches that non-professionals may be responsive to subcultural elements in crises which the professional less attuned to such themes would fail to address.

The crisis intervention movement itself has played a considerable role in shaping trends. In such crises as disasters and concentration camps, cooperation among the afflicted often held the key to survival.[14] Community self-help movements, such as Alcoholics Anonymous, have laid stress on emergency responses of fellow sufferers to individuals in crisis.[15] And lay therapeutic movements, such as "switchboards," were designed to respond to the needs of individuals who had nowhere to turn for assistance.

Such enterprises not only make a case for the deployment of nonprofessionals but also provide models for "teaming" lay resources with professional staff. Lay groups, for instance, use professional consultants, and invoke specialists for clients who need them. Conversely, such groups may accept referrals from professionals who see the activities of these groups as therapeutically relevant. Such relationships set precedents for new functional arrangements—such as teams of mental health specialists, nonprofessional staff, and peers—which can jointly address the problems of clients.

In the context of these developments, the prison looms large among institutions that have minimally exploited the range of their human resources in rendering aid to inmates. While job descriptions of custodial officers stress skills and qualities relevant to dealings with the personal problems of inmates, norms and formal role classifications tend to relegate the officer to his traditional security functions. It is these functions which provide the key to an officer's status. Guards who discuss their work at the neighborhood tavern are most apt to stress the risk of their job (which is small) rather than to boast about help rendered to distressed inmates. In interactions with professionals, officers find that despite their constant contact with inmates their opinions are neither sought nor respected. When an officer escorts an inmate to a psychiatric interview, his role is that of a nonparticipant in an alien ritual. Such features of the professional-nonprofessional interface produce a situation in which the relationship between members of potential treatment teams is fraught with suspicion and lack of trust.

Though prisons permit inmate self-help groups, they assign them restricted roles—such as talking about alcohol problems—or see them as social outlets. Group counseling is designed to subserve a vaguely rehabilitative goal. And inmate councils become loud spokesmen for minor bread-and-butter grievances. In practice, inmate representatives are informal "power" figures who are tied into negative peer-influence groups, or staff-related individuals who are not sociometrically linked to their peers.

Inmate subcultures (whose norms we discussed in Chapter 1) militate against therapeutic concern for fellow inmates. Not only is therapy viewed as a staff function, and therefore resisted, but the premium set on "doing one's time" discourages involvement with the problems of one's peers. Moreover, inmates and staff share the view that the man in crisis is a special type of person who falls under the purview of professional staff. And the professionals—who are seen as crisis interventionists—reject the assignment. They view themselves as Healers of the Sick, and they deal at best perfunctorily with men who fail to meet the established criteria of pathology.

The "nonsick" inmate is presumed self-sufficient, equipped with resources and means of survival. He is in no position to challenge this assumption. If he does protest it, he is deemed exploitative (malingering, self-seeking), or he risks his reputation, or both. He cannot be a man with problems, because ordinary men are not conceived of as in trouble. The recognition of problems implies special handling. Beyond lies the world of the Manliness Myth.

There are also powerful resistances among inmates to the initiation of interactions that could open the possibility of constructive intervention by anyone. Such resistances—which were freely discussed by our subjects —reinforce the self-insulating processes of crises and produce a chasm that surrounds men and keeps their problems invisible to the breakdown point, and sometimes beyond it.

A powerful source of resistance to the sharing of problems is the sense of privacy of the man in crisis, which may prevent him from approaching sources of help. This resistance may be operative for most persons, but it tends to be especially acute in individuals who are introspective or who have limited verbal skills. A problem is also created for men who are strongly wedded to a self-image that excludes feelings of despair:

34:   They asked me what was wrong. You know, "None of your business."
      I had this attitude where they were invading something that was private
      and personal, you know? Which it was. . . . When a cat masturbates, he
      takes that as a private thing—it's private and it's personal. Same as one
      taking his life—if he feels that he wants to kill himself, it's a private and
      personal thing.

cx 2: Some people won't tell other people their problems, not even a
       psychologist or psychiatrist or anyone. And these people I really feel
       sorry for, because they're even a lot worse off than I am. A friend of
       mine is like that, in here, and its really too bad. . . . His sister died.
       She got stabbed in the heart five times while he was in here, right? And
       the chaplain called him up, and he said, "Well, you know, we just got
       word that your sister was murdered." He sat back and said, "Yeah."
       The priest thought he was crazy. He's not crazy. It's just that he can't
       talk to anybody. He hates feelings.

Another concern that keeps men in crisis from sharing their problems is the fear of being taken lightly or of being viewed as immature, defective, or weak. This concern is especially common in subcultural contexts such as prison, where manliness or inviolability is a positive norm.

d 28: What I learned about jail, which isn't very much, you won't go to
       another inmate and tell him something like this. He'll probably think
       you're a punk or a sissy or something like that, which I really am.

cx 13: I try to stuff it off, try to keep my mind off it, while I'm out here, so people don't think you're weak or something. They won't take advantage of you, but they won't give you respect. I just kept it into myself. Then I start thinking about it again when I'm locked up in my cell.

Another reason for resistance to meaningful communication is the fear of having one's problem become public property. In institutions this reason may become particularly salient, because it ties into concerns about stigmatization by staff and exploitation by peers.

gm 1: Well, by not relating to a lot of people, it probably keeps down a lot of static. Or you tell some people too much, you give them an opening for them to punch. And I don't intend to be punched.

cx 23: And, like, I didn't speak to anybody about my sister or anything. Because I didn't want to put anything on the street, you know, as they would say in jail. Like, let everybody know about my problems and everything. So I sort of held it in, you know?

cx 29: I couldn't open up because everything I say he's writing down on paper, and I was afraid, you know? I don't want everybody to know. I just want to talk to somebody that would understand and would try to help without letting everybody else know. . . . So he wrote out a report that I couldn't open up and give it to the psychiatrist. The same thing with him. The only thing I could tell him was that I was nervous.

Another reason for resistance to intervention is the premise, based on noncrisis experiences, that one is self-sufficient and capable of attending to his own affairs. A related assumption is a normative one—it holds that to be worthwhile, men must deal independently with their difficulties. A second variation is that personal problems are not amenable to outside help because they are tied to one's makeup. Curiously, no single version of the independence premise is very widely held. The crisis experience is such that it tends to produce, in most people, substantial feelings of un-self-sufficiency.

a 4: I'm a funny guy. I have funny ways about me. I'm used to taking care of my own problems. I don't try to tell nobody my problems to take care of them. In other words, I would sit down all night and think about how to cope with this problem. This is me. I don't tell nobody else my problems. . . . I would rap; I would talk with the dudes; I talked sensible to them.

D 5:   See, I'm not going to say they couldn't help me, but I'm just that
type of person. I like to try to rationalize things by myself. I feel like
I'm getting older, and I ain't got no more mamas and daddies and aunt-
ies to sit down and put me on their lap and say, "Well, look, this is the
way you've got to do this." You know, I'm getting to be a man, and I've
got to start acting like a man. And if I have a problem I have to learn
to solve it myself. Because, like they say, mama's not always going to be
around, daddy's not always going to be around. And right now they're
not around.

A common reservation about the interpersonal climate as it bears on the
possibility of sharing problems is that men who face unique and different
versions of stress are apt to center on their own concerns. This makes the
man in crisis feel that he is likely to mobilize resentment or to elicit unsolicited accounts of the other man's troubles if he attempts to discuss his
difficulties.

GM 3:   I started thinking, "Damn, what's the matter with these people?
I'm talking plain English, and nobody seems to understand what I'm
saying. Or maybe they're not even trying to understand!"

MHDM 14:   Sometimes he comes over and he tells me, "Don't give up."
He'll be talking to me. But, like, he'll be worrying me more about his
case than I am worrying about mine. Do you know what I mean?

Some persons feel that they are cut off from meaningful communication
because they are forced to associate with individuals with whom they have
little in common. This difficulty might be overcome by systematic socio-
metric or subcultural pairing of persons who face stress.

MHDM 3:   There ain't nobody to talk to. You got a cell partner, right?
You get a cell partner like I get, one time I had a Spanish cat that
didn't speak English. Another time I had a Chinese guy, and he didn't
speak English, you know? Another time I had a guy that was so ignorant—this guy just got off the bus from Mississippi somewhere—this
guy was so ignorant, he couldn't understand nothing I said. I could
understand what he said, but he couldn't understand what I said. So
they stick anybody they can. They don't make no—or like this, you're
facing armed robbery, you've got a heavy charge, right? And they stick
a guy in there with a petty larceny. And he says, "Ha, ha, I'm going
home tomorrow. Ha, ha, I'll be home next week. I'll be out there in
New York, man. Let's see, I'm going to do this and I'm going to do
that." What kind of shit is that? There's a guy in here for homicide, and
they stick a guy in his cell that's got petty larceny. They do that. They

don't separate nobody. Or then you get the little kid, right? He might be as old as you, but he ain't growed up yet. I've had people with little kid minds, you know, and they played little kid games. Throwing water on you and doing dumb shit, tickling your toes and shit when you're sleeping.

GM 8:   There's a lot of people that you can't relate to. The best way I can describe it to you is me taking a child that's born blind from birth and then when you could explain it to him you would try to explain the color green to him. Well, you can't because there's nothing you can associate it to. There's no approach that you can take to say, "Well, it's this or that." There's no way possible.

Traditional staff roles may pose problems for persons who require assistance with developing crises. Routine responses may be geared to staff functions, such as classification, investigation, or discipline, and may close off or discourage open communication. Such responses may leave the man in crisis with the feeling that he is faced with rejection, obtuseness, or at best, indifference:

CX 60:   You know, I wanted to talk to somebody that's going to at least listen to me. I don't want to go to no dep that's just going to say, "Well, somebody wrote you up, you're wrote up, that's all there is to it." I want somebody who's going to listen to me, you know?

CX 7:   They tell you something like, "We're going to send you to this institution. This is a very good institution. It has this and this." They say that about all institutions, and they don't know what's going on inside the institution. . . . They say that just to make somebody happy. Like, "Don't worry."

V: I said, "Why you asking me all this? There's nothing wrong with me, man." I started asking the person back. I said, "Do you hear things?" He said no. I said, "Do you hate your mother?" He said no. I said, "I'm asking you the same things you asked me. I got good sense just like you got good sense. There's nothing wrong with me."

CX 5:   So he asked me questions similar to you. "Why did you cut up" and "was your grandfather ill?" And all this. Then he asked me have I ever attempted to have a sexual relationship with my mother. And shit, when he said that, I jumped up and started to grab him. When he said that, I just jumped up. And he backed up against the wall, and I said, "Look, man, I think you better be cool." And he said, "Don't be upset." And he said, "I'm just interviewing you" and stuff. I said, "You don't ask me no questions like this, man." And then he said, "If you walk out, I'm going to write you up." And I said, "You know what, you can take those papers and whatever else you got in your desk and stick it up your ass and shit." And then I walked out.

A specific staff role which poses problems for crisis intervention is that of prevention. Men perceived as future dangers are apt to see themselves as currently unresponded to. The reaction to a man's potential acts may precipitate self-fulfilling responses which culminate in breakdowns. This holds particularly for situations where staff not only communicate lack of interest, but transfer men to settings which narrow their options and increase their stress.

MHDM 28:   When I came in here, the guy asked me have I attempted to commit suicide? And I said, "Yes. I drank a bottle of Clorox." So they sent me to the tenth floor. Then that day had passed, and the following day that's when I decided to hang up.

D 26:   They brought a nurse up here in the ward, and a group counselor happened to ask me a question, "Well, what do you think about her?" I said, "Well, seeing she is a woman, she wears glasses, she reminds me of my wife." So right away they shot me on medication. It's supposed to decrease your sex, I guess. Then I said, "I didn't say that with any intentions of harming her, you know, or anything."

A common staff reaction which the troubled individual may find unhelpful is the way in which medication is used to cope with the mood-control aspects of crises. Persons who feel themselves not-listened-to are apt to equate medication with unresponsiveness. It is hard for them to see the relevance of drugs if these are not "aimed" at the content of a problem that has been shared and explored with staff.

A 6:   I saw Mr. G——————, my counselor, and told him that I was thinking about suicide, and I told the psychiatrist that I was thinking about suicide. And he put me on medication that helped me to commit suicide. . . . Psychiatrists, they can't talk to you because they're too busy. They have too much work to do. He says, "How's the medication doing, and how are you feeling?" I tell him, "Not too good." "Well, you got certain problems. I don't have much time right now, but this medication should help you along."

M 32:   He talks to me for a little while, and then after that he gives me some medication and it puts me to sleep. . . . He gives me the medicine, but I don't take it.

I: You don't take it? What do you do with it?

M 32: Throw it away.

I: You don't like the medicine?

M 32: Tastes nasty.

Custodial officers may respond to inmates in crisis as standard control problems, and this response, even if it is appropriate elsewhere, may produce unscheduled reactions. For example, teasing a self-possessed inmate may avoid a confrontation, but a man in crisis may see the same ploy as an act of cold, premeditated sadism.

MHDM 10: I had a cat there tell me, he said, "Why didn't you cut your jugular vein? All you got to do is cut it over there." And I said, "That's a joke; I don't know what side it's on." He said, "No, it's on this side. What you should do is cut down this way. This way, if you cut the vein, they can't stitch it up." He says, "Tell them other people down there that." I told him, "I'll do you one better. You put it down in writing, and I'll bring it down there." He said, "Ah, no, that wouldn't be right." I said, "No, it wouldn't be right, and you wouldn't have that badge either!"

MHDM 6: And I explained that to him, and he said, "I don't care about your wife." I realize he don't care about my wife, man, but the attitude he had taken—"Fuck you," that's the kind of attitude he had took. So then I started to snatch the phone, and the other guy said, "No, the other inmates, they want to use the phone. They might have problems like yours." I said, "Why don't you crack my cell?" He said no. He knew I was mad. I don't know, when I get mad, you can look at my face and tell I'm mad. He had a big smile on his face to think he had me there. I just walked in the back, broke the light bulb, and cut up.

The ledger has another side, however, which permits us to visualize the possibility that, handled with skill, staff interventions could reduce the impact of stress immeasurably. There are inmates who not only recall being helped by professionals or by staff-administered programs, but who can spell out ways in which their difficulties were successfully addressed:

AC 8: Well, the psychiatrist was a female, she was a psychologist. And, you know, it's always good to rap to a female in jail. And, you know, like, she used to listen to me, and she'd have, like, some kind of sympathy for me. And, like, I'd tell her, "I'm thinking about this, it's on my mind," and so on and so forth. And she'd sit there and actually feel for

my problem. You know, it's nice to have sympathy from a woman when
you're in jail.

P: I just be talking to her. She be shooting a couple of questions at me, I
be popping them back. I be giving her the answers if I know them. She
be saying, "What if you do kill yourself? You know you're not coming
back." "So what?" Stuff like that, she'll be getting deep down. These
other guys, "You want to kill yourself, huh? Oh, wow, let me put you
on medication." The first thing they say is medication. If you talk to
Miss _____, you don't need no medication. Because she's got
a deep conversation, you understand?

GM 3:   When I got to court, the court didn't thump on me, that court
talked to me as one individual to another, and didn't use my record as a
crutch. They talked to just me, and they asked me why and all this here.
And I said, "Here's the situation. I got shafted so many times, I don't
like this. I feel it's unfair." So they seemed to understand.

In our interviews, the guard frequently appeared as villain, but guards
were also often portrayed as sympathetic, effective intervention agents.
The potential use of the guard in crisis intervention efforts is documented
by inmates who were assisted at crucial junctures by humane and concerned officers:

4:   He started telling me, you know, do I got any kids on the outside. And
I said, "Yes, four months old." So the officer told me, "Think about him.
If you go, what then is he going to do? Don't think about your wife and
your mother. They don't care. Think about your kid." Then I said,
"You're right." I started crying, and he kept talking to me. He started
saying, "Well, you do your own thing, and do the bit the best way you
can. You know, alive, not hanging, not cutting up. Someday you'll be
out there." And I said, "Yeah, you're right." So I went down to my bunk
and started thinking, "The officer's right in what he's telling me." So I
just went and fell asleep.

CX 27:   So he came over, you know? He told me—he started rapping. He
says, "What's wrong?" again, and I says, "Nothing." He says, "Come
on." He says, "Why don't you let me come on in and rap to you." He
says, "I think you need some help." He says, "I can help you." He said,
"You and me been all right. We good friends, aren't we?" I says, "Yeah."
He says, "Well, let me come on in." I says, "No, don't come in." I says,
"I might hurt you. Please don't come in, OK?" He says, "Now I'm going
to come in." He says, "I don't think you'll hurt me." He says, "You and
me all right, aren't we?" I looked at the man, you know, and I said to

myself, "Will I hit him if he come in?" I didn't know what I was going to do, you know? My mind kept spinning around, "Should I hit him or don't hit him?" And I like the guy, you know, I respect him. He is an all right officer.

So he just sat there, and he looked at me. So I even let him crack the gate. He cracked the gate, and he came inside, and I raised the thing like this to hit him, and he looked at me, and he put his hand out, and he says, "Come on," he says, "You don't want to hit me, you don't want to hit me, come on." I looked at him, you know? I dropped the glass. He came over and took me by the hand, you know? He said, "Let's grab this." He said, "Somebody scattered some matches," something like that. The whole place was ransacked, you know? So he took me out. That's when I really broke hysterical, you know? Like when I get sad I cry, you know? I started to cry, I started to shake. I couldn't talk, you know? They took me over in the rec room, you know, talk to me for a few minutes, you know, waited until I calmed down a little and took me up, you know, to the nearest hospital and got me some medication.

In interviews with nonprofessional staff, one discovers evidence of the sort of empathy which confirms the impression that custodial and quasi-custodial personnel are a pool of untapped therapeutic skills. While some guards may characterize "weak" inmates in contemptuous and superficial terms, other guards show considerable empathy and surprising diagnostic acumen:

PO 1:   I would say that I think they feel just about as low as the bottom of the ocean. Of course, you can notice it, working with them. They'll come in the shop, and they'll sit right down and won't talk, don't feel good today. I usually let them go for a while and then sit down and ask, "What's the matter?" And usually they'll come out with it. It might be a letter from home. Maybe somebody's come in that's a parole violator, or somebody has just come in the population and they found that somebody else is going with their girl friend, or something of this nature. Or they had a death in the family, somebody that they're close to.

PO 2:   And you sort of watch him and see how he's going. Because you're in the yard—all you've got to do is watch. And you can pick out one guy that you know—like him, you know he had that Dear John letter, and you watch, see? And the first time you see his eyes getting all red. So then you don't let him see you talking to the other guys that he hangs around with, and you tell them, "See what you can do." You'd be surprised. . . . You get to know their friends, you understand? And you say, "Straighten him out, help him out. Tell him she's not the only girl." And I go along with it too. And then sometimes you can help him. You see something going on there now. You know he's a bunch of nerves, so you put him on the floor. Waiting on the other fellows. Giving the hot water, handing towels, passing cigarettes. Running around back and forth, doing a little work. And he gets his mind going, and you'd be surprised how he snaps out of it. I've got one in my division now—when he came in, I wouldn't give two cents to put him on the floor because he's highstrung, got a bad temper, and he flies off the handle like that. But now I let him on the floor because he's calmed down.

The use of peers as intervention agents is a strategy that must be used with cognizance of its limitations. For one, there are inmates who have strong and specific objections to the concept of peers in therapeutic roles. At minimum, these resistances must be dealt with before meaningful and effective interactions can occur:

GM 3:   See, the inmate population down there is more or less kids. And the majority of them, like, are too immature. But with this action there, I didn't feel that some one of them could help me out, whereas a professional counselor or something like this could.

MHDM 32:   The officer said . . . , "Can't you speak to one of the inmates?" I said, "Inmates have just as much problems as I have. They don't want to hear my problems, just like I don't want to listen to their problems." Because I feel it's none of my business, their problems. And then my problems is none of their business. They're men just like me inside the place, they're just like inmates.

Some complaints about peer interactions relate not to the principle of using peers as intervention agents, but to the fact that, left to their own devices, untrained men may intervene in clumsy, unskilled fashion:

A 1:   I would talk to him. And he would say, "Don't cut up. I don't want to have to mop up all that blood." And, you know, you're supposed to say, like a doctor would say, "Why do you want to cut up? Why do you want to hurt yourself?" And then I could talk my problem, why do I want to cut up.

ARS A: They got these suicide squads. The suicide squads put you under pressure. . . . They argue with you, they give you all this bullshit. They're junior pigs. They put you under too much pressure. They're inmates like I am, and they tell you, "You hang up, I'm gonna bust your ass. You cut up, I'm gonna bust your ass." I don't want to hear this, because the next one that tells me that, I'm gonna bust his ass. He talks a lot of bullshit. And they tell you a lot of things, they got you under pressure twenty-four hours a day. Psychologically and physically.

E 2: My cell partner, _____, says to me, "What do you want to do that for, man?" I told him what was the use of me keep on living without nothing to fight for, without any family. And he gave me some pretty good advice, which I cannot remember at this time.

On the positive side, peers who share a problem similar to that of the man in crisis are apt to prove helpful. They may capture appropriate feelings and concerns. They may provide hope, or demonstrate the feasibility of solutions. And they furnish perspective—particularly if their own difficulties are comparatively serious. A lifer, for example, may be a peculiarly effective change agent:

A 15: There's one particular inmate who has a life that's sort of molded on the same principle as mine was. I can relate to him. And he's got twenty-five years. And when I see him, I'm really down—if I can see him laugh—and shit, he's got twenty-five years. And I figure, "Wow, and I'm feeling bad?" Now I can argue and argue with myself long enough to pull myself out a little bit, to do something else that'll pull me out more and then something else that'll bring me out more, you know, till I'm all the way out.

D 31: He showed me that his position was worse than mine and that if I tried to hang on, that things could improve in time. I mean, he didn't tell me this in words. But I was thinking to myself, "He got life, and he never tried it. He's hanging on, and he's going to live life for all it's worth." Then I said, "Life is sweet. I ain't got but a year. Even if nobody talks to me, even if I never make a friend while I'm in here, maybe I'll get through the year. And when I get back to the street I know I'll have friends because I left friends out there."

I: So that like opened up your mind to different ways of looking at that?

D 31: Right, yeah, that's what happened. It came so I seen a whole lot of different ways of looking at it. And then that's when I finally settled down and started to go on and do my time.

The following example shows how an inmate can capitalize on his experience to help others. Here, a psychotic in remission skillfully attacks the delusions of a disturbed fellow inmate:

D 5: The thing is he thought that Elvis Presley was his father and Marilyn Monroe was his mother. He would talk to them, but he had enough sense to know that they wasn't, but he said that they was in his head. Like, he'd talk to them, and they would tell him to break a window, or tell him to kill himself, you know, stuff like this. So I told him, "When you was in the street, did you hear voices?" Not that I was trying to psychoanalyze the guy, but just trying to be a little helpful to him. So he would not hurt himself. So he says, "No, I didn't hear voices when I was in the street." I said, "Well, do you hear voices now?" He said, "Well, that's what I don't understand." I said, "Do you ever think, like, the devil was in your head, and it's just you talking to yourself?" "You know," he says, "what do you mean by that?" I said, "Do you know what subconscious is?" He said no. Well, I had to start breaking it down for him. I said, "well, your subconscious is really yourself talking to yourself. You know, just like thinking to yourself, that's all." He says, "No, Marilyn Monroe, she keeps telling me that she's my mother, and Elvis Presley is my father." And I said, "But you didn't hear Elvis Presley in the street." I said, "This is only because you're doing time. You're under a lot of pressure. Some people can deal with this pressure, and some can't." I said, "You cannot deal with this pressure, so you're giving yourself this delusion—in your mind. Some people's in your head, which is nobody. It's just you talking to yourself." And he said, "Well, I don't know." He say, "I still say they're trying to kill me." He was really kind of jammed.

The deployment of an experience-based strategy requires the training of inmates in differential diagnosis, so as to assure the appropriateness of their response:

D 19:   I was talking to this guy about a week ago. He was telling me that he didn't feel right, and I was trying to find out where he was coming from. And he finally told me that he felt that people want to fuck him, you know? And I told him, "Just get your mind together and relax, because this is all in your mind."

I: Yeah, well, some of it isn't, though, because in some cases guys have gotten raped, you know? And so it's a real kind of fear.

D 19:   Yeah, right.

An important aspect of peer intervention is its therapeutic benefits for the person who intervenes—and these benefits are emphasized in "free world" self-help movements. Reaching out provides a meaningful role, distracts a man from dysfunctional concern with his own difficulties, and leads to rewarding social interaction. This fact is intuitively obvious to inmates who seek out peers in need when they feel the onset of depressions or crises:

MHDM 14:   You see, like, when I have a problem, I generally go until I find somebody that has a problem, and I try to talk to them. There's a saying that you can always tell somebody else and help them sometimes, but you can't help yourself. And this is how I do it. . . . At one time here I might feel depressed. So I know a guy, I see him sitting down, and I know he's got something bothering him on his mind. So I say, "Hey, what's happening?" He says, "This place, man, I don't feel like I can take it no more. I just want to end it." I say, "Wow, you can't do that." He look at me and says, "Why?" I say, " 'cause you can't. Number one, you'll be cheating yourself," He says, "What have I got to lose?" I say, "A whole lot. Look, I did eleven years crossed out of my life, locked up." I said, "If anybody should be snuffed, it would be me. I don't have no family, nobody." And this kind of builds the guy up. I say, "Look at you, you got family, you got somebody coming to visit you every week, you can call somebody, make a phone call." I say, "You, it's beautiful," I say, "and furthermore, if you feel like talking about your case, let's talk about it." Now during that time while I'm doing this, I've done forgot about my problems, I'm really involved in this person. Really involved. So when I get through rapping with him, and I can see maybe a smile on his face or something, I feel that I accomplished something. This makes me feel good inside, and then my problem's gone.

There is a growing pool of inmates who have experienced breakdowns. These men have knowledge and credentials. They have reason to care. They can be selected for use in peer intervention on the basis of their interpersonal skills, then trained and monitored. The role of such inmates obviously requires thought. The model of the "suicide squad," which has been implemented in New York City, is one possible strategy. In this operation, team members counsel high-risk inmates against suicidal acts. But this model is tied to risk and broadly focused. What we may want instead are typologically grounded teams which permit the matching of problem and experience. The aim could be to provide the inmate in trouble with a fellow sufferer who has survived comparable difficulties. The role of such persons would *not* be the direct confrontation of self-destructive intent. Rather, it would be (1) to permit the inmate in trouble to voice feelings, thereby reducing his explosive potential; (2) to communicate to the inmate in trouble the nonunique character of some of his dominant concerns; and (3) to provide the inmate in trouble with a framework for a more open and realistic perspective.

In other instances, nonproblem inmates could play roles. They could be physically invoked, for example, to assuage fear of threatening peers. This might require grouped assignments or transfers, formal networks of communication, and peer mediation.

A variety of ancillary benefits could accrue from such strategies. Exploitive inmates could be neutralized by grouped victims. Many inmates now poorly integrated into prison society could acquire a useful and meaningful place in it. There could also be self-image and status benefits. The English-speaking inmate of Latin extraction, for example, could have a "bridging" function in counseling. This would be a particularly vital role, since Latins (like Blacks, Indians and others) have concerns whose translation requires an "inside" perspective not often available to the prison staff.

A vital communication-facilitating resource is the correctional officer. Guards are not merely discipline-enforcers and order-keepers. They are presumed to have a generalist role, which includes rehabilitative and human relations functions. But some guards have greater interest and ability in these areas than do others. Such guards can be pinpointed through procedures that include peer and inmate nominations and supervisory ratings. They can be set apart administratively as generalist-specialists, somewhat along the lines of the family crisis policemen who are assigned to family fight calls. This requires informal allocations of duties, permitting the invocation of a qualified man when his presence is required.

Training could be continuous, and could involve meetings in groups; guards specializing in the rehabilitative and human relations areas could pool their experiences and thinking with or without professional assistance. Such guards could contribute to the training of other guards, and could evolve manuals and lesson plans related to the management of inmates with problems. To be sure, the role of the guard, like that of the inmate, is fraught with ambiguity and risk. One difficulty is the problem of appeals for favors or administrative requests. The problem is a familiar one. Family crisis officers, for instance, encounter requests for arrests; psychotherapists are subjected to dependency bids and exploitative moves. Here, training and role definition would provide means of redefining guard-inmate interactions to encourage an honest presentation of inmates' problems.

So far in our discussion, we have been using the expression *crisis intervention* loosely, and sometimes with varying connotations. What do we really have in mind when we use this term? The concept that seems most compatible with our experience is one that views the target of intervention generously, specifies long-term and short-term intervention goals, and deploys different strategies for different types of crises. Defining the target generously means that crisis intervention should be used with *any* individual who *through actions* conveys the message that he is not surviving with integrity in his situation. In prison, this would include inmates who injure themselves, request segregation, succumb to predatory fellow inmates, insulate themselves from others, or, according to officers or fellow inmates, show marked changes for the worse in their demeanor. We feel that men who act troubled deserve at least the opportunity to ventilate their concerns, if they desire to do so.

Using crisis intervention for long-term and short-term goals means that such intervention should provide people with assistance in maximizing their chances of survival *not only* in their *immediate* setting but also in subsequent life situations. For instance, if an inmate is slated for return to the community, interventions designed to build up his resources for coping with prison should transfer at least partially to his prospective encounters with free world stresses. Though our focus is on a man's concerns in the here and now, these concerns must be sufficiently central to a man's personality to be mobilized in other areas of his life.

The formal definition of crisis intervention would be that of a process which ameliorates discomfort at junctures in which men are disturbed, and in which they are prevented by their despair from freely responding to their surroundings.[16] Ideally, such treatment should *postdate* behavioral manifestations of crisis. This timing is dictated not only by diagnostic considerations—the availability of indices—but also by the need to protect the unafflicted from unwarranted intrusion.[17] Moreover, there is the matter of amenability to treatment. Men in crisis are rarely reachable at early stages of crisis development because these early stages tend to include the emergency use of last-ditch defenses. On the other hand, during a short period immediately following breakdown a man's defenses are generally disrupted. At this critical point most individuals seem able —even eager—to participate in personal reevaluations.

If crisis intervention is aimed at core difficulties of men in crisis, its goals must vary with the nature of these difficulties. In Table 13.1 we provide a suggestion or two of some implications that our themes might have for differential disposition. The table traces crisis themes to intervention goals. It also suggests that each goal involves an intervention modality, and calls for differences in the type of staffing. For instance, mental health experts seem superfluous in addressing coping difficulties but are essential in interventions addressed at impulse-management problems. Impulse-control management would require a special milieu—a therapeutic community—in which trained nonprofessionals could be teamed with psychiatric staff. On the other hand, the intervention settings required to deal with non-psychotic problems could be routinely accommodated by most institutional contexts.

Our model presupposes a classification system of the type we have described, including a milieu inventory, and also presumes an effort to promote a supportive climate. In prisons, specifically, crisis intervention as we see it would be hard to implement as long as inmates and staff stigmatize or reject the targets of intervention. While an ideal climate is not required, the suspension of unrealistic norms, such as the Manliness Myth, must be possible in sub-environments.

A modest first step—the halfhearted legitimation of personal problems— can prove critical. For if men listen to the despair of others, they may

TABLE 13.1 *Intervention Implications of the Typology of Crises*

Nature of Crisis	Goal of Intervention	Setting and Process	Primary Intervention Agents
Sanctuary Search and Self-Victimization	Helping the person to sort through his problems and regain perspective	Problem-solving groups or dyads	Trained and monitored peers
Isolation Panic	Removing the person from stressful setting; providing social support	Social contact; constructive activity; reassurance	Peers and nonprofessional staff
Self-Classification and Aid Seeking	Exploring susceptibilities and adjustment problems; placing the person in ameliorative setting	Supportive contact in line with dependency state; gradual weaning and building of internal supports	Nonprofessional staff
Self-Deactivation, Self-Sentencing and Self-Retaliation	Reinterpreting past career (including the working through of guilt and shame); building favorable self-image; providing help in goal-setting	Psychological exploration in depth; career counseling and training	Professional and nonprofessional staff, with possible peer assistance
Fate Avoidance	Providing group membership in relatively noncompetitive, nonviolent settings; building self-confidence through personal and social achievements	Reduction of fear in non-threatening context; building self-esteem and social skills	Staff and peer self-help groups
Self-Linking and Self-Certification	Mobilizing external supports or building substitute networks; providing training in self-reliance	Reduction of separation anxiety; providing supportive structure; cementing internal supports	Significant others from the "outside world," staff, and peers

Nature of Crisis	Goal of Intervention	Setting and Process	Primary Intervention Agents
Self-Alienation and Self-Release	Rebuilding brittle defenses; working through confusions about reality	Formal therapy in therapeutic milieu	Professional staff, with team assistance
Self-Escape and Self-Preservation	Dealing with panic and destructive impulses; building a flexible system for self-control and self-tolerance	Minimizing danger cues; formal therapy in therapeutic milieu	Professional staff, with team assistance
Self-Intervention	Providing insight into scope of problem; addressing problem through therapy	Response to mood-control request; formal therapy in therapeutic milieu	Professional staff, with team assistance

begin to empathize. And when men acknowledge the feelings of others, they may discover their own. With defensive postures unfrozen, further change becomes possible. And if men permit themselves to respond to their own humanity, even environments of stress such as prisons can become settings for survival and milieus for personal growth.

NOTES

1. E. Lindemann, "Symptomatology and Management of Acute Grief," *American Journal of Psychiatry*, 1944, *101*, 141–48.

2. M. Bard, *Training Police as Specialists in Family Crisis Intervention*, Final Report to Office of Law Enforcement Assistance, Department of Justice, mimeographed, undated.

3. One of the main proponents of a taxonomy that makes attempted suicides a separate category is E. Stengel ("Attempted Suicides," in *Suicidal Behavior: Diagnosis and Management*, ed. H. Resnick [Boston: Little, Brown, 1968]). Other discussions of classification include E. Cohen, "Self-Assault in Psychiatric Evaluation," *Archives of General Psychiatry*, 1969, *21*, 64–67; A. G. DeVries, "Definition of Suicidal Behaviors," *Psychological Reports*, 1962, *22*, 1093–98; P. T. Dorpat and E. S. Ripley, "The Relationships between attempted Suicide and Committed Suicide," *Comprehensive Psychiatry*, 1967, *8*, 74–79; E. H. Schmidt, P. O'Neal, and E. Robins, "Evaluation of Suicide Attempts as a Guide to Therapy," *Journal of the American Medical Association*, 1954, *155*, 549–57; A. T. Beck and R. Greenberg, "The Nosology of Suicidal Phenomena: Past and Future Perspectives," *Bulletin of Suicidology*, 1971, *8*, 10–17. E. S. Shneidman has noted that the assumption that one deals with *mere* "suicide attempts" produces "tendencies to assume a pejorative attitude toward these behaviors." He states that "it is all too easy to say that an individual only attempted suicide or to dismiss the case as beneath the need for human compassion." He points out that "meaningful treatment has to be essentially in terms of the person's personality and the frustrations, duress, fears, and threats which he experiences in his living relationships" ("Orientation Toward Death: A Vital Aspect of the Study of Lives, in *The Study of Lives*, ed. R. W. White, [New York: Prentice-Hall, 1936], p. 201).

E. L. Ansel and R. K. McGee note that "a suicide attempt frequently creates negative attitudes in others, and thus the helper often responds to an attempter with hostility and rejection, perhaps failing to effect a change desired by the attempter, which was indeed the reason for the attempt. Such reaction may then prompt the attempter to engage in further suicidal behavior" ("Attitudes Toward Suicide Attempters," *Bulletin of Suicidology*, 1971, *8*, p. 22).

4. It is ironic, in this regard, that one of the most reliable predictors of suicide is a past suicide attempt.

5. T. S. Szasz, *Ideology and Insanity: Essays on the Psychiatric Dehumanization of Man* (Garden City, N.Y.: Doubleday Anchor, 1970).

6. S. Martin points out that of thirteen suicides in New York City correctional facilities between October 1970 and September 1971, "eleven took place in cells where the prisoner was alone . . . [while] generally the tendency is for at *least* two inmates to occupy a cell." Memorandum dated 4 October 1971 to Alan J. Gibbs, City of New York, Health Services Administration (mimeographed).

7. R. Moos recently noted that "more books treating man and his environment from a holistic and ecological viewpoint have appeared within the past four years than have appeared during the prior three decades" ("Conceptualizations of Human Environments," *American Psychologist*, 1973, *28*, p. 652). A newly published volume on the subject is W. Ittelson, et al., *An Introduction to Environmental Psychology*, (New York: Holt, Rinehart and Winston, 1974). Although research on the ecology of prisons has not reached the level of sophistication of other studies, there is evidence that ecological dif-

ferences exist between prisons and among different environments within the same prison (eg., R. Moos, "The Assessment of Social Climates of Correctional Institutions," *Journal of Research in Crime and Delinquency*, 1968, *5*, 174–88).

8. T. B. Palmer, "Matching Worker and Client in Corrections," *Social Work*, 1973, *18*, 95–103; J. Grant and M. Q. Grant, "A Group Dynamics Approach to the Treatment of Nonconformists in the Navy," *Annals of the American Academy of Political and Social Science*, 1959, *322*, 126–235; M. Q. Warren, "Classification of Offenders as an Aid to Efficient Management and Effective Treatment," *Journal of Criminol Law, Criminology, and Police Science*, 1971, *62*, 239–58.

9. Among such statements are the following: Board of Directors, National Association of Social Workers, *Standards for Social Service Manpower*, Washington, D.C., June 1973; National Association of Mental Health, Policy Statement on Manpower, April 1968; G. Grosser, et al., *Non-Professionals in the Human Services* (San Francisco: Jossey-Bass, 1969); Roche Report, "Can 'Subprofessionals' Solve Human Services Needs?" *Frontiers of Psychiatry*, 1970, *7*, 1–2, 5–6; *Action for Mental Health: Final Report of the Joint Commission on Mental Illness and Health* (New York: Basic Books, 1961); National Committee on Employment of Youth, *Pros and Cons: New Roles for Non-Professional in Corrections* (Washington, D.C.: U. S. Government Printing Office, 1966).

10. Thus L. M. Roberts points out that "some would include all human affairs within the borders of community psychiatric practice, since all men's activities are relevant to his present and future mental health." Having said this, Roberts goes on to define "all social, psychological and biological activity affecting the mental health of the populace [as] of interest to the community psychiatrist, including programs for fostering social change, resolution of social problems, political involvement, community organization planning, and clinical psychiatric practice" ("Introduction" to L. M. Roberts, S. L. Halleck, and M. B. Loeb, *Community Psychiatry* [Garden City, N.J.: Doubleday Anchor, 1969, p. 7]). Similar comprehensive definitions are available elsewhere.

11. M. Jones, *Beyond the Therapeutic Community* (New Haven, Conn.: Yale University Press, 1968), pp. xx, 76 ff.

12. A. Bandura, *Principles of Behavior Modification* (New York: Holt, Rinehart and Winston, 1969), pp. 104 ff.; B. G. Guerney, *Psychotherapeutic Agents: New Roles for Non-Professionals, Parents and Teachers* (New York: Holt, Rinehart and Winston, 1969).

13. Note 8 above. See also D. R. Cressey, "Changing Criminals: The Application of the Theory of Differential Association," *American Journal of Sociology*, 1955, *61*, 116–20; L. Empey and J. Rabow, "The Provo Experiment in Delinquency Rehabilitation," *American Sociological Review*, 1961, *26*, 679–96.

14. B. Bettelheim observed that the Communist inmates of concentration camps, who were well organized, had a relatively good chance of psychological survival ("Individual and Mass Behavior in Extreme Situations," *Journal of Abnormal and Social Psychology*, 1943, *38*, 417–52); L. J. Killian points out that disasters evoke loyalties to one or another of one's membership groups ("The Significance of Multiple Group Membership in Disasters," *American Journal of Sociology*, 1952, *57*, 3–14); Stouffer et al. show that "pride in one's outfit" was a factor protecting soldiers against fear in combat (*The American Soldier: Combat and Its Aftermath* [Princeton, N.J.: Princeton University Press, 1949]).

Self-help movements among disaster victims have been described by L. Logan, L. M. Killian, and W. Mars, *A Study of the Effect of Catastrophe on Social Disorganization*, Memorandum ORO-T-194, Operations Research Office, Chevy Chase, Md., 1952; and J. B. Taylor, L. A. Zurcher, and W. H. Key, *Tornado: A Community Responds to Disaster* (Seattle: University of Washington Press, 1970).

15. *Alcoholics Anonymous* (New York: Works Publishing Company, 1950). For a more extended discussion, see H. Toch, *The Social Psychology of Social Movements* (Indianapolis: Bobbs-Merrill, 1965), chap. 4.

16. E. Shneidman, "Crisis Intervention: Some Thoughts and Perspectives," in *Crisis Intervention*, ed. G. A. Spector and W. L. Clairborn (New York: Behavioral Publications, 1970), pp. 9–15.

17. N. A. Kittrie, *The Right to be Different: Deviance and Enforced Therapy* (Baltimore: Penguin Books, 1973); T S. Szasz, *Ideology and Insanity: Essays on the Psychiatric Dehumanization of Man* (New York: Doubleday, 1970).

Index